▌▌▌ Health International

Health International is a nationally based utilization review/disease management services company that provides a comprehensive managed medical care program for employers and plan administrators to assist employees and their dependents in improving the quality of their health care and reducing unnecessary medical costs.

Health International offers a comprehensive managed care program that includes the following services:

- Outpatient Surgery Precertification
- Inpatient Precertification/Concurrent Review/Discharge Planning
- Second Opinion/Consultations
- Psychiatric/Substance Abuse Precertifications/Concurrent Review/Discharge Planning
- High Risk OB Management
- Specialized Disease Management Programs:
  - Endocrine Diseases
  - Respiratory Diseases
  - Cardiac Diseases
  - Cancer
  - Musculoskeletal
  - Neurological
  - Immune
  - Transplants
- Short/Long Term Disability Management
- Workers Compensation Medical and Disability Management
- Catastrophic Medical Case Management
- 24 Hour Nurse HelpLine

We also offer a number of administrative services to assist employees and employers:

- Medical Claims Analysis
- Pharmacy Claims Analysis
- PPO Directory System including Telephonic Access
- HILink which can telephonically link multiple vendors with one 800 number

Health International is always looking for excellent, highly motivated individuals to join us. Primarily, we are looking for:

- Physicians
- Nurses
- Computer Programmers/Analysts

We provide a professional environment where your medical education and experience can be utilized to the fullest extent for improving the quality and appropriateness of patient care.

Health International has continuously been granted full URAC accreditation in:

- Health Utilization Management Standards
- Workers' Compensation Utilization Management Standards
- 24-Hour Telephone Triage and Health Information Standards
- Case Management Organization Standards

14770 North 78th Way
Scottsdale, Arizona 85260

Telephone: (800) 333-3760
Fax: (480) 948-3797

Website: www.health-intl.com

The HIPAA Handbook:

What Your Organization Should Know About The Federal Privacy Standards

Editors:
Dennis Melamed
Alexander J. Brittin

Important Note to Readers

The views in this reference book represent only the views of the authors and not the organizations with whom they are affiliated. This entire book is for informational purposes only. No part of this book is intended to be used as a substitute for specific legal or consulting advice or opinions. This book does not create an attorney-client relationship.

URAC has published this book with the understanding that the publisher, the editors and the authors are not engaged in rendering legal, accounting, consulting, information technology, or other professional services.

Purchase or use of this book does not create an attorney-client relationship. Anyone using this book, or any information found within it, should not act upon anything found in this book without first seeking professional counsel or advice.

Editors: Dennis Melamed, Alexander J. Brittin
Assistant Editors: Garry Carneal, Lani Caprio, David I. Korsh

©2001   **URAC/American Accreditation HealthCare Commission**
12 75 K Street NW, Suite 1100
Washington, DC 20005
Phone: 202-216-9010; Fax: 202-216-9006; Web site: *www.urac.org*

About the Editors

Dennis Melamed, MA

Dennis Melamed is editor and publisher of *Health Information Privacy Alert*, the first business-to-business publication focused on managing the privacy, confidentiality and security of health information. He is currently working on two other volumes related to the Health Insurance Portability & Accountability Act (HIPAA) security and transaction standards for URAC.

Mr. Melamed is also co-founder of PrivacySecurityNetwork.com, an Internet resource for HIPAA compliance and related topics. He is a frequent lecturer on the HIPAA Administrative Simplification provisions and other business and regulatory issues.

Mr. Melamed has served as a regulatory affairs consultant and contributing author for projects sponsored by the Ford Foundation and the National Science Foundation. A veteran business editor and reporter, he was a Washington Correspondent for *Business Week* and has written extensively for a variety of national publications on business and regulatory issues.

Mr. Melamed also has served as a legislative and regulatory analyst for a nonpartisan congressional caucus and as Vice Chairman of the Board of the National Press Club. He received his undergraduate degree in Government from the College of William and Mary and his Master's Degree in Journalism from the Pennsylvania State University. Mr. Melamed can be contacted at hipalert@aol.com.

Alexander J. Brittin, JD, MA, LLM

Alexander J. Brittin, Esq., is principal member of the Brittin Law Group, P.L.L.C., Washington, DC. Before forming his own firm, he was a partner with McKenna & Cuneo, L.L.P. Mr. Brittin wrote *The HIPAA Handbook: What Your Organization Should Know About The Proposed Security Standards*. He also writes a monthly column called "Rules & Regs," for the magazine *E-Business Strategist*. A complete listing of his works and background can be found at www.privacysecuritynetwork.com/healthcare/brittinbio1.htm.

Mr. Brittin's practice specializes in healthcare and government contract counseling and litigation, with an emphasis on information privacy and security. His clients include PROs and health plans. He has established compliance programs, supervised voluntary disclosures, and conducted compliance assessments and reviews.

Under contract with the Center for Medicare and Medicaid Services, he prepared a compliance guide for all Medicare fee-for-service contractors. He has also written compliance plans for healthcare contractors. Mr. Brittin was recently appointed to a three-year term as a Council Member of the ABA's Public Contract Section (2001-2004).

About the Authors

Victor Blanchard

Victor Blanchard is a Senior Manager in the Technology Risk Consulting practice in Arthur Andersen LLP's Mid-Atlantic region, and is the Security, Privacy & Infrastructure service line leader. He is Arthur Andersen's representative to the Workgroup for Electronic Data Interchange (WEDI) Policy Advisory Groups on Security and Privacy, as well as the Strategic National Implementation Project (SNIP) where he supports the education initiative.

Joseph Braun, MD, JD, MPH, MBA

Joseph L. Braun is an assistant professor of Emergency Medicine at George Washington University. Prior to this he was the Chief Medical Officer at the George Washington University Health Plan having served in the same position at UnitedHealthCare of Texas for three years and at NYlCare for two years. Previous to this he ran a primary care clinic in Alvin, Texas, and worked as a health regulations attorney with Wood Lucksinger and Epstein. He is an Air Force Reserve Officer assigned to the Surgeon General's Office at the Pentagon. Dr Braun is currently finishing his Ph.D. in Public Policy at George Washington University.

Lani Caprio, BA

Lani Caprio has over 15 years of experience in the health care field. Prior to joining URAC, she worked in medical records at Queen's Medical Center in Honolulu, the Chairman's Office of the Department of Medicine at Georgetown University Medical Center, and was on the staffs of the American Dental Association, the National Association of Children's Hospitals, and the public policy practice of The Lewin Group.

John Conniff

John Conniff has been an expert on health care and insurance issues for nearly 20 years. From 1993 through 2000, he served as Deputy Insurance Commissioner for Health Policy for the State of Washington. During that time, he chaired various committees for the National Association of Insurance Commissioners including the task force that developed the model health information privacy law. From 1986 until 1993, he served as attorney to the Washington State House of Representatives advising on insurance, banking, and health care.

Guy D'Andrea, BA

Guy D'Andrea is senior vice president for URAC, where he oversees URAC's standards development process. He is a frequent speaker on the topic of health care quality and oversight, and has authored numerous articles on accreditation issues. He is a member of the editorial board of the newsletter *BNA's Health Plan and Provider*. Mr. D'Andrea has served as Director of the American Association of Health Plans' State Services Department and Director of State Health Policy for the American Managed Care and Review Association.

Tom Hanks

Tom Hanks is the Practice Director, Enterprise Security & HIPAA Compliance for Beacon Partners. Mr. Hanks is a past board member of the Workgroup for Electronic Data Interchange (WEDI), member of the WEDI/SNIP (Strategic National Implementation Plan) steering committee, co-chair of the WEDI Privacy Policy Advisory Group (PAG), the WEDI Security PAG, and the WEDI Internet Work Group. He is also a commissioner for the Electronic Health Network Accreditation Commission and chairs their Security Standards Criteria Committee.

James M. Jacobson, JD

James M. Jacobson is a partner in the National Health Law Group of Holland & Knight LLP, working out of the firm's Boston and Washington offices. He is the Chair of the firm's Managed Care Team, and a member of the firm's Corporate Compliance and HIPAA Teams. He also serves as General Counsel to the Disease Management Association of America.

David I. Korsh, JD, MA

David I. Korsh is Associate General Counsel for URAC. Before joining URAC, Mr. Korsh served as Legislative Counsel for the National Association of Insurance Commissioners and held a variety of legislative positions on Capitol Hill.

Theodore T. Martin, JD

Ted Martin is a partner in the law firm of Baker & Hostetler LLP. A trial lawyer, Mr. Martin's practice focuses on complex commercial cases. He also regularly counsels clients on legal issues relating to information technology issues, including privacy and security matters. Prior to joining Baker & Hostetler, he served as general counsel for Digineer, Inc., a technology company that provides solutions to the digital health care market.

Karen Milgate, MA

Karen Milgate is a Research Director at the Medicare Payment Advisory Commission (MedPAC). She is responsible for their research and policy analysis on quality and access issues. Prior to her work at MedPAC she served as the Deputy Executive Vice President for the American Health Quality Association (AHQA). Before that, she was Senior Associate Director for Policy Development with the American Hospital Association.

Janet Newberg, JD

Janet Newberg is a partner in the law firm of Felhaber, Larson Fenlon & Vogt, based in Minnesota. She practices primarily in the area of health care regulatory compliance. From 1992 through 1998, she served as Criminal Health Care Fraud Coordinator for the U.S. Attorney's Office, District of Minnesota. From 1992 through 1999 she also served as the Director of Minnesota Health Care Fraud Task Force.

Mark L. Schuweiler

Mr. Schuweiler is the Director of Global Information Assurance Services at EDS Corporation for Insurance, Finance, Banking and Health Care, and as such, is the owner of EDS' HIPAA security and privacy practice as well as the privacy services responsive to Gramm-Leach-Bliley. He has more than 27 years experience in defining and managing the delivery of technical and information security services to companies world-wide and has served in a variety of executive capacities including CEO and owner of two technical service companies.

About URAC

URAC (also known as American Accreditation HealthCare Commission) is a 501(c)(3) non-profit charitable organization founded in 1990 to establish standards for the health care and managed care industries. URAC's broad-based membership includes representation from all the constituencies affected by health care, such as employers, consumers, regulators, health care providers, and the workers' compensation and managed care industries. Member organizations of URAC participate in the development of standards and are eligible to sit on the Board of Directors.

URAC offers 12 different accreditation programs for health care organizations.

- Case Management Organization Standards
- Core Standards
- Credential Verification Organization Standards
- External Review Organization Standards
- Health Call Center Standards
- Health Network Standards
- Health Plan Standards
- Health Utilization Management Standards
- Health Web Site Standards
- Network Practitioner Credentialing Standards
- Workers' Compensation Network Standards
- Workers' Compensation Utilization Management Standards

Since 1991, URAC has issued more than 2000 accreditation certificates to over 500 organizations doing business in all 50 states. URAC-accredited organizations provide health care services to over 120 million Americans.

Because of URAC's broad-based standards and rigorous accreditation process, purchasers and consumers look to URAC accreditation as an indication that a managed care organization has the necessary structures and processes to promote high quality care and preserve patient rights. In addition, regulators in 30 states recognize URAC's accreditation standards in the regulatory process.

URAC's quality mission also has diversified and expanded in recent years. For example, URAC is engaged in several research projects to assess and identify new approaches to improve performance measurement in a variety of health care settings.

URAC also publishes cutting-edge books on the health care delivery system such as *The Utilization Management Guide: Second Edition, The PPO Guide, Case Management State Laws: A 50-State Survey of Health & Insurance Statutory Codes, Models of Care: Case Studies in Healthcare Delivery Innovation, The Credentialing Guide, Rise to Prominence: The PPO Story,* and the *URAC Directory of Accredited Organizations.*

URAC now offers over 40 days of educational conferences, workshops, and seminars annually on issues ranging from accreditation to best practices.

URAC Corporate Members

- American Association of Health Plans (AAHP)
- American Association of Preferred Provider Organizations (AAPPO)
- American College of Physicians/American Society of Internal Medicine (ACP/ASIM)
- American Health Quality Association (AHQA)
- American Hospital Association (AHA)
- American Insurance Association (AIA)
- American Medical Association (AMA)
- American Nurses Association (ANA)
- American Psychiatric Association (APA)
- Blue Cross Blue Shield Association (BCBSA)
- Employers' Managed Health Care Association (EMHCA)
- Health Insurance Association of America (HIAA)
- International Union, UAW
- National Association of Insurance Commissioners (NAIC)
- National Association of Manufacturers (NAM)
- Washington Business Group on Health (WBGH)

Table of Contents

Part III: Compliance

Part IV: Enforcement

Part V: Appendices

Foreword

This publication provides an overview and explains the privacy regulations issued in 2000 under the Health Insurance Portability and Accountability Act (HIPAA) of 1996.

The implementation of HIPAA during the next few years represents both the best and the worst relating to government oversight of health care operations.

On the bright side, the HIPAA Privacy Rule addresses an important need to preserve the confidentiality of patients' health care information in the new electronic environment. Traditionally, medical records were stored in the physician's file cabinet and claims information often traveled through the U.S. postal service. In today's innovative eHealth marketplace through IT and Web enabled systems, the protection of personal health information has become much more complicated. The HIPAA Privacy Rule attempts to address this in a serious and comprehensive manner.

Due to the dynamic nature of the health care marketplace, the application of uniform Privacy Principles has been difficult. This struggle to create comprehensive privacy protection was evident in the disheveled and lengthy rulemaking process, which did little to alleviate the confusion and anxiety over what the industry would be required to do. As a result, the regulation is not always clear about the scope and coverage in a given circumstance. In addition, a number of court actions are being filed challenging the legitimacy of all or parts of HIPAA.

Maintaining patient trust and confidence in how medical information is used, transmitted and stored should remain a fundamental goal. Yet, HIPAA provides an illustrative example of how the road to privacy protection can be bumpy and filled with curves.

The goal of this book is to smooth over the potholes and straighten out the bends. The authors of the book have spent a considerable amount of time studying the scope and applicability of HIPAA and the Privacy Rule for a wide range of health care organizations.

As a result, this publication is a "must-read" for health care professionals from all areas of the industry. Its analysis provides practical insight on how a comprehensive and successful compliance strategy can be developed for health care organizations and their business partners. Additionally, this book provides an excellent starting point for organizations that want to adopt good business practices as they migrate towards eHealth applications.

Dennis Melamed and Alexander Brittin should be congratulated for putting together such a dynamic team of experts to answer our questions. In my opinion after reading this book, the journey towards HIPAA compliance will be a little easier.

Garry Carneal, JD, MA
President and Chief Executive Officer
URAC

Part I

Privacy and the
New Patient Landscape

Section 1.0 - Privacy and the New Patient Landscape

Dennis Melamed

1.1 The Move to Electronic Transactions

Growing reliance on electronic data technologies such as automated claims processing coupled with the expansion of information technology (IT) and Web-enabled applications have had a profound effect on the U.S. health care system. These changes and advancements have been driven in part by the desire to reduce medical and insurance costs and take advantage of the efficiencies promised by technological solutions to improve the health care system. The result: a new model for health care business and delivery systems based on unencumbered and expanded access to patient data.

In 1996 alone the health care industry invested an estimated $10 to $15 billion in information technology.[1] And while various surveys and studies suggest that health care organizations generally are lagging in their adoption of electronic strategies, no one is suggesting that spending will abate anytime soon. In fact, reliance on electronic applications in a wide array of health care settings is now growing exponentially.

1.2 The Fundamental Issue – Patient Privacy versus Business Needs

As a consequence, the U.S. health care system will become more technologically sophisticated and generate increasingly large amounts of data that will be shared by a growing number of entities that do not readily – or overtly – appear on the patient's radar.

Because of these trends, a new contract between the patient and the health care system is emerging. And it is this renegotiation that is substantially driving the debate over patient privacy and data security.

Prior to the electronic revolution, patient data had little economic value beyond the treatment of the patient. Now, however, the new abilities to aggregate and analyze patient data provide new medical and business opportunities for all health care companies, including providers, insurers and product manufacturers.

Among other things, this now usable stream of information enables:

- Providers to identify trends and make more effective treatment decisions;
- Insurers to make more informed assessments in underwriting health risks;
- Product manufacturers to prioritize and tailor their R&D and marketing efforts; and
- Regulators to identify health threats more rapidly.

The benefits are largely undisputed. However, the drive for electronic systems and the expansion of the health care infrastructure were premised on free access to this business asset, i.e. patient data.

With more than $1 trillion spent annually on health care in the U.S., these kinds of decisions not only have significance for maintaining the health of the citizenry and improving efficiency, they also have serious business implications. Individually identifiable health information has evolved into a bona fide business asset, and thus is highly sought after.

The economic value of this information has not only prompted the creation of new business activities throughout the health care industry. The ability to collect, aggregate and tailor new services for the nation's patients and health care consumers also provoked strong and deep concerns over patient privacy and confidentiality.

To be sure, concerns over privacy and confidentiality are not confined to the health care system. The issue shadows computer technology throughout the business world. However, no area delves so deeply into the intimate details of a person's life than health care.

1.2.1 A New Definition of Efficiency

Congress explicitly recognized this confluence of events when it included the Administrative Simplifications provisions into the Health Insurance Portability & Accountability Act of 1996 (HIPAA). As a direct result of this law, the health care industry faces a new set of regulatory challenges in balancing the desire and need to optimize the use of technology to improve the delivery of services and keep costs under control with the need to assure patients that the intimate details of their lives will remain private and confidential.

A primary focus of this resource guide is to explain how the definition of "efficiency" has changed because of the Administrative Simplification provisions and what the health care industry must do to adapt.

The HIPAA Administrative Simplification provisions are intended to change the way health care generates, maintains and shares personally identifiable health information. These changes were sought by the health care industry to streamline transaction processing. However, once Congress examined the issue, it also decided to mandate changes in direct response to a significant structural problem in the technological and process renovation in health care: the lack of effective patient privacy protections.

Prior to HIPAA, new systems for sharing and tracking data and transactions were developed, and the hope was for a technically more efficient way of providing health care services, executing routine administrative transactions, and collecting data to make better health care – as well as business – decisions.

Unfortunately, in the case of health care, electronic data systems were premised on largely unfettered access to patient health care data. Assuming that patients were only interested in the narrow issues of efficient delivery of health care services and cost, health care providers, insurers and the rest of the industry forged ahead in the name of efficient data and transaction processing and research.

As the debate over the HIPAA Privacy Rule proceeded, it was clear that this assumption was false. The availability of powerful and inexpensive computers

and the development of data networks made patient data a new and valuable commodity. New business applications became feasible, allowing health care and other industries to use health and medical records for a variety of purposes beyond treatment and payment. These innovations, in turn, raised new concerns over medical privacy.

1.2.2 The Move Away from Paper-Based Records

Before the proliferation of computers, patients provided the personal details of their medical histories and status with the understanding that the physician would keep the information private and confidential. Paper-based records provided further assurances that personally identifiable information would remain reasonably – if imperfectly – protected because of the cumbersome efforts required to gain access to those documents.

However, this paper-based system fostered an insular world view in which patient privacy and records security were not high on anyone's agenda. After all, the medical profession has had a long and deep commitment to the confidentiality of the doctor-patient relationship. This environment also meant that the health care system infrequently confronted other societal or business goals outside its primary and highly defined mission of treating patients. HHS noted:

> Until recently, health information was recorded and maintained on paper and stored in the offices of community-based physicians, nurses, hospitals, and other health care professionals and institutions. In some ways, this imperfect system of record keeping created a false sense of privacy among patients, providers, and others. Patients' health information has never remained completely confidential. Until recently, however, a breach of confidentiality involved a physical exchange of paper records or a verbal exchange of information.[2]

The transition to electronic data processing fundamentally changed this health care working environment. Not only did the free access to patient data become a pre-requisite for efficient operations, but electronic data processing brought down or made irrelevant many of the functional barriers that so imperfectly protected sensitive health information in a paper-based system.

This change in environment now has forced the health care community to become more sensitive to issues beyond its core mission of providing health services because the data it is generating is being used in a multitude of new and diverse ways. Some of these new uses are welcome; others, as it turns out, are not.

The unencumbered access to data and blurrier lines between health care and other industries – to the surprise of many in health care – aroused new fears among the patients over the use of their medical records.

1.3 The Passage of HIPAA

The federal government response to these fears came in 1996 when Congress adopted HIPAA to improve health insurance coverage in the United States. At the time, the public viewed the law as one primarily empowering employees and their families to transfer health care insurance benefits from one employer to another, or to continue coverage when the employee left a job or was terminated.

Tucked away in the law were provisions known as Administrative Simplification. Lawmakers recognized that computers and electronic transmission of data were having profound effects on the health care system. They and the health care industry also recognized that the use of computers and the electronic processing and transmission of health data could save billions of dollars in administrative costs for processing routine transactions.

However, there would be a price to be paid if the industry wanted to realize those benefits and savings: the public had to be assured that patient privacy would be strengthened, preserved and protected.

Health care organizations were put on notice that they could no longer take a myopic view of what constituted efficiency. Evaluating the efficiency of operations strictly from health care delivery and business perspectives was not enough.

The industry discovered that the public – its patients – viewed privacy as a fundamental right, a right that was implicitly endorsed and deepened in a paper-based world. Equally important to the conventional or paperwork view of efficiency, policymakers

feared that without guarantees of privacy, the health care system would ultimately become less efficient in its core mission because patients would start withholding information from their health care providers. The development of the Privacy Rule is based in substantial part on this premise.

> In short, the entire health care system is built upon the willingness of individuals to share the most intimate details of their lives with their health care providers.[3]

1.4 The Side of Effects of Waiting

As HIPAA was being debated and signed into law, the Millennium Bug exploded onto the world stage. Dire predictions of catastrophic failures across the full spectrum of human existence forced every industry – including health care – to drop everything to prevent the disaster. As a result, Y2K diverted money from other needed infrastructure programs, and privacy and other important issues were shunted aside.

The Millennium Bug not only diverted resources, it provoked serious side effects in the public's computer consciousness. The alarm over a mass failure of computer systems because of the lack of two digits stoked fears and skepticism over the use of electronic processing generally.

This concern has been fueled continuously by the almost daily stories about computer viruses, hacker attacks and mistakes making data vulnerable or resulting in accidental release. National media accounts over successful hacker attacks into the Pentagon computer system in 1998 and other systems that were perceived to be state-of-the-art only deepened the distress the public felt toward the protection of computer databases holding the details of their lives.

The health care community was not immune. For example, Wisconsin physicians in the spring of 1998 opposed state requirements to report every patient encounter. In fighting the requirement – the physicians wanted hospitals to take on the task – they raised questions about the state's ability to protect the information from computer hackers.[4]

Concern over privacy continued to grow as the public was fed a steady diet of media reports that health data was not secure. In 1998, a public uproar ensued after the *Washington Post* reported that CVS, a national pharmacy chain, had allowed its prescription customer list to be used for refill reminders subsidized by drug companies.

Media interest in privacy only grew. Computer glitches at the University of Michigan Health system in 1999[5] and at a Kaiser Permanente facility in California in 2000[6] and even a 1999 truck accident in Connecticut[7] involving processed health insurance forms made headlines.

These stories pointed HHS to one thing:

> No matter how or why a disclosure of personal information is made, the harm to the individual is the same. In the face of industry evolution, the potential benefits of our changing health care system, and the real risks and occurrences of harm, protection of privacy must be built into the routine operations of our health care system.[8]

The industry did little to fundamentally address privacy in the face of a growing public relations problem. The deadline for Y2K was quickly approaching, and the media attention over the possibility of disaster was increasingly hyped. However, the industry had other reasons to wait. Congress said it would enact specific legislation governing medical privacy by August 1999. That commitment, in fact, was enshrined in HIPAA.

1.5 The Price for Uniformity

In HIPAA, Congress promised to give the industry national administrative and financial health care transactions standards because the market had failed to provide this necessary step in the new world of computers.[9] Electronic processing demands interoperability and compatibility, and health care organizations were loath to spend the substantial resources needed to overhaul their proprietary computer systems. No one but the federal government had the clout to enforce uniform transactions.

The "price" for these federal standards, however, would be new rules for protecting the privacy and security of electronic health care information.

However, the privacy issue became so knotty and controversial during the legislative debate that Congress deferred the issue. And it did so in an unusual way. It promised – in the law – to enact a separate

privacy law by August 1999. To add credibility to that promise, Congress statutorily required HHS to issue a privacy regulation if the legislature did not provide more comprehensive and well thought out instructions. Health care companies took that legislative commitment seriously as Congress rarely likes to delegate authority over such large issues to the Executive Branch.

After HIPAA was signed into law, HHS pursued development of the generally noncontroversial transaction standards as Congress intermittently struggled with the privacy issue. When HHS started to issue these standards, it cautioned that they must be accompanied by the HIPAA privacy and data security regulations.

While working on the transaction standards, industry and government policymakers starkly discovered that the public cared about privacy as well as the efficient delivery of health care and transaction processing. In June 1998, the medical privacy issue made national news as a result of a public hearing by the National Committee on Vital & Health Statistics on the creation of a unique patient identifier.

1.5.1 Unique Patient Identifier is Rejected

The hearings in Chicago revealed that many people were extremely concerned over the privacy implications of a national health ID. Civil libertarians and others feared that in reality it would create a national citizens database. The efficiency and cost savings promised by the transaction standards and even the promise of better health care services were of little interest to a wide range of political interests in the evolving world of electronic processing if the price was the loss of privacy and tools that could allow the government or business to become too intrusive.

There was virtual unanimity among the health care organizations and privacy advocates that a unique patient identifier would be helpful in facilitating transaction processing and health care delivery. However, privacy advocates maintained – and others in the public agreed – that the possibility of creating a national database for health care was too high a price to pay for this kind of efficiency.[10]

Whether or not this identifier actually would create a national database was irrelevant. The hint of such a project provoked strong political reactions. Congress responded to the public outcry by imposing a funding moratorium on work on the unique patient identifier.

1.5.2 Public Concerns Grow

HHS acknowledged growing public worry in its proposed privacy rule in 1999, stating:

> The risk of improper uses and disclosures has increased as the health care industry has begun to move from primarily paper-based information systems to systems that operate in various electronic forms. The ease of information collection, organization, retention, and exchange made possible by the advances in computer and other electronic technology afford many benefits to the health care industry and patients. At the same time, these advances have reduced or eliminated many of the logistical obstacles that previously served to protect the confidentiality of health information and the privacy interests of individuals.[11]

In the Privacy Rule, HHS summed up the tension resulting from the growing use of interconnected electronic information systems and privacy:

> Use of electronic information has helped to speed the delivery of effective care and the processing of billions of dollars worth of heath care claims. Greater use of electronic data has also increased our ability to identify and treat those who are at risk for disease, conduct vital research, detect fraud and abuse, and measure and improve the quality of care delivered in the U.S.

> At the same time, these advances have reduced or eliminated many of the financial and logistical obstacles that previously served to protect the confidentiality of health information and the privacy interests of individuals. And they have made our information available to many more people...

> In the potential near future, when technology makes it almost free to send lifetime medical records over the Internet, the risks may grow rapidly. It may become cost-effective, for instance, for companies to offer services that allow purchasers to obtain details

of a person's physical and mental treatments. In addition to legitimate possible uses for such services, malicious or inquisitive persons may download medical records for purposes ranging from identity theft to embarrassment to prurient interest in the life of a celebrity or neighbor....

> The growing level of trepidation about privacy in general... has tracked the rise in electronic information technology. Unless public fears are allayed, we will be unable to obtain the full benefits of electronic technologies.[12]

1.5.3 Congress Fails to Act – HHS Assumes Lead

Congress failed to act by the end of 1999. The Senate Health, Education, Labor & Pensions Committee held several hearings in 1998 and 1999, and Sens. James Jeffords (R-Vt.), Patrick Leahy (D-Vt.) and Robert Bennett (R-Utah) drafted comprehensive legislative proposals. However, agreement could not be reached on a handful of controversial areas, including minors' rights to privacy and parental notification requirements (abortion) and whether to pre-empt state law.

The issue generated little traction in the House of Representatives although a coalition of health care organizations tried to tack on legislation – bitterly denounced by privacy advocates – on a government spending bill in 1998.

With no congressional action by the statutory deadline, HIPAA required HHS to act. With incomplete instructions from Congress, the department issued its 600-page privacy proposal on Nov. 3, 1999.

The response was predictable; HHS was inundated with more than 50,000 comments. Interest was so intense, the department extended the public comment deadline for an additional 45 days into February 2000 to accommodate the public and industry's desire to have a say.

The final rule was published Dec. 28, 2000.

However, that was not the last word.

After eight years out of office, the Republicans captured the White House in 2000, and the Privacy Rule was trapped in the transition. One of the first actions of the new administration was to halt and review all pending proposed and final regulations issued by the outgoing Clinton Administration.

At the time it was unclear whether the Privacy Rule would be affected by this review of "midnight regulations" issued by the departing Democrats. However, the issue was rendered moot after it was discovered that HHS had made a technical misstep under an obscure law, known as the Congressional Review Act, which gave Congress 60 days to approve or reject major regulations.

Under this law, major regulations, such as the Privacy Rule, had to be officially delivered to the Congress and the Comptroller General of the U.S. HHS failed to deliver a copy of the regulation to the Comptroller General until Feb. 14. As a result, the effective date of the regulation was delayed to April 14, 2001, when the two-year transition period for health care to get prepared would start.

During this time, newly installed HHS Secretary Tommy Thompson responded to industry arguments to re-open the Privacy Rule for further changes. Industry groups maintained that the Clinton Administration had made unexpected and unsupported changes in the final regulation and many new implementation problems already had been discovered.

Thompson ultimately rejected the need to further delay the rule. Instead, he promised what the Clinton Administration promised: the Office of Civil Rights, tasked with enforcing the rule, would issue guidance to clarify ambiguities and internal conflicts with the rule. In addition, he promised a new targeted round of rulemaking to make more substantive changes to the regulation.

However, he did not suggest that the Privacy Rule's essential thrust would be changed.

In July, HHS issued its first set of clarifications to the Privacy Rule.

1.6 Candid Concerns and Next Steps

In both the proposed and final rules, HHS's stated intention was to provide a balance between the need to run health care operations and meet national priorities with the need to protect the privacy, confidentiality and security of patient data.

This new contract between the patient and the health care system over the use of health information gives patients new rights to control the flow of their health data, access their medical records and hold companies accountable for failing to protect their data. The Privacy Rule also requires covered health care organizations and their partners to adopt and enforce new policies and procedures to ensure that personally identifiable information is used in line with patient expectations

With 1,500 pages of regulatory explanations and text, the Privacy Rule can be easily seen as the definitive word in this area. However, that would be a mistake. There is near unanimity that the regulation is flawed. For example, many in the health care industry believe that Congress must pre-empt state laws while others would like to see patients have a private right of action to sue over violations.

Regardless of the competing agendas, the pervasiveness of health data in the economy means that protecting privacy will be an iterative and ongoing process. Although the concepts are relatively easy to grasp, the fact that HHS needed almost 400,000 words to state and explain what it was requiring should disabuse anyone of the notion that the regulation will be simple to implement.

1.7 The Purposes of This Reference Book

The purpose of this reference book is to help health care organizations and their partners develop reasonable and effective policies and procedures that meet the compliance requirements of the Privacy Rule. To help health care providers, health plans and their partners, we have divided the discussion of the HIPAA Privacy Rule into as many discrete sections as possible to allow readers to find answers quickly.

In addition, information is repeated in several sections when appropriate. This was done to reduce the distraction resulting from the reader's need to continually refer to other parts of the reference. In other instances, the reader is guided back to a specific section for a broader discussion of a related concept.

Endnotes

[1] Standards for Privacy of Individually Identifiable Health Information, 65 Fed. Reg. 82,462, 82,465 (Dec. 28, 2000)(to be codified at 45 C.F.R. pts. 160, 164).

[2] *id.* at 82,465.

[3] *id.* at 82,467

[4] *Health Info. Privacy Alert.* May 1998, at 3.

[5] *Health Info. Privacy Alert.* February 1999, at 8.

[6] Kaiser's Quick Action Curbs Criticiam Over Release of Data. *Health Info. Privacy Alert.* August 2000 at 7.

[7] Aetna's Trash Problems May Prove Illustrative. *Health Info. Privacy Alert.* April 1999, at 5.

[8] 65 Fed. Reg. at 82,467.

[9] These transactions are: health claims and equivalent encounter information, enrollment and disenrollment in a health plan, eligibility for a health plan, health care payment and remittance advice, health plan premium payments, health claim status, referral certification and authorization, and coordination of benefits and will be the subject of another volume in this book series, *What Your Organization Should Know About the Federal Transactional Standards.*

[10] The response to the controversy over the unique patient identifier in Washington was a political one: Congress stopped funding work on the standard and has continued the moratorium through Sept. 30, 2001.

[11] Standards for Privacy of Individually Identifiable Health Information, 64 Fed. Reg. 59,918, 59.920 (proposed Nov. 3, 1999) (to be codified at 45 C.F.R. pts. 160-164).

[12] 65 Fed. Reg. at 82,465-66.

Section 2.0 - The Lay of the Land: Who is Covered by HIPAA

David I. Korsh

2.1 Introduction

When the Department of Health and Human Services (HHS) released the Privacy Rule[1] in April 2001, official statements and media accounts may have left the impression that a comprehensive federal system for protecting health data and medical records had finally been erected. That is far from true, and therein lies the root of much confusion and uncertainty.

The Privacy Rule resulted from an incomplete set of congressional instructions to HHS, and the result is a regulation that left everyone with some degree of dissatisfaction.

To be sure, the reach of the Privacy Rule is far and wide but not all-encompassing. It does not cover all health-related information, and it does not cover all individuals and organizations that generate, maintain, or share this information. Consequently, as companies and individuals strive to meet the goals of this evolving regulatory structure, it is important to understand the limits of its coverage.

2.2 Who Is Covered?

The universe of organizations and individuals covered by the Privacy Rule is referred to as "covered entities."[2] Generally, these people and organizations are *health plans, health care clearinghouses, and health providers who transmit any health information electronically* in connection with administrative and financial transactions specified in HIPAA. The Privacy Rule applies generally to "protected health information" regardless of the form in which it is generated.

However, the rule leaves many other entities that generate and handle protected health information outside its reach. Those not covered by the Privacy Rule include: property and casualty lines of insurance such as workers' compensation and automobile,

disability, liability, and other policies offering limited benefits coverage, even when such arrangements provide coverage for health care services. The rule also specifically excludes nursing home fixed indemnity policies.

Though not specifically excluded, but omitted by the way HHS defined covered entities are: employers, unions, and others acting as plan sponsors, self-administered group plans with fewer than 50 participants, government programs not specifically listed in the rule, and financial institutions.

It is important to remember that although these entities are not directly covered by the Privacy Rule, in many instances, they are affected by the rule and will have new responsibilities for protecting individually identifiable health information.

2.2.1 Health Plans

The Privacy Rule lists 15 specific categories and other entities in the broad definition of "health plan."[3] These are:

- Group health plans;
- Health insurance issuers, which means an insurance company, insurance service, or insurance organization, including a health maintenance organization (HMO), licensed to engage in the business of insurance in a state and subject to state law that regulates insurance;
- HMOs, which means federally qualified HMOs, organizations recognized as an HMO under state law, or a similar organization regulated for solvency under state law in the same manner and to the same extent as an HMO;

The Paper-Ploy: HIPAA's Effect on Paper-Based Providers

One underlying assumption of the Privacy Rule is that ultimately the entire health care system will use electronic technologies and engage in one or more of the HIPAA-mandated standardized transactions. However, for now, some health care providers may try to avoid the HIPAA privacy standards by conducting their operations only through paper-based systems.

The Privacy Rule only applies to covered entities that are defined as health plans, health care clearing houses and health care providers that transmit any health information in electronic form in connection with a transaction covered by the Privacy Rule. In the case of health care providers, the Privacy Rule does not impose any of its requirements if they engage only in paper-based transactions, and as a result do not use the standardized electronic transactions.

However, once a covered health care provider electronically uses one of the standard transactions or has another entity use one of the standardized transactions on its behalf, then the Privacy Rule also applies to the provider's entire operation. The Privacy Rule does not enable a covered entity like a provider to segregate its practices to impose the regulatory requirements only on those patients or cases that involve the use of the HIPAA standards.

- Dennis Melamed

- Part A or Part B of the Medicare program;
- Medicaid program;
- Issuers of Medicare supplemental policy;
- Issuers of a long-term care policy, excluding nursing home fixed indemnity policies;
- Employee welfare benefit plans or any other arrangements that are established or maintained for the purpose of offering or providing health benefits to the employees of two or more employers;
- Health care program for active military personnel;
- Veterans health care program;
- Civilian Health and Medical Program of the Uniformed Services (CHAMPUS);
- Indian Health Service program under Indian Health Care Improvement Act;
- Federal Employees Health Benefits Program;
- Approved state child health plans providing benefits for child health assistance;
- Medicare+Choice program;
- High risk pools established under state law to provide health insurance coverage or comparable coverage to eligible individuals; and
- Any other individual or group plan or combination of individual or group plans that provides or pays for the cost of medical care.[4]

2.2.2 Health Care Clearinghouses

The Privacy Rule also includes "health care clearinghouses" as covered entities. HHS defined such entities as "a public or private entity, including billing services, repricing companies, community health management information systems or community health insurance systems, and 'value-added' networks and switches"[5] that performs either of two functions.

The two functions are:

- Processes or facilitates the processing of another entity's health information that is in a nonstandard format or contains nonstandard data content into standard data elements or a standard transaction or
- Receives a standard transaction from another entity and processes or facilitates the processing of health information into nonstandard format or nonstandard data content for the receiving entity.[6]

2.2.3 Health Care Providers

The Privacy Rule contains a broad and somewhat complex definition of covered health care providers. First, these are health care providers who transmit any health information in electronic form in connection with a HIPAA electronic transaction. Second, a health care provider is a provider of services, a provider of medical or health services, and any other person or organization who furnishes, bills, or is paid for health care in the normal course of business.[7]

2.2.4 Affiliated Entities

The provision of health care services takes many shapes. Recognizing this, HHS took additional steps to ensure that the Privacy Rule accounted for the creativity of the market place by adopting specific rules that apply to organizations that do not fit easily in the definition of a covered entity. For example, HHS adopted the concept of "affiliated entities."[8]

Some legally distinct covered entities may share common administration of organizationally discrete but similar activities. A good example of this is a hospital chain. The Privacy Rule allows legally distinct covered entities that share common ownership or control to designate themselves, or their health care components, together to be a single covered entity. In such a case, all affiliates can use and share protected health information as if a single covered entity.

The rule also notes a covered entity may – as a single legal entity, affiliated entity, or other arrangement – combine the functions or operations of providers, plans and clearinghouses.[9] Integrated health plans and health care delivery systems that may function as both health plans and health care providers are examples.

These kinds of organizations with multiple covered functions may use or disclose the protected health information who receive the covered entity's health plan or health care provider services, but not both. This data use is confined, however, to the purposes related to the appropriate function being performed. For example, an HMO may integrate data about health plan members and clinic services to members, but a health care system may not share information about a patient in its hospital with its health plan if the patient is not a member of the health plan.

2.2.5 Hybrid Entities

Another example of HHS's attempt to address the multiplicity of structures within health care is the "hybrid entity."[10] Under the regulation a "hybrid entity" is a single legal entity that includes a health plan, clearinghouse, or health care provider, but whose primary function(s) is not the provision of these services. For example, a school with an on-site health clinic or an employer that self-administers a sponsored health plan might be considered hybrid entities as their primary purpose for existence is not the provision of health care and related services.

The Privacy Rule covers the entire hybrid entity. Consequently, the entire hybrid entity must ensure compliance with the regulation and develop and implement protections – firewalls – to protect against the improper use or disclosure within or by the organization. In other words, the health care component within a larger organization is prohibited from sharing protected health information with the larger entity unless an individual has authorized the disclosure or the regulation otherwise permits the disclosure.

2.2.6 Business Associates

The limits of the Privacy Rule are most telling in HHS's adoption of the concept of "business associates"[11] of covered entities. As defined in the rule, a business associate is someone other than a member of the workforce of a covered entity or organized health care arrangement who performs or assists in a "function or activity involving the use or disclosure of individually identifiable health information, including claims processing or administration, data analysis, processing or administration, utilization review, quality assurance, billing, benefit management, practice management, and repricing...."[12]

A business associate is also someone besides an employee of the covered entity who provides "legal, actuarial, accounting, consulting, data aggregation [citation omitted], management, administrative, accreditation, or financial services" where the provision of the service includes the disclosure of protected health information.[13]

The Privacy Rule requires covered entities to have contracts with these business associates to ensure the safekeeping of protected health information (For a more detailed discussion of Business Associates, see Section 6.0.)

2.2.7 Data Aggregators

HHS specifically addressed another business associate relationship – data aggregation – that focuses on the collection and use of protected health informa-

Accreditation Organizations

The Privacy Rule contains a number of references to accreditation organizations and their involvement with the health care system. Nevertheless, the regulation does not treat accreditation organizations, including URAC (also known as the American Accreditation HealthCare Commission), Joint Commission on the Accreditation of Healthcare Organizations (JCAHO), or National Committee for Quality Assurance (NCQA) as covered entities.

Although state governments as well as the federal government have "deemed" or "recognized" private accreditation organizations by statute or regulation, essentially treating accreditation organizations as health care oversight agencies, HHS did not include accreditation organizations in the definition of "health oversight agency." The department stated in the Privacy Rule's preamble that accreditation organizations perform health care functions on behalf of health plans and covered health care providers. So, "in order to obtain protected health information without individuals' authorizations, accrediting groups must enter into business associate agreements with health plans and covered health care providers for these purposes."[1] To that, HHS added:

> While their work can promote quality in the health care delivery system, private accreditation organizations are not authorized by law to oversee the health care system or government programs in which health information is necessary to determine eligibility or compliance, or to enforce civil rights laws for which health information is relevant. Under the final rule, we consider private accrediting groups to be performing a health care operations function for covered entities. Thus, disclosures to private accrediting organizations are disclosures for health care operations, not for oversight purposes.[2]

HHS tried to clarify the distinction stating that when "performing accreditation activities for a covered entity, private accrediting organizations will meet the definition of business associate, and the covered entity must enter into a business associate contract with the accrediting organization in order to disclose protected health information."[3]

Another provision in the Privacy Rule applies specifically to accreditation organizations and "whistleblower" protection. A covered entity does not violate the regulation when a member of the covered entity's work force or a business associate discloses protected health information to an "appropriate health care accreditation organization for the purpose of reporting the allegation of failure to meet professional standards or misconduct by the covered entity."[4]

- Dennis Melamed

[1] 65 Fed. Reg. at 82,492.
[2] 65 Fed. Reg. at 82,610-11.
[3] 65 Fed. Reg. at 82,611.
[4] 65 Fed. Reg. at 82,807 (to be codified at 45 C.F.R. pt. 164.502(j)).

tion from more than one covered entity for purposes, such as quality assurance, benchmarking and other comparative analyses.

The Privacy Rule defines "data aggregation" in the following way: "with respect to protected health information created or received by a business associate in its capacity as the business associate of a covered entity, the combining of such protected health information by the business associate with the protected

health information received by the business associate in its capacity as a business associate of another covered entity, to permit data analyses that relate to the health care operations of the respective covered entities."[14]

This is also one activity in which HHS makes an exception to its prohibition on business associates from further disclosing protected health information.[15] As an example, HHS cited the situation in which a state hospital association could act as a business associate of its member hospitals and combine data provided to it to help the hospitals evaluate their relative performance in areas such as quality, efficiency and other patient care issues. In this instance, however, the business associate contracts of each of the hospitals would have to permit the activity, and the protected health information of one hospital could not be disclosed to another hospital unless the disclosure is otherwise permitted by the Privacy Rule.

HHS also noted that there may be other situations in which a business associate may combine or aggregate protected health information received in its capacity as a business associate of different covered entities, such as when it is performing health care operations on behalf of covered entities that participate in an organized health care arrangement.

A business associate that is performing payment functions on behalf of different covered entities also may combine protected health information when necessary, such as when the covered entities share financial risk or otherwise jointly bill for services.[16]

2.3 What Information is Covered?

At the center of the Privacy Rule is the definition of exactly what is protected. HHS crafted three definitions for various concepts to ensure that the appropriate information will be safeguarded. HHS provided definitions of *health information, personally identifiable health information,* and *protected health information.* The Privacy Rule applies not only to electronic records, but extends to paper records that might have been in electronic format at one time, oral communications, and such electronic media as magnetic tapes, electronic mail, compact disks, voicemail, facsimile, etc.

2.3.1 Health Information

The term "health information" means:

any information, whether oral or recorded in any form or medium, that:

(1) Is created or received by a health care provider, health plan, public health authority, employer, life insurer, school or university, or health care clearinghouse; and

(2) Relates to the past, present, or future physical or mental health or condition of an individual; the provision of health care to an individual; or the past, present, or future payment for the provision of health care to an individual.[17]

2.3.2 Individually Identifiable Health Information

The Privacy Rule defines "individually identifiable health information" as:

information that is a subset of health information, including demographic information collected from an individual, and:

(1) Is created or received by a health care provider, health plan, employer, or health care clearinghouse; and

(2) Relates to the past, present, or future physical or mental health or condition of an individual; the provision of health care to an individual; or the past, present, or future payment for the provision of health care to an individual; and

(i) That identifies the individual; or

(ii) With respect to which there is a reasonable basis to believe the information can be used to identify the individual.[18]

2.3.3 Protected Health Information

In addition, "protected health information" is defined as:

individually identifiable health information:

(1) Except as provided in paragraph(2) of this definition, that is:

(i) Transmitted by electronic media;

(ii) Maintained in any medium described in the definition of *electronic media* at § 162.103 of this subchapter; or

(iii) Transmitted or maintained in any other form or medium.[19]

The definition of protected health information specifically excludes several categories of individually identifiable health information. The exclusions are for education records covered by the Family Educational Right and Privacy Act[20] and certain other specified educational records at 20 U.S.C. § 1232g(a)(4)(B)(iv).[21]

2.3.4 Special Classes of Information

With the exception of psychotherapy notes, the Privacy Rule does not draw any distinction among different classes of protected health information. In other words, the Privacy Rule does not impose new requirements for protecting genetic, Human Immuno-deficiency Virus/Acquired Immune Deficiency Syndrome (HIV/AIDS), cancer, or other types of information.[22]

At the same time, covered entities should remember that the Privacy Rule does not preempt state laws that are more protective of privacy than the federal frame-work. Because many states have enacted special protections for a variety of classes of information, such as HIV/AIDS and genetics, as a practical matter, covered entities are likely to face differing require-ments based on state law.

2.3.5 Psychotherapy Notes

The Privacy Rule provides a higher standard of protection for psychotherapy notes, which are "notes recorded (in any medium) by a health care provider who is a mental health professional documenting or analyzing the contents of conversation during a private counseling session or a group, joint, or family counsel-ing session and that are separated from the rest of the individual's medical record."[23]

The Privacy Rule excludes from the definition "medication prescription and monitoring, counseling session start and stop times, the modalities and frequencies of treatment furnished, results of clinical tests, and any summary of the following items: Diagnosis, functional status, the treatment plan, symptoms, prognosis, and progress to date."[24]

With a few exceptions, the Privacy Rules requires a covered entity to receive a separate patient authoriza-tion to use or disclose psychotherapy notes to carry out treatment, payment, or health care operations.

A covered entity must get the patient's consent, not an authorization, for the person who originated the psychotherapy notes to use these notes to carry out treatment and for the covered entity to use or disclose

psychotherapy notes for undertaking training pro-grams for students, trainees, or practitioners in mental health learning under supervision to practice or improve their skills in group, joint, family, or indi-vidual counseling. In addition, a covered entity may use psychotherapy notes to defend against a legal action or other proceeding brought by the indi-vidual.[25]

According to HHS, psychotherapy notes are not part of the medical record and are never intended to be shared with anyone else. While the Privacy Rule treats all protected health information as sensitive, HHS provides a greater degree of protection for psycho-therapy notes because of a federal psychotherapist-patient privilege created by the U.S. Supreme Court in *Jaffee v. Redmond*[26] and the "unique role of this type of information."[27]

2.4 Key Points

- Although employers and unions are not directly covered by the Privacy Rule, they will be affected by the new requirements, particularly when they offer health benefits or on-site health services for their employees or members.
- The Privacy Rule does not create special classes of information with the exception of psychotherapy notes.
- HIPAA does not pre-empt state laws that are more protective of privacy, and many states have imposed stricter controls in a number of areas, such as HIV/AIDS and genetic infor-mation.
- Private sector accrediting bodies are not automatically excluded from Privacy Rule coverage because they are not always consid-ered health oversight bodies.

Endnotes

[1] 65 Fed. Reg. at 82,462.

[2] 65 Fed. Reg. at 82,798 (to be codified at 45 C.F.R. pt. 160.102)..

[3] *id.* at 82,799 (to be codified at 45 C.F.R. pt. 160.103).

[4] *id.*

[5] *id.*

[6] *id.*

[7] *id.*

[8] *id.* at 82,808 (to be codified at 45 C.F.R. pt. 164.504(d)).

[9] *id.* at 82,509.

[10] *id.* at 82,807-08 (to be codified at 45 C.F.R. pt. 164.504(a)-(c)).

[11] *id.* at 82,798-99 (to be codified at 45 C.F.R. pt. 160.103).

[12] *id.* at 82,798.

[13] *id.*

[14] *id.* at 82,803 (to be codifed at 45 C.F.R. pt. 164.501).

[15] *id.* at 82,505.

[16] *id.* at 82,506

[17] *id.* at 82,799 (to be codified at 45 C.F.R. pt. 160.103).

[18] *id.* at 82,804 (to be codified at 45 C.F.R. pt.164.501).

[19] *id.* at 82,505.

[20] 20 U.S.C. § 1232g.

[21] 65 Fed. Reg. at 82,805 (to be codified at 45 C.F.R. pt. 164.501).

[22] In discussing genetic information in the Privacy Rule's preamble, HHS stated: "We agree that the definition of protected health information includes genetic information that otherwise meets the statutory definition. But we believe that singling out specific types of protected health information for special mention in the regulation text could wrongly imply that other types are not included." 65 Fed. Reg. at 82,621.

[23] 65 Fed. Reg. at 82,805 (to be codified at 45 C.F.R. pt. 164.501).

[24] *id.*

[25] *id.* at 82,811 (to be codified at 45 C.F.R. pt. 164.508(a)(2)).

[26] 518 U.S. 1 (1996).

[27] 65 Fed. Reg. at 82,652.

Section 3.0 - The New Patient Rights to Controlling Health Information

Joseph Braun

3.1 A New Definition of Efficiency

The administrative savings promised by the HIPAA electronic transactions come at a price: the creation of new patient rights to privacy, confidentiality and access to medical records and other health information. As a result, compliance with the Privacy Rule must be based on an understanding of these patient rights. For example, the Privacy Rule gives individuals new rights to challenge the use and accuracy of protected health information. Therefore, it is important for heath care providers, plans, insurers and other covered entities to understand how individuals may exercise those rights under the new federal rule.

The HIPAA Administrative Simplification provisions created new federal privacy rights for patients to enable them to exert more control over their personal health information. The Privacy Rule makes this goal plain by incorporating the concepts of patient privacy and data security in its definition of efficiency of the health care system.

HHS states in the Privacy Rule that the regulation has three purposes to:

(1) Protect and enhance the rights of consumers by providing them access to their health information and controlling the inappropriate use of that information;

(2) Improve the quality of health care in the U.S. by restoring trust in the health care system among consumers, health care professionals, and the multitude of organizations and individuals committed to the delivery of care; and

(3) *Improve the efficiency and effectiveness of health care delivery by creating a national framework for health privacy protection that builds on*

efforts by states, health systems, and individual organizations and individuals. (emphasis added)

Improving the health care system in this new context of efficiency is not a simple task as personally identifiable health information is generated and used in a wide variety of tasks in and out of the health care system.

3.2 Medical Records

Billions of medical-related records are created every year which must be retained anywhere from seven to 30 years. This material contains important and sensitive information that can range from mental health records, substance abuse records, genetic information as well as a broad range of other data that may or may not be important to an individual.

3.2.1 Access to Medical Information

New universes of individuals and organizations now routinely access this information as well. A study by the American College of Hospital Administrator estimates that, on average, 75 people have access to any one record.[1] This expanded data sharing was occurring even before the development and expanding use of utilization management, quality studies, disease management, pharmacy management and use of the chart for billing questions.[2]

Patients now face higher risks of devastating financial and emotional consequences if health information is inappropriately disclosed. To reduce those risks, the Privacy Rule imposes new legal liabilities on health care providers and insurers for failing to safeguard this information properly.

3.2.2 Confidentiality beyond the Doctor-Patient Relationship

The intrinsic nature of the patient-physician relationship is based on the concept of confidentiality. The patient must be free to tell the physician items of an intimate and personal nature without fear of this information being disclosed to the public. The physician likewise must be unfettered in being able to probe into these areas and know that the resulting answers will be protected. This, of course, is not a new phenomenon.[3]

However, the managed care system and the computer revolution have made the patient's interaction with the health care system vastly more complex.

3.2.3 Patient's Rights to Access Medical Record

The confluence of computer use and managed care prompted confusion over some of the most basic structures of the health care system. For example, the question frequently arises over the rights patients have in regard to medical records. The Privacy Rule does not directly address this issue, but as discussed later, the burden to comply with the new requirements falls with those who generate, maintain and use the information.

At the same time, ownership of the medical record is an important issue to explore as state laws have spoken on this issue, and those statements affect the interactions among patients, health care providers and insurers.[4]

Medical records traditionally have been regarded as the property of the institution or practitioner that creates and maintains them.[5] The courts, however, also have recognized a limited property right of the patient to the information in the record.[6]

Media accounts suggest that the right to medical privacy is new, however, that is not true. This right has a long line of legal precedents. Warren and Brandeis, in their article *The Right to Privacy* state that this right can be linked to the fundamental rights of life, liberty and the pursuit of happiness.[7] This right has been confirmed by the courts in *Planned Parenthood of S.E. Penn. v Casey*[8] and *Estate of Behringer v Medical Center of Princeton*.[9] The second case is particularly germane as it verified the right of patients to have their medical records remain confidential.

Furthermore, cases from state courts have ruled patients have a right to review their records, a right of access or privacy and the right to copy records.[10] Many state laws also allow patients the right of access to their medical records. What has been lacking has been a statutory federal right of patients to control and monitor access to their records.

The Privacy Rule changes this landscape. It now creates a series of federal rights for patients in areas, such as notice, consent, access and inspection, accounting, amendment of their personal medical information.

3.3 What HIPAA Covers: The Rights of Patients

Before discussing the new rights granted to patients, it is important to understand what actually is being protected and subject to those rights.

3.3.1 Definitions

HHS provided definitions of *health information, personally identifiable health information* and *protected health information* to assure the proper use of patient health information. The department crafted a broad definition of health information to ensure that any information that could reflect an individual's health or medical condition would be covered.

Health information means:

(A)ny information, whether oral or recorded in any form or medium, that:

    (1) Is created or received by a health care provider, health plan, public health authority, employer, life insurer, school or university, or health care clearinghouse; and

    (2) Relates to the past, present or future physical or mental health or condition of any individual; or the past, present, or future payment for the provision of health care to an individual.[11]

Individually identifiable health information means:

(i)nformation that is a subset of health information, including demographic information collected from an individual, and:

    (1) Is created or received by a health care provider, health plan, employer, or health care clearinghouse; and

(2) Relates to the past, present, or future physical or mental health or condition of an individual; the provision of health care to an individual; or the past, present, or future payment for the provision of health care to an individual; and

    (i) That identifies the individual; or

    (ii) With respect to which there is a reasonable basis to believe the information can be used to identify the individual.[12]

Protected health information means individually identifiable health information:

(1) Except as provided in paragraph (2) of this definition, that is:

    (i) Transmitted by electronic media;

    (ii) Maintained in any medium described in the definition of *electronic media* at § 162.103 of this subchapter; or

    (iii) Transmitted or maintained in any other form or medium.

(2) *Protected health information* excludes individually identifiable health information in:

    (i) Education records covered by the Family Educational Right and Privacy Act, as amended, 20 U.S.C. 1232g; and

    (ii) Records described at 20 U.S.C. 1232g(a)(4)(B)(iv). This section deals with the definition of what constitutes an educational record and what is not included.[13]

3.3.2 The Need for Fair Information Practices

The Privacy Rule establishes four new and broad patient rights in regard to medical privacy and confidentiality. Patients have the right to:

- Notice of use and disclosures;
- Consent to the use and disclosures;
- Access records for inspection and amendment; and
- An accounting of how the protected health information was used and shared.

These new rights are necessary because of the expanded uses of protected health information. This data is no longer used simply by the physician for purposes of patient care or for billing. Instead, it is used for a wide variety of management and business endeavors.

Furthermore, personal health information has become a valuable commodity that is used, sold and otherwise transferred to other companies who then could put it to use in a broad number of marketing, research or other business applications.

For example, large health care companies and their suppliers use protected health information to forecast usage trends and make decisions regarding individual treatment decisions and resource utilization. Pharmacy benefits managers use the information to personally contact health plan members and their physicians to help in making decisions about the use of one medication over another. Life and health insurance also use this information in data banks to verify that information given on application is accurate. As described in more detail in Section 8.0, disease management vendors also use medical information to coordinate care for certain chronic disease states.

These expanded uses – often invisible to the patient – have generated both public and political concern. The rights granted under HIPAA are designed to give patients a better knowledge of the uses of this information and provide an element of control over that information.

3.3.3 The Right of Notice

The right of notice refers to an obligation on the part of a covered entity to inform patients about potential uses of their protected health information and their rights to limit uses. In most instances, health care providers who have direct treatment relationships with their patients obtain the consent of their patients to use and disclose protected health information for treatment, payment and health care operations.

While concern about the "coerced" nature of these consents remains, both patients and practitioners believe that patient consent is an important part of the current health care system and should be retained. By "coerced," the Privacy Rule means that the provision of health care services is conditioned on this permission from the patient.

Providing notice and obtaining consent have special significance for patients and practitioners. Patient advocates argue that the act of signing these consent and authorization forms focuses the patient's attention on the substance of the transaction and creates an opportunity for patients to ask questions about or seek modifications in the provider's practices.

To encourage a more informed interaction between the patient and the provider during the consent process, the Privacy Rule requires that the consent form be accompanied by a notice that contains a detailed discussion of the provider's health information practices. The consent form must reference the notice and must inform patients that they have the right to ask the health care provider to request certain restrictions as to how the information will be used or disclosed.

Global consents, i.e. a document that consolidates permissions for all uses, are not allowed. While these may be more efficient from an administrative perspective, the new definition of efficiency under the Privacy Rule incorporates the need for patients to be informed and more in control of data practices.

3.3.4 The Right of Consent

The right of consent refers to obtaining the informed permission of patients for the use of their health information based on the notice provided by the covered entity.[14] The consent form must be written in plain language to ensure that it is understood by all patients.

The Privacy Rule draws a distinction between consent and authorization for use and disclosure of protected health information. However, they represent the basic premise of the rule that patients must grant permission for the use of their information. (See Section 5.0 for a broader discussion of consents and authorizations.)

The consent must inform the patient that protected health information may be used and disclosed by the covered entity to carry out treatment, payment, or health care operations.[15] The covered entity must determine which of these elements (use and/or disclosure; treatment, payment, and/or health care operations) to include in the consent document, as appropriate for the covered entity's practices.

For covered health care providers that are required to obtain consent, the requirement applies only to the extent the covered provider uses or discloses protected health information. For example, if all of a covered provider's health care operations are conducted by members of the covered provider's own workforce, the covered provider may choose to obtain consent only for uses, not disclosures of protected health information to carry out health care operations.

If an individual pays out of pocket for all services received from the covered provider and the provider will not disclose any information about the patient to a third party payer, the provider may choose not to obtain the individual's consent to disclose information for payment purposes.

If the covered entity has reserved the right to change its privacy practices in accordance with the rule, the consent must indicate that the terms of the notice may change and must describe how the individual may obtain a revised notice.[16]

The consent must inform individuals that they have the right to request restrictions on uses and disclosures of protected health information for treatment, payment, and health care operations purposes. It also must state that the covered entity is not required to agree to an individual's request, but that if the covered entity does agree to the request, the restriction is binding on the covered entity.[17] The consent must indicate that the individual has the right to revoke the consent in writing, except to the extent that the covered entity has taken action in reliance on the consent.

3.3.5 The Right of Access and Inspection

The right of access refers to the ability of the patient to inspect, copy and otherwise have knowledge of any health information that could be potentially used or disclosed by a covered entity.[18] This provision gives patients the right to access protected health information that is maintained in a designated record set.

This right applies to health plans, covered health care providers, and health care clearinghouses that create or receive protected health information other than as a business associate of another covered entity. Under the Privacy Rule, patients have a right to access any protected health information that is used, in whole or in part, to make decisions about them. This information includes, for example, information used to make health care decisions or information used to determine whether an insurance claim will be paid.

Covered entities often incorporate the same protected health information into a variety of different data systems, not all of which will be used to make decisions about individuals. For example, information systems that are used for quality control or peer review analyses may not be used to make decisions about individuals. In that case, the information systems would not fall within the definition of a designated record set. It is not required that entities grant an individual access to protected health information maintained in these types of information systems.

3.3.6 Verifying the Identity of a Requestor

Under the general verification requirements of the Privacy Rule, the covered entity is required to take reasonable steps to verify the identity of the individual making the request.[19] The Privacy Rule does not mandate particular identification requirements (e.g., drivers license, photo ID). That decision is left to the discretion of the covered entity.

However, the covered entity must establish and document procedures for verifying the identity and authority of personal representatives, if not known to the entity. For example, a health care provider can require a copy of a power of attorney or can ask questions to determine that an adult acting for a young child has the requisite relationship to the child.

Similarly, the Privacy Rule requires covered entities to have policies and procedures for assuring individuals access to protected health information about them. While such policies and procedures must include documentation of the designated record sets subject to access, who is authorized to determine when information will be withheld from an individual, and similar details, the notice need only explain generally that individuals have the right to inspect and copy information about them, and tell individuals how to exercise that right.

3.3.7 Duration of the Right of Access

The Privacy Rule requires that covered entities must provide access to individuals for as long as the protected health information is maintained in a designated record set.

3.3.8 Exceptions to the Right of Access

The Privacy Rule specifies three types of information to which individuals do not have a right of access, even if the information is maintained in a designated record set. They are:

- Psychotherapy notes;
- Information compiled in reasonable anticipation of or for use in a civil, criminal, or administrative action or proceeding; and
- Certain protected health information maintained by a covered entity that is exempted under the Clinical Laboratory Improvements Amendments of 1988 (CLIA).

It is important to note that this provision is not intended to require covered entities to provide access to documents protected by attorney work-product privilege nor should this be construed as an alteration of the rules of discovery.

3.3.9 The Right of Accounting

The right of accounting refers to the individual's right to receive a listing of all disclosures and other releases of any protected health information for purposes other than treatment, payment and health care operations for the previous six years that the data has been maintained.[20] This includes the right to receive an accounting of disclosures made by a covered entity, including disclosures by or to a business associate of the covered entity subject to certain exceptions as discussed in this chapter.

The accounting must include all disclosures. including disclosures authorized by the individual and must contain the date of each disclosure; the name and address of the organization or person who received the protected health information; and a brief description of the information disclosed. For disclosures other than those made at the request of the individual, the accounting also must include the purpose for which the information was disclosed.

Individuals *do not have a right* to an accounting of disclosures:

- To health oversight or law enforcement agencies if the agency provided a written request for exclusion for a specified time period and the request stated that access by the individual during that time period would be reasonably likely to impede the agency's activities

- To the individual for disclosures used for facility directories,
- To persons involved in the individual's care,
- For other disclosures for notification purposes;
- To national security or intelligence purposes;
- To correctional institutions or law enforcement officials; or
- Made by the covered entity before the compliance date of the rule for that covered entity.

Covered entities must provide a requested accounting no later than 60 days after receipt of the request. If the covered entity cannot meet the deadline, the covered entity may extend the deadline by no more than 30 days.

The covered entity must inform the individual in writing, within the standard 60-day deadline, of the reason for the delay and the date by which the covered entity will provide the request. A covered entity may only extend the deadline one time per accounting request.

Individuals have a right to receive one free accounting per 12-month period. For each additional request by an individual within the 12 month period, the covered entity may charge a reasonable, cost-based fee. If it imposes such a fee, the covered entity must inform the individual of the fee in advance and provide the individual with an opportunity to withdraw or modify the request in order to avoid or reduce the fee.

3.3.10 The Right of Amendment

The right of amendment refers to the individuals ability to request a change to their protected health information if they feel it is incorrect[21] This is an important right in that it allows the individual to challenge the accuracy of any protected health information.

The individual has a right to request a covered health care provider or health plan to amend protected health information about the individual for as long as the information is maintained in the designated record set.

A. The Denial of an Amendment Request: A covered health care provider or health plan may deny a request

for amendment if it determined that the protected health information was not created by the covered provider or health plan, or if it was accurate and complete. A covered entity is permitted, but not required, to deny a request if any of these conditions is met.

However, there is one exception. If the individual provides a reasonable basis to believe that the originator of the protected health information is no longer available to act on the requested amendment, the covered entity must address the request for amendment as though the covered entity had created the information.

A covered entity also may deny a request for amendment if the protected health information is not part of a designated record set or would not otherwise be available for inspection [22]

Moreover, a covered entity may deny a request for amendment if the covered entity determines that the information in dispute is accurate and complete. This concept comes from the Privacy Act of 1974, governing records held by federal agencies, which permits an individual to request correction or amendment of a record "which the individual believes is not accurate, relevant, timely, or complete." [23]

This right, however, is not intended to interfere with medical practice or to modify standard business record keeping practices. Perfect records are not required. Instead, a standard of reasonable accuracy and completeness should be used.

In addition, this right is not intended to provide a procedure for substantive review of decisions such as coverage determinations by payers. It is intended only to affect the content of records, not the underlying truth or correctness of materials recounted therein. Attempts under the Privacy Act of 1974 to use this mechanism as a basis for collateral attack on agency determinations have generally been rejected by the courts. The same results are intended here.

B. Requests for Amendment and Timely Action:[24] Covered entities must permit individuals to request that the covered entity amend protected health information about them. The Privacy Rule also permits certain specifications for the form and content of the request.

If a covered entity informs individuals of these requirements in advance, a covered entity may require individuals to make requests for amendment in writing and to provide a reason to support a requested amendment. If the covered entity imposes such a requirement and informs individuals of the requirement in advance, the covered entity is not required to act on an individual's request that does not meet these requirements.

Covered entities must act on a request for amendment within 60 days of receipt of the request. The covered entity must inform the individual, as described below, that the request has been either accepted or denied, in whole or in part. It also must take certain actions pursuant to its decision to accept or deny the request, as described below.

If the covered entity is unable to meet the deadline, the covered entity may extend the deadline by no more than 30 days. The covered entity must inform the individual in writing, within the initial 60-day period, of the reason for the delay and the date by which the covered entity will complete its action on the request. A covered entity may only extend the deadline one time per request for amendment.

C. Accepting the Amendment: If a covered entity accepts an individual's request for amendment or correction, it must make the appropriate amendment. At a minimum, the covered entity must identify the records in the designated record set that are affected by the amendment and must append or otherwise provide a link to the location of the amendment.

Covered entities should not expunge any protected health information. Covered entities may expunge information if doing so is consistent with other applicable law and the covered entity's record keeping practices. The Privacy Rule contemplates that a complete record includes all changes, modifications and amendments.

The covered entity must inform individuals about accepted amendments and get permission from the individual to share the information. If the individual agrees, the covered entity must make reasonable efforts to provide a copy of the amendment within a reasonable time to: (1) Persons the individual identifies as having received protected health information about the individual and needing the amendment;

and (2) Persons, including business associates, that the covered entity knows have the unamended information and who may have relied, or could reasonably expect to rely on the information to the detriment of the individual.

D. Actions on Notices of Amendment: If a covered entity receives a notification of amended protected health information from another covered entity as described above, the covered entity must make the necessary amendment to protected health information in designated record sets it maintains. In addition, covered entities must require their business associates who receive such notifications to incorporate any necessary amendments to designated record sets maintained on the covered entity's behalf.

3.3.11 The Right to Restrict

The right to restrict under the Privacy Rule enables patients to seek limits on the sharing of protected health information by *all covered entities*. However, the Privacy Rule does not require covered entities to agree to those restrictions.

If the covered entity agrees to the restriction, then it becomes binding but it applies only to the covered entity. At the same time, HHS encourages covered entities to inform others of the restriction, but noted that this could be problematic as well. In acknowledging a restriction, covered entities risk *de facto* disclosure of the information itself.

If a restriction is agreed to by the covered entity, health care providers can breach that agreement in emergency health care situations. However, HHS said it expected that health care providers would foresee this possibility and include an "emergency" provision when negotiating these restrictions.

A covered entity may terminate a restriction with the individual's written or verbal agreement. If agreement is made verbally, then the covered entity must document it. In addition, if the covered entity wishes to terminate the restriction unilaterally, it must inform the patient and can share only the information generated after the termination.

The covered entity's ability to decline restrictions is far from open-ended. For example, covered health care providers must agree to "reasonable requests" to limit communications of protected health information. For example, patients may request that information not be sent to specific individuals (including those assisting in the patient's care), and that communications be sent to locations other than the patient's home.

3.4 Key Points

- HIPAA created a new definition of efficiency for the health care system which includes the privacy, confidentiality and security of protected health information.
- The Privacy Rule creates new patient rights obligating covered entities to seek permission to use protected health information and to allow access and changes to be made to medical and other health records.
- Covered entities are under no obligation to agree to restrictions on the use of data beyond what is required under the Privacy Rule. However, they are required to accommodate reasonable requests to ensure communications are kept confidential.
- The Privacy Rule does not create a new ownership right for patients over their medical records.

Endnotes

[1] American College of Hospital Administrators, Medical Confidentiality, Can It Be Protected? 2-3(1983).

[2] Peter R. Kongstvedt, P., The Managed Health Care Handbook (1996).

[3] Tom L. Beauchamp, & James F. Childress, Principles of Biomedical Ethics (4th ed. 1994).

[4] For example, in 1998, the Florida Insurance Commission told Aetna USHealthcare that it could not jointly own medical records generated by physicians. Flordida law states that the physician owns the medical record.
Insurer Contracts Come Under Attack by Physicians over Confidentiality, Ownership of Medical Records, *Health Info. Privacy Alert*, Aug. 1998, at 1.
Ultimately, Aetna rewrote its contracts, maintaining that access to the record was key, not ownership.
Aetna USHealthcare Rewrites Contract In Plain English to Avoid Misunderstandings over Confidentiality, Records Ownership, *Health Info. Privacy Alert*, Oct. 1998, at 1.

[5] *McGarry v. J.A. Mercier Co.*, 262 N.W. 296 (Mich. 1935).

[6] *Pyramid Life Ins. Co. v. Masonic Hospital Assoc.* 191 F. Supp. 51 (D. Okla. 1961)

[7] Warren and Brandeis, "The Right to Privacy"

[8] 505 U.S. 833 (1992)

[9] 249 N.J. Super. 597, 595 A.2d 1251 (1991).

[10] *Pierce v. Penman* 515 A.2d 948(Pa. Super. 1986).

[11] 65 Fed. Reg. at 82,799 (to be codified at 45 C.F.R. pt. 164.501).

[12] *id.*

[13] *id.*

[14] *id.* at 82,810 (to be codified in 45 C.F.R. pt. 164.506(c)).

[15] *id.*

[16] *id.* at 82,821 (to be codified at 45 C.F.R. pt. 164.520(b)(1)(v)(C)). Also see *id.* (to be codified as 45 C.F.R. pt.164.520) and the corresponding preamble discussion regarding notice requirements.

[17] *id.* at 82,822 to be codified at 45 C.F.R. pt. 164.522(a)).

[18] *id.* at 82,823 to be codified at 45 C.F.R. pt. 164.524(a)).

[19] *id.* at 82,800 (to be codified at 45 C.F.R. pt. 164.514(h)).

[20] *id.* at 82,826 (to be codified at 45 C.F.R. pt. 164.528).

[21] *id.* at 82,824-26 (to be codified at 45 C.F.R. pt. 164.526).

[22] id. at 82,823-24 (to be codified at 45 C.F.R. pt.164.524).

[23] *See* (5 U.S.C. 552a(d)(2)).

[24] *id.* (to be codified at 45 C.F.R. pt. 164.526(b)).

Section 4.0 - Giving Notice:
What Patients Have a Right to Know
Tom Hanks

4.1 Introduction

At the core of the HIPAA Privacy Rule are require-ments for health care providers and other covered entities to get permission for using protected health information. As the previous section discussed, the Privacy Rule provides patients and consumers with new rights to control and access their individually identifiable health information.

Four principles make up the engine for this patient control of protected health information: *notice, patient consent, patient authorization*, and determining the *minimum necessary* amount of information to accom-plish the task.

This section discusses the basic requirements placed on covered entities to provide notice of the data usage and sharing policies to fulfill the notice requirements to inform patients. Section 5.0 discusses the other three principles.

4.2 Understanding the Notice Requirement

Notice refers to the requirement that health care providers and health plans inform patients of how they will use, maintain, and share protected health informa-tion.[1]

The requirement applies to providers and plans, but there are two types of special entities within these categories which reap special benefits under the Privacy Rule that should be discussed first: organized health care arrangements and affiliated entities

4.2.1 Organized Health Care Arrangement

An organized health care arrangement is one that allows unique covered entities to operate under a joint notice and consent so that a single notice and consent serves all the covered entities.[2] To qualify as an Organized Health Care Arrangement, individuals who obtain services from these entities have to expect that these arrangements will be integrated with jointly managed operations. An example of such an arrange-ment is a hospital, with its staff physicians and all of its clinical departments that may use contracted or outsourced providers. This may include its emergency department, clinical laboratory, radiology, pharmacy, and all physicians on staff.

Although each department or staff provider could be a separate entity, the patient would expect that all of these departments and physicians are jointly integrated and managed. In this case, a single, joint notice and consent, that was agreed upon by all the members of the arrangement, serves to allow all the components of the entity to be able to use, disclose and share informa-tion for the purpose of treatment, payment or health care operations.

4.2.2 Affiliated Entities

Affiliated entities are those entities where there is common control or ownership (greater than five percent) that binds the entities together.[3] An example could be a group of hospitals managed by a single entity. For purposes of HIPAA compliance, these entities could declare themselves a single Affiliated Entity and operate under a single joint notice and consent process.

4.3 Notice of Privacy Practices

All individuals, except prison inmates, have a right to receive a notice from any covered entity regarding that entity's privacy practices.[4] The individual does not need to have a customer or patient relationship with the covered entity to receive a notice. Instead, the covered entity's notice is intended to be a public document. This means that covered entities must be prepared to share their data practices with anyone who requests a copy.

All covered entities, including group health plans (and self-insured plans), must provide a notice to individuals of how they plan to use and disclose the individual's protected health information, and of the individual's rights with respect to that information.

If a covered provider, who is part of an organized health care arrangement, has different privacy practices at their office then the practices described in the joint notice, they are required to produce a separate notice that accurately describes their privacy practices.

Correctional institutions and clearinghouses that only use or disclose protected health information only as business associates of other covered entities do not have to produce a notice.

4.3.1 The Amount of Detail Required

A covered entity's notice does not need to document all of the entity's privacy practices. Rather, it only needs to explain the entity's privacy practices in general terms.[5] For example: while the Privacy Rule requires detailed policies and procedures regarding the implementation of the individual's right to access and amend their records, the covered entity only has to explain generally that individuals have the right to inspect, copy and amend information about them and tell them how to exercise that right.

4.3.2. The Need for More than One Notice

Covered entities may be required to produce more than one notice. A governing principle is that notices must accurately convey the privacy practices that are relevant to the individuals receiving them. For example, covered entities operating in more than one state may produce a separate notice for each state that they operate in to reflect the unique laws of those states. In another example, a covered entity that has both provider and health plan components would produce separate notices for each component.

The covered entity, however, makes binding commitments in its notice. It is not permitted to use or disclose protected health information beyond what is stated in the notice. In the event the entity materially changes its privacy practices, polices or procedures, the notice must be revised to reflect those changes. See **Reservation of Rights to Revise** below.

4.3.3. Notice as a Public Document

The notice is intended to be a public document available to anyone making a request. It is HHS's intention that it be available for people to make informed decision about purchasing health care products.[6]

4.3.4 Electronic Delivery of Notice

Notices can be delivered electronically if the individual has agreed to receive materials electronically. However, any covered entity providing notices electronically also must be able to provide one on paper, if requested, and state in the notice the individual's right to receive a paper copy.[7]

All covered entities that obtain consent must provide notice in conjunction with obtaining consent.

4.4 Deadlines for Providing Notice

4.4.1 Health Plans

Health plans must provide notice to all enrollees by the April 2003 deadline and, after the compliance date, to all new enrollees when they join the plan. Health plans also must inform enrollees at least once every three years on how to obtain a copy of the notice.[8] One copy to the member (name insured) also serves for all dependents.

4.4.2 Providers with Direct Relationships

Health care providers with direct treatment relationships must provide notice by the first day of service, whether delivered on-site or electronically, after the compliance date. The notice, and any revisions to the notice, must be promptly and prominently posted at the site of service and be available for individuals to receive on request.[9]

4.4.3 Providers with Indirect Relationships

Health care providers with indirect relationships are required only to produce notices on request.[10] In the event an individual's first service from a covered provider is electronic, then the notice must be automatically provided to the individual, concurrently with the request for service. If any covered entity included in a joint notice distributes the notice, then the notice has been distributed for all the entities included in the joint notice.

4.5 Specific Notice Requirements

4.5.1 Plain Language

The notice must be written in plain language.[11] Plain language means a reasonable effort to:

1. Organize material to serve the needs of the reader;
2. Write short sentences in the active voice, using "you" and other pronouns;
3. Use common, everyday words in sentences; and
4. Divide material into short sections.

Concerning non-English speaking populations, there is some expectation for covered entities to provide notice in the language of the recipient. This is a requirement under The Civil Rights Act of 1964 for covered entities receiving federal assistance.

Likewise, in the Privacy Rule, HHS communicates an expectation that covered entities will accommodate the needs of individuals who cannot read.

4.5.2 Header Wording

The header of the notice must contain the specific wording:

THIS NOTICE DESCRIBES HOW MEDICAL INFORMATION ABOUT YOU MAY BE USED AND DISCLOSED AND HOW YOU CAN GET ACCESS TO THIS INFORMATION. PLEASE REVIEW IT CAREFULLY.[12]

4.5.3 Uses and Disclosure Under Law

The notice must inform individuals of all the uses and disclosures that the covered entity is required or permitted to make under all applicable state and federal laws.[13] However, covered entities should not include statements that limit their ability to use or disclose information required by law or necessary to avoid a serious and imminent threat to health or safety. Instead, the notice should:

1. Clearly, describe all the uses and disclosures of protected health information they are permitted or required to make under the Privacy Rule without individual authorization or consent. Each use and disclosure must be described separately.
2. Clearly describe all the uses and disclosures of

protected health information, including at least one example of each, that they are permitted to make with consent for treatment, payment, and health care operations.

If any other applicable law prohibits or limits the covered entity's ability to use or disclose protected health information that would be permitted under the Privacy Rule, the notice must describe only the uses and disclosures permitted under the more stringent law.

4.5.4 Authorization

The notice must state that any uses and disclosures other than those in the section on **Uses and Disclosure** will be made only with the individual's authorization, and that the individual has the right to revoke these authorizations.[14]

4.5.5 Separate Statements of Use and Disclosure

If the covered entity intends to conduct any of the following uses and disclosures, a separate statement is required for each.

1. The covered entity may contact the individual to provide appointment reminders or information about treatment alternatives or other health-related benefits and services that may be of interest to the individual.
2. The covered entity may contact the individual to raise funds for the covered entity.
3. A group health plan, health insurer, or HMO may disclose protected health information to the sponsor of the plan (employer).[15]

4.5.6 Statement of Individual Rights

As discussed in Section 3, the Privacy Rule created new patient rights over the use of protected health information. Covered entities are required to inform their patients, members or customers of those rights The statement of individual rights is a brief description of how the individual may exercise each of those rights as follows:

1. Right to request restrictions on specific uses and disclosures of protected health information *and* a statement that the covered entity may refuse the request.
2. Right to receive confidential communications.

3. Right to inspect and copy their protected health information.
4. Right to amend their protected health information.
5. Right to receive an accounting of disclosure of protected health information not for the purpose of treatment, payment, and health care operations.
6. Right to receive a paper copy of their notice upon request.[16]

4.5.7 Entity's Requirements under Law

The notice must state that the covered entity has a legal requirement to maintain privacy of protected health information, provide a notice of its duties and privacy practices, and to abide by the terms of the notice.[17]

4.5.8 Reservation of Right to Revise

The notice should state that the covered entity reserves the right to change and revise its privacy practices to protected health information previously created or received and how it will provide individuals with a revised notice.[18] *If this statement is not included in the notice, and the covered entity changes its privacy practices, any protected health information previously created or received prior to the date of the revision, cannot be included in any use or disclosure which was not contained in the notice prior to the changes.*

If there is no reservation of right to revise stated in the notice, then the records must be segregated so that any information created or received prior to the revision date would be prevented from being used for any additional uses and disclosures contained in the revised notice.

4.5.9.Complaint Procedures

The notice should include a statement on how an individual who believes his or her protected health information has been improperly used or disclosed may file a complaint with the covered entity.[19] This should include the name and telephone number of the contact person.

There also must be a statement that the individual has a right to file a complaint with the HHS Secretary and that there will be no retaliation for filing such a complaint.

4.5.10 Effective Date

The notice must state the date the notice went into effect, not the date it was produced. The effective date cannot be earlier than the date the notice was published.[20]

4.5.11 Special Requirement for Joint Notices

A joint notice must meet all requirements cited above, plus it must reasonably identify all of the covered entities, or class of covered entities, to whom the joint notice applies.[21] It must list the service delivery sites or classes of delivery sites. If the covered entities will share protected health information to perform treatment, payment, and health care operations, then that statement must be included in the notice

4.6 Key Points

- The covered entity makes binding commitments in its Privacy Notice.
- A covered entity may have to produce more than one version of its Privacy Notice if it operates in more than one state to reflect the differences in state law.
- If other applicable laws further restrict the collection and/or sharing of personally identifiable information, the HIPAA Privacy Notice must describe only the uses and disclosures permitted under the more stringent law.
- The notice should state that the covered entity reserves the right to change and revise its privacy practices.
- The Privacy Notice must state the date the notice went into effect, not the date it was produced.

Endnotes

[1] 65 Fed. Reg. at 82,820 (to be codified at 45 C.F.R. pt. 164.520).

[2] *id.* at 87,804 (to be codified at 45 C.F.R. pt. 164.501).

[3] *id.* at 82,808 (to be codified at 45 C.F.R. pt. 164.504(d)(1)).

[4] *id.* at 87,821 (to be codified at 45 C.F.R. pt. 164.520).

[5] *id.* (to be codified at 45 C.F.R. pt. 164.520 (b)(1)(ii)).

[6] *id.* at 82,821-22 (to be codified at 45 C.F.R. pt. 164.520 (c)).

[7] *id.* at 82,822 (to be codified at 45 C.F.R. pt. 164.520 (c)(3)(ii)).

[8] *id.* (to be codified at 45 C.F.R. pt. 164.520 (c)(1)(ii)).

[9] *id.* (to be codified at 45 C.F.R. pt. 164.520 (c)(2)).

[10] *id.* (to be codified at 45 C.F.R. pt. 164.520 (c)(3)(iii)).

[11] *id.* at 82,821 (to be codified at 45 C.F.R. pt. 164.520 (b)(1)).

[12] *id.* (to be codified at 45 C.F.R. pt. 164.520 (b)(1)(i)).

[13] *id.* (to be codified at 45 C.F.R. pt. 164.520 (b)(1)(ii)(D)).

[14] *id.* (to be codified at 45 C.F.R. pt. 164.520 (b)(1)(ii)(E)).

[15] *id.* (to be codified at 45 C.F.R. pt. 164.520 (b)(1)(iii)).

[16] *id.* (to be codified at 45 C.F.R. pt. 164.520 (b)(1)(iv)).

[17] *id.* (to be codified at 45 C.F.R. pt. 164.520 (b)(v)(A)).

[18] *id.* (to be codified at 45 C.F.R. pt. 164.520 (b)(1)(v)(C)).

[19] *id.* (to be codified at 45 C.F.R. pt. 164.520 (b)(1)(vi)).

[20] *id.* (to be codified at 45 C.F.R. pt. 164.520 (b)(1)(viii)).

[21] *id.* at 82,822 (to be codified at 45 C.F.R. pt. 164.520 (d)).

Section 5.0 - Getting Permission: Patient Consent and Authorization

Tom Hanks

5.1 Introduction

HIPAA's privacy notice requirements discussed in Section 4.0 requires covered entities to develop policies and procedures for handling personally identifiable health information. As stated earlier, however, the Privacy Rule crafted three other mechanisms to drive patient control of protected health information and which mandate what many of the policies described in the notice should address.

This section discusses these three other mechanisms: *patient consent, patient authorization*, and determining the *minimum necessary* amount of information to accomplish the task.

5.2 Minimum Necessary Disclosure/Use Provision

Before discussing HIPAA's requirements addressing how to obtain the appropriate consents or authorizations from patients, health care providers and other covered entities first should understand the principle of "*minimum necessary*."[1]

Under this regulatory concept, health care providers and other covered entities may only share the minimum amount of information necessary to conduct an activity where protected health information is used or disclosed.

5.2.1 Internal Business Use

The minimum necessary requirement also covers internal uses by the covered entity so that each entity must define what information will be made available to each employee based on specific business functions and needs. For example, a billing clerk may have access to the information needed to perform the billing role that would not include the clinical information that would be available to a coding specialist.

This can be accomplished through "role-based" access controls where each function is assigned certain "roles" or classes that allow access to information assigned to that role. Employees then are assigned those roles and their access to information is restricted to that needed only for the roles or functions that they perform.

This also means each covered entity must develop policies and procedures that define the protected health information that an employee needs to perform his or her job and limit access to only that information. These determinations are based on reasonableness and the technical feasibility of controlling such access. Reasonableness and technical feasibility are not defined, however, the expectation is that covered entities will develop the proper justifications for their decisions.

5.2.2 Clinical Settings

In a treatment context, the *minimum necessary* provision does not apply. Health care providers do not have to think about whether they are sharing too much information. Providers are free to share whatever information they wish with another provider for the purpose of providing treatment.

For example, providers are meant to have the freedom to exchange information, consult, and review other patient records for comparison purposes (e.g., radiologist looking at the last 10 MRIs for a particular diagnostic scan). There is no intent in the Privacy Rule to impose unreasonable barriers to the provision of health care.

5.2.3 Requests from Covered Entities and Health Oversight Agencies

When requesting information from another covered entity, the covered entity requesting the information must ask for only the minimum amount necessary to perform the function in question. Conversely, covered entities receiving requests for information from other covered entities can assume that information requested is the minimum necessary.

In this context, the decision on what is deemed minimally necessary falls to the requesting entity.

This is also true for requests from state and federal health care oversight agencies, such as the Food & Drug Administration and Center for Disease Control.

5.2.4 Standard Transaction Exemption

The minimum necessary provision does not apply to the uniform electronic transaction standards created by the Administrative Simplification provisions of HIPAA. As a result, covered entities can conduct these standard transactions without regard to whether the information disclosed is appropriate for the purpose of disclosure.[2]

5.2.5 Interaction with the HIPAA Security Rule

Operationally, the minimum necessary provision is an opportunity for covered entities to streamline its workflow and business processes. As job functions are studied, some covered entities may find that their job descriptions bear little relationship to the work performed. It makes sense at this time for covered entities to perform workflow analyses while they are studying their job functions. This gives covered entities an opportunity to realign workflow to improve processes, reclassify job functions, and rewrite job descriptions.

Because of the role-based access to information implicit in the minimum necessary provision, it is also an area in which the HIPAA Privacy Rule interacts with the HIPAA Security Rule. Consequently, when an organization constructs and implements privacy policies to comply with the Minimum Necessary provisions, it also should make sure those policies are consistent and integrated with its security policies. (See Section 15.0, for a broader discussion of how the Privacy and Security Rules overlap)

5.3 Patient Consent

Another one of the mechanisms under HIPAA to control the use and disclosure of personal health care information is the *patient consent* requirement.

Consent refers to patient agreement to use protected health information for *treatment, payment,* and *health care operations.* This provision broadly reflects what

most patients expect when they encounter the health care system for services. The consent requirement is not intended to restrict the ability of providers to consult with other providers about the patient's condition.

5.3.1 Treatment

Treatment refers to the provision, coordination, or management of health care and related services by one or more health care providers, including the coordination or management of health care by a health care provider with a third party; consultation between health care providers about a patient; or the referral of a patient for health care services from one provider to another.[3]

At the same time, the Privacy Rule tries to recognize and accommodate situations in which the patient receives services from medical professionals who work in support of or in conjunction with the health care provider who actually communicates with the patient directly.

As a result, the Privacy Rule draws a distinction between *direct treatment,* in which providers typically provide direct, face-to-face care and *indirect treatment.* Indirect treatment refers to situations in which providers act on orders from another provider and may not directly see the patient. It also refers to situations in which a provider acts under the direction of a provider's order and where the results are typically furnished to the ordering provider and not the patient. Examples of an indirect treatment relationship include: radiology, pathology, clinical laboratory analyses, and hospital pharmacies.

Generally, health care providers who are in a *direct treatment relationship*[4] *must obtain consent* from the individual to use and disclose protected health information for the purpose of treatment, payment, and health care operations. Providers in an *indirect treatment relationship*[5] *are not required to obtain consent,* but are not prohibited from obtaining consent.

Other covered entities, at their option, may obtain consent, but a covered entity that tries to obtain consent and is refused, cannot use or disclose any protected health information for the purposes included in the consent.

In situations in which providers with direct treatment relationships, such as a specialist or hospital, to whom a patient has been referred for the first time, the referred provider or hospital cannot use protected health information to schedule appointments or surgery before getting the patient's written consent. HHS plans to issue new regulations modifying the Privacy Rule to rectify the situation.[6]

[*A. Oral Exchanges:* See sidebar on page 49.]

5.3.2 Payment

Payment generally is any activity by a health plan to seek payment of premiums, fulfill its responsibility for coverage or health care providers' activities undertaken to obtain or provide reimbursement for the health care services rendered to the patient.[7] This includes

1. Determination of eligibility and coverage (e.g. coordination of benefits); and adjudication or subrogation of health benefit claims;
2. Adjusting risk based on enrollee health status and demographics;
3. Billing, claims management, collection activities, obtaining payments from reinsurance, and related health care data processing;
4. Reviewing health care services, with respect to medical necessity, coverage, appropriateness of care, or justification of charges;

5. Reviewing utilization, including pre-certification and preauthorization of services, concurrent and retrospective review of services.

A. Disclosure for Payment Processing: Any disclosure for payment processing to a financial institution may include only the following information:

1. Name and address of the account holder;
2. Name and address of the payer or provider;
3. Amount of the charge for health services;
4. Date on which health services were rendered;
5. Expiration date for the payment mechanism, if applicable; and
6. Individual's signature.

B. Disclosures to Consumer Reporting Agencies: Only the following protected health information may be disclosed to a consumer-reporting agency relating to collection of premiums or reimbursement:

1. Name and address;
2. Date of birth;
3. Social Security Number;
4. Payment history;
5. Account number and
6. Name and address of the health plan or health care provider.

Unintended Consequences

In a regulation as far-reaching as the Privacy Rule, some provisions may have unintended consequences. HHS identified at least two instances of this problem in its first round of clarifications.[1] The problem centers on when and how to require consent for first time referrals to health care providers and pharmacies.

As the regulation is written now, a health care provider with a direct treatment relationship cannot use protected health information when the patient is first referred to the provider without first getting written consent from the patient. That means the information cannot be used to schedule appointments, surgery and other activities that fall under the definitions of treatment, payment or health care operations until the patient provides written consent to the referred provider.

The same problem arises when a patient is referred to a pharmacy for the first time. The pharmacy cannot use protected health information that was telephoned in by a patient's physician if the patient is a new customer without getting consent from the patient first.

HHS said it did not intend to interfere in these ways and will propose new regulations to fix the problems.

–Dennis Melamed

---

[1] *Guidance/Q&As*, Standards for Privacy of Individually Identifiable Health Information (45 C.F.R. pts. 160 and 164), *available at* http://www.hhs.gov/ocr/hipaa (last revised July 6, 2001).

5.3.3 Health Care Operations

The Privacy Rule provides a list of activities that are included as health care operations. This is an area of continued confusion and concern and as experience with the regulation is gained, a more refined view of health care operations is expected to emerge.[8]

In the meantime, the Privacy Rule lists the following activities as covered under the umbrella of health care operations.

1. Conducting quality assessment and improvement activities, including outcomes evaluation and development of clinical guidelines, provided that the obtaining of generalizable knowledge is not the primary purpose of any studies resulting from these activities; population-based activities relating to improving health or reducing health care costs, protocol development, case management and care coordination, contacting of health care providers and patients with information about treatment alternatives; and related functions that do not include treatment;

2. Reviewing the competence or qualifications of health care professionals, evaluating practitioner and provider performance, health plan performance, conducting training programs in which students, trainees, or practitioners in areas of health care learn under supervision to practice or improve their skills as health care providers, training of non-health care professionals, accreditation, certification, licensing, or credentialing activities;

3. Underwriting, premium rating, and other activities relating to the creation, renewal, or replacement of a contract of health insurance or health benefits, and ceding, securing, or placing a contract for reinsurance of risk relating to claims for health care (including stop-loss insurance and excess of loss insurance). If a health plan receives protected health information for these purposes, and if benefits are not placed with the plan, then the plan may not use or disclose the protected health information received for that purpose.

4. Conducting or arranging for medical review, legal services, and auditing functions, including fraud and abuse detection and compliance programs;

5. Business planning and development, such as conducting cost-management and planning-related analyses related to managing and operating the entity, including formulary development and administration, development or improvement of methods of payment or coverage policies; and

6. Business management and general administrative activities of the entity.

Furthermore, other business management activities which fall under the health care operations definition in the Privacy Rule include:

1. Customer service, including the provision of data analyses for policy holders, plan sponsors, or other customers, as long as that protected health information is not disclosed to the policy holder, plan sponsor, or customer;

2. Resolution of internal grievances;

3. Due diligence in connection with the sale or transfer of assets to a potential successor in interest, if the potential successor in interest is a covered entity or, following completion of the sale or transfer, will become a covered entity; and

4. Creating de-identified health information, fundraising for the benefit of the covered entity, and marketing for which an individual authorization is not required under the marketing provisions of the Privacy Rule.

5.3.4 Transferability

With the exception of business associates, a consent generally obtained by one covered entity may not be used for another covered entity.[9] The only exception is the "joint consent" in which covered entities that participate in an "organized health care arrangement" may develop a joint consent. In this case, the individual consents to the uses and disclosures of protected health information by each of the covered entities in the arrangement. A joint consent must identify either the individual covered entities or class of covered entities to which the consent applies.

5.3.5 Consent as a Condition for Treatment

Health care providers may require a patient to provide consent as a condition of providing treatment.[10] Although consent is optional for health plans, if a health plan chooses to obtain consent, then the health plan may condition enrollment on consent, if consent is sought in conjunction with enrollment.[11]

5.3.6 Revocation

Once obtained, the consent is valid until revoked by the patient in writing. Patients may revoke their consents at any time.[12] However, a health care provider may refuse to continue to treat an individual who revoked consent, and a health plan may disenroll an individual – again provided that the consent was sought in conjunction with the individual's enrollment.

Upon receipt of a revocation, the covered entity must stop processing the protected health information for use or disclosure, except to that extent that it has taken action by relying on the consent. One example would be continuing to use the information in billing for treatment already performed before the consent was revoked.

5.3.7 Exceptions

The Privacy Rule contemplates situations in which obtaining consent is not feasible or reasonable and therefore suspends the requirement.[13] These are:

1. Emergency treatment situations. However, the health care provider must try to obtain consent as soon as reasonably practical;
2. Where the health care provider is legally required to treat the individual and the health care provider attempts to obtain consent; or
3. Where there are substantial barriers to communication and in the provider's professional judgment, the circumstances infer the individual's consent.

In all of these cases, if consent is not obtained, the provider must document the attempt and the reason consent was not obtained.

A. Consent and Pharmacies: A pharmacist may provide advice about over-the-counter medicines without getting the customer's prior consent if the pharmacist does not create or keep a record of any protected health information. In this case, the only

---

Attorney/Client Privilege versus Doctor/Patient Confidentiality

Covered entities should not confuse the doctor-patient relationship with the attorney-client relationship. Although both are premised on strong claims of confidentiality they are not interchangeable. Covered entities that obtain information under the doctor-patient relationship cannot turn around and share that information with their attorneys without first obtaining patient consent. The Privacy Rule does not generally allow the consent given to one covered entity to automatically allow access by another entity.

The Ohio Supreme Court, however, clarified the issue even more for hospital administrators who may mistakenly rely on their attorney-client privilege to share patient records under the treatment, payment and health care operations provisions of the Privacy Rule.[1] In *Biddle v. Warren Gen. Hosp.*[2], the Ohio Supreme Court ruled that a hospital violated a patient's common law right of privacy when it allowed the hospital's law firm access to patient records to determine if any of the patients qualified for supplemental Social Security benefits to help pay for treatment bills. The Ohio court explicitly rejected arguments from Warren General Hospital and the Ohio State Bar Association that an attorney-client privilege existed between the hospital and law firm that kept the patient records confidential. The court also rejected the hospital's contention that patients had given consent when they signed a general authorization to allow the hospital to release information to process and pay claims.

The Ohio Supreme Court concluded that the authorization "does not authorize the release of medical information to the hospital's lawyer, and certainly not for the purpose of determining the patient's status as a Social Security claimant."[3] Also of major significance, the Court recognized that breaches of confidentiality can be used by patients as an independent common law cause of action to sue in Ohio state court. While the case directly affects only the citizens of Ohio, covered entities should recognize that courts in other states frequently look to published opinions when formulating legal theories.

– Dennis Melamed

[1] Consent generally obtained by one covered entity may not be used for another covered entity 65 Fed. Reg. at 82,810 (to be codified at 45 C.F.R. pt. 164.506(a)(3)(ii)(5))).
[2] 86 Ohio St. 3d 395, 715 N.E. 2d 518 (1999).
[3] *Biddle* at 86 Ohio St. 3d 406, 715 N.E. 2d at 527.

---

interaction or disclosure of information is a conversation between the pharmacist and the customer. The pharmacist may disclose protected health information about the customer to the customer without obtaining his or her consent but may not otherwise use or disclose that information.

Friends and family members may pick up prescriptions from a pharmacy without written consent by the patient. Based on the circumstances, a pharmacist (or any other provider) may use professional judgment and experience with common practice to make disclosures that are in the patient's best interest. As an example, HHS, in its clarifications, stated that the fact that a relative or friend arrives at a pharmacy and asks to pick up a specific prescription for an individual infers that he or she is involved in the individual's care. The Privacy Rule allows the pharmacist to give the prescription to the relative or friend. The individual does not need to provide the pharmacist with the names of such persons in advance.

5.3.8 Content of the Consent Document

The Privacy Rule establishes specific rules and parameters concerning the content of the consent document.[14] These are:

1. Consent must reference and refer the individual to the covered entity's notice of privacy practices. *Consent may not be combined in a single document with the notice.*

2. Consent must indicate that the individual has the right to review the notice before signing it. If the provider has reserved the right to change its privacy practices, the consent must state that the notice may change and describe how to obtain a revised notice.

3. In addition to treatment, payment, and health care operations, the consent may combine other forms of legal permission. For example, the consent may be combined with a state law requirement for consent to use or disclose HIV/AIDS information.

4. If other legal permission is combined in the consent document, then the permissions must be visually and organizationally separate from the consent for treatment, payment, and health care operations and require separate signatures and dates. For example, this could include consent for release of HIV/AIDS

related information as required by a state law or an assignment of benefits to a provider.

5. Where research includes treatment of the individual, consent may be combined with an authorization for the use or disclosure of protected health information created for the research. *Note: This is the only circumstance in which consent may be combined with an authorization.* (See Section 9.0 on Research)

6. Consent must state that the individual has the right to request restrictions on the use and disclosure of protected health information, but must also state that the covered entity may refuse the request.

7. *If the consent lacks a required element, it is not valid.*

8. Covered entities must document and retain any consents.

5.4 Authorization Requirements

Generally, authorizations are required for all uses and disclosures not required by law and uses beyond treatment, payment, and health care operations. Authorizations must be obtained by covered entities even to use the protected health information for their own use.[15]

The Privacy Rule also requires a covered entity to document and retain the signed authorizations it obtains.

If a covered provider seeks an authorization from a patient, then the authorization must contain a statement that treatment may not be conditioned on the authorization, except when providing research-related treatment as in obtaining a history.

If the authorization is for the use of the covered entity, the entity must describe any possible uses or disclosures of the information, including such things as research when approved by an Institutional Review Board that does not require the individual's authorization.

5.4.1 Research

For the purposes of research, covered health care providers must obtain separate authorizations for:

1. The use of protected health information created during the research;

2. Any historical information that was gathered

by the covered entity before the research started if the covered entities want access to that data; and

3. A description of each purpose for which the protected health information will be used or disclosed. For example, the covered entity would describe the type of data expected to be derived from the research and what they are going to do with it.

For a broader discussion on research, see Section 9.0.

5.4.2 Health Plans

Authorizations issued by a health plan must include a statement that enrollment or benefits eligibility may not be conditioned on an authorization, and are sought for the health plans eligibility or enrollment determinations or for its underwriting or risk rating determinations. [16]

Minor's Rights to Privacy

The issue of parental access to protected health information of children is a politically sensitive area of the Privacy Rule because it encompasses such issues as abortion, mental health and substance abuse.

Of particular concern to the Bush Administration is a provision that may enable doctors to avoid state parental notification laws that require that parents be informed when their minor children are getting abortions. The Privacy Rule allows doctors to use their professional judgment in determining whether to notify parents or other personal representatives of patients when disclosure may cause harm to the patient.[1] As a result, HHS may revisit the issue.[2]

HHS addresses the issue of minors' rights to privacy generally in the context of outlining requirements for personal representatives to make decisions for a patient.[3] Because parents usually have the authority to make health care decisions about their minor children, parents are generally personal representatives of their children. As a result, the Privacy Rule anticipates that parents usually will have the right to access health information about their minor children. This also is the case for guardians or others acting *in loco parentis* of a minor.

The Privacy Rule, however, also defers to state law in determining what rights minors have to privacy vis-à-vis their parents.[4] For example, when a state law provides an adolescent the right to consent to mental health treatment without the consent of his or her parent, and the adolescent obtains treatment without parental consent, the parent is not the personal representative under the Privacy Rule for that treatment and will not have access to that information.[5]

A parent also is not a child's personal representative when a court determines or other law authorizes someone other than the parent to make a treatment decisions for a minor. This would be true under the rule when a court gives the authority to make health care decisions for a minor to an adult other than the parent, to the minor, or reserves the power for itself.

HHS also explained in its first round of clarifications that parents are not considered the child's personal representative when a parent agrees to a confidential relationship between the minor and the physician. For example, if a physician asks the parent of a 16 year-old if the physician can talk with the child confidentially about a medical condition and the parent agrees, the parent would not have acces to the protected health information that was discussed during that confidential conference.

- Dennis Melamed

---

[1] 65 Fed. Reg. at 82,823 (to be codified at 45 C.F.R. pt. 164.524(a)(3)(i)).

[2] *Guidance/Q&As*, Standards for Privacy of Individually Identifiable Health Information (45 C.F.R. pts. 160 and 164), *available at* http://www.hhs.gov/ocr/hipaa (last revised July 6, 2001) (hereinafter "Guidance/Q&As").

[3] *id.* at 82,806 (to be codified at 45 CFR pt.164.502(g)).

[4] *id.* at 82,800 (to be codified at 45 CFR §160.202.

[5] *Guidance/Q&As*.

However, health plans may condition payment of a claim for specific benefits on an authorization, if the authorization is not for psychotherapy notes and is needed to determine payment of a claim.

Health plans may not ask for or use psychotherapy notes for any reason. An authorization for a health plan to obtain psychotherapy notes is not a valid authorization.

A covered entity may condition the provision of health care that is solely for the purpose of creating protected health information for disclosure to a third party. For example, if an employer paid a provider to perform physical exams on its employees, then the provider could condition his or her services on the employee authorizing release of the information to the employer.

As with consents, individuals may revoke an authorization in writing at any time. If the authorization was obtained as a condition of obtaining insurance coverage, the health insurer has the right under other law to contest the claim.

5.4.3. Content of the Authorization Document

The Privacy Rule imposes specific requirements on the content of patient authorizations.[17] They are:

1. A specific description of the information to be used or disclosed;
2. The identify, name or class of persons to whom the protected health information will be disclosed;
3. An expiration date or event that relates to the purpose;
4. The defined purpose of disclosure;
5. A statement that the individual has the right to revoke the authorization in writing a description of how it may be revoked;
6. A statement that the protected health information used or disclosed may be subject to re-disclosure and may no longer be protected;
7. The signature of the individual or personal representative (including a description of the personal representatives authority) and date. A copy must be provided to the individual;
8. The content is written in plain language – see Plain Language in Notice above.
9. A statement that, if any remuneration results from the use or disclosure, that the covered

entity will receive remuneration;

10. A statement that, if the covered entity has received consent or provided notice, refers to the consent and/or notice and states that any respective statements are binding; and

11. A statement that individuals may refuse to sign and that they may inspect or copy the protected health information to be used or disclosed.

5.4.4 Special Considerations

A. Marketing: Marketing is defined as a communication about a product or service, which encourages recipients of the communication to buy or use the product or service. There is no limit to the type or means of communication.

Generally authorization must be obtained for any marketing activities. However, the Privacy Rule gives providers and health plans substantial leeway in discussing treatment-related services or products.

The exceptions to marketing that do not require authorization are:

1. Activities related to treatment, payment or health care operations;
2. Communications made by a health care provider as part of the treatment and for the purpose of furthering the treatment of that individual. This means that health care providers are free to use or disclose protected health information as part of a discussion of its products and services, or the products and services of others, and to prescribe, recommend or sell products and services as part of the treatment. This includes referrals, prescriptions, recommendations and other communications that describe how a product or service may relate to the health of the individual; and
3. Communications tailored to an individual made by a health plan or health care provider to an individual in the course of managing treatment, including recommending alternative treatments, therapies, providers, or settings of care.

For a broader discussion of marketing, see Section 7.0.

B. Psychotherapy Notes: Psychotherapy notes must be separated from the rest of the individual's medical record to qualify as psychotherapy notes. Health plans may not request authorization to use or disclose psychotherapy notes for determination of benefits, underwriting, issuing insurance or payment of claims. Authorizations for psychotherapy notes may not be combined with any other authorization or consent.

5.4.5 Revocation

Covered entities are responsible for implementing a revocation of an authorization only if they have direct knowledge of the revocation. If a covered entity is aware of a revocation, then they have to honor the revocation, including informing any applicable business associates. However, there are no provisions for covered entities to proactively determine the status of current authorizations before disclosing the information.[18]

For example, a government agency may obtain an authorization for all providers who have seen the individual in the past year. If the individual sends a written revocation to the agency, the Privacy Rule does not require the agency to inform all of the providers that there as been a revocation. Therefore, if a covered entity does not know about a revocation, it is not violating the rule by acting on the authorization.

5.4.6 Exceptions

A. Fundraising: Fundraising is a named health care operation and for these purposes listed in the health care operation definition. As a result, no authorization is required, even to release demographic information to a third party raising funds on behalf of the covered entity.

For a fuller discussion of fundraising, see Section 7.0 on Marketing.

B. Disaster Relief: There is no requirement to obtain authorization for the purpose of disclosing protected health information to federal, state, local, or private agencies engaged in disaster relief activities.

5.5 Uses and Disclosures Requiring an Opportunity for the Patient to Agree or Disagree

While the Privacy Rule details formal requirements for advanced consent and authorization over the use of protected information, HHS also recognized that many situations occur in which information agreements are required for the smooth operation of the health care system. These situations include listing the patient in a facility directory and access to information by clergy and family members.[19] In the preamble to the Privacy Rule, HHS stated:

> The final rule addresses situations in which the interaction between the covered entity and the individual is relatively informal and agreements are made orally, without written authorizations for use or disclosure. In general, under the final rule, to disclose or use protected health information for these purposes, covered entities must inform individuals in advance and must provide a meaningful opportunity for the individual to prevent or restrict the disclosure.[20]

However, covered entities should remember that an agreement by the individual to disclose protected health information at one point in time does not imply disclosure indefinitely.

For example, if a patient is admitted on Monday, discharged Wednesday, and readmitted on Friday, an agreement to be included in the patient directory on Monday is not valid for the same patient to be included in the patient directory when readmitted on Friday. The patient can also revoke permission for disclosure at any time.

As detailed below there are several circumstances and situations in which patients must have an opportunity to agree or object are.

5.5.1 Facility Directories

The Privacy Rule allows health care providers (typically facilities) to include patient information in their directories only if:

1. They inform incoming patients of their directory policies and the patient does not object; and
2. They give patients an opportunity to opt out of the directory listing or restrict some of the information to be included.

If the patient is incapacitated or in emergency treatment circumstances, the health care provider can use his or her professional judgment to decide whether to include the individual's information and what information to include in the facility directory.

However, the individual must be given the opportunity to object as soon as practical after the individual is capable of making a decision. Additionally, if the provider learns of an incapacitated individual's prior wish not to be included in the directory, the facility must not include the individual's information in the directory.

5.5.2 Clergy

Subject to the individual objecting, a covered entity may disclose, the individual's name, general condition (in terms that do not communicate specific medical information, individual's location, and religious affiliation) to clergy. This disclosure can be made without the clergy inquiring by patient name.

5.5.3 Third Parties Involved in the Patient's Care

Covered entities may disclose protected health information to a person involved in the current health care of an individual. This includes family members, relatives, close friends, boy/girl friends, roommates, neighbors, colleagues, or any other person named by the individual.

The drafters of the Privacy Rule intended for this provision to maintain current practices with respect to the involvement of other persons in an individual's care and the sharing of protected health information to a contact person during a disaster.

The Privacy Rule gives the health care provider latitude to involve other persons that in his or her professional judgment are appropriate and may be needed to participate in the individual's care. If the individual has the capacity to make his or her own decisions, then the patient must be consulted and given an opportunity to agree or object to disclosure of protected health information to third parties.

If the individual is incapacitated, the provider can use his or her best professional judgment and is cautioned to take circumstances into consideration that may put the individual at risk. For example, providers may not want to give out this information if the third parties were the perpetrators of abuse to the individual.

Generally, the provider is to exercise his or her professional judgment to determine whether disclosures are in the individual's best interest.

Providers can make reasonable inferences, such as when a friend shows up at the pharmacy to pick up a prescription or sharing information with the person showing up to drive the individual home from the hospital.

5.5.4 Verification Requirements

While the Privacy Rule gives the health care provider latitude to disclose protected health information to an individual's relatives and other people providing care, there is no requirement to verify the identify of those relatives or other persons involved in the patient's care. Providers can rely on the verbal authorization of the patient and use their professional judgment consistent with the circumstances.

5.6 Individual Right to Request Restrictions

Generally, an individual has the right to ask covered entities to restrict the use or disclosure of protected health information covered under a consent or authorization. [21]

The individual must make this request, however, to the covered entity directly responsible for the information. For example, in the case where a clearinghouse is the business associate of a hospital, the individual could not ask the clearinghouse to restrict the individual's uncle, who was a staff physician at the hospital, from seeing the information. The business associate (in this case, a clearinghouse) would not typically have control over the circumstances in which the information could be disclosed.

The Privacy Rule, however, also states that the covered entity may refuse to agree to the restrictions. While there is some skepticism about the utility of this provision from the patient's perspective, it is more than conceivable that large organizations of patients, such as unions, may have enough influence to make such requests meaningful.

If the covered entity agrees to the restrictions, then they are binding. Restrictions must be documented and any documentation regarding restrictions must be retained for six years. With the exception of providing restricted protected health information to providers for emergency treatment, *there is no requirement to notify other entities to which they disclose protected health information of the existence of any restrictions.* For example, in the case where a hospital accepted a patient's request to restrict his or her uncle, also a staff physician, from access to their information, the hospital would not be responsible if they then sent that information in a claim form to a health plan that subsequently contracted the patient's uncle to perform case review or management using the patient's information.

A covered entity may override any agreed upon restrictions in the event of an emergency treatment situation. If the information is disclosed to a provider for emergency treatment, the covered entity must request the provider to not further use or disclose the information.

A covered entity may terminate an agreed upon restriction by written or oral agreement that is documented. If the covered entity terminates the agreement unilaterally, the removal of restrictions only applies to information received after the termination.

5.7 Confidential Communication Requirements

Individuals may request covered entities to communicate his or her protected health information on a confidential basis. [22] For example, patients who do not want family members to know about a certain treatment can request that the covered entity communicate with them at their places of employment, by mail to a designated address or by phone to designated numbers. An individual also can request that mail be sent in a closed envelope and not by postcard.

Covered health plans and health care providers must accept any reasonable request. However, there is a proviso: when the request is to a health plan, the individual must clearly state that the disclosure of all or part of the protected health information may endanger the individual. For example; if a dependent of the insured represented to the health plan that the insured would injure the dependent if the insured found out about his or her treatment, then the dependent could request the health plan to not send the EOB (explanation of benefits), which contained that treatment information, to the insured. If it were administratively reasonable to implement the request, the health plan would have to comply.

Covered entities can judge the reasonableness of any request based on administrative difficulty and not on the perceived merits of the request. That is, if it is administratively reasonable, a covered entity must comply with a request that has an unreasonable foundation. However, as applicable, a request may be refused if the individual does not provide information as to how payment will be made or has not specified an alternative address or method of contact.

5.8 Use and Disclosure of Information Not Requiring Consent, Authorization or Agreement

Covered entities do not need individual authorization to release protected health information for the following purposes:

- Statutory mandates;
- Public health activities;
- Victims of abuse, neglect or domestic violence;
- Health oversight activities;
- Judicial and administrative proceedings;
- Law enforcement purposes;
- Decedents;
- Cadaveric donation of organs, eyes, or tissues;
- Research purposes;
- Serious threats to health and safety;
- Specialized government functions; and
- Workers compensation; and
- Research performed under the purview of an Institutional Review Board (IRB) or private Privacy Board. These boards must be set up to conform to the Common Rule and at least one individual of the board must be independent of any entity with interest in the research. [23]

The specific details of disclosures are as follows:

A. Disclosures Mandated by Law: All covered entities may respond to disclosure requirements required by any law, provided the use or disclosure meets and is limited to the relevant requirements of those laws.

B. Uses and Disclosures for Health Oversight Activities: The Privacy Rule allows disclosure to an agency or authority of US, state, territory, political subdivision of state or territory, or Indian Tribe, that is authorized by law to oversee the health care system or government programs in which protected health information is necessary to determine eligibility, compliance or to enforce civil rights laws for which health information is relevant.

This includes agencies such as the Equal Employment Opportunity Commission, Food and Drug Administration (FDA), Public Health Service, US Dept. of Labor's Pension and Welfare Benefits Administration, etc. This also includes disclosures for health care fraud investigations. *This provision does not automatically include private sector organizations such as accrediting organizations or coding committees that help government agencies.*

Furthermore, an investigation or activity is not considered oversight and is considered law enforcement if:

1. The individual is the subject of the investigation; or
2. The investigation does not directly relate to the receipt of health care or a claim/ qualification for public benefits.

C. Uses and Disclosures to Avert a Serious Threat to Health and Safety:

1. *When to Disclose:* A covered entity may, consistent with applicable law and standards of ethical conduct, use or disclose protected health information, if the covered entity in good faith believes the use or disclosure:

   a. Is necessary to prevent or lessen a serious and imminent threat to the health or safety of a person or the public and is to a person reasonably able to prevent or lessen the threat, including the target of the threat; or
   b. Is necessary for law enforcement authorities to identify or apprehend an individual:
      - Because of a statement by an individual admitting participation in a violent crime that the covered entity believes may have caused serious physical harm to the victim; or
      - Where it appears that the individual has escaped from a correctional institution or from lawful custody.

   A use or disclosure is not permitted if information learned by the covered entity is gained:

   a. In the course of treatment to affect the propensity to commit the criminal conduct that would be the base for

disclosure above, or from counseling or therapy; or

   b. Through a request by the individual to initiate or be referred for treatment, counseling or therapy.

For example, in the case of a clinical psychologist who is treating a person for kleptomania, that provider would not be allowed to disclose to law enforcement that the person stole an item from a store.

Disclosure made for this purpose shall contain only:

a. ABO blood type and Rh factor;
b. Date and time of death;
c. Scars,
d. Tattoos,
e. Height,
f. Weight,
g. Gender,
h. Race,
i. Hair,
j. Eye color, and
k. Presence or absence of facial hair.

2. *Communicable Disease:* The Privacy Rule allows disclosure to a person who may have been exposed to a communicable disease or may be at risk of contracting or spreading a disease or condition – provided that covered entity or public health authority is authorized by law to notify such a person.

3. *Public Agencies:* The public health activities provision allows disclosures to U.S. public health authorities and, at the direction of a public health authority, to an official of a foreign government agency that is acting in collaboration with a U.S. official. This includes statutorily mandated or government ordered disclosures to the FDA to report adverse events, product defects or problems, or biologic product deviations to enable recalls, repairs, or replacement, including locating and notifying individuals who have received those products, or to conduct post marketing surveillance.

Other agencies covered under this provision are the Occupational Safety and Health

Administration, Federal Mine Safety and Health Act, Centers for Disease Control and Prevention, and state and local public health departments for public health purposes.

5.8.1 Government Programs Providing Public Benefits

A health plan that is a government program providing public benefits may disclose protected health information relating to eligibility for enrollment to another agency providing the public benefits if sharing the information is required or expressly authorized by law or regulation. That is, government agencies that perform eligibility or enrollment functions can share the information with other agencies that are authorized by law to have access to the information.

5.8.2 Employers and Plan Sponsors

A. Disclosures to Employers: Health care providers who make disclosures to employers under this provision must provide notice to the individuals that it discloses protected health information to employers related to the medical surveillance of the workplace and work-related illnesses and injuries.

This notice is separate from the notice of privacy practices as discussed above. Disclosures may be made to an employer about an individual who is a member of the workforce of the employer, if:

1. The covered entity is a health care provider who is member of the workforce of the employer or who provides the health care at the request of the employer; to conduct an evaluation relating to medical surveillance; or to evaluate whether the individual has a work-related illness or injury;
2. The protected health information that is disclosed consists of findings concerning a work-related illness or injury or medical surveillance;
3. The employer needs these findings in order to comply with law requiring recording illness or injury or workplace medical surveillance; or
4. The covered health care provider provides a written notice to the individual that protected health information relating to the medical surveillance or work-related illness and injuries is disclosed to the employer.

B. Summary Reports to Plan Sponsors: Health plans may provide summary report data to their plan sponsors, even if the data does not meet the definition of de-identified. However, such usage must be included in the covered entity's notice of privacy practices.

5.8.3 Victims of Abuse, Neglect or Domestic Violence

This provision allows disclosure to public health authorities authorized to receive reports of child abuse or neglect. In addition, it allows — if expressly authorized by statute or law - disclosure to any governmental authority authorized by law to receive reports of abuse, neglect or domestic violence if required by law, and limited to the requirements of the law.

Disclosure of information also is allowed if:

1. The individual agrees to disclosure;
2. The covered entity believes in its best judgment that disclosure is necessary to prevent serious harm;
3. The victim is incapacitated; or
4. If the law enforcement or other public official represents that the protected health information disclosed is not intended to be used against the individual and that an immediate enforcement activity would be materially damaged by waiting until the individual is able to agree.

The covered entity must inform the individual of all disclosures to report abuse, neglect, or domestic violence with two exceptions. These are when:

1. The covered entity believes that informing the individual would place him or her at risk of serious harm; or
2. The covered entity would be informing a personal representative and the covered entity reasonably believes that informing that person would not be in the individual's best interest.

5.8.4 Judicial Proceedings and Law Enforcement

A. Judicial and Administrative Proceedings: Protected health information may be disclosed if the request is made pursuant to a court order, response to subpoena, or discovery request from a party to the proceeding. If there is no subpoena or order from the court, the covered entity can only disclose protected health information if there are satisfactory assurances that reasonable efforts have been made to notify the individual or the parties, and secure a protective order to guard the confidentiality.

For example, in the case where a covered entity receives a subpoena for information, the covered entity should ask for some form of proof that the individual has been notified of the subpoena and given opportunity to object. Alternatively, the covered entity may ask for a copy of the court protective order that would "seal" the information and order that the parties to the legal proceedings not disclose it.

The minimum necessary disclosure requirements do not apply in the case of a court order or order from administrative tribunal. That is, the covered entity can comply with the request without determining the appropriateness of the information requested in relation to the purpose for which it is requested.

B. Law Enforcement Purposes: Covered entities may disclose protected health information only to the extent limited by the relevant requirements of the legal process or other laws. This means that providers and plans can respond to a warrant, subpoena or other order issued by a judicial officer, state, federal, or grand jury subpoena. This also holds true for administrative requests such as a subpoena, summons or civil investigation.

However, in both instances, the information sought must be relevant; the request must be narrowly drawn and specific as reasonably practical; and it is determined that de-identified information cannot reasonably be used.

C. Information about Suspects, Fugitives, Material Witnesses and Missing Persons: Information about suspects, fugitives, material witnesses, and missing persons may be disclosed for both cases in which law enforcement officials are seeking to identify and/or locate the individual. However, only the following information may be disclosed:

1. ABO blood type and Rh factor;
2. Date and time of death;
3. Scars,
4. Tattoos,
5. Height,
6. Weight,
7. Gender,
8. Race,
9. Hair,
10. Eye color, and
11. Presence or absence of facial hair.

Covered entities cannot disclose DNA data, dental records, or typing, samples or analyses of tissues or body fluids other than blood.

Under the law enforcement provision, a covered entity *can only respond to a law enforcement request.* However, the request can be made orally.

D. Correctional Institutions and Law Enforcement Custodial Situations: A covered entity may disclose protected health information to a correctional institution, correctional psychiatric institution, or a law enforcement official having custody of an inmate or other individual if the law enforcement official represents that the protected health information is necessary for:

1. The provision of health care to such individuals;
2. The health and safety of such individual or other inmates;
3. The health and safety of the officers or employees of the correctional institution;
4. Law enforcement on the premises of the correctional institution; and
5. Administration and maintenance of the safety, security, and good order of the correctional institution.

E. Other Communications with Law Enforcement: Covered entities may initiate disclosure with law enforcement if the covered entity believes that the protected health information constitutes evidence of a crime committed on the premises.

In the event of a medical emergency on the premises of the covered entity, the entity may disclose protected health information if it is necessary to alert law enforcement to:

- The commission of a crime and its nature;
- The locations of the crime or victims; and
- Identity, description, and location of the perpetrator.

If the individual is a victim of a crime, a covered entity may disclose protected health information if the individual agrees to the disclosure or the covered entity is unable to obtain the individual's agreement due to an emergency circumstance.

The law enforcement official must represent that the information is needed to determine whether a crime has occurred by someone other than the victim. Law enforcement also must state that the information is not intended to be used against the victim and that immediate law enforcement activity would be materially harmed by a delay in receiving the protected health information.

A covered entity may disclose protected health information about an individual to law enforcement officials to alert them to the death of the individual if the covered entity suspects that the death may have resulted from criminal conduct.

A covered entity may release protected health information that a covered entity believes in good faith provides evidence of criminal conduct on the premises of the covered entity.

Similarly, a covered health care provider giving health care in a medical emergency – other than an emergency on the premises of the provider – may disclose protected health information to law enforcement if the disclosure is necessary to alert law enforcement to:

1. The commission and nature of a crime,
2. The location of the crime and the victims, or
3. The identity, description, and location of the perpetrator.

In the event the covered entity believes the emergency is the result of abuse, neglect, or domestic violence, then the disclosure falls under the control the provisions governing "Victims of Abuse, Neglect or Domestic Violence" (see above)

5.8.5 Other Permissible Disclosures Not Requiring Authorization or Consent

A. Disclosures about Decedents: This provision allows covered entities to disclose protected health information to funeral directors and public hospitals with on-staff medical examiner functions as necessary to carry out their duties, consistent with applicable law. This includes psychotherapy notes.

B. Disclosures for Cadaveric Donation of Organs, Eyes, or Tissues: A covered entity may use or disclose protected health information to organ procurement organizations or other entities engaged in the procurement of banking or transplantation of cadaveric organs, eyes, or tissue for the purpose of eye or tissue donation and transplantation.

C. Uses and Disclosures for Research Purposes: A covered entity may use or disclose protected health information for research when an Institutional Review Board or Privacy Board approve the changes or waivers in the individual's authorization.

D. United States and Foreign Military Authorities: A covered entity may disclose the protected health information of individuals who are US Armed Forces personnel or foreign military personnel for activities deemed necessary by the appropriate US or foreign military command authorities. However, the purposes and the command authorities for such disclosures must be published in the *Federal Register.*

E. Department of Veterans Affairs: A component of the Department of Veterans Affairs that is a covered entity may use or disclose protected health information to components of the department that determines eligibility benefits under the Secretary of Veterans Affairs.

F. Protective Services for the President and Others: Covered entities may disclose protected health information to authorized federal officials for the provision of protective services to the President and other persons, or to foreign heads of state or for the conduct of investigations.

G. National Security and Intelligence Activities: A covered entity may disclose protected health information to authorized federal officials for the conduct of lawful intelligence, counter-intelligence, and other national security activities authorized by the National Security Act.

H. Medical Suitability Determinations: Covered entities that are components of the Department of State may use protected health information to make medical suitability determinations and may disclose whether the individual was medically suitable to the officials of the Department of State for: (1) conducting required security clearances, to determine worldwide availability for mandatory service abroad; or (2) for a family to accompany a Foreign Service member abroad.

I. Disclosures for Workers' Compensation: A covered entity may disclose protected health information as authorized by and to the extent necessary to comply workers' compensation laws or other similar programs established by law, that provide benefits for work-related injuries or illness without regard to fault.

5.9 When Consent and Authorizations Conflict

There may be occasions where an individual has signed multiple consents and/or authorizations that may conflict. The covered entity must abide by the most restrictive consent or authorization. For example, a nursing home may have had an individual sign an authorization to obtain a copy of her medical records from her physician.[24]

However, the physician may have previously obtained consent from the individual for treatment purposes. If the nursing home authorization granted permission for the physician to disclose genetic information but the consent excluded such information, then the physician must adhere to the more restrictive consent. When there is such a conflict, a covered entity may resolve the conflict by obtaining either a new written or oral consent – oral consent must be documented.

5.10 The Need for Consents versus Authorizations

Consent is only obtained for a use or disclosure of protected health information for the purposes of treatment, payment and health care operations. An authorization is required for uses and disclosures that are *not* for the purpose of treatment, payment, and health care operations.

For example, for the purpose of subrogation, a health plan may desire additional protected health information from a physician who rendered the health care services. In this case, the disclosure of the information by the provider is not for the purpose of treatment, payment and health care operations by the provider. That is, the disclosure is: (1) Not needed for treatment, (2) Not required for payments to the provider, and (3) Not part of the provider's health care operations. Therefore, the provider's disclosure is for the payment or health care operations of the health plan, it would not be covered by the patient's consent obtained by the provider. Rather, an authorization, and not a consent, would be the proper document for the plan to use when requesting such a disclosure.

5.11 Transition Rules

Providers in direct treatment relationships have been concerned about their ability to use and disclose a patient's health information after the Privacy Rule's compliance date if they had not seen the patient and had an opportunity to obtain a HIPAA compliant consent.

HHS has clarified that after the Privacy Rule's compliance date, providers can continue to operate under pre-HIPAA consents until their first opportunity to obtain a HIPAA compliant consent. That is, if before the Privacy Rule's compliance date, a provider that has obtained a pre-HIPAA consent giving them the ability to use and disclose a patient's health information, can operate as if that were a HIPAA compliant consent until the next time they see the patient. For example, if a provider were to obtain a pre-HIPAA consent in March of 2003 and did not see the patient until June of 2003, they could operate under the pre-HIPAA consent from April 14, 2003 until they saw the patient and had an opportunity to obtain a HIPAA compliant consent.

5.12 Key Points

- The patient consent requirements apply only to the use and disclosure of protected health information for treatment, payment and health care operations. Authorizations apply to other uses of protected health information.
- Patient consents and authorizations can be waived in emergency situations.
- The Minimum Necessary provisions of the Privacy Rule do not apply to the HIPAA electronic transaction standards.
- The Minimum Necessary requirement covers internal uses so that each entity must define what information will be made available to each employee by role.
- Providers in an indirect treatment relationship are not required to obtain consent.
- Patients must be given the opportunity to object to the disclosure of protected health information in facilities directories and to clergy and family members.
- Accrediting bodies do not have an automatic authorization to access protected health information. They may need a business associate contract.
- When consents and authorizations conflict, the

more privacy-protective statement prevails.

- Covered entities must accommodate reasonable requests to provide confidential communications regarding protected health information when requested by a patient.

- Providers, who provide protected health information to employers in regard to medical surveillance of the workplace, must give patients separate notice to the patient informing them of this disclosure.

- When subpoenas not ordered by a court or administrative body are served on a covered entity, the subjects of those subpoenas must be given notice and an opportunity to object.

Endnotes

[1] 65 Fed. Reg. at 82,805 (to be codified at 45 C.F.R. pt. 164.502(b)).

[2] *id.* at 82,806 (to be codifed at 45 C.F.R. pt. 164.502(b)(2)(v). These transactions are: health claims and equivalent encounter information, enrollment and disenrollment in a health plan, eligibility for a health plan, health care payment and remittance advice, health plan premium payments, health claim status, referral certification and authorization, and coordination of benefits and will be topic of another volume in this book series, *What Your Organization Should Know About the Federal Transactional Standards*.

[3] *id.* at 82,805 (to be codified at 45 C.F.R. pt. 164.501).

[4] *id.* at 82,803.

[5] *id.* at 82,804.

[6] *Guidance/Q&As*, Standards for Privacy of Individually Identifiable Health Information (45 C.F.R. pts. 160 and 164), *available at* http://www.hhs.gov/ocr/hipaa (last revised July 6, 2001).

[7] 65 Fed. Reg. at 82,804-805 (to be codified at 45 C.F.R. pt. 164.501).

[8] *id.* at 82,803-804

[9] *id.* at 82,810 (to be codified at 45 C.F.R. 164.506(a)(3)(ii)(5)).

[10] *id.* (to be codified at 45 C.F.R. pt. 164.506(b)(1)).

[11] *id.* (to be codified at 45 C.F.R. pt. 164.506(b)(2)).

[12] *id.* (to be codified at 45 C.F.R. pt. 164.506(c)(5)).

[13] *id.* (to be codified at 45 C.F.R. pt. 164.506(a)(3)(i)).

[14] *id.* (to be codified at 45 C.F.R. pt. 164.506(c)).

[15] *id.* at 82,811 (to be codified at 45 C.F.R. pt. 164.508).

[16] *id.* (to be codified at 45 C.F.R. pt. 164.508(b)(4)(ii)).

[17] *id.* at 82,811-12 (to be codified at 45 C.F.R. pt. 164.508(c)).0

[18] *id.* (to be codified at 45 C.F.R. pt. 164.508(b)(5)).

[19] The issue of access to patients by family members has been problematic for states who have enacted comprehensive medical privacy laws as well. For example the state of Maine rescinded its comprehensive medical privacy law after press accounts revealed that hospitals would not let close family members know the status of their relatives or allow them to send flowers. Maine Law Deferred in Wake of Litigation Fears, Media Gripes, *Health Infor. Privacy Alert*, Jan. 1999 at 1.

[20] 64 Fed. Reg. at 82,521

[21] *id.* (to be codified at 45 C.F.R. pt. 164.522(a)).

[22] *id.* (to be codified at 45 C.F.R. pt. 164.522(b)).

[23] *id.* (to be codified at 45 C.F.R. pt. 164.512).

[24] *id.* (to be codified at 45 C.F.R. pt. 164.506(e)).

Frank Exchanges: The Rules on Oral Communications

The Privacy Rule applies to protected health information in all forms including that communicated verbally.[1] HHS's goal was to ensure protected health information is safeguarded when it is discussed or read aloud from a computer screen or a written document.[2] HHS noted in the Privacy Rule that it did cover oral communications, i.e., "a conversation about a person's protected health information could be shared with anyone."[3]

At the same time, HHS does not expect absolute protection of protected identifiable information in regard to oral communications. Covered entities must have policies and procedures in place that reasonably address the specific concerns around this issue. As mentioned frequently through this reference book, HHS's intention is not to compromise patient treatment or safety in the name of privacy

In its clarifications, HHS acknowledged that talking among providers must not be prohibited. Generally, discussions among providers about the treatment of patient is allowed because these communications fall under the definition of treatment.

In its clarifications, HHS said the following practices are permissible if reasonable precautions are taken to prevent inadvertent disclosures:[4]

- Health care staff may orally coordinate services at hospital nursing stations.
- Nurses or other health care professionals may discuss a patient's condition over the phone with the patient, a provider, or a family member.
- A health care professional may discuss lab test results with a patient or other provider in a joint treatment area.
- Health care professionals may discuss a patient's condition during training rounds in an academic or training institution.

Reasonable precautions would include such practices as using lowered voices and talking away from other people. To assure that the Privacy Rule does not inhibit legitimate conversation, HHS said it will propose regulatory language to reinforce and clarify that these and similar oral communications (such as calling out patient names in a waiting room) are permissible.

Facility Modifications

HHS also explained that it does not intend to require hospitals and doctors' offices to be modified to provide private rooms and soundproof walls to avoid any possibility that a conversation may be overhead. The Privacy Rule only requires covered entities to take reasonable measures. "The Department does not consider facility restructuring to be a requirement under this standard. In determining what is reasonable, the Department will take into account the concerns of covered entities regarding potential effects on patient care and financial burden."[5]

The Privacy Rule *does not require* the following types of structural or systems changes:

- Private rooms.
- Soundproofing of rooms.
- Encryption of wireless or other emergency medical radio communications that can be intercepted by scanners.
- Encryption of telephone systems.

Covered entities must provide reasonable safeguards to avoid prohibited disclosures. That does not mean all risks must be eliminated to satisfy this standard. Instead, the Privacy Rule requires covered entities to review their policies and procedures to ensure reasonable protections.[6]

For example, HHS said that the following changes may constitute safeguards:

- Pharmacies could ask waiting customers to stand a few feet back from a counter used for patient counseling.
- Providers could add curtains or screens to areas where oral communications often occur between doctors and patients or among professionals treating the patient.
- In an area where many patient-staff communications routinely occur, use of cubicles, dividers, shields, or similar barriers may constitute a reasonable safeguard. For example, a large clinic intake area may reasonably use cubicles or shield-type dividers, rather than separate rooms. [7]

In assessing what is "reasonable," covered entities may consider the viewpoint of prudent professionals.

Access to Oral Information

The Privacy Rule does not require entities to grant patients with access to all oral information. The rule applies only to "designated records sets." This definition does not include oral information. At the same time, if a covered entity tapes or digitally records oral communications, these may meet the definition of designated record set.

For example, a health plan is not required to provide a member access to tapes of a telephone "advice line" interaction if the tapes are only maintained for customer service review and not to make decisions about the member.

The Privacy Rule also does not require covered entities to document any information – including oral information – that is used or disclosed for treatment, payment or health care operations.

The Privacy Rule, however, requires covered entities to document some information disclosures for other purposes. For example, some disclosures must be documented to meet the standard for providing a disclosure history to an individual upon request. For example, if a covered physician discloses information about a case of tuberculosis to a public health authority,[8] then he or she must maintain a record of that disclosure regardless of whether the disclosure was made orally by phone or in writing.

– Dennis Melamed

---

[1] 65 Fed. Reg. at 82,799, 82,805 (to be codified at 45 CFR pts. 160.103, 164.501).

[2] *id.* at 82,827 (to be codified at 45 C.F.R. pt. 164.530(c)(2)).

[3] *id.* at 82,620.

[4] *Guidance/Q&As*, Standards for Privacy of Individually Identifiable Health Information (45 C.F.R. pts. 160 and 164), *available at* http://www.hhs.gov/ocr/hipaa (last revised July 6, 2001).

[5] *id.*

[6] Such precautions are also required under the proposed HIPAA data security regulation.

[7] *id.*

[8] 65 Fed. Reg. at 82,813-18 (to be codified at 45 C.F.R. pt. 164.512). This section details the circumstances under which protected health information may disclosed without consent, authorization or an opportunity for the patient to object.

Section 6.0 - Closing the Loop: Business Associates and Privacy Protection

Alexander J. Brittin

6.1 Introduction

The Administrative Simplification provisions under HIPAA apply to covered entities that engage in electronic standard transactions.[1] This limited statutory authority means that whenever protected health information is transferred or made available to a non-covered entity, it is beyond the direct reach of HIPAA. Recognizing the inherent limitations of the law, HHS concluded that to prevent the unauthorized use or disclosure of protected health information, it must impose certain requirements on covered entities that have business relationships with non-covered entities.

By doing so, HHS is not regulating non-covered entities. Rather, HHS is placing contractual restrictions on the flow of information from covered entities to non-covered entities. In essence, HHS extended the scope and reach of the Privacy Rule by requiring the use of business associate contracts when covered entities transfer protected health information to non-covered entities.

The following describes those situations when a business associate contract relationship arises, when it does not and mandatory requirements of a business associate contract. As with any contract, one should seek competent legal advice to fully understand all of the legal and business ramifications of entering into a binding legal commitment.

6.2 Who is a Business Associate?

A business associate is an organization or person, other than a member of the covered entity's workforce, who receives protected health information from a covered entity to provide services to or on behalf of a covered entity.[2] Within the specific realm of health care, business associate services include claims processing or administration, utilization reviews, quality assurance, billing, benefits management, practice management, repricing, or any other activity regulated by the Privacy Rule.

A business associate also can be a person or organization that provides the following professional services:

- Legal,
- Actuarial,
- Accounting,
- Consulting,
- Management,
- Administrative accreditation,
- Data aggregation, and
- Financial.

However, merely providing a service to or on behalf of a covered entity does not create a business associate relationship by itself. There must also be a transfer of protected health information with an intent to allow the business associate to perform a service for or on behalf of the covered entity. The implications of these requirements as well as others described below mean that the use of a business associate contract is not as prevalent as one would think.

6.2.1 When a Business Associate Relationship is Not Created

Vendors, subcontractors, other business associates and even covered entities acting as business associates must act on behalf of or provide a service to a covered entity and intend to disclose protected health information to create a business associate relationship that triggers the regulatory mandate for a contract under the Privacy Rule.[3]

However, not every use or disclosure triggers a business associate relationship. For example, when a health care provider discloses protected health information to a health plan for payment purposes no business associate relationship is established. This is because neither is acting on behalf of nor providing a service to the other.

Other examples of when business associate relationships are *not* created include:

- When a covered entity *furnishes protected health information to a conduit for transport* (e.g., the U.S. Postal Service, certain private couriers and their electronic equivalents). Because the covered entity does not intend to disclose the information and the probability of exposure of protected health information is very small, the conduit is not a business associate of the covered entity. However, covered entities should remember that the probability of exposure of protected health information is not usually a criterion used under the Privacy Rule.[4]

- When a financial institution, acting on behalf of a covered entity, *processes consumer-conducted financial transactions* by debt, credit other payment card, or clears checks, initiates or processes electronic funds transfer, or conducts any other activity that directly facilitates or effects the transfer of funds for compensation.[5]

- *Typical consumer conducted payment transactions* that may include some health information (e.g., diagnosis or procedure) that may be implied through the name of the health care provider or health plan being paid. While this does not create a business associate relationship, the Privacy Rule requires that the covered entity meet the minimum necessary disclosure requirements. In other words, a covered entity processing a consumer-conducted financial transaction should disclose only the minimum necessary information to accomplish the transaction.[6]

- When a covered entity *discloses protected health information to a health oversight agency as part of a federal program.* A typical example of this occurs when a peer review organization (PRO) engages in health oversight activities as part of its Medicare contract. In this situation, no business associate relationship is created

between the PRO and the covered provider furnishing the protected health information. The PRO is not performing services for or on behalf of the covered entity and therefore no business associate relationship is created.[7]

- *Responses to a law enforcement request* or a subpoena issued by a court of administrative body.[8]

6.2.2 Disclosures within a Covered Entity

Sometimes a business associate relationship does not arise simply because no disclosure occurs outside of the covered entity. The "legal bounds" of a covered entity are defined by the "health care component" which includes all parts of the entity that perform covered or health care functions.[9] An entity's workforce includes employees, volunteers, trainees and other persons whose conduct is under the direct control of the coved entity, even if they are not paid by the covered entity.[10]

The Privacy Rule also recognizes that in some situations the legal bounds of the covered entity may extend beyond just the corporate structure. For example, in the case of an organized health care arrangement,[11] a provider in a clinical setting may be engaged in joint activities with other providers. If these providers are participating in joint activities that meet the requirements of an organized health care arrangement, then no business associate relation arises among the participants.

6.2.3 Disclosures Related to Treatment

One of the broadest exclusions of business associate contracts is when the transfer of protected health information is related to treatment.[12] Disclosures by a covered entity to a health care provider concerning the treatment of an individual do not create a business associate relationship. For example, when a covered entity sends a specimen to a laboratory for analysis, no business associate relationship is created. The laboratory is a health care provider and the laboratory analysis relates to treatment of the individual.

On the other hand, if a transfer occurs between covered health care providers, a business associate relationship may arise if the service being provided is not concerning treatment. For example, if a hospital offers to perform a billing service for physician, then the hospital is a business associate of the physician and a business associate contract is required.[13]

6.3 The Business Associate Contract

When a business associate relationship exists, the Privacy Rule requires a covered entity to enter into a business associate contract before disclosing protected health information. [14]

While the exact terms of a business associate contract are left to the discretion of the covered entity and its business associate, HHS outlined the mandatory elements that the contract must contain. These elements are:[15]

1. A definition of the permitted and required uses and disclosures of protected health information by the business associate. The parties must provide a general description of the business associate's permitted uses and disclosures of protected health information.

2. Prohibition on the business associate to use or further disclose protected health information in a manner that would violate the regulation if done by the covered entity.

3. An explicit agreement from the business associate that it will not use or further disclose the protected health information other than as permitted or required by the contract or as required by law.

4. An explicit agreement that the business associate will use appropriate safeguards to prevent use or disclosure of the protected health information other than as provided for by its contract. This requirement generally imposes the soon-to-be finalized security regulation upon a business associate.

5. An explicit agreement that the business associate will report to the covered entity any use or disclosure of the protected health information not provided for by its contract of which it becomes aware.

6. An explicit agreement that the business associate will ensure that any agents, including any subcontractor, to whom it provides protected health information received from, or created or received by the business associate on behalf of the covered entity agrees to the same restrictions and conditions that apply to the business associate.

7. A requirement that the business associate will make available protected health information if requested by an individual in accordance with the individual's right to access the information for review purposes.

8. A requirement that the business associate will make available protected health information for amendment and incorporate any amendments to protected health information in accordance with an individual's right to amend health records.

9. A requirement that the business associate will make available the information required to provide an accounting of disclosures in accordance with the Privacy Rules requirements for providing patients with an accounting of disclosures.

10. A requirement that the business associate will make its internal practices, books, and records relating to the use and disclosure of protected health information received from, or created or received by the business associate on behalf of, the covered entity available to HHS for purposes of determining the covered entity's compliance. A covered entity should never include a clause that gives it the right to audit a business partner's compliance with the regulation. The reason is that audits are very expensive and such audits are unlikely to be conducted. If a breach occurs and the covered entity failed to exercise its audit rights, then the business associate can assert as a defense that the covered entity contributed to the breach or disclosure by its failure to audit the business associate. Therefore, it is sufficient to simply include a clause that gives HHS the right to audit the books and records of a business associate.

11. A requirement that at the contract's termination, the business associate will, if feasible, return or destroy all protected health information received from, or created or received by the business associate on behalf of, the covered entity and retain no copies. If the return or destruction is not feasible, the agreement must include a provision that will extend the protections of the contract to the information and limit further uses and disclosures to those purposes that make the return or destruction of the information infeasible.

12. A requirement that the business associate will authorize termination of the contract by the covered entity, if the covered entity determines that the business associate has violated a material term of the contract.

The contract may permit the business associate to use and disclose protected health information for the proper management and administration of the business associate. Furthermore, it may permit the business associate to provide data aggregation services relating to the health care operations of the covered entity.[16]

The Privacy Rule recognizes that in those situations where a business associate is required by law to perform a function or activity on behalf of a covered entity or to provide a service to the covered entity, the business associate may refuse to enter into a business associate contract. According to the rule, in those limited circumstances where the business associate is required to perform the work for the covered entity, disclosure may occur even without a business associate contract provided the covered entity can show that it attempted in good faith to enter into a business associate contract but was unsuccessful.[17]

For example, a covered entity may attempt to enter into a business associate contract when a state agency or its contractor is licensing the covered entity. If the licensure activities are required by law (in other words, not a health care operation that would trigger the need for a business associate contract), then the covered entity may not be able to get the agent or contractor to enter into a business associate agreement. In this situation, the Privacy Rule will excuse the covered entity, provided it made a good faith attempt to secure a business associate agreement with the entity.

6.4 Negotiating a Business Associate Contract

Business associate contracts have provisions that must be included before the agreement is considered compliant with the Privacy Rule. However, there is still a lot to negotiate between the affected parties.

For example, should a business associate contract be incorporated into the underlying agreement between a covered entity and its business partner? On the other hand, should it be a freestanding agreement? There are pluses and minuses to either approach.

By using only one contract, there is the preexisting agreement that can be used with modifications to accommodate HIPAA requirements. Some have also suggested that it makes the negotiation easier and keeps contract administration requirements to a minimum.

On the other hand, using a separate contract has advantages. By having a separate HIPAA business associate contract, it is easier to limit liability to just the HIPAA related issues. Likewise, arguments by business associates that they must be compensated to comply with the HIPAA requirements are more easily handled if the HIPAA contract is kept separate and left just to the regulatory requirements.

Aside from the question of one agreement or two, substantive issues involve terms and conditions that are in addition to those required by the Privacy Rule. For example, most vendors who perform services for covered entities will try to limit their liability to the value of the contract or one month of service. The covered entity, however, will not want to limit the liability of its business associate because it does not know the extent of the liability created by a breach. Thus, liability must be carefully considered and addressed by each party.

Ownership of the data is another important question. As a general proposition, the health care professional that made the observation owns the data. What if a business associate gets the data and then de-identifies it? Can the business associate use the de-identified data for any purpose it chooses, including profiting from the data? Covered entities should clearly assert their ownership rights to the data.

Covered entities also should consult with state privacy laws. State laws that are not preempted by the Privacy Rule may have an impact on the business associate contract. Likewise, a number of other standard issues should be addressed as part of the negotiation of a business associate contract.

Keep in mind that each business relationship is unique. Legal counsel should be consulted, as with any contract.

A sample business associate contract with mandatory and suggested clauses is found in Appendix C.

6.5 Business Associate Relationships between Government Agencies

While the Privacy Rule applies to most government agencies that provide or administer health care services, some aspects of the business associate provisions cannot be applied. For example, when both the covered entity and its business associate are government agencies, it is not feasible to impose the business associate contract requirements. As a general proposition, it may not be possible for one government agency to contract with another. Also, it may not be proper to suggest that one agency is acting on "behalf of" another agency. Likewise, it may not be possible for one agency to authorize the other to terminate the contract.

Recognizing these obstacles, HHS imposes a more limited requirement on a covered government agency when it transfers protected health information to another government agency. A government agency can stay in compliance with the privacy regulation by entering into a memorandum of understanding (MOU). These MOUs contain the terms of a business associate contract as described above to comply with the Privacy Rule. Although they are not binding contracts, these MOUs afford the necessary adequate assurances that a government agency needs to be in compliance before it can transfer protected health information to another government agency.[18]

Alternatively, a government agency may satisfy its obligations if there are other laws or regulations that contain requirements that accomplish the objectives of the business associate contract. For example, the Privacy Act imposes a number of obligations on a government that may, depending upon the way the agency implements these requirements, accomplish the objectives of a business associate contract.

6.6 Remaining in Compliance

Once a business associate contract is in place, the respective parties must diligently monitor the use of protected health information to ensure it complies with the terms of the contract. If a covered entity becomes aware of a material breach of the contract by its business associate, it must take reasonable steps to cure the breach or the covered entity will itself be in non-compliance with the Privacy Rule.[19]

If the covered entity is not successful in curing the breach then it must terminate the business associate contract, if feasible, or report the problem to the Secretary of HHS.[20] As a practical matter, covered entities must remain vigilant to breaches by its business associates, however, there are limits to what any contractor is expected or can accomplish. A covered entity is not strictly liable for the actions or inactions of its business associate. Rather, a covered entity is only required to exercise reasonable care when disclosing protected health information to a business associate. Reasonable care is demonstrated by entering into a business associate contract and taking reasonable steps to monitor compliance with the contract.

6.7 Key Points

- Carefully assess whether a business associate relationship is created. Merely contracting with a covered entity does not trigger the need for a business associate contract. Likewise, merely receiving protected health information does not necessarily prompt the need for a Business Associate Contract either.
- Under some circumstances, covered entities may be required to enter in Business Associate Contracts with other covered entities.
- If a Business Associate Contract is required, make sure all of the regulatory requirements of the Privacy Rule are made part of the agreement between the parties.
- Carefully describe a business associate's uses and disclosures
- Consider the use of additional terms and conditions in a business associate contract.
- Covered entities should refer to their respective state laws in drafting Business Associate Contracts because HIPAA does not pre-empt all state laws.

Endnotes

[1] A *covered entity* under HIPAA is a "health plan, health care clearinghouse or a health care provider who transmits any health information in electronic form in connection with a transaction covered by [the privacy regulation]." 65 Fed. Reg. 82,798 (to be codified at 45 C.F.R. pt. 160.102).
[2] The full definition of a *business associate* is found at 65 Fed. Reg. 82,798-99 (to be coified at 45 C.F.R. pt. 160.103).

[3] According to the definition of a *business associate*, it is a person who acts "[o]n behalf of such covered entity" or "[p]rovides [certain services] to or for such covered entity." *id.*

[4] 65 Fed. Reg. at 82,476.

[5] *id.*

[6] *id.*

[7] *id.*

[8] 65 Fed. Reg. at 82,477.

[9] A description of the legal bounds of a covered entity are described at 65 Fed. Reg. at 82,807 (to be codified at 45 C.F.R. pt. 164.504(a-c)).

[10] 65 Fed. Reg. at 82,800 (to be codified at 45 C.F.R. pt. 160.103).

[11] *id.* at 82,804 (to be codified at 45 C.F.R. pt. 164.501).

vv [13] 65 Fed. Reg. at 82,476.

[14] The HIPAA privacy regulation speaks in terms of being in compliance, as opposed to being liable. In other words, if a covered entity does not enter into a business associate contract it does not necessarily create a liability issue. Rather, it suggests that the covered entity may be in non-compliance with the regulation.

[15] A full listing of the elements of a business associate contract is found at 65 Fed. Reg. at 82,808 (to be codified at 45 C.F.R. pt. 164.504(e)(2)).

[16] *id.* at 82,808-09 (to be codified at 45 C.F.R. pt. 164.504(e)(4).

[17] *id.* at 82,808 (to be codified at 45 C.F.R. pt. 164.504(e)(3)(ii)).

[18] *id.* (to be codified at 45 C.F.R. pt. 164.504(e)(3)).

[19] *id.* (to be codified at 45 C.F.R. pt.164.504(e)(1)).

[20] *id.* (to be codified at 45 C.F.R. pt. 164.504(e)(1)(ii)).

Part II

Situational Privacy: How HIPAA Affects Common Health Care Activities

Section 7.0 - Marketing

Dennis Melamed and Alexander J. Brittin

7.1 Introduction

After the fear over discrimination in the work place and the insurance market, perhaps the most significant public concern over the use of individually identifiable health information revolves around the unsolicited marketing of products and services.

HHS recognized this public concern, observing in the preamble to the Privacy Rule:

> The incentives facing a company that acquires individually identifiable health information also discourage privacy protection. A company gains the full benefit of using such information, including its own marketing efforts or its ability to sell the information to third parties. The company, however, does not suffer the losses from disclosure of protected health information; the patient does. Because of imperfect monitoring, customers often will not learn of, and thus not be able to take efficient action to prevent uses or disclosures of sensitive information.[1]

The Privacy Rule does not entirely preclude the use of the protected health information for marketing without patient authorization. Some forms of marketing are clearly permitted under the regulation as HHS attempted to accommodate the need for a free flow of information within the health care system and to the patient to provide and discuss treatment and explain and discuss health benefits.

7.2 What Is Marketing?

The Privacy Rule defines marketing as: ". . . a communication about a product or service a purpose of which is to encourage recipients of the communication to purchase or use the product or service."[2]

The Privacy Rule does not limit the type or means of communication that are marketing.[3] In other

words, whether the marketing is communicated electronically, orally or in writing is irrelevant in determining when marketing occurs.

Generally, a covered entity may not use or disclose protected health information for marketing without an authorization that meets the requirements of the authorization section of the Privacy Rule.[4] For a more detailed discussion on consents and authorizations, see Section 5.0.

However, the Privacy Rule carved out specific exemptions from this requirement. In its first round of clarifications, HHS acknowledged this area is murky and intends to adjust the regulation as more experience is gathered with the regulations.[5]

7.3 Marketing Activities Exempted from Patient Authorization Requirements

To clarify the Privacy Rule's intent to not inhibit patient treatment, HHS defined those activities that would be considered marketing, but are exempt from the authorization requirement. These exemptions generally apply to certain types of activities that would fall under the definitions of treatment, payment, or health care operations.

Those marketing activities that are not specifically exempted but still fall under treatment, payment or health care operations are presumed to be marketing and require patient authorization.

To ensure that covered entities can freely discuss treatment with patients, the Privacy Rule does *not* consider marketing to be communications that are:

- Part of a provider's treatment of the patient and for the purpose of furthering that treatment. This would include making recommendations of specific brand-name pharmaceuticals or referrals to other providers; or

- Made in the course of managing the patient's treatment or recommending alternative treatment. For example, reminder notices for appointments, annual exams, or prescription refills are not marketing. Similarly, informing an individual who is a smoker about an effective smoking-cessation program is not marketing, even if that program is offered by someone other than the provider or plan making the recommendation.[6]

In addition, the Privacy Rule includes other types of marketing that would be permissible without patient authorization. However, the following criteria must be met:

- The communication occurs in a face-to-face encounter between the individual and the covered entity.[7] This provision enables a covered entity, such as a physician or insurer, to discuss any services and products, including those of a third-party, without restriction when covered entities meet with patients.
- The marketing takes the form of providing products or services of *only nominal value*.[8] HHS explained that this provision ensures that covered entities do not violate the Privacy Rule when they distribute calendars, pens and other merchandise that generally promotes the covered entity. This also allows covered entities to give patients free drug samples.
- The covered entity is marketing its own health-related products or services or those of a third party if the communication complies with the following requirements:
  1. Identifies the covered entity as the party making the communication;
  2. Prominently states that the covered entity is receiving direct or indirect remuneration from a third party for making the communication;
  3. Except in the case of a general communication (such as a newsletter), contains instructions describing how the individual may opt-out of receiving future communications about health-related products and services; and

  4. Where protected health information is used to target the communication about a product or service to individuals based on their health status or health condition, explains why the individual has been targeted and how the product or service relates to the health of the individual.[9]

HHS explained in the Privacy Rule's preamble that remuneration from a third party includes payments such as a fixed price per disclosure, compensation for the costs of compiling and sending the information to be disclosed, and, with respect to marketing communications, a percentage of any sales generated by the marketing communication. As an example, HHS cited the situation in which a device manufacturer offers to pay a fixed price per name and address of individuals with a particular diagnosis, so that the company can market its new device to those people.

The goal behind divulging the fact that the covered entity is receiving remuneration, according to HHS, is to provide individuals with the opportunity to weigh the covered entity's potential conflict of interest when deciding to authorize the covered entity's use or disclosure of protected health information.

Furthermore, HHS said that the Privacy Rule clarifies its intent to cover "a direct, tangible exchange, rather than the mere fact that parties intend to profit from their enterprises."[10]

7.4 Disclosures to Business Associates

Disclosure of protected health information to business associates for marketing is limited to those business associates that conduct marketing activities on behalf of the covered entity. Marketing by business associates must meet the guidelines discussed in Section 7.3. No other disclosure for marketing is allowed without patient authorization. In other words, protected health information cannot be given to a business associate for the business associate's own purposes without approval from the patient. As with any disclosure to a business associate, the covered entity must obtain a business associate's agreement.

7.5 Marketing versus Disease Management

The issue of marketing is particularly sensitive in the context of disease management programs. The difficulty in drawing distinctions between disease management and marketing prompted HHS to drop plans to define disease management. HHS stated in the final rule's preamble: "Rather than provide a definition of disease management, this final rule defines marketing. We note that overlap between disease management and marketing exists today in practice and they cannot be distinguished easily with a definitional label." [11]

As with marketing, HHS also relied, in part, on its definitions of treatment, payment and health care operations, to address disease management. For a fuller discussion of disease management, see Section 8.0.

7.6 Key Points

- Not all marketing uses of protected health information require patient authorization.
- Covered entities are free to discuss their health benefits and patient treatment options with patients without a marketing authorization.
- When covered entities receive remuneration for marketing uses of protected health information, they must inform patients and provide them with an opportunity to opt-out.
- Covered entities may provide marketing materials of nominal value, such as drug samples, pens and calendars, without patient authorization.
- General communications, such as newsletters, do not require opt-out mechanisms. HHS relies substantially on the definitions of treatment, payment and health care operations for regulating marketing and disease management. Because marketing is defined in the Privacy Rule, when covered entities evaluate disease management operations, they should take into account the regulation's marketing provisions.

Endnotes

[1] 65 Fed. Reg. at 82,761-62
[2] *id.* at 82,804 (to be codified at 45 C.F.R. pt. 164.501).
[3] *id.* at 82,493-94.
[4] *id.* at 82,819 (to be codified at 45 C.F.R. 164.514(e)(1)).
[5] *Guidance/Q&As*, Standards for Privacy of Individually Identifiable Health Information (45 C.F.R. pts. 160 and 164), *available at* http://www.hhs.gov/ocr/hipaa (last revised July 6, 2001)

[6] *id.*
[7] 65 Fed. Reg. at 82,819 (to be codified at 45 C.F.R. pt. 164.514(e)).
[8] *id.*
[9] *id.*
[10] Health care researchers conducting clinical trials also are governed by financial disclosure requirements under various federal laws to prevent conflicts of interest.
[11] 65 Fed. Reg. at 82,718.

Section 8.0 - Disease Management

James M. Jacobson

8.1 Introduction

Disease management (DM) may be one of the most confusing areas in the Privacy Rule. A key problem is that HHS could not arrive at a definition for DM organizations.[1]

This confusion, in part, exists due to concerns expressed by HHS officials over the use of protected information for marketing purposes. Because many companies that offer DM services also may be engaged in marketing, the department took a function-by-function approach to ensure that protected health information was appropriately handled in any given situation. For a broader discussion of marketing, see Section 7.

As a result, regardless of whether a division or company calls itself a DM organization, the covered entity must examine the specific activities and the target of those activities to determine how the Privacy Rule may apply.

8.2 What is Disease Management?

The Privacy Rule provisions relating to DM are based on two general categories of activity: patient-specific and population-based activities. Many DM programs identify patients in a covered population, such as members of a managed care organization, who have a specific chronic disease (such as diabetes or asthma) that requires substantial management. Under these programs, patient management may include regular patient condition monitoring, medication compliance advice and recommendations to the physician for adjustments and self-management training.

The DM organization also may operate a system in which it advises health professionals on "best practices" or evidence-based treatment guidelines devel-

oped from outcomes research. They also may include telephone and web-based interactions with patients to monitor their progress and allow them to seek further information.

As discussed in Section 5.0, covered entities generally are required to obtain patient authorizations for uses and disclosures of protected health information other than for treatment, payment or health care operations.

The challenge for covered entities is determining when DM activities qualify as treatment or health care operations, which will not require patient authorization, as opposed to marketing or some other non-treatment, non-health care operations activity, which will require patient authorization for the use and disclosure of protected health information.

8.3 Application to the Privacy Rule

Covered entities may use or disclose protected health information to DM organizations without patient authorization for treatment and health care operations. Treatment in this context generally refers to activities directed toward a specific patient. Health care operations in this context generally refers to activities that are aimed at populations of patients.

8.3.1 Patient-Specific Activities

Covered entities may use or disclose protected health information to their DM organizations without patient authorization under the treatment exception if the DM services are directed toward a particular individual and if a provider is involved in the use or disclosure.

The Privacy Rule defines treatment to mean:

> ... the provision, coordination, or management of health care and related services by one

or more health care providers, including the coordination or management of health care by a health care provider with a third party; consultation between health care providers relating to a patient; or the referral of a patient for health care from one health care provider to another.[2]

DM activities involving a nurse or other clinician aimed at specific individuals generally would fall under the Privacy Rule's definition of treatment and thus would not require patient authorization. Some common activities in this area include:

- Nurse chat;
- Patient self-management coaching;
- Medication usage and compliance information (which also may fall within the definition of health care operations);
- Interactions with patients via telephonic or Web-based DM tools; and
- Other activities that engage the patient in individualized health care improvement.

It is still unclear whether health plans (both staff model plans, which really are providers, and group model or other non-staff plans which are not) may take advantage of the treatment exception. Recent guidance has shed no light on this aspect of the rule. The treatment definition says nothing about health plans, and the preamble states that "Activities of health plans are not considered to be treatment."[3]

Until further guidance is provided, health plans cannot be assured that that they may use and disclose protected health information for those DM activities focused on specific individuals under the treatment exception. However, health plans may still use and disclose protected health information for most DM purposes under the health care operations exception to the patient authorization requirements.

8.3.2 Population-Based Activities

Covered entities also may use or disclose protected health information to their DM vendors without patient authorizations if the activity falls under health care operations. In other words, the Privacy Rule authorizes covered entities such as HMOs, insurers, and employer ERISA health plans to use and disclose protected health information for DM activities that are population-based without patient consent or authorization.

Some common activities in this area, as described in the definition of health care operations, include:

- Quality assessment and improvement, including outcomes evaluation and development of clinical guidelines;
- Population-based activities related to improving health or reducing health care costs;
- Protocol development;
- Case management and care coordination;
- Contacting health care providers and patients with information about treatment alternatives; and
- Related functions that do not include treatment.

8.4 Compliance Considerations

Until HHS offers guidance or modifications to the final rule, covered entities should take the following steps to achieve compliance with the patient authorization and consent provisions of the rule:

8.4.1 Covered Entities

A. Patient Authorizations and Consents: All covered entities should:

- Determine which exceptions to patient authorization and consent might apply to internal and outsourced DM programs.
- If patient authorization or consent is required or desired for any DM uses or disclosures, ensure that the patient forms specifically permit access to protected health information for DM purposes, and otherwise conform to regulatory requirements for consent forms.
- Review and conform compliance to state laws that are more stringent.

B. Health Care Providers: Health care providers, when acting as covered entities, should:

- Obtain patient consent when using or disclosing protected health information for DM purposes, regardless of whether the DM activities are focused on a particular patient (treatment) or a population (health care operations).
- To avoid the need for obtaining a patient authorization when using or disclosing protected health information for DM activities focused on a specific patient, ensure that

providers develop the protected health information themselves or receive it directly from a patient.

If providers receive the protected health information at any point from a health plan or other non-provider covered entity, it is not clear whether such providers, as Business Associates to the health plan covered entity, could use it for a "treatment" purpose without patient authorization, because the health plan arguably could not do so.

C. Health Plans: Health plans, when acting as covered entities, should:

- Determine whether specific uses or disclosures of protected health information for DM activities come within the treatment or health care operations exceptions. If they are not specifically enumerated items in the health care operations definition, opinion of counsel should be sought regarding whether patient authorizations are required.

- For patient and employer relations and for risk management purposes, determine whether to seek patient consents for those DM activities within treatment and health care operations even though not required by the Privacy Rule. HHS recognized in the Preamble that health plans, including ERISA welfare benefit plans, may have a higher comfort level that they will not be sued under state tort or contract law for violating HIPAA provisions (e.g., when a state has set HIPAA compliance as the state standard of privacy compliance) when they have a tangible patient consent on file especially when authorizations are not required.

8.4.2 "Minimum Necessary" Disclosure and DM

A covered entity must ensure that no more than the "minimum necessary" protected health information is used or disclosed, and must implement appropriate policies and procedures to carry out this purpose. Comments on the Privacy Rules specifically state that the "minimum necessary" standard is intended to reflect and be consistent with, not override, professional judgment and standards.

However, there will be a substantially greater liability risk for covered entities that are used to disclosing entire medical records to their DM vendors or pharmacy benefit managers if they do not carefully analyze whether continuing that practice would comply with the rule's intent. HHS's first round of clarifications significantly relaxes may of these concerns by establishing a "reasonable" business practices standard.[4]

For DM purposes, the Privacy Rule distinguishes between the use, request, and disclosure of protected health information:

- Use: A covered entity must identify and document whether its DM programs, internal or outsourced, have a need for protected health information and the categories of protected health information to which such programs need access.

- Disclosure: A covered entity must implement policies and procedures that limit the routine and recurring disclosure of DM information to the minimum that is necessary for the particular DM purpose. The covered entity is not required to review each routine and recurring disclosure individually.

- Request: For all other disclosures, a covered entity must develop criteria that limit disclosure to that necessary to comply with a specific request by a DM vendor. The covered entity must individually review every request for disclosure according to the developed criteria. Disclosures to health care providers for treatment purposes are not subject to these requirements.

8.4.3 DM and Business Associate Agreements

Generally, a covered entity may disclose protected health information to a Business Associate, or hire a Business Associate to obtain or create protected health information for it, but only if the covered entity obtains specified satisfactory assurances through a written agreement that the Business Associate will appropriately handle the information. (See Section 6.0 for a fuller discussion of Business Associate agreements).

Covered entities offering DM programs through outsourced DM organizations, PBMs, and others generally will have to have Business Associate contracts with them.

Covered entities should:

- Ensure that the Business Associate agreement includes a statement of the specific DM activities to be delegated, with vendor assurances that it will safeguard such protected health information as required by contract and by the use and disclosure rules applicable to the covered entity;

- Determine whether to limit disclosures of protected health information to DM Business Associates only for the purposes of carrying out those DM activities that are listed within the treatment or health care operations exceptions to patient authorization. With such limitations, the covered entity may avoid potential liability for the DM organization's failures to obtain authorizations on its behalf.

- If the covered entity does not wish to limit protected health information disclosures to its DM organization to those within the exceptions to patient authorization, the Business Associate contract should:

  1. Ensure that the DM organization will obtain a patient authorization as required by the rule for all uses or redisclosures for DM purposes that are not treatment and health care operations; or
  2. Require consultation between the covered entity and the DM organization's legal staff to make a determination as to whether patient authorizations are required; or
  3. Require an opinion of outside counsel or, if possible, advice from HHS itself.

- Ensure that the contract requires DM vendors to include all of the same provisions of the Business Associate agreement in any subcontracts it enters into on behalf of the covered entity. For example, DM vendors may themselves outsource to web-enabling firms to add Internet care management tools, home monitoring device companies, and nurse triage/demand management firms.

- Strict scrutiny of the vendor's subcontracting agreements should be mandated in the Business Associate agreement. The covered entity may wish to go even further by requir-

ing the DM vendor to get its approval before redisclosing protected health information to subvendors (other than to providers), or by requiring the use of covered entity-prepared Business Associate contracts for use with subvendors.

- Require DM vendors to report any known misuse of protected health information by itself or a subvendor to the covered entity.

- Require termination of the contract if the covered entity has substantial and credible evidence of a pattern or practice of the DM vendor that is a material breach of the agreement related to the use or disclosure of protected health information and the minimum necessary rule.

- Require the DM vendor, upon termination, to return or destroy all protected health information provided to it by the covered entity.

- Require the DM vendor to name the covered entity as an insured on its errors and omissions policies, and ensure that the policies cover HIPAA and state privacy law breaches.

- Require the DM vendor to comply with all state laws that are not preempted.

- Require careful indemnification provisions that specifically indemnify the covered entity from liabilities incurred due to DM vendor uses and disclosures of protected health information.

8.4.4 DM and Administrative Obligations

Other sections have already described the administrative and consumer protection requirements. While only a few of these provisions have specific implications for DM programs, they are significant. First, because there is so much confusion about whether a covered entity may use or disclose to the vendor protected health information for DM services that are not specifically enumerated in treatment or health care operations, the following are among those most critical for covered entities to consider:

- Covered entities must train their workforce appropriately concerning which protected health information, and for which purposes protected health information, may be disclosed. For example, marketing staff or other business people usually will not have enough clinical information to know whether certain databases of claims, laboratory, and prescribing data or medical records will be used by the DM vendor for enumerated treatment or health care operations purposes.

- Because privacy practices are likely to change frequently with respect to DM programs as the industry itself matures, covered entities should include in the patient notice of information practices a provision that expressly reserves the right to change its privacy practices. Otherwise, the covered entity will be required to follow the burdensome procedures outlined in the Privacy Rule to make changes.

8.5 Key Points

The following key points were made in this section:

- Because HHS did not define DM, covered entities must take a function-by-function approach in determining how to comply with the Privacy Rule.
- DM activities generally fall into two categories: patient specific and population based. Patient-specific activities are likely to be deemed treatment while population-based activities are likely to be deemed health care operations.
- Covered entities generally will require Business Associate contracts with their DM vendors.
- Covered entities should be sure to include in their notices on privacy practices that they reserve the right to change those policies as DM services are likely to change as they mature.

Endnotes

[1] HHS stated in the preamble: "Many commenters recommended adding the term disease management to health care operations. We were unable, however, to find a generally accepted definition of the term. Rather than rely on this label, we include many of the functions often included in discussions of disease management in this definition or in the definition of treatment." 65 Fed. Reg. at 82,490.

[2] *id.* at 82,805 (to be codified at 45 C.F.R. pt. 164.501).

[3] 65 Fed. Reg. at 82,498.

[4] *Guidance/Q&As,* Standards for Privacy of Individually Identifiable Health Information (45 C.F.R. pts. 160 and 164), *available at* http://www.hhs.gov/ocr/hipaa (last revised July 6, 2001)

Section 9.0 - Research

Dennis Melamed

9.1 Introduction

Access to protected health information and medical records is the lifeblood of biomedical and health services research. While the Privacy Rule acknowledges this, it also recognizes that privacy has been a relatively low priority in this area.[1] To ensure the issue receives attention, HHS developed a framework that obliges covered entities and researchers to pay specific attention to and make explicit decisions on privacy.

The Privacy Rule deals with the two major types of research:

- Research involving the treatment of human subjects; and
- Records-based research.

Each incurs separate requirements. However, both sets of requirements are premised on the principle that individuals should have more information and control over the use of protected health information.

9.2 What Is Research?

Research takes many shapes and has many objectives. For example, clinical trials testing experimental treatments on humans are not the same as records-based research to determine disease trends. In addition, comparative studies used to assess the relative effectiveness of products for marketing is not the same as determining the health effects of environmental pollutants for new regulatory standards.

Consequently, under the Privacy Rule, HHS established a definition of research to accommodate the wide range of activities that may occur in the pursuit of knowledge. It did so by borrowing the definition for research used in the Federal Policy for the Protection of Human Subjects, also known as the "Common Rule", which governs federally funded research involving human subjects.[2] The Privacy Rule thus defines research as a "systematic investigation, including research development, testing and evaluation, designed to develop or contribute to generalizable knowledge."[3]

This definition applies to the two general categories of research, i.e., research involving human subjects and records-based research.

9.3 Research Involving Treatment[4]

Although the Common Rule addresses privacy, in the past, attention focused overwhelmingly on the safety of the patient.[5] One consequence of the Privacy Rule is an attempt to redress the neglect and ensure that patients know how their protected health information will be used by the researchers and with whom it will be shared to make an informed decision on whether to participate in the research.

9.3.1 Researchers as Covered Entities

Frequently, research involves providing treatment for patients in the form of clinical trials. In these cases, researchers generally can expect to be considered covered entities because they provide treatment and are likely to engage in one of the covered electronic standards. The researcher (e.g., physician) does not have to engage in one of the covered electronic transactions in the course of administering the clinical trial to be deemed a covered entity. Instead, if the researcher uses the electronic transactions anywhere in his or her practice, the entire practice is deemed to be covered under HIPAA.

9.3.2 Authorizations[6]

As with other uses and disclosures of protected health information, researchers must provide a notice of what information they want and how they will use the information and obtain an authorization from the patient. The individual's authorization for research involving treatment generally tracks the requirements for obtaining authorizations generally. A valid authorization for research must:

- Describe the information to be used and disclosed;
- Identify the person authorized to make the requested use and/or disclosure;
- Identify the person to whom the covered entity may make the requested use and/or disclosure;
- Include an expiration date or an event that triggers the expiration;
- A statement of the individual's right to revoke the authorization in writing and the exceptions to the right to revoke, together with a description of how the individual may revoke the authorization;
- A statement that information used or disclosed under the authorization may be subject to re-disclosure by the recipient and no longer be protected by Privacy Rule; and
- The signature of the individual and date; or if the authorization is signed by a personal representative of the individual, a description of the representative's authority to act for the individual.[7]

For a broader discussion of authorizations, see Section 5.0.

Covered entities also must explain the extent to which some or all of the protected health information will be used or disclosed for purposes of treatment, payment, and health care operations. For example, if a provider intends to seek reimbursement from the individual's health plan for the routine costs of care associated with the research, the authorization must explain the types of information that it will provide to the health plan for payment purposes.

This treatment, payment and health care operations provision is important as the federal government and covered entities increasingly are financing the normal costs of care associated with the research.

If the covered entity gets or intends to get an authorization to use and disclose the information under the consent for treatment, payment and health care provisions, the authorization must refer to that consent or notice, and state that the limits of the research authorization are binding.

9.3.3 Combining Consent with Authorization for Research Involving Treatment

To minimize the amount of documentation from the individual (subject), the Privacy Rule permits the covered entity to combine the individual's authorization with the consent to carry out treatment, payment or health care operations or with its notice of privacy practices if the covered entity's primary interaction with the patient is the research. [8]

9.3.4 Conditioning Experimental Treatment on Authorization

The Privacy Rule allows covered entities to condition participation in research involving treatment on the patient agreeing to authorize the use and disclosure of protected health information.[9]

If a covered entity has an existing relationship with the patient prior to the research, the entity can combine the research authorization to use protected health information with other authorizations (except for psychotherapy notes.). However, the research treatment cannot be premised on agreeing to the authorization.

Thus, as a practical matter, this means providers and insurers who wish to recruit patients for clinical trials must get two separate authorizations: one for the use and disclosure of protected health information that will be created for the research and treatment; and one for the use of the individual's existing protected health information prior to the research. [10]

9.3.5 Clinical Trial Recruitment of Existing Patients

Covered entities, who want to give their patients or members the opportunity to participate in clinical trials, first must get authorization from the patient to use the protected information for trial recruitment purposes. In this case, the provider or insurer would be seeking authorization from the patient for its own use and disclosure.

However, the Privacy Rule allows covered entities to review medical records to determine if its patients or members fit the needs of the clinical trial without an authorization from the patient. See Section 9.6.5 - Reviews Preparatory to Research.

9.4 Permissible Disclosures

The Privacy Rule does not prevent researchers from making disclosures to federal or state authorities required by law. For example, under the Food, Drug, and Cosmetic Act, sponsors of clinical trials, such as pharmaceutical and medical device manufacturers[11] are required to inform the Food and Drug Administration of adverse events resulting or suspected of resulting from their experimental treatments.

9.5 Patient Access to Protected Health Information in Research

Patient access to protected health information is one of the foundations of the Privacy Rule, but in the research context, it is where HHS decided to balance the rights of the patient with the needs of the research. As a result, researchers do not have to provide access to the protected health information generated by the research as long as the research is in progress and the patient agrees to the denial of access when consenting to participate.

The consent to participate in the research, however, must state that the patient has the right to access protected health information re-instated once the research is completed. In other words, once the research is completed, the patient must be given the right to access his own information.[12]

9.6 Records Based Research

Records-based research is another area in which HHS tried to balance the researchers' need for access to data with the new privacy rights of patients. The Privacy Rule created a system in which a covered entity may use or disclose an individual's protected health information without the individual's consent or authorization, and without providing the individual an opportunity to object to the disclosure.

9.6.1 Research versus Health Care Operations

Not all examinations of protected health information qualify as research. HHS found it necessary to draw a distinction between research and health care operations. In the definition of health care operations, the Privacy Rule specifically excludes activities designed to develop or contribute to generalizable knowledge.[13]

For example, a researcher who sought medical records to compare the effectiveness of two treatments for publication in a peer-reviewed journal must comply with the research provisions of the regulation. However, a business manager accessing the same data with the purpose of developing new clinical guidelines for patients within his organization would be covered by the health care operations provisions.

If quality assessment and improvement activities change into research, the covered entity must document that change "as proof that, when initiated, the primary purpose was health care operations," HHS explained in the preamble.[14]

9.6.2 Institutional Review Boards and Privacy Boards

Gaining access to protected health information for research is not an automatic process. It requires the covered entity to evaluate the relative merits of the research versus the privacy intrusion through the use of Institutional Review Boards (IRBs) or Privacy Boards. These boards are empowered to grant waivers of patient authorizations to enable researchers to access protected health information.

To receive a waiver of the patient authorization requirements to access patient records, researchers – regardless of whether they are affiliated with a covered entity or not – must submit their proposals to an IRB or a Privacy Board.

The Privacy Rule requires that a covered entity obtain documentation that an IRB or Privacy Board has approved the waiver or alteration of an individual's authorization. This process also is borrowed from the Federal Policy for Protection of Human Subjects (the Common Rule).

Covered entities do not have to use IRBs and can create Privacy Boards to review research proposals. However, the expectation is that IRBs will be conducting the bulk of the oversight of research. The concept of the Privacy Board was developed by HHS to allow organizations without access to IRBs to oversee and evaluate research proposals.

In its first round of clarifications, HHS explained that in cases in which research requires protected health information from two or more covered entities, covered entities may accept the documentation of IRB or Privacy Board approval from a single IRB or Privacy Board.[15]

The composition of IRBs is covered under the Common Rule.

The Privacy Rule establishes general requirements on who should sit on the Privacy Boards. Membership should include people with "varying backgrounds and appropriate professional competency as necessary to review research protocols and the effects on the individual's privacy rights. It also should include at least one member who is not affiliated with the covered entity, not affiliated with any entity conducting or sponsoring the research, and not related to any person who is affiliated with such entities. [16]

9.6.3 Waivers of Authorizations

A covered entity may use or disclose protected health information for research purposes if it gets a waiver of the authorization requirements from an IRB or Privacy Board. To obtain this waiver, the covered entity must secure:

- A statement that the alteration or waiver of authorization was approved by an IRB or Privacy Board in compliance with the requirements of the Privacy Rule (including the Privacy Board's composition);
- A statement identifying the IRB or Privacy Board and the date on which the alteration or waiver of authorization was approved; and
- A written statement from the IRB or Privacy Board that the research meets eight specific criteria.
- The eight criteria are:
  1. The use or disclosure of protected health information involves no more than minimal risk to the individuals;
  2. The alteration or waiver will not harm the privacy rights and the welfare of the individuals;
  3. The research could not practicably be conducted without the alteration or waiver;
  4. The research could not practicably be conducted without access to and use of the protected health information;
  5. The privacy risks to individuals whose protected health information is to be used or disclosed are reasonable in relation to the anticipated benefits if any to the

individuals, or the importance of the knowledge that may reasonably be expected to result from the research;
  6. There is an adequate plan to protect the identifiers from improper use and disclosure;
  7. There is an adequate plan to destroy the identifiers at the earliest opportunity consistent with conduct of the research, unless there is a health or research justification for retaining the identifiers, or retention is otherwise required by law; and
  8. There are adequate written assurances that the protected health information will not be reused or disclosed to any other person or entity, except as required by law, for authorized oversight of the research project, or for other research for which the use or disclosure of protected health information would be permitted by the rule.[17]

The IRB or Privacy Board waiver/alteration documentation also must:

- Identify the reviewing board and give the approval date;
- Describe the protection health information to be disclosed; and
- Contain the signatures of board chairman or member designated by the chairman.

9.6.4 Expedited Reviews

For the IRB, the Common Rule's procedures regarding expedited review apply. For the Privacy Board, the Privacy Rule's review procedures apply. An expedited review under the Privacy Rule allows one or more members of the Privacy Board to waive the need for patient authorization when the research involves no more than a minimal risk to individual privacy.[18]

9.6.5 Reviews Preparatory to Research

Sometimes access to records that contain protected health information is necessary to enable researchers to formulate hypotheses to test in research. "The intent of this provision is to permit covered entities to use and disclose protected health information to assist in the development of a research hypothesis and aid in the recruitment of research participants,"[19] HHS said.

The Privacy Rule allows a covered entity to disclose protected health information to a researcher during the preparation of the research proposal without the individual's authorization. However, the covered entity must obtain assurances from the researcher that:

- The use and disclosure are only for the purposes of reviewing protected health information to prepare a research protocol or for similar purposes;
- No protected health information will be removed from the covered entity by the researcher; and
- The protected health information is necessary for the research. [20]

The researcher may only record the protected health information in a de-identified format.

9.7 Research on the Deceased

The Privacy Rule permits the use and disclosure of individually identifiable health information of a deceased individual. Access to this information may be obtained without the prior authorization of a legal representative provided that the covered entity obtains assurances that the information is necessary for the research and is solely sought for research. In addition, the covered entity may require the researcher to provide documentation of the death of the individual.

9.8 Minimum Necessary Information

The Privacy Rule allows the covered entity to rely upon the documentation received from the IRB or Privacy Board describing the privacy review of the use of protected health information when applying the minimum necessary standard for research purposes.

The rule also permits the covered entity to rely upon the written assurances received from the researcher for the use of protected health information for reviews preparatory to research and for research on decedent information when applying the minimum necessary standard.

9.9 Liability Issues

Some areas of research still remain confused within the Privacy Rule. For example, it is still unclear how the Privacy Rule deals with researchers who seek to interview patients for research purposes but who do not provide treatment.

Presumably, the researchers will have gone through an IRB or Privacy Board approval process, committing themselves to protecting the information they gathered. However, further guidance is pending in this area.

Another concern is over the liability of the covered entities and the boards who grant researchers access to protected health information. Once the information is in the hands of the researcher, the Privacy Rule does not apply because the regulatory requirements do not follow the information. In other words, the researcher is not covered by HIPAA.

This has led to some discussion within health care organizations about the need to require records-based researchers to agree to indemnity clauses in addition to the assurances required under the waiver provisions of the Privacy Rule. Indemnity clauses are not required under the Privacy Rule, but covered entities may want to consider them to limit their legal liabilities in the event researchers or the researchers' organizations misuse the protected health information they receive.

9.10 A HIPAA Escape Route: De-Identified Data

The Privacy Rule creates a framework to de-identify health and medical records for use in medical research and business applications that significantly reduces the possibility of re-identifying patients. The Privacy Rule also provides significant incentives: the use of de-identified data largely dispenses with the need for the policies, procedures, and documentation required to use individually identifiable health information.

The Privacy Rule adopts two methods for de-identifying protected health information:

- One based on a safe harbor; and
- One based on statistical expertise.

9.10.1 Safe Harbor for De-Identifying Protected Health Information

The regulation establishes a safe harbor under which a covered entity will be deemed to have de-identified a record containing protected health information if all of a list of 19 specified items of information have been removed. In addition, the covered entity cannot have "actual knowledge that the information could be used alone or in combination with other information to identify an individual who is a subject of the information."[21]

The 19 items that must be stripped from a record to be considered de-identified under the Safe Harbor are:

(A) Names;

(B) All geographic subdivisions smaller than a state, including street address, city, county, precinct, zip code, and their equivalent geocodes, except for the initial three digits of a zip code if, according to the current publicly available data from the Bureau of the Census:

    (1) The geographic unit formed by combining all zip codes with the same three initial digits contains more than 20,000 people; and

    (2) The initial three digits of a zip code for all such geographic units containing 20,000 or fewer people is changed to 000.

(C) All elements of dates (except year) for dates directly related to an individual, including birth date, admission date, discharge date, date of death; and all ages over 89 and all elements of dates (including year) indicative of such age, except that such ages and elements may be aggregated into a single category of age 90 or older;

(D) Telephone numbers;

(E) Fax numbers;

(F) Electronic mail addresses;

(G) Social security numbers;

(H) Medical record numbers;

(I) Health plan beneficiary numbers;

(J) Account numbers;

(K) Certificate/license numbers;

(L) Vehicle identifiers and serial numbers, including license plate numbers;

(M) Device identifiers and serial numbers;

(N) Web Universal Resource Locators (URLs);

(O) Internet Protocol (IP) address numbers;

(P) Biometric identifiers, including finger and voice prints;

(Q) Full face photographic images and any comparable images; and

(R) Any other unique identifying number, characteristic, or code.[22]

Eliminating all 19 elements is not always necessary, however. For example, age or year of birth may be retained for most uses. At the same time, extreme ages,

e.g. 90 and above, may require broader aggregation as such samples represent a limited population where the potential for re-identification is increased.[23]

9.10.2 Geographic Indicators

Geographic indicators represent another area that may be retained with some limitations. Rather than specifying the use of 3 or 5 number zip codes, HHS determined that geographic identifiers could be retained if those identifiers represented populations of more than 20,000 people.

In practical terms this creates a list of forbidden 18 three-digit zip codes. They are: 022, 036, 059, 102, 203, 555, 556, 692, 821, 823, 830, 831, 878, 879, 884, 893, 987, and 994. This means covered entities must replace these zip codes with zeros and treat them as a single geographic entity. HHS will maintain a list of the forbidden zip codes.

9.10.3 Any Other Unique Code

The safe harbor for de-identified data includes an omnibus category: "Any other unique identifying number, characteristic, or code." HHS specifically cites clinical trial record numbers and medical device serial numbers as examples, but this also includes any unique number that is generated with the intention of identifying an individual. This also includes patient invoices even if the invoice numbers are randomly generated.

The underlying principle governing this category is that a number or code that is uniquely generated to identify an individual fails to enter the safe harbor. This includes payment invoices and any other number that was generated with the primary purpose of identifying an individual.

9.10.4 Prohibition Against Re-Identification

The Privacy Rule prohibits covered entities from attempting to re-identify the de-identified data they receive.

The fact that records or keys that re-identify the data may be under tight legal or logistical restrictions is of no consequence in the Privacy Rule. Instead, HHS presumes that such obstacles represent little more than a leaky ship in which data has an unacceptable likelihood of escaping.

The clear message from HHS is that the legality or ease of accessing information that can be used to re-identify a record is of no consequence in determining the status of information as de-identified.

9.10.5 Statistical Expertise Exemption

The second method of de-identification relies on a covered entity's expertise and experience in statistics to remove or encrypt a combination of information different from the list of 19 items. This method is based on using commonly accepted scientific and statistical standards for preventing rediscslosure. The covered entity must document the analysis and results that justify the determination.

In the original privacy proposal, HHS provided examples of the kinds of entities that would have the necessary statistical experience and expertise to make these judgments. They include: large health research institutions, such as medical schools with epidemiologists and statisticians on the faculty; federal agencies such as the National Center for Health Statistics, the Agency for Health Care Policy and Research, FDA, the Bureau of the Census, and NIH; and large corporations that conduct health research such as pharmaceutical manufacturers with epidemiologists and statisticians on staff.[24]

HHS refers to two reports from the Office of Management for determining commonly accepted scientific and statistical standards:

- Statistical Policy Working Paper 22 – Report on Statistical Disclosure Limitation Methodology, prepared by the Subcommittee on Disclosure Limitation Methodology, Federal Committee on Statistical Methodology *(www.fcsm.gov/working-papers/wp22.html)*
- The Checklist on Disclosure Potential of Proposed Data Releases, prepared by the Confidentiality and Data Access Committee, Federal Committee on Statistical Methodology *(www.fcsm.gov/docs/checlist_799.doc)*.

The first report concludes that the two main risks for re-identification are the existence of records with unique characteristics, such as unusual occupations or very high salaries or very old ages, and the existence of external sources of records with matching data elements that can be used to link with the de-identified data to re-identify the data.

HHS said in the preamble in the Privacy Rule that it anticipated the need to issue further guidance in this area.

9.10.6 Using Protected Health Information to Create De-Identified Data

Covered entities and their business partners who receive protected health information can use the protected health information to create de-identified information. However, they would be required not to disclose the key or other mechanism that would enable the information to be re-identified.

9.11 Clinical Laboratory Improvements Amendments of 1988 (CLIA)

The Privacy Rule does not require research laboratories that are exempt from the CLIA regulations and are also a covered health care provider to provide individuals with access to protected health information. HHS acknowledged that requiring this access might result in the research laboratory losing its CLIA exemption.[25]

9.12 Transition Rules

Researchers may rely on current authorizations and consents from patients for research purposes obtained before the compliance date of the Privacy Rule for use in the specific research project after the compliance date. However, the covered entity must abide by all limitations in that consent or authorization.

9.13 Key Points

- The Privacy Rule addresses two major categories of research: research involving human subjects and records-based research.
- If clinical trial researchers engaged in the covered electronic transactions in their medical practice, they will be considered covered entities because they provide treatment.
- The Privacy Rule draws a distinction between research and health care operations. If an activity that started out as health care operations turns into research, that change must be documented to indicate the original purpose.
- Covered entities are permitted without patient authorization to review patient records to determine if their membership or patient population includes individuals who may qualify for clinical trials.

- Patient authorizations for the use of protected health information in clinical trials cannot prevent legally mandated disclosures to local, state or federal agencies. However, the possibility of this disclosure must be in the authorization form.

- Research involving treatment frequently involves the payment for routine costs of care by third parties. Consequently, covered entities must inform trial subjects that protected health information will be shared under the treatment, payment and health care operations provision of the Privacy Rule.

- Covered entities may accept the documentation of IRB or Privacy Board approval from a single IRB or Privacy Board when research requiring protected health information is obtained from two or more covered entities.

- All 19 data elements that make up the Safe Harbor for de-identification of protected health information do not always have to be removed.

- Invoices and other records that may be generated using random numbers are still identifiable records because they were generated to identify an individual.

- Covered entities can use protected information to generate de-identified data that can be shared

Endnotes

[1] The Privacy Rule also represents another element in an ongoing reassessment of the safety and oversight of biomedical and health research. Media reports about the 1999 death of Jessie Gelsinger, who died while participating in a genetic therapy trial conducted by the University of Pennsylvania, focused even more attention on the way human subjects are protected in biomedical research. In response to Gelsinger's death and other problems reported in other clinical trials, HHS consolidated several other offices and created the Office of Human Research Protections in June 2000. To emphasize the increased importance of human subject safety, HHS placed the new office in the Office of the Secretary. In addition, the Institute of Medicine, the HHS Inspector General and the National Bioethics Advisory Commission have issued reports in recent years warning that institutional review boards are being overwhelmed and may not be able to provide the required oversight of research protocols. These warnings came before the Privacy Rule was issued and imposed yet another responsibility – privacy protection – on IRBs.

[2] Basic HHS Policy for Protection of Human Research Subjects, 45 C.F.R. § 46.102 *et seq.* (2001). The Common Rule governs substantial amounts of federally-sponsored research, but not all federally funded research. Thus, the Privacy Rule expands the universe of researchers who must start paying closer attention to privacy issues. At the same time, the Common Rule is frequently used in the private sector as a model.

[3] 65 Fed. Reg. at 82,805 (to be codified at 45 C.F.R. pt. 164.501).

[4] The proposed privacy regulation contained a provision on research unrelated to treatment, which was an attempt by HHS to deal with genetic testing and genetic information. That provision was dropped by HHS as it was confusing and cumbersome. For the purposes of this chapter, treatment refers to the provision of health care in conducting clinical trials involving human subjects.

[5] Research involving the treatment of humans, such as in clinical trials, is governed by other statutes as well, such as the Food, Drug, and Cosmetic Act, U.S.C.A. § 301 *et seq.* (2001), administered by the Food and Drug Administration.

[6] The requirements for authorization to use or disclose individually identifiable health information are not the same as the requirements of the Common Rule for obtaining a research subject's informed consent.

[7] 65 Fed. Reg. at 82,811-12 (to be codified at 45 CFR pt. 164.508(c)).

[8] *id.* at 82,812 (to be codified at 45 CFR pt. 164.508(f)(2)).

[9] *id.* at 82,810 (to be codified at 45 CFR pt. 164.506(b)(4)(ii)).

[10] HHS noted in the preamble:"…we anticipate that covered entities will almost always, if not always, condition the provision of research-related treatment on the individual signing the authorization…for the covered entity's use or disclosure of protected health information created for the research." 65 Fed. Reg. at 82,520-21.

[11] Medical product manufacturers generally are not considered covered entities under the Privacy Rule. At the same time, they are involved in the development of research protocols for both clinical trials involving humans and records-based research. These companies frequently use independent investigators to conduct trials, and these investigators send back records that identify patients by codes maintained by the investigators.

[12] 65 Fed. Reg. at 82,823 (to be codified at 45 C.F.R. pt. 164.524(a)(2)(iii)).

[13] *id.* at 81,803 (to be codified at 45 C.F.R. pt. 164.501).

[14] *id.* at 82,490.

[15] *Guidance/Q&As*, Standards for Privacy of Individually Identifiable Health Information (45 C.F.R. pts. 160 and 164), *available at* http://www.hhs.gov/ocr/hipaa (last revised July 6, 2001).

[16] 65 Fed. Reg. at 82,816 (to be codified at 45 C.F.R. pt. 164.512(i)(1)(B)).

[17] *id.* (to be codified at 45 C.F.R. pt. 164.512(i)(2)). The first four waiver requirements already are required under the Common Rule. The requirement to determine that the benefits of the research outweigh the privacy intrusion also is frequently included in reviews under the Common Rule. The requirements for demonstrating adequate protection of the identifiers, an adequate plan to destroy the identifiers, and written assurances that protected health information will not be reused or disclosed to others are not currently required under the Common Rule.

[18] *id.* at 82,817 (to be codified at 45 C.F.R. pt. 164.512(i)(2)(iv)(C)).

[19] *id.* at 82,537

[20] *id.* at 82,816 (to be codified at 45 C.F.R. 164.510(i)(1)(ii)).

[21] *id.* at 82,819 (to be codified at 45 C.F.R. pt.164.514(2)(i)).

[22] *id.* at 82,818 (to be codified at 45 C.F.R. pt. 164.514(2)(i)).

[23] *id.* at 82,710.

[24] 64 Fed. Reg. at 59,936.

[25] CLIA regulations exempt the components or functions of "research laboratories that test human specimens but do not report patient specific results for the diagnosis, prevention or treatment of any disease or impairment of, or the assessment of the health of individual patients" from the CLIA regulatory scheme. 42 C.F.R. § 493.3(b)(2)(2001).

Section 10.0 - Peer Review Organizations

Karen Milgate

10.1 Introduction

Patient rights to health privacy raises new issues for the health care industry as its shares information with external organizations who assist the providers or plans with utilization and quality improvement analysis. The complexity of the Privacy Rule, particularly as it interacts with Medicare and Medicaid programs and other covered entities may present special challenges to Peer Review organizations (PROs).

At the same time, as the public is concerned about privacy, it is also concerned over the quality and safety of patient care. The Privacy Rule attempts to balance these competing demands.

The Federal Government also has made it clear that it does not want to compromise the quality of care in the name of privacy.

10.1.1 Quality Improvement Organizations

Quality Improvement Organizations (QIOs) perform a wide variety of services for many different covered entities. They conduct medical reviews, assist providers (including practitioners, hospitals, skilled nursing facilities, home health agencies, and nursing homes) and plans in analyzing and improving the quality of care they deliver and assessing the appropriateness of billing and payment.

The primary role for most QIOs is through Medicare as a Peer Review Organization (PRO). However, they also have contracts with Medicaid, public and private employers, and other federal agencies.

10.1.2 How QIOs Do Their Jobs

The QIOs perform their work in a variety of ways. Sometimes they analyze specific medical records for the purposes of medical necessity determination, and other times they are asked to analyze aggregate samples of claims to identify patterns.

The largest portion of their work in Medicare relies on hospitals and other providers to share individually identifiable patient information to identify quality improvement opportunities. The result of this information sharing is the implementation of improved health care services.

The complexity of the Privacy Rule may provoke some reluctance on the part of the providers and plans to provide this protected health information. As a result, QIOs need to become familiar with the requirements to anticipate these concerns.

10.2 Sharing Health Information with QIOs

The Privacy Rule directly affects QIOs because of their need to obtain protected health information from providers and plans. The primary question for external organizations like QIOs that rely on provider data for data analysis is: *Under what circumstances are covered entities allowed to give them protected information without individual authorizations?*

There are three primary roles in which QIOs would be able to obtain protected health information:

- Oversight,
- Business associate, or
- Research.

All QIO work in Medicare is likely to be considered oversight under the Privacy Rule. However, the private sector activities of QIOs will fall under either the requirements for business associates or research. The regulation's coverage of Medicaid work will be determined on a state-by-state basis.

10.2.1 Oversight Role

A. Medicare: Congress created the PRO program for Medicare and gave these organizations the authority to review individual patient records. Congress also required institutional providers and others with Medicare agreements to disclose protected health information to the PROs for utilization and quality of care review. With this authority came strict confidentiality and disclosure protections.

The Privacy Rule does not pre-empt the mandatory requirements for information sharing mandated by laws, such as in the Medicare program.

Although the PROs are performing this oversight function for HCFA, *the regulation does not specifically clarify whether a HCFA contractor would be included within the definition of an oversight agency.*[1] Given that the government contracts with many other entities to assist them in performing numerous oversight functions it would seem reasonable for PROs to be included as a government "agent."

However, until clarifications are provided in this area, PROs should discuss the situation with HCFA (now known as the Centers for Medicare and Medicaid Services or CMS) personnel. If that clarification is not forthcoming, PROs may need to develop business associate relationships with CMS and/or with providers, or become researchers.

Because of current Medicare requirements, PROs generally have strong safeguards in place to protect the privacy and confidentiality of individually identifiable health information.

B: State Law and Medicaid Oversight: State laws play a significant role in this rule. For QIOs, state law will determine whether QIO contracts with Medicaid also would be considered "oversight" for the purposes of complying with the Privacy Rule. If providers or plans in the state are required to give the PROs the information and the purpose for the disclosure falls within the definition of oversight, the functions the QIOs are performing could be considered oversight. The issue of whether the QIO would be considered an "agent" of the Medicaid agency for purposes of oversight is the same for Medicaid as it is for Medicare.

10.2.2 Business Associate Role

In situations in which QIOs are not deemed to be operating in an oversight capacity, they will be able to obtain protected health information from health care providers and other covered entities through business associate relationships with them.

As discussed in previous sections, the Privacy Rule allows the disclosure of protected health information to entities termed "business associates" if the external organization assists the health care provider or other covered entity in performing one of three authorized functions:

- Payment,
- Treatment, or
- Health care operations.

The definition of health care operations in the Privacy Rule contains much of the work a QIO performs, including quality assessment and improvement, the development of clinical guidelines, medical review and the review of the competence of provider/practitioners.

QIO work related to utilization management and correct billing would fall under the authorized function of payment. Consequently, most QIOs could operate as business associates under the Privacy Rule.

In this context, the Privacy Rule limits the ways in which QIOs can use the health care operations data they receive from health care providers and other covered entities. QIOs are allowed to aggregate data from different covered entities. However, the Privacy Rule allows business associates only to use the protected health information for purposes specific to each entity's patients or covered population.

This limitation may make it more difficult for QIOs to apply findings from Medicare work to broader populations and to publish analysis of their findings. The Privacy Rule states in the definition of health care operations that protected health information may only be disclosed to business associates as long as the "obtaining of generalizable knowledge is not the primary purpose of any studies resulting from the activities."

Generalizable knowledge is considered research and any entity using information for research purposes would have to comply with the research requirements.

For a more in-depth discussion of business associate contracts, see Section 6.0.

10.2.3 QIOs and Research

Another way in which covered entities may disclose protected health information to QIOs without individual authorization is to obtain it for research. This may be necessary if a QIO wants to use the data for a function broader than that contained in the definition of oversight or through a business associate agreement.

For example, if a QIO wants to use the information it receives from providers for the benefit of a broader population than the ones for which they have a business associate agreement, the purpose might be deemed a pursuit of "generalizable knowledge" and not permitted under the business associate agreement for health care operations.

A QIO acting as a research entity still must specify how it will protect and use the information. QIOs also must follow either the institutional review board review process for certain federally funded research or establish an internal privacy board to determine the appropriateness of the disclosure. In most cases the researchers would be required to destroy the identifiers at the earliest opportunity.

10.3 Key Points

- Providers may hesitate to work with QIOs, but should bear in mind that many of these data requests may be statutorily required and not pre-empted by HIPAA.
- QIOs working with Medicaid should discuss the issue with their Medicaid contractors and examine state law to determine whether the state has a mandate to perform the function and whether the providers or plans are required to share data for that purpose.
- Without an oversight role, QIOs will need to obtain protected health information through either a business associate or research relationship.

Endnotes

[1] For purposes of the Medicare contract, QIOs are termed Peer Review Organizations (PROs) to recognize that clinical peers should perform the services described above.

Section 11.0 - Employers

Dennis Melamed and Alexander J. Brittin

11.1 Introduction

Employers – including covered entities acting in their capacity as employers – are not directly covered by the Privacy Rule. However, that does not mean they avoid Privacy Rule requirements. The Privacy Rule creates a new framework for managing protected health information that reverberates throughout the business enterprise.

For example, many employers will be affected by the Privacy Rule when they provide or pay for medical care for their employees as part of a qualified group health plan.

11.2 Group Health Plans and Their Employer Sponsors

Employers, including covered entities, are likely to be affected by the Privacy Rule if they provide or pay for medical care for their employees. As discussed in Section 2.0, the Privacy Rule covers "health plans," which includes group health plans sponsored by employers. Although the Privacy Rule does not directly cover sponsors of group health plans, i.e. employers, it gets around this limitation by imposing restrictions when insurance companies, health maintenance organizations (HMOs) and third party administrators (TPAs) may disclose protected health information to them. The Privacy Rule also imposes restrictions on the use of protected health information once sponsors receive it from insurance companies, HMOs and TPAs.

The U.S. Department of Health and Human Services (HHS) explained in the Privacy Rule's preamble:

> Neither employers nor other group health plan sponsors are defined as covered entities. However, employers and other plan sponsors

– particularly those sponsors with self-insured group health plans – may perform certain functions that are integrally related to or similar to the functions of group health plans and, in carrying out these functions, often require access to individual health information held by the group health plan.[1]

11.2.1 The Privacy Rule Covers ERISA Group Health Plans

Many group health plans are regulated under the Employee Retirement Income Security Act of 1974 (ERISA). However, there has been much confusion over whether ERISA plans are covered by the Privacy Rule.

The short answer is: Yes, ERISA plans are covered under the Privacy Rule because they are health plans. Specifically, funded and self-funded plans with 50 or more participants and plans of any size if administered by an entity other than the employer are group health plans covered by Privacy Rule.

Under ERISA, a group health plan must be a separate legal entity from its plan sponsor. ERISA-covered group health plans usually do not have a physical presence as they may not have their own employees and sometimes do not have their own assets (i.e., they may be fully insured or the benefits may be funded through the general assets of the plan sponsor, rather than through a trust).

Often, the only evidence of the existence of a group health plan is the contract and related plan documents that describe the rights and responsibilities of covered participants, including the benefits that are offered and the eligible recipients.

From a practical perspective, however, someone or some office in the company interacts with the health insurer, HMO or TPA. In most situations, this means that someone in the employer's organization will have access to protected health information in the context of negotiating with insurance companies and HMOs, or providing or paying for employee medical care.

11.2.2 Restrictions on Group Health Plan Sponsors Receiving Protected Health Information

A primary purpose of the Privacy Rule is to protect the privacy and confidentiality of information to ensure that patients are not discriminated against because of their health status.

Under the regulation, a basic reason why group health plans are defined as covered entities is to ensure that employers may not use protected health information in making employment-related functions except as authorized by law.

At the heart of the Privacy Rule's approach to group health plans are the plan documents, which explain the legal obligations of the plan and provide notice to the plan members – employees and their dependents – of the access and uses the employer will make of the protected health information.

A group health plan can authorize an insurance company, HMO or TPA to disclose protected health information to the plan sponsor for administrative functions only. Administrative functions are payment and health care operations. Disclosure to a plan sponsor for administrative functions can occur only if:

1. The group health plan documents are amended to describe the permitted uses and disclosures of protected health information;
2. Specify that disclosure is permitted only upon receipt of a certification from the plan sponsor that the plan documents have been amended and the plan sponsor has agreed to certain conditions regarding the use and disclosure of protected health information; and
3. Provide adequate firewalls to: identify the employees or classes of employees who will have access to protected health information; restrict access solely to the employees identified and only for the functions performed on behalf of the group health plan; and provide a mechanism for resolving issues of noncompliance.

In its explanation of this third point, HHS acknowledged that organizations frequently reorganize and change personnel. As a result, it suggested that companies do not need a high degree of specificity in identifying the employees or class of employees who will have access to this information.

11.2.3 Certification to Insurers, HMOs, and TPAs

The second restriction listed above is a certification that a plan sponsor must prepare and send to an insurance company, HMO or TPA before it may receive protected health information.

That certification is "a simple statement," according to HHS, that must include statements from the sponsor that the plan documents establishing the health plan include the following provisions:

- Not use or further disclose the information other than as permitted or required by the plan documents or as required by law;
- Ensure that any agents, including subcontractors, to whom they provide protected health information received from the group health plan, agree to the same restrictions and conditions that apply to the plan with respect to this information;
- Not use or disclose the information for employment-related actions and decisions or in connection with any other benefit or employee benefit plan;
- Report to the group health plan any use or disclosure of the information that is inconsistent with the uses or disclosures provided for of which it becomes aware;
- Allow employees to access and request changes to their protected health data;
- Make available the information required to provide an accounting of disclosures of the protected health information
- Make internal practices, books, and records relating to the use and disclosure of protected health data received available to HHS for compliance purposes for the group health plan; and
- If feasible, return or destroy all protected health information received from the group health plan that you still maintain in any form.

This certification provides a sufficient basis under the Privacy Rule for the health insurance issuer, HMO or other TPA to disclose protected health information to the plan sponsor under the Privacy Rule.

11.2.4 Ways to Avoid Plan Sponsor Restrictions

An insurer, HMO or other TPA may disclose *summary health information* to a group health plan and its sponsor without invoking the restrictions described above (amending the plan, certification and firewalls). Summary information, as opposed to protected health information, merely summarizes claims history, claims expenses, or types of claims experienced by individuals for whom the plan sponsor has provided health benefits under a group health plan.

Summary information is not the same as de-identified data. Summary information contains certain identifiers, but HHS makes a special exception for group health plans/sponsors and allows them to receive summary information without having to comply with above described restrictions or: de-identifying the data first.

11.2.5 TPAs and Business Associate Contracts

Because employers are in businesses for reasons other than providing health benefits to their employers, many health plans are designed to have relatively few employees. As a result, plans are likely to outsource these activities to insurance companies, HMOs, and TPAs

The issues center on when does the group health plan need to enter into a business associate contract with these entities. As described in Section 6.0 on business associate contracts, these agreements are required under certain circumstances when a person provides a service to or on behalf of a covered entity.

For example, when a group health plan purchases insurance, no business associate relationship is created because the insurance company is acting on behalf of the employees, not the group health plan. On the other hand, if a group health plan contracts with an insurer or TPA for services that are "in addition to or not directly related to the provision of insurance,"[2] then a business associate relationship arises and the group health plan must enter into a business associate contract with the insurer, HMO or TPA. The reason is that the insurer, HMO or TPA is providing, in this later case, a service to or on behalf of the group health plan.

11.2.6 Providing Notice of Information Practices

As a covered entity, a group health plan must provide its employees with notice of its information practices. This requirement is triggered whenever protected health information or summary information is furnished by an insurance company, HMO, or TPA to a group health plan and its sponsor. The only exception is when a group health plan does not receive any protected or summary health information, e.g., it simply purchases insurance/HMO coverage and does not get protected or summary health information even for negotiation purposes.

11.2.7 Changes to Health Plans

When plan sponsors change their policies on the use and disclosure of protected health information, they must make those changes in their plans and give notice to the plan members.

11.3 Beyond the Health Plan

Beyond their role as sponsors of health plans, health care executives should remember that they also have other employer responsibilities that may require the use and disclosure of protected health information. As a result providers, plans and insurers should take a broader view of compliance beyond the specific operational areas addressed by the Privacy Rule.

11.3.1 HIPAA and Other Federal Laws

A host of other federal laws come into play and interact with the Privacy Rule. HHS attempts to address the issue in its discussion on how health care providers, health plans and clearinghouses generally should approach other federal and state requirements. The Privacy Rule contains examples of where it already anticipates the Privacy Rule will interact with other laws and regulations. These include:

- Americans With Disabilities Act
- Clinical Laboratory Improvement Act
- Department of Transportation regulations
- Employee Retirement Income Security Act
- Environmental Protection Act and its accompanying regulations
- Family and Medical Leave Act
- Federal Aviation Administration

- Federal Educational Rights & Privacy Act
- Federal Highway Administration rules
- Food, Drug & Cosmetic Act
- Freedom of Information Act
- Gramm-Leach-Bliley Act
- National Labor Relations Act
- Privacy Act
- Public Health Service Act
- Rehabilitation Act
- Social Security Act (including its Medicare and Medicaid provisions)
- Workers Compensation laws

This list is certainly not exhaustive and does not include the large number of state and local laws that also may come into play. (See Section 16.0 on Pre-emption.)

11.3.2 A Balancing Act: Permissible versus Mandated Disclosures

HHS recognized that a rule dealing with such a fundamental commodity as protected health information would be complicated. In the preamble to the Privacy Rule, the department advised providers, plans and clearinghouses that when faced with the question of whether other laws require disclosure, they should determine whether the disclosure is required or merely permitted.

In those cases in which another law requires disclosure, the Privacy Rule permits the covered entity to share the information with the relevant organization without patient authorization.

However, if another federal law prohibits a covered entity from using or disclosing information that also is protected health information, but the Privacy Rule permits the use or disclosure, a covered entity must comply with the other stricter federal law. They should not use or disclose the information.

If another federal law merely permits the disclosure, the covered entity must refer to the Privacy Rule's list of permissible disclosures. If it is listed there, patient authorization is not required. If not, patient authorization is required.

Generally, permissible disclosures that do not require patient authorization include the following areas:

- Public health activities;
- Domestic violence, neglect or abuse;

- Judicial and administrative proceedings;
- Law enforcement;
- Organ transplantation;
- Serious threats to health or safety; and
- Workers compensation.

For a more in-depth discussion of permissible disclosures, refer to Section 5.0 on Consent and Authorizations.

11.4 Americans with Disabilities Act

HHS said that employers are not directly covered by the Privacy Rule, but they are subject to the federal disability nondiscrimination laws and, therefore, must protect the confidentiality of all medical information concerning their applicants and employees. The law specifically cites the Rehabilitation Act of 1973 and the Americans with Disabilities Act (ADA).

To illustrate the interaction generally, the rest of this discussion focuses on the ADA.

The ADA covers employers of 15 or more employees, employment agencies, labor organizations, and joint labor-management committees. The focus of this law is to prevent discrimination against individuals with qualifying disabilities.

It is also important to remember that the federal courts have ruled that the ADA applies to both the able bodied and the disabled. In a 10th Circuit Court of Appeals case in 1998, the judges ruled 2-1 that non-disabled people may sue employers under the ADA when employers ask questions regarding their medical history or condition on employment applications.[3]

In that case, the worker did not get a job because he answered a question regarding whether he had ever received workers compensation benefits.

Employers subject to ADA nondiscrimination standards have confidentiality obligations regarding applicant and employee medical information. For example, employers must treat medical information, including medical information from voluntary health or wellness programs and any medical information that is voluntarily disclosed as a confidential medical record, subject to some exceptions.

In the context of the Privacy Rule, HHS explained in its preamble that the transmission of health information by an employer to a covered entity, such as a group health plan, is governed by the ADA confidentiality restrictions.

The transmission of job applicant or employee health information by the employer's management to the group health plan may be permitted under the ADA standards as the use of medical information for insurance purposes. Similarly, disclosure of this medical information by the group health plan, under the limited circumstances permitted by the Privacy Rule, may involve use of the information for insurance purposes.

HHS concluded in the Privacy Rule preamble that the ADA regulation is not intended to disrupt the regulatory structure for self-insured employers or current industry practices in sales, underwriting, pricing, administrative and other services, claims and similar insurance-related activities based on classification of risks as regulated by the states.[4]

If an employer-sponsored group health plan is closely linked to an employer, HHS explained, the group health plan might be subject to ADA confidentiality restrictions, as well as the Privacy Rule.

Nothing in the Privacy Rule will prevent an employer from conditioning a final offer of employment based on a fitness or health report from the prospective employee. The ADA, however, does preclude employers from seeking medical information prior to a job offer.

Similarly, the Privacy Rule does not preclude employers from requesting protected health information when they receive requests for reasonable accommodations from an employee invoking the ADA. Under the ADA, an employee, who can demonstrate a qualifying disability, can require the employer to provide reasonable job accommodations for that position.

If an employer receives a request for a reasonable accommodation, the employer – under the Privacy Rule – still will be able to require reasonable documentation about the employee's disability and the functional limitations that require the reasonable accommodation, if the disability and the limitations are not obvious.

With all that said, the Privacy Rule and ADA regulations do not always reign supreme either individually or together in managing protected health information. As discussed in Section 12.0, the requirement of other federal laws may take precedence.

11.5 Key Points

- Employers are not directly covered by the Privacy Rule, but are likely to come under its regulatory umbrella if they sponsor health plans.
- Changes in the use and disclosure of protected health information must be reflected in the plan documents.
- Employers may share protected health information under the authority of other laws without patient authorization if those laws statutorily mandate disclosure.
- The Privacy Rule does not prevent employers from conditioning employment on providing health information if a job offer has been made and the medical information is necessary to confirm the applicants ability to do the job.
- The Privacy Rule does not prevent employers from requiring protected information to substantiate and address the need for a reasonable accommodation under the Americans with Disabilities Act when the disability is non-obvious.

Endnotes

[1] 65 Fed. Reg. at 82,507.

[2] *id.* at 82,509.

[3] *Griffin v. Steeltek, Inc.* , 160 F.32 591 (10th Cir. 1998).

[4] 65 Fed. Reg. at 82,486.

Section 12.0 - Labor Relations

Dennis Melamed

12.1 Introduction

The main focus of the Privacy Rule is on the protection of patient privacy. However, it also addresses some issues in the context of privacy for workers. Public concern over employer access to protected health information was a significant motivation for the U.S. Department of Health and Human Services (HHS) in developing the Privacy Rule. The department tried to directly confront the fear that there was "…no comprehensive protection prohibiting the employer from using that information to make decisions about promotions or job retention."

Furthermore, as discussed in Section 11.0, employers, while not directly covered by the Privacy Rule, will be affected by it to the extent they offer health plans and manage their employees.

In addition, the Privacy Rule covers some aspects of workers compensation and provides organized labor with a new tool to limit the disclosure and use of protected health information by employers.

12.2 Workers' Compensation

Workers compensation programs are statutorily exempt from the Privacy Rule.[1] Under the Privacy Rule, a covered entity may disclose protected health information about an individual to a party responsible for payment of workers' compensation benefits to the individual, and to an agency responsible for administering and /or adjudicating the individual's claim for workers' compensation benefits.[2]

Workers' compensation benefits include benefits under programs such as the Black Lung Benefits Act, the federal Employees' Compensation Act, the Longshore and Harbor Workers' Compensation Act, and the Energy Employees' Occupational Illness Compensation Program Act.

Although covered entities are allowed to disclose protected health information for workers compensation purposes, the Privacy Rule does impose the Minimum Necessary requirement on these disclosures.

The workers compensation program has generated some labor controversy over the nature of the authorizations some insurers have required. As a result, employers and covered entities in their employer capacities, should be aware of this contention in developing their strategic plans for HIPAA and the overall management of protected health information and the minimum necessary requirement in the Privacy Rule.

In the spring of 1998, the Montana AFL-CIO successfully challenged one workers compensation insurer and the state-run program over authorizations the union said were too broad.[3] Labor argued that requiring employees to sign these broad authorizations violated the Americans with Disabilities Act, the Family Medical Leave Act and general state privacy protections.

Then in late 1998, the AFL-CIO started waging a quiet legislative campaign to insert more stringent limits on disclosure authorizations in every state's workers compensation program. In starting that campaign, it also developed a model privacy law that included the concepts of sharing only the minimum necessary information to process a claim and giving workers access to their health records.

When the unions released the model, it cited the Montana case and several employers who sought "virtually unlimited information about an individual's medical history."[4] The lobbying effort met with little success in state legislatures around the country in 1999. But the AFL-CIO continued its campaign.

For employers with unionized work forces, deciding if and when to share protected health information can be even more confusing. The prohibition against using protected health information in employment-related decisions is straightforward in and of itself. However, it does not exist in a vacuum.

HHS's intention and rulings by administrative and judicial bodies also indicate that employers will not always be allowed to use Privacy Rule to prevent the sharing of protected health information with their unions.

At the same time that labor unions are starting to insert medical privacy provisions into their contracts, they also desire access to protected health information as well. Consequently, employers should examine the specific laws and issues under discussion in preparing their policies and procedures over the handling of this information.

12.3 Right to Restrict Uses

As discussed in Section 5.0 on Consent & Authorization, the Privacy Rule provides patients with the right to seek restrictions on the use of protected health information. However, individuals are not the only ones who can request such restrictions.

Unions can be expected to exercise this new right as the AFL-CIO has placed a high priority on medical privacy above and beyond the issues involved in workers compensation programs.

In November 1999, the issue of medical privacy went beyond the rhetoric and into contractor negotiations as the United Auto Workers inserted specific medical privacy provisions in their labor contracts with General Motors, DaimlerChrysler and Ford.[5] Those contract provisions required the employers to use the information gathered on their employees only for the stated purposes under which the data was obtained.

Neither the unions nor the companies said that this reflected new policy. However, the unions expressed concern over the "prevalence of electronic processing and computer access to medical records," and they wanted explicit assurances for the protection of their members' medical privacy.

Although the Privacy Rule does not directly address many of these labor-related issues, covered entities and employers should recognize their connection to the Privacy Rule when developing their strategies for managing protected health information.

12.4 National Labor Relations Act

HHS addresses the National Labor Relations Act specifically in its discussion of the Privacy Rule. The Act created a framework under which workers are allowed to organize into collective bargaining units and band together to seek redress of grievances against employers.

HHS stated that the Privacy Rule does not prohibit disclosures of protected health information to collective bargaining representatives under that law.

To the extent a covered entity is required by law to disclose the information to collective bargaining representatives, it can do so without an authorization from the employee. The definition of health care operations also allows disclosures to employee representatives for grievance resolution purposes.

The National Labor Relations Board (NLRB), created by the National Labor Relations Act, is likely to be first administrative body to consider these issues under the Privacy Rule. In fact, it addressed the issue of medical privacy and union access to protected health information in a case decided in August 2000, four months before the final HHS regulation was published.[6]

Adding some complexity to the issue, this case also involved the Americans with Disabilities Act (ADA). A union sought information about one of its members after the member was given a job to accommodate his non-obvious disability under the ADA. The union was concerned that the accommodation was used by the company to circumvent its negotiated labor contract.

The union member refused to authorize the sharing of his medical records with the union, and company management did not share the records with the union out of deference to the ADA and medical privacy.

The NLRB noted that the employee's disability was not an obvious one, and the union had a right to see the employee's file. The board relied on an Equal Employment Opportunity Commission decision, when it concluded that when the need for an accommodation is not obvious, the employer and union may share reasonable documentation explaining the need for the accommodation.

The Privacy Rule will have the same effect as the NLRB decision in allowing unions reasonable access to employee records without patient authorization under similar circumstances.

12.5 Key Points

- Workers compensation programs are exempted from the Privacy Rule, but HHS expects covered entities to share only the minimum amount of protected health information necessary to fulfill its obligations.
- The Privacy Rule is not the pre-eminent regulation in labor relations and frequently will not serve as a legitimate reason for not sharing protected health information with unions.

Endnotes

[1] Health Insurance Portability and Accountability Act of 1996, § 706, 29 U.S.C. § 1186 (2001). Although the state program is exempted from the Privacy Rule, it is important to remember that one of the mandate transaction standards under the Administrative Simplification provisions is the First Report of Injury, a workers compensation report, which arguably contains protected health information. It is far from clear whether the program will remain exempt once the electronic standard is developed and finalized.

[2] 65 Fed. Reg. at 82,818 (to be codified at 45 C.F.R. pt. 164.512(l)).

[3] Montana Unions Irate Over Insurer Release Authorization. *Health Info. Privacy Alert*, Apr. 1998 at 4.

[4] AFL-CIO to Start State Campaign on Privacy in Workers Comp. *Health Info. Privacy Alert*, Dec. 1998 at 1.

[5] Auto Workers Emphasize Medical Privacy in New Contracts. *Health Info. Privacy Alert*, Nov. 1999 at 1.

[6] *Roseburg Forest Products Co. and Western Council of Industrial Workers*, 331 N.L.R.B. 124 (2000).

Section 13.0 - The Internet

Dennis Melamed

13.1 When Online Companies are Covered Entities

Although the electronic revolution and the use of the Internet were two of the primary motivations behind the Privacy Rule, HHS does not generally single out Web-based health care organizations for special coverage.[1] However, it does address some issues specific to the conduct of health care services on line.

HHS explained that online companies are covered entities under the Privacy Rule if they otherwise meet the definition of health care provider or health plan and satisfy the other requirements of the rule, i.e., providers must also transmit health information in electronic form in connection with a HIPAA transaction.

To ensure that there was no confusion on this point, HHS restated this position, first enunciated in the preamble to the proposed rule: "An individual or organization that bills and/or is paid for health care services or supplies in the normal course of business, such as...an 'online' pharmacy accessible on the Internet, is also a health care provider for purposes of this statute ."[2]

13.2 Providing Notice

This treatment is explicitly borne out by HHS's clarification that covered health care providers who provide services to individuals over the Internet have direct treatment relationships with those individuals. That means covered Internet-based providers must distribute a notice of privacy practices after the compliance date by automatically and contemporaneously providing the notice electronically in response to the individual's first request for service, if the individual agrees to receive the notice electronically.[3]

For example, the first time an individual requests to fill a prescription through a covered Internet pharmacy, the pharmacy must automatically and contemporaneously provide the individual with the pharmacy's notice of privacy practices. An individual that receives a covered entity's notice electronically retains the right to request a paper copy of the notice as described above. This right must be described in the notice.[4]

13.3 Internet Service Providers

Merely operating on the Internet or other electronic environment does not automatically trigger the Privacy Rule, even if the organization handles covered transactions. There was some concern that the transmission of the HIPAA transaction standards would designate telecommunications companies, such as Internet Service Providers (ISPs), as covered health care clearinghouses. However, HHS said that the definition of a health care clearinghouse excludes those organizations that merely provide connectivity or mechanisms to convey information.[5]

For a further discussion of ISPs and business associates, see Section 6.0.

13.4 Key Points

- The fact that a covered entity engages in covered activities on the Internet does not exempt those activities from the Privacy Rule.
- Internet service providers are not covered by the Privacy Rule unless they engage in covered activities, such as treatment, payment or health care operations and engage in the HIPAA electronic transactions.

Quality Also Means Confidentiality: URAC's Health Web Site Accreditation Program

Central to the mission of the Privacy Rule is the strengthening of public trust in the health care system. As discussed throughout this book, the new definition of health care efficiency includes the preservation of privacy, confidentiality, and data security. However, the increasing importance of the Internet as an avenue for sharing health care information with consumer also raises other issues about the management and quality of that information.

In response, URAC created the Health Web Site Accreditation Program to provide health care consumers with a tool to help identify Web sites that adhere to industry quality standards. The URAC accreditation program is designed to dovetail with and enhance the consumer privacy protections of HIPAA.[1]

The URAC accreditation program is targeted at consumer-oriented, Web-based activities of the health care industry. Because of the rapid evolution of Web technology and its impact on Web operations, the term of an organization's Health Web Site Accreditation will last only one year, an accreditation period shorter than URAC's usual two years for other health care organizations.

In the area of privacy and confidentiality, the URAC program contains standards specifically related to privacy that expand on the Privacy Rule. The URAC Web standards require that the Web site:

- Informs users of how and for what purposes personally-identifiable information (including personal health information) is collected.
- Allows users to opt-out of the collection and use of personally-identifiable information and describes the consequences both of providing and not providing such information.
- Permits users to opt-in for the collection and use of personal health information and describes the consequences both of providing and not providing such information.
- Obtains opt-in from users prior to the collection and use of personal health information.
- Limits the use of personal health information for any purpose outside the scope of the original opt-in without first obtaining additional opt-in (unless required by law).
- Provides information to users about how to access, supplement, and amend user-provided personal health information.
- Obtains specific, voluntary opt-in from the user prior to disclosure of patient health information unless required for: health care operations; treatment; payment; internal quality management activities; or legal requirements (public health reporting, fraud and abuse investigations, court orders and warrants).
- Allows users to opt out of the continued collection and use of their personal health information.
- Develop and implement policies and procedures for the management of personal health information of users who have opted out of providing additional information, or who no longer have access to their personal health information on the Web site.
- Develop and implement policies and procedures for the deletion of personal health information for which the user has opted-out:
- Furthermore, if the Web site uses passive tracking mechanisms, such as "cookies" or "web bugs," the Web site:
- Discloses the use of passive tracking mechanisms to users and the purpose(s) for which the passive tracking mechanisms will be used;
- Provides users an opportunity to opt-out of the use of passive tracking mechanisms; and
- Informs users of the consequences of opting out of the use of passive tracking mechanisms (for example, restricted access to the Web site).

URAC's privacy standards also call for the data owner (the entity that either directly or indirectly owns or operates a Web site) to require a business partner agreement from any third parties who have access to personal health information on or obtained through the Web site, holding the partner to the same (or higher) privacy standards as the owner.

While privacy is a necessary component of public trust in health web sites, it is not the only factor. URAC's Health Web Site Accreditation standards also require an organization to demonstrate the development and maintenance of policies and procedures that govern all aspects of its Web-based health activities, including:

- Quality oversight
- Disclosure
- Health content and service delivery
- Linking
- Security
- Accountability

URAC's Health Web Site Accreditation program was launched July 30, 2001. For additional information about the program, see www.urac.org.

- Guy D'Andrea and Lani Caprio

---

[1] Although accreditation from URAC or any other accrediting body is not automatically deemed as compliance with the Privacy Rule or other regulatory requirements, HHS has expressed its desire to coordinate with the accrediting bodies to assist with compliance. HHS said in its explanation of the rule: "HIPAA does not give the Secretary the authority to delegate her responsibilities to other private or public agencies . . . However, we plan to explore ways that we may benefit from current activities that also serve to protect the privacy of individually identifiable health information . . . In developing its enforcement program, we may explore ways it can coordinate with other regulatory or oversight bodies so that we can efficiently and effectively pursue our joint interests in protecting privacy." 65 Fed. Reg. at 82,604-605.

Endnotes

[1] HHS stated in the preamble to the Privacy Rule:

> In the potential near future, when technology makes it almost free to send lifetime medical records over the Internet, the risks may grow rapidly. It may become cost-effective, for instance, for companies to offer services that allow purchasers to obtain details of a person's physical and mental treatments. In addition to legitimate possible uses for such services, malicious or inquisitive persons may download medical records for purposes ranging from identity theft to embarrassment to prurient interest in the life of a celebrity or neighbor.

65 Fed. Reg. at 82,465.

[2] *id.* at 59,930 *cited in* 65 Fed. Reg. at 82,574.

[3] *id.* at 82,725.

[4] *id.* at 82,551.

[5] *id.* at 82,477.

What Your Organization Should Know about the Federal Privacy Standards

Part III

Compliance

Section 14 - Gaining Control: Compliance Programs

Victor Blanchard

14.1 The Purpose of a HIPAA Privacy Compliance Program

The Privacy Rule, in many respects, represents best practices for data management. Consequently, covered entities will be forced to reexamine most – if not all – of their operations. This is likely to be an intricate effort consisting of numerous tasks.

This section discusses the key elements for developing and implementing a Privacy Rule Compliance Program.

14.1.1 Compliance Program

For many organizations, a formally documented HIPAA Privacy Compliance Program will be the key effort to address the public's need for greater privacy and meet the mandates of the Privacy Rule. However, documenting an organization's privacy program should not be viewed as the end, but more as the means to ensure appropriate privacy controls are put in place.

Briefly, a covered entity's compliance plan should be viewed as senior management's position regarding how each patient's, member's and customer's health information will be protected, and only disclosed to those with legitimate reasons to view it.

The following points outline the purposes behind a privacy compliance strategy. The Compliance Program should:

- Limit the release of protected health information without consent or authorization to only those purposes that do not require patient assent;
- Inform consumers about how their health information is being used;
- Give an individual access to his or her own health records and the right to request amendments or make corrections;
- Restrict the amount of information used and disclosed to the "minimum necessary;"
- Require that information be disclosed only for research that is conducted in a responsible manner; and
- Create new penalties for improper use or disclosure of information.

14.2 Planning an Effective Program

For a Compliance Program to be effective, covered entities should consider the following as part of planning, development, and implementation:

- Direct the program to meet the customer's expectations;
- Minimize capital expenditures and related costs;
- Keep doing what you do well;
- Integrate privacy into your strategic plan; and
- Document and communicate your compliance effort.

A. Know Your Customer: Direct the Program to Meet the Customer's Expectations

The Compliance Program should be directed at the audience that drove the need for the regulations: the patient.

Knowing what the customer (patient) expects can be identified in many ways. These include reviewing the original comments to the draft Privacy Rule, studying the comments in the preamble of the final Privacy Rule, monitoring privacy forums in person or via the Internet, or by communicating directly with your customer community regarding privacy views, concerns, and needs. This knowledge can further ensure that the solutions implemented by the covered entity meet requirements, but are tempered with the understanding of expectations of the customers.

B. Be Reasonable - Minimize Capital Expenditures and Related Costs: The Privacy Compliance Program should be based on a clear understanding of the implementation standards, the related implementation requirements, and how they apply to a particular covered entity's business.

The Privacy Rule uses the word "reasonable" more than 250 times, and in various sections uses language such as "The policies and procedures must be reasonably designed, taking into account the size of and the type of activities that relate to protected health information undertaken by the covered entity...."[1]

Recognize that more than one solution exists for every problem and that the regulation speaks to implementation requirements. Each covered entity must determine the best solution based on its activities dealing with protected health information, as well as the operational and strategic initiatives affecting the covered entity's business.

C. Keep Doing What You Do Well: Every organization can claim to perform certain processes or functions in a manner that might be considered best practice or world class. The Privacy Compliance Program should not undermine that value, but should embrace and leverage it into the new processes.

In the Privacy Rule, HHS expresses its intention to improve the effectiveness and efficiency of health-related services. In other words, keep what you already do well, and use that knowledge to design other processes and functions that concurrently meet compliance requirements.

In a provider setting, the growth of the electronic medical record (EMR) has forced both the medical records and information systems personnel to think more about who has access to patient information. For those providers that have recently implemented an EMR system, the opportunity was presented then to design and implement a privacy and security model to control access to confidential data. That model can be reapplied to other information system environments involving patient data.

For a health plan, new processes and systems are being developed constantly to receive, adjudicate, and pay claims more efficiently and effectively. The investments made in these processes should be pre-served, with additional considerations being worked into the solution to meet HIPAA privacy requirements. An example may be paying claims via the Internet. While a wide variety of privacy and security issues come to mind, this capability does coincide with the objectives of the regulations.

D. Integrate Privacy into the Organization's Strategic Plan: The Compliance Program should not be developed or allowed to exist in a vacuum. Instead, covered entities should look for ways to integrate privacy protection into their longer range planning.

Many health care organizations engage in or plan to implement e-health initiatives to exploit the benefits of various new technologies. But whether it is e-health, critical pathways, or new compliance requirements, these strategic initiatives must be considered in the development of the Compliance Program.

For example, new technological advances may simplify or ease the development of technical implementation requirements, while the redesign of the admissions process could be enhanced in conjunction with the implementation of new consent requirements.

Developing the Compliance Program in conjunction with existing strategic projects or initiatives could provide the leverage needed to get a certain project moving. Some organizations have chosen not to view HIPAA as a compliance exercise at all, and intend to implement the requirements almost entirely through efforts already underway. Using HIPAA as the means of getting a strategic initiative moving more quickly and effectively may be the most cost-effective and easily accepted method for some organizations.

E. Document and Communicate Your Compliance Effort: The Compliance Program must be documented and should be easily accessible to those who will be expected to operate under these policies and procedures. The Compliance Program can be documented in either written or electronic form, and should be retained for a minimum of six years. However, beyond these guidelines, a variety of options exist.

One effective way of documenting the Compliance Program is by making the information available over the organization's Intranet. This approach can make the information more easily available to all individuals subject to the provisions.

This approach can make education and understanding of the policies easier by also incorporating functionality for individuals to submit questions regarding the effect of a given policy or procedure. It makes access to policies and procedures ubiquitous, thus further reducing an individual's claim of not knowing a certain activity was considered unacceptable and subject to sanctions. Finally, the dissemination of new policies and procedures can be centralized enabling more effective means of communicating management's new view of certain activities.

A thoroughly documented and effectively communicated compliance plan can serve as an effective form of due diligence as well. If management develops the policies and procedures, makes them available on the company's Intranet, and effectively communicates this program to the affected individuals, then when an infraction does occur, management can point to the process that was followed to address the situation proactively.

14.3 The Process for Developing a Compliance Program

The specific process by which each organization chooses to develop its own Compliance Program will vary. Many organizations decided early in this process that they did not want to be on the "bleeding" edge regarding privacy, forging new territory potentially to be replicated or refuted by later entrants.

Yet others recognize the potential value of Privacy Rule for demonstrating to customers and to the public how important the protection of personal information is to the organization. As a result, the effort becomes a marketing opportunity. Regardless of the view taken, the major tasks or steps in process of developing a Compliance Program remain the same.

A. Designate a Privacy Official: At the outset, the HIPAA Coordinator or Steering Committee Leader may initially fill the position of a privacy official. Regardless of the title, having an individual with the appropriate background, skills, and authority to start an effective Compliance Program is key. The Privacy Rule indicates that this responsibility is anticipated to be an additional responsibility for an existing employee.[2] However, the size and complexity of the organization will be a better barometer for determining how to fulfill this function.

This perception will clearly depend upon the size and complexity of the covered entity and the extent to which privacy and security compliance policies, procedures, and practices are already in place and being monitored.

B. Evaluate Existing Processes, Procedures, and Data Flows: To determine the most effective path to take, a clear understanding of where the covered entity currently sits is crucial. Factors include:

- The need to understand how information enters the covered entity's environment;
- How that information is used and maintained while under the covered entity's control; and
- Where that information is disseminated.

Assessing management's current position with regard to privacy- and security-related policies and procedures is a second area that is critical to understand, if for no other reason than for the documentation requirements under the Privacy Rule.

The final area to address is the understanding of real-world practices – the day-to-day processes involving confidential information regardless of the documented policies and procedures.

Not having this level of understanding of the basics affecting the privacy of protected health information dooms the covered entity's attempt to develop an effective Compliance Program. Take the time to understand the current environment, processes, and practices before venturing down a new path.

C. Assess What You Need with What You Have: Once a clear understanding exists regarding the way information is handled and the policies and procedures are understood affecting those processes, management will want to determine how those policies, procedures, and practices compare to the Privacy Rule and implementation requirements.

This will require capturing the results of the comparison of current processes to the regulation at a level sufficient to facilitate a plan to reach compliance by the April 2003 deadline. Generally, this will involve either time studying the regulations and developing a custom assessment approach or using the services of a third party. Both approaches have a cost attached to them, and each covered entity must

A New Gatekeeper? The HIPAA Privacy Official

The Privacy Rule requires covered entities to designate a Privacy Official, who is responsible for developing and implementing the policies and procedures of the regulation. [1]

However, the regulation does not necessarily require all affiliated entities to name their own Privacy Officials. HHS explained in its preamble that the number of Privacy Officials for a covered entity's subsidiaries will be determined by how the covered entity designates those components.[2] In other words, that decision to name Privacy Officials for each subsidiary or affiliated organization relies on the documented designation of those organizations by the covered entity.

For example, if several subsidiaries are designated as a single covered entity, then they need only name a single Privacy Official. Likewise, if several covered entities share a notice for services provided on the same premises, only one Privacy Official is required.

To the extent that group health plans do not provide health benefits through an insurance contract, they too are required to designate a Privacy, HHS explained in the preamble.

The Privacy Rule does not preclude the Privacy Officer from having other duties. HHS tries to accommodate small covered entities, such as small group practices, by crafting the concept of scalability. In fact, HHS states in its regulatory impact analysis of the rule that it "assumes the privacy official role will be an additional responsibility given to an existing employee in the covered entity, such as an office manager in a small entity or compliance official in a larger institution."[3]

Job Description

The duties of the Privacy Official are broadly defined, leaving substantial flexibility for organizations to tailor the position to their specific circumstances. The American Health Information Management Association (AHIMA) issued a model senior management job description that may assist the covered entity in creating their own position. It also recommends the creation of a privacy oversight committee, consisting of relevant senior management. An URL to the AHIMA model is located in the Internet Resources Appendix at the end of this book.

Under the AHIMA model, the Privacy Official's responsibilities would include:

- Providing guidance and assisting in the identification, implementation, and maintenance of privacy policies and procedures.
- Performing periodic privacy risk assessments and related ongoing compliance monitoring in coordination with the entity's other compliance and operational assessment functions.
- Working with legal counsel and management, key departments, and committees to ensure the organization maintains appropriate privacy and confidentiality consent, authorization forms, and information notices and materials.
- Overseeing and ensuring delivery of privacy training and orientation to all employees, volunteers, contractors, alliances, business associates, and other appropriate third parties.
- Participating in the development, implementation, and ongoing compliance monitoring of all trading partner and business associate agreements.
- Establishing, in conjunction with management and operations, a mechanism to track access to protected health information, within the purview of the organization and as required by law and to allow qualified individuals to review or receive a report on this activity.
- Establishing and administering a process for receiving, documenting, tracking, investigating, and taking action on all complaints concerning the organization's privacy policies and procedures in coordination and collaboration with other similar functions and, when necessary, legal counsel.
- Ensuring compliance with privacy practices and consistent application of sanctions for failure to comply with privacy policies for all individuals in the organization's workforce, extended workforce, and for all business associates, in cooperation with human resources, the information security official, administration, and legal counsel as necessary.

- Serving as a member of, or liaison to, the organization's IRB or Privacy Board should one exist.
- Reviewing all system-related information security plans throughout the organization's network to ensure alignment between security and privacy practices, and acts as a liaison to the information systems department.
- Working with all personnel involved with any aspect of release of protected health information, to ensure full coordination and cooperation under the organization's policies and procedures and legal requirements.
- Cooperating with the Office of Civil Rights, other legal entities, and organization officials in any compliance reviews or investigations.

- Dennis Melamed

[1] 65 Fed. Reg. at 82,876 (to be codified at 45 C.F.R. pt. 164.530(a)(1)).

[2] *id.* at 82,807 (to be codified at 45 C.F.R. pt. 164.504(b)).

[3] *id.* at 82.768.

determine the most effective and efficient method for its situation.

The need for an effective assessment approach does not change though. The covered entity must know precisely where gaps exist between current practices and the Privacy Rule and the options for attaining compliance.

D. Budgeting: Regardless of the size or complexity of the entity, effective budgeting will be critical. The health care industry has no more money to waste than any other industry.

One strategy is making HIPAA's privacy requirements a component of other pre-existing strategic initiatives that already have a budget for dollars and other resources. This also may alleviate concerns of certain covered entities that regard HIPAA solely as a compliance issue. This approach may communicate that some or all of the HIPAA requirements, including privacy, may be compulsory but serve an important strategic purpose as well.

Another example is not to have a HIPAA budget at all. Some organizations take the approach of developing a new business model (addressing operational, administrative, and technological components) to be rolled out to the covered entity's various departments or facilities. Thus, a budget would be developed to support the new business model, possibly never mentioning HIPAA.

And of course depending on the organization's corporate culture and resources, a stand-alone or supplementary budget earmarked as a HIPAA compliance budget may be the best way to mobilize the

organization to implement the appropriate privacy and security protocols.

No matter how the budget is couched, the components of that budget should be substantially the same. More than just an estimate of dollars, the budget or resource plan should focus on several other components as well.

To start, qualitative and quantitative benefits of a particular budget line item should be outlined. As the budget request comes together for presentation to management for approval, having information aimed at answering management's question of "why" will be key.

In addition, components of the budget may include additional full- or part-time employees broken down into person-days, cost factors for each labor category, cost estimates for new technological resources (e.g. hardware, software), estimates for consulting assistance, and confidence factors for each budget component depicting the level of assurance of each number's accuracy.

E. Proactively Train the Organization's Audience: Depending upon the nature of the covered entity's operations, the audience or audiences to be trained will vary. Regardless, the value of keeping all of the affected parties informed about the regulations improves the likelihood of positive "buy-in" to new processes and policies. These parties will certainly include employees, but should potentially also include outsourcing service providers, other key vendors that are affected, and external legal counsel.

The training need not be formal or time-consuming, but it should be informative and specific to the covered entity. Spending some additional time educating the right audience will have a positive effect on the Compliance Program from its inception well into the future compliance phase.

F. Obtain Senior Management's Commitment: Senior management must understand HIPAA and its potential impact on the covered entity's operational, administrative, and technological environment. Senior management should be kept informed from the beginning on what the privacy issues entail, what they mean to the business, and how they are going to change operations in the near future. When management understands the impact these regulations are going to have on current business practices, the approval of budgets and similar requests can be expected to move more smoothly.

G. Integrate Internal Audit and/or Regulatory Compliance: The Privacy Rule provides few details on the implementation requirements or their effects on a covered entity's internal audit or regulatory compliance areas. Clearly, these functions should be included in any education efforts and should be included as members of a HIPAA Steering Committee because of their knowledge about the operations and technologies already in place. One or both of these value-added functions also should be integrated into the current assessment process, as well as any ongoing monitoring activities.

The organization's privacy officials also should give strong consideration to the need to perform compliance-type audits of some third parties to the covered entity. In other words, if a third party provides a service to the covered entity that is considered critical, and the loss of that support would have a significant operational impact on the covered entity, then that third party should be included in the internal audit plan. This addresses the business need to ensure that key third parties are meeting the HIPAA requirements.

In addition, the compliance plan will have an impact on the internal audit or regulatory compliance staffing, as well as the need to ensure that a "right to audit" clause is included in service contracts and business associate agreements, enabling the covered entity to perform audit activities of the third party's environment with proper notice.

H. Communicate Your Efforts: The privacy official should take the lead in working with senior management and the marketing staff on how most effectively to communicate the entity's efforts. This can take a variety of forms, but will likely include the following groups: senior management, employees, customers, consultants, vendors, business associates, and possibly the media.

14.4 Elements of the Privacy Compliance Program

The following section provides some of the more commonly recognized components of an organization's Privacy Compliance Program.

A. Designation of a Privacy Official and the Related Duties: Every covered entity must designate a privacy official who will be responsible for the development and implementation of the privacy policies and procedures that will guide and govern that organization's approach to compliance. Depending on the size and complexity of the organization, the duties of the privacy official may require a new employee be added to the work force or the responsibilities be absorbed by an existing employee.

Regardless of whether this is a new duty or a new full-time equivalent, the designated privacy official and his or her job responsibilities are expected to be a full time commitment for most organizations to ensure the proper development, implementation, and maintenance of the Privacy Compliance Program. In addition to the development of the privacy policies and procedures, this function will likely be responsible for other duties including relevant training, coordination between different departments or entities, the evaluation of current procedures, and assuring compliance.

For a further discussion of the Privacy Officer position, go to page 96.

B. Dissemination of Privacy Notice: The "notice of privacy practices"[3] provides an individual the right to an adequate notice of the uses and disclosures of protected health information that may occur as part of a covered entity's operations. It also must address the individual's rights and the covered entity's legal responsibilities with respect to protected health information.

For health service providers, the notice of privacy practices must be provided to patients with direct treatment relationships no later than the first visit following the compliance date. For practical purposes, hospitals and similar providers are expected to provide a copy of the privacy notice as part of the admission process regardless of the number of times a patient makes a visit.

Because the regulations do not explicitly require that the notice be mailed to each individual, health plans should be able to cover this requirement by including the privacy notice in an existing communication process. For practical purposes, the notice could be mailed to members as part of a planned mailing, such as by adding it to an existing booklet being distributed anyway.

C. Identification of Safeguards to Protect Privacy: Both the final Privacy Rule and draft Security Rule speak to the need to identify and implement reasonable safeguards. In the Privacy Rule, the purpose of the safeguards is to ensure the integrity and confidentiality of every individual's protected health information, protect against reasonably anticipated threats or hazards to that information, and to protect against any inadvertent disclosure of protected health information.

The Privacy Rule, however, does not provide specific implementation requirements regarding safeguards. Rather, this is expected to be a common sense and scalable standard adapted to each covered entity's business. The regulation also requires the covered entity to develop and implement administrative safeguards.

The general requirement of documenting policies and procedures has received substantial attention. The Privacy Rule recognizes and encourages organizations to rely on two levels of development: the industry/ trade association level and the covered entity's level.

By encouraging associations to develop and adopt model policies, individual members can then pull those policies into their own Privacy Compliance Program by reference, needing only to fill in gaps. Clearly this approach will take time. The associations will need to develop or redevelop policies and guidelines, followed by consensus building among the membership.

The individual covered entity remains the responsible party for development, implementation, and

education about privacy policies and procedures. Whether these guidelines can be pulled in by reference or need to be developed by the covered entity, it will be the privacy official's responsibility to determine the organization's need and ensure that a complete privacy program is in place.

D. Ability to Receive and Respond to Complaints: Beginning with the relationship between the right to lodge a complaint and the privacy notice, individuals must be informed of their rights to complain to the covered entity and the Secretary of HHS if they believe their privacy rights have been violated.

In support of these rights, covered entities must identify a contact person or function and tell patients how to lodge complaints. This person or function also must be prepared to provide further direction and information about the management and escalation of complaint procedures. All of the complaints received must be documented, along with the disposition of the complaint. All of that documentation is subject to the same retention standards as outlined for other privacy-related documentation.

E. Definition and Application of Sanctions: Covered entities are not only required to implement privacy policies and procedures to address proactively risks and controls over protected health information. A plan must define a covered entity's reaction to situations where a policy has been violated. The ability to apply appropriate sanctions for inappropriate activity is required.

The sanctions for privacy violations must be documented and should be communicated in the same manner and in conjunction with the education process for the entire Privacy Compliance Program. If a sanction is applied, that activity also must be documented and retained.

In the case of whistleblowers, individuals generally cannot be sanctioned for releasing protected health information, assuming the provisions for "whistleblowing" are followed. This also should be clearly communicated in the policies, procedures, and privacy notice.

F. Mitigation Procedures: When a covered entity becomes aware of a use or disclosure of protected health information that violates its own policies and procedures or the Privacy Rule, it must take prudent measures to mitigate or minimize the harmful effects of the infraction. The nature of the infraction does not make a practical difference with regard to this requirement. It can be an accidental or intentional violation.

Further, this requirement extends to the business associates of the covered entity. In other words, the third party that is given access to the covered entity's protected health information must have policies and procedures in place to address the need to mitigate the effects of a violation of the Privacy Compliance Program. The covered entity may choose to include this particular requirement in audit procedures of the business associate to ensure that data will be protected. However, when a breach occurs, appropriate action and escalation procedures must be applied.

G. Document Retention Requirements: A covered entity must retain the documentation required, whether in written or electronic form, for a minimum of six years from the date of its creation or the date when it last was in effect, whichever is later.[4]

That means an effective program for storing written and electronic copies of required documentation must be established and maintained. One good reason for ensuring compliance with this requirement is the ability to prove some level of due diligence and to demonstrate that the organization addressed the Privacy Rule.

H. Use and Disclosure Policy: See Sections 4.0 and 5.0 on appropriate use and disclosure policies.

Less is More: Sharing the Minimum Amount of Information Necessary

The Privacy Rule requires covered entities to take reasonable steps to limit the use or disclosure of, and requests for protected health information to the minimum necessary to accomplish the intended purpose.[1] However, the minimum necessary provisions do not apply to the following:

- Disclosures to or requests by a health care provider for treatment purposes.
- Disclosures to the individual who is the subject of the information.
- Uses or disclosures made under an authorization requested by the individual.
- Uses or disclosures required for compliance with the standardized HIPAA transactions.
- Disclosures to HHS when disclosure of information is required under the rule for enforcement.
- Uses or disclosures that are required by other law.[2]

A covered entity's policies and procedures must identify the persons or classes of people who require access to protected health information to do their jobs. This process also must determine the types of protected health information needed and the appropriate condition for access. HHS does not expect covered entities to conduct a case-by-case review of each instance of access to information.

For example, hospitals may have policies that allow doctors, nurses, or others involved in treatment to have access to the entire medical record. Case-by-case review of each use is not required. However, where the entire medical record is needed, the covered entity's policies and procedures must state so explicitly and include a justification.

For routine or recurring requests and disclosures, the policies and procedures may be standard protocol. However, these policies and procedures must limit the protected health information disclosed or requested to the minimum necessary for that particular type of disclosure or request.

For non-routine disclosures, covered entities must develop reasonable criteria for determining, and limiting disclosure to, only the minimum amount of protected health information necessary. Non-routine disclosures must be reviewed on an individual basis in accordance with these criteria. When making non-routine requests for protected information, the covered entity must review each request to ensure it seeks only that information reasonably necessary.

Reasonable Reliance

The Privacy Rule allows a covered entity to rely on the judgment of the party requesting the disclosure as to the minimum amount of information that is needed under the following situations:

- A public official or agency for a disclosure permitted under § 164.512 of the rule;
- Another covered entity;
- A professional who is a workforce member or business associate of the covered entity holding the information; and
- A researcher with appropriate documentation from an Institutional Review Board (IRB) or Privacy Board.

The Privacy Rule does not require such reliance, however, and the covered entity has the discretion to make its own determinations.

Determining Minimum Necessary Information

The Privacy Rule requires a covered entity to make reasonable efforts to limit use, disclosure of, and requests for protected health information to the minimum necessary to accomplish the intended purpose. This leaves it to the covered entities to take reasonable steps to limit data sharing as appropriate.

The standard is intended to make covered entities evaluate their practices and enhance protections to prevent unnecessary or inappropriate access to protected health information. "It is intended to reflect and be consistent with, not override, professional judgment and standards," HHS said in its first round of clarifications.

The requirements do not prohibit medical residents, medical and nursing students, and other medical trainees from accessing patient information in the course of their training. However, policies and procedures must be developed to account for their access.

Covered entities are not required to restructure their current systems to comply with the minimum necessary requirements. In its clarifications, HHS said it does not generally consider facility modifications as necessary. However, they may want to make some adjustments to minimize access, such as isolating and locking file cabinets or records rooms, or providing additional security on computers maintaining personal information.

The Privacy Rule also acknowledges the wide variation in covered entities. HHS advises that covered entities take into account their ability to configure the records systems to restrict access. As an example, HHS said it may not be reasonable for a small, solo practitioner who has largely a paper-based records system to limit access of employees with certain functions to only limited fields in a patient record, while other employees have access to the complete record. On the other hand, a hospital with an electronic patient record system may reasonably implement such controls, and therefore, may choose to limit access in this manner to comply with the rule.

Expected Changes to the Minimum Necessary Provision

The provision does not prevent covered entities from maintaining patient medical charts at bedside, require that covered entities shred empty prescription vials, or require that X-ray light boards be isolated. The Privacy Rule only requires reasonable precautions to prevent inadvertent or unnecessary disclosures. HHS said in its first round of clarifications that it will issue further modifications to the Privacy Rule to further reassure providers

HHS also said it did not intend to ban the use of sign-in sheets in waiting rooms, and the department intends to issue regulatory modifications to clarify that this and similar practices are permitted. As more questions arise, HHS said it will provide more detailed guidance and clarification.

- Dennis Melamed

---

[1] 65 Fed. Reg. at 82,805 (to be codified at 45 C.F.R. pts. 164.502(b), 164.514(d)).

[2] *Guidance/Q&As*, Standards for Privacy of Individually Identifiable Health Information (45 C.F.R. pts. 160 and 164), *available at* http://www.hhs.gov/ocr/hipaa (last revised July 6, 2001).

I. Business Associates and Compliance: As discussed in more detail in Section 6.0, a business associate could be any third party with whom a covered entity shares protected health information.

In the case of health plans, the need to have contracts with potentially hundreds or thousands of providers could result in a voluminous process of renegotiating some or all of these contracts. Some of those agreements are referred to as "evergreen" contracts, renewing year after year with minimal or no modifications. The need to renegotiate for certain HIPAA considerations could open the discussion to the reconsideration of other terms and conditions, a process most parties would prefer to avoid.

Some organizations are considering the use of term sheets and contract addenda to sidestep the possibility of new contract negotiations. Some proactive vendors are developing term sheets that explain the new authorities and responsibilities that they will contractually need to comply with their activities that fall under the Privacy Rule.

Other organizations are considering strict limits for reopening contracts that confine negotiations to only those matters that are affected by the Privacy Rule.

J. Authorization Forms: See Sections 4.0 and 5.0 on the appropriate use of authorization forms.

K. Access to Protected Health Information by Individuals: Access to one's own protected health information is one of the individual rights mandated by the Privacy Rule.[5] This requirement gives every individual the right to access his or her own health information.

Administratively, the covered entity has 30 days in which to act upon a request for access. If the entity grants the access, the individual must be informed of that acceptance.

If the covered entity decides to deny access, a written explanation must be provided to the individual. Further, if the request is denied, the covered entity still must make other protected health information available that was not explicitly excluded in the explanation of the denial.

The information that the individual has access to is limited to a "designated record set."[6] A designated record set includes any information used by the covered entity to make decisions about the individual.

In the case of a *health plan*, that data would minimally include enrollment, payment, adjudication, and medical management data. For *providers*, this would involve the medical record and billing record for the individual.

In addition to these data elements, the designated record set includes any other group of records that the covered entity uses, in whole or in part, to make decisions about individuals.

Data that is used for decision-making purposes that is held by a business associate also is included in the designated record set. For the privacy official, the challenge is determining if data that is part of the designated record set is held by business associates, and then developing a strategy for accessing that information expeditiously when an individual makes an access request.

Exceptions to what is included in the designated record set also exist. They include psychotherapy notes, information gathered for civil or criminal proceedings, and data related to the Clinical Laboratory Improvements Amendments of 1988.[7]

Finally, the process by which the covered entity makes protected health information accessible to individuals must be documented. The entity must document the designated record set that will be subject to access by individuals, along with the titles of the persons or functions responsible for receiving and responding to requests for access by individuals.

L. Denial of Request for Inspection and Copying: The Privacy Rule not only provides for access, but also defines the circumstances under which access may be denied.[8] If an individual is denied access to his or her protected health information, specific requirements must be met. They include making other relevant information available to the individual and supplying the individual with a documented explanation for the denial of access.

Minimally, the denial explanation must include:

- The basis or reasoning for the denial;
- A statement of the individual's review rights, and how the individual can exercise those rights; and
- How the individual may complain to the covered entity.

M. Amendments to Records: In addition to an individual's right to access his or her health information, the Privacy Rule dictates the means by which the covered entity must make the corrections to that information.[9]

A covered entity has 60 days to act on a request for amendment or correction.[10] *The privacy official is strongly encouraged to discuss this entire section with the chief medical officer or equivalent function in the organization.* The focus of this discussion will be on the need to maintain a record of the amendments and corrections made to an individual's protected health information.

If an amendment is requested and accepted by the covered entity, the entity must make the correction by minimally identifying the records in the designated record sets that are affected. Then, the correction should be made by appending or linking the current record set to the amendment. This sounds convoluted, and it is.

The bottom line is that an effective audit trail must be maintained for any amendments and corrections. The original errant data or record must be discernible from the correction or amendment.

In addition, all of the documentation related to a requested amendment or correction must be maintained and in some manner linked to the individual's protected health information. This may include the individual's request for a correction, the covered entity's denial of a request, the individual's statement of disagreement with the denial, and any ensuing rebuttals.

N. Required Accountings of Disclosure: Another right granted to an individual is the ability to request and obtain an accounting of disclosures of his or her protected health information to third parties.[11] As with the other individual rights, the covered entity has a limited amount of time to act on an individual's request. In this case, the covered entity has a 30-day deadline from the date the request is received.

The content of the accounting itself is well-defined. That alone will not make it any easier for privacy officials or information technology personnel to identify and implement a solution for responding to these requests, but it does provide the framework for the information that must be captured to meet this requirement.

The accounting must include disclosures of an individual's protected health information. This includes:

- Disclosures made to or by business associates;
- Disclosures made during the six years prior to the request beginning at the date of compliance for the Privacy Rule;
- Dates of the disclosure;
- Name and address of the entity that received the protected health information;
- A brief description of the information disclosed; and
- A brief statement of the purpose of the disclosure.

All of the aforementioned components of the accounting of disclosures must be documented, along with the written accounting itself provided to individuals, and the titles of the person or function responsible for receiving and processing requests for accountings of disclosures.

O. Training: The training requirements[12] require training on the entity's policies and procedures for every employee anticipated to have contact with protected health information. This training must be conducted for current employees by the compliance date and repeated whenever a significant change occurs in the policies and procedures of that entity. The Privacy Rule leaves room for the employer or privacy official to determine the most effective means of providing that training.

Employees hired after the compliance date that are anticipated to come into contact with protected health information will need to be trained within a reasonable period of time.

P. Policy Change Policy: Covered entities need a policy for changing other policies. Many organizations already have a procedure for amending or modifying existing policies. In this context, it will need to be made part of the privacy policies and compliance plan.

When a change is made to a policy or procedure, that change must be evaluated to determine if changes to the privacy notice are needed to reflect the new thinking. If the privacy notice must be updated, the new policy cannot be implemented until the privacy notice has been communicated and made effective as of an explicit date. In addition, if the change is significant it may require retraining of all or some the employees to change certain functions or behaviors.

14.5 Key Points

- Senior management must be involved in the development of a covered entity's compliance plan.
- Using HIPAA as way of getting a strategic initiative moving more quickly and effectively may be the most cost-effective and easily accepted method for some organizations.
- If the privacy notice must be updated, the new policy cannot be implemented until the privacy notice has been communicated and made effective as of an explicit date. If the change is significant, it may require retraining of all or some the employees to change certain functions or behaviors.
- A covered entity must retain the documentation required, whether in written or electronic form, for a minimum of six years from the date of its creation or the date when it last was in effect, whichever is later.
- The privacy official is strongly encouraged to discuss the issue of changes and amendments to records with the chief medical officer or equivalent function in the organization. The focus of this discussion should be on the need to maintain an appropriate record.

Endnotes

[1] 65 Fed. Reg. 82,827 (to be codified at 45 C.F.R. pt. 164.530(h)(i)(1)).

[2] *id.* at 82,826. (to be codified at 45 C.F.R. pt. 164.530).

[3] *id.* at 82,820 (to be codified at 45 C.F.R. pt. 164.520).

[4] *id.* at. 82,828 (to be codified at 45 C.F.R. pts. 164.530(j)(1) and (2)).

[5] *id.* at 82,823 (to be codified at 45 C.F.R. pt.164.524).

[6] "Designated record set" is defined at 65 Fed. Reg. 82,803 (to be codified at 45 C.F.R. pt. 164.501).

[7] The CLIA, 42 U.S.C. § 263a, and accompany regulations, 42 C.F.R. § 493, require clinical laboratories to comply with standards regarding the testing of human specimens. The law requires clinical laboratories to disclose test results or reports only to authorized persons, as defined by state law. If a state does not define the term, the federal law defines the term as the person who orders the test.

[8] 65 Fed. Reg. 82,823 (to be codified at 45 C.F.R. pt. 164.524).

[9] *id.* at 82,824-26 (to be codified at 45 C.F.R. pt. 164.526).

[10] *id.* at 82,825 (to be codified at 45 C.F.R. pt. 164.526).

[11] *id.* at 82,826 (to be codified at 45 C.F.R. pt. 164.528).

[12] *id.* at 82,826 (to be codified at 45 C.F.R. pt. 164.530(b)).

Section 15.0 - Where Privacy Meets Security

Mark L. Schuweiler

15.1 The Relationship Between Privacy and Security

The Privacy Rule and the proposed Security Rule represent the first nationwide effort to protect an individual's personal health information from unwarranted access and disclosure. Both sets of regulations make up the two critical sides of the patient information confidentiality coin. Privacy regulations focus on the application of effective policies, procedures and business service agreements to control the access and use of patient information. The proposed security regulations address the organization's infrastructure requirements to assure secure and private communication and maintenance of confidential patient information

Yet, the Privacy Rule and the proposed Security Rule overlap in a number of areas. Consequently, attention to privacy policies and practices alone are not enough to ensure compliance with HIPAA or ensure the protection of health data.

Organizations may seek to protect personal patient information, but without effective security and privacy policies, procedures, services, and mechanisms in place, they cannot guarantee confidentiality. Data security is a necessary component of data protection and data integrity, and health care organizations should harmonize their actions so that security and privacy policies and procedures are consistent.

15.2 Overview of the Combined Security/Privacy Requirements

The proposed Security Rule is consistent with what has come to be known as "industry best practice" for information security. One of the definers of "best practice" is the U.S. National Security Agency (NSA). This agency is the world's leader in defining practice

for security of information. In the NSA Information Security Assessment Methodology, which the agency requires to be used in the assessment of the Federal Government, 18 baseline categories are examined to evaluate information security practice. Of those 18 baseline categories, 13 are also common to information privacy best practice and can be used as the basis for identification of the common touch points between the Privacy Rule and the proposed Security Rules. The 18 baseline categories are:

1. Documentation*
2. Roles and Responsibilities*
3. Identification and Authentication*
4. Account Management*
5. Session Controls*
6. External Connectivity*
7. Telecommunications*
8. Auditing*
9. Virus Protection
10. Contingency Planning
11. Maintenance
12. Configuration Management*
13. Back-ups
14. Labeling*
15. Media Sanitization/Disposal*
16. Physical Environment*
17. Personnel Security
18. Training and Awareness*

The categories marked with an asterisk are the 13 that are addressed by both privacy and security.

15.2.1 Information Security Documentation.

The documentation of information security practices encompasses administrative and security policies, guidelines and requirements, system security plans and standard operating procedures. Particular attention should be paid to the quality and quantity of these documents and of user procedure security manuals and how well users understand all of the above.

Both the Privacy Rule and the proposed Security Rule have substantial requirements for documentation. Both also emphasize maintenance of records and tracking. This would include, for example, tracking who and when patient information is used and disclosed, or tracking the attendance for security awareness training, or effectively tracking document configuration management, etc.

15.2.2 Information Roles and Responsibilities.

Three governing administrative and security issues should be examined to obtain a basis for an analysis of identification and authentication practices. Those analyses will be: 1) upper level management's perception and actions relating to privacy and security; 2) systems operation; and 3) how the user community functions with respect to privacy and security.

The Privacy Rule and the proposed Security Rule make it clear that policy and procedures must spell out responsibilities for protection and disclosure of patient information, and that minimum necessary access (least privileges in security parlance) should be the ruling guidance in every situation.

15.2.3 Identification and Authentication.

The fundamental building block of information privacy and security is the identification and authentication of the people that use the information infrastructure. This includes what is required of the user to use its system, e.g. something you know (passwords); something you have (smart cards); or something you are (biometrics).

Policy, procedures and mechanisms for both privacy and security must ensure proper identification and authentication. A good example of where this is paramount is in how call centers are able to identify and authenticate callers.

15.2.4 Account Management

The way accounts are initialized, terminated, maintained, and the way special accounts are handled should be analyzed to assure the accounts are safe, are

Information Security Documentation:
HIPAA Privacy and Security Regulation Touch Points

Privacy Rule	Security Rule
Uses and Disclosures	Administrative
Permitted Uses	Certification
Minimum Necessary	Chain of Trust Partners Agreements
Notices	Contingency Plan
	Formal Mechanisms for Records
	Processing
	Information Access Control
	Internal Audit
	Personnel Security
	Security Configuration Mgmt
	Security Incident Procedures
	Security Management Process
	Termination Procedures
	Training
	Physical Safeguards
	Physical Access Controls
	Policy Guidelines for WS
	Technical Services
	Access Controls

Information Roles and Responsibilities:
HIPAA Privacy and Security Regulation Touch Points

Privacy Rule	Security Rule
Uses and Disclosures	Administrative
Permitted Uses	Certification
Minimum Necessary	Chain of Trust Partners Agreements
Consents	Contingency Plan
Authorizations	Formal Mechanisms for Records
Minimum Necessary	Processing
De-Identification	Information Access Control
Privacy Officer	Internal Audit
	Personnel Security
	Security Configuration Mgmt
	Security Incident Procedures
	Security Management Process
	Termination Procedures
	Training
	Physical Safeguards
	Assigned Security Responsibility
	Physical Access Controls
	Security Awareness Training
	Technical Services

Identification and Authentication:
HIPAA Privacy and Security Regulation Touch Points

Privacy Rule	Security Rule
Authorizations	Administrative
	Chain of Trust Partners Agreements
	Information Access Control
	Personnel Security
	Security Management Process
	Termination Procedures
	Training
	Physical Safeguards
	Media Controls
	Physical Access Controls
	Secure Workstation Location
	Technical Services
	Access Control
	Audit Controls
	Authorization Control
	Data Authentication
	Entity Authentication
	Technical Mechanisms

documented, and that those policies and procedures are proactively managed.

Unlike Y2K, HIPAA is ongoing and dynamic. Policies and procedures must be continuously monitored and updated to prevent unauthorized use or disclosures. Similarly, user accounts need to be consistently and carefully monitored.

Activities that address these concerns include: management of user lists; processes by which terminated employees access is removed; and changes to access privileges when individual roles change.

15.2.5 Session Controls

Computer operations should be observed to insure that all workstations logged-on are protected. For example, health care organizations should determine whether time-outs are managed, locked-screen capability with passwords exist, the existence of warning banners, unsuccessful log-on can disable accounts, and whether there is limited use of privileged accounts.

As with Account Management, networks and applications require management as well. Warning banners aid in user awareness and in enforcement to ensure that users cannot say that they were not notified. Similarly, putting into effect automatic log-off after a period of inactivity is specified by the proposed Security Rule.

15.2.6 External Connectivity

Vulnerabilities should be identified with regard to the Internet, modems, and dedicated circuits. The enterprise boundary should be identified and issues such as firewall operations, application port control, and authentication to the firewalls are considered in a holistic manner. The degree to which the internal enterprise architecture is hidden from the outside also should be evaluated. Backdoor activity is an important issue with regard to external connectivity.

Communications with business associates must be secure and the nature and extent of such communications must be defined by service agreements.

Electronic communication (e.g., dial-up point-to-point and Internet-based email) under the proposed Security Rule must be encrypted. This is one of the highest risk areas for unintended access.

15.2.7 Telecommunications

There is a real danger to patient privacy in the telecommunications arena. Consequently, evaluation of the level of encryption used must be considered.

Account Management:
HIPAA Privacy and Security Regulation Touch Points

Privacy Rule	Security Rule
Uses and Disclosures Permitted Uses Minimum Necessary Consents	Administrative Chain of Trust Partners Agreements Formal Mechanisms for Records Processing Information Access Control Security Configuration Mgmt Security Management Process Termination Procedures Physical Safeguards Assigned Security Responsibility Media Controls Physical Access Controls Policy/Guidelines Technical Services Access Controls Authorization Controls

Session Controls:
HIPAA Privacy and Security Regulation Touch Points

Privacy Rule	Security Rule
Uses and Disclosures Permitted Uses Minimum Necessary	Administrative Formal Mechanisms for Records Processing Information Access Control Security Management Process Physical Safeguards Policy/Guidelines on Workstation Use Technical Services Access Control Authorization Control Technical Mechanisms

External Connectivity:
HIPAA Privacy and Security Regulation Touch Points

Privacy Rule	Security Rule
Uses and Disclosures Permitted Uses Minimum Necessary	Administrative Chain of Trust Partners Agreements Information Access Control Security Configuration Mgmt Security Management Process Technical Services Access Control Authorization Control Entity Authentication Technical Mechanisms

Telecommunicatons:
HIPAA Privacy and Security Regulation Touch Points

Privacy Rule	Security Rule
Uses and Disclosures Permitted Uses Minimum Necessary	Administrative Chain of Trust Partners Agreements Information Access Control Security Configuration Mgmt Security Management Process Technical Services Access Control Authorization Control Entity Authentication Technical Mechanisms

15.2.8 Auditing

Audit operations (e.g. what is audited and who analyzes the audit logs) should be reviewed to determine the maturity of the audit procedures. Intrusion detection issues should be identified and reviewed.

15.2.9 Configuration Management

Like maintenance above, failure to tightly control all changes to privacy and security procedures, systems, software, and hardware can result in the generation of additional vulnerabilities. This area should be reviewed to insure that the organization has proactive controls of the relocation and reconfiguration of system resources.

Processes, hardware and software must be continuously monitored to assure that adds, changes, and deletes do not adversely affect security and privacy features.

15.2.10 Labeling

This area deals with what information and why that information is classified and or sensitive. Additionally, employee awareness of data sensitivity needs to be studied. Appropriate labels on all media can assist with preventing accidental disclosures.

15.2.11 Media Sanitation and Disposal

This refers to the standard operating policy and procedure with regard to media sensitization and how much understanding the end user must have about that policy. This critical area is frequently overlooked. Not only does the paper document need to be sanitized prior to disposal or public disclosure, but so does electronic media. For example the proposed Security Rule specifically suggests degaussing of tapes and disk media.

15.2.12 Physical Environment

The point with physical security is that the physical environment can be used to offset a lack of other privacy procedures and system security capabilities. For example, health care organizations must control access of individuals to facilities or areas within a facility where protected information is stored and/or used.

15.2.13 Training and Awareness

The end user is usually the weakest link in privacy and security. Statistically, 85% of all incidents are

Auditing:
HIPAA Privacy and Security Regulation Touch Points

Privacy Rule	Security Rule
Authorizations	Administrative Formal Mechanisms for Records Processing Internal Audit Security Configuration Mgmt Security Management Process Physical Safeguards Media Controls Physical Access Controls Technical Mechanisms

Configuration Management:
HIPAA Privacy and Security Regulation Touch Points

Privacy Rule	Security Rule
Minimum Necessary	Administrative Formal Mechanisms for Records Processing Security Configuration Mgmt Security Management Process Physical Safeguards Media Controls

Labeling:
HIPAA Privacy and Security Regulation Touch Points

Privacy Rule	Security Rule
Authorizations Notices	Administrative Information Access Control Security Configuration Mgmt Security Management Process Physical Safeguards Media Controls

Media Sanitation and Disposal:
HIPAA Privacy and Security Regulation Touch Points

Privacy Rule	Security Rule
De-Identification	Administrative Chain of Trust Partners Agreements Formal Mechanisms for Records Processing Information Access Control Security Configuration Mgmt Security Management Process Termination Procedures Physical Safeguards Media Controls Physical Access Controls

internally generated. Formal information privacy and security training programs for users and administrators are required to have an effective security environment.

15.3 Finding The Right Solution

Achievement of an effective program to comply with the Privacy Rule and proposed Security Rule requires consideration of several issues, including:

- There is not one single solution for every organization;
- Determining the best solutions requires a clear understanding of the issues involved and the requirements of both rules; and,
- The role of the organization's mission, market sector, complexity and size play an important role in determining the most appropriate course and required actions to ensure patient information confidentiality.

Organizations seeking to address areas in which they are not in full compliance with both the Privacy Rule and the proposed Security Rule must consider both when determining a solution that provides compliance. In many cases a satisfactory solution may be found with the application of either a procedural solution as suggested by the Privacy Rule or a technical security solution suggested by the proposed Security Rule. Both solutions should be cconsidered. The best one will be the one that offers the least complexity and exposes your organization to the lowest business risk.

15.4 Key Points

- Compliance with the Privacy Rule is not enough to ensure the protection of individually identifiable heal th information. The proposed Security Rule plays an integral part in assuring adequate safeguards are in place.
- The Privacy Rule and the proposed Security Rule overlap in many areas, and decisions in one area will affect decisions in another. Consequently, health care organizations should ensure that both sets of policies and procedures are harmonized.
- Health care organizations should be alert to the possibility that a solution to complying with the Privacy Rule may provide the solution to complying with the proposed Security Rule.

Physical Environment:
HIPAA Privacy and Security Regulation Touch Points

Privacy Rule	Security Rule
Authorizations	Administrative Chain of Trust Partners Agreements Information Access Control Personnel Security Security Configuration Mgmt Security Management Process Physical Safeguards Media Controls Physical Access Controls Secure Workstation Location

Training and Awareness:
HIPAA Privacy and Security Regulation Touch Points

Privacy Rule	Security Rule
Training	Administrative Chain of Trust Partners Agreements Contingency Plan Formal Mechanisms for Records Processing Information Access Control Personnel Security Security Configuration Mgmt Security Incident Procedures Security Management Process Termination Procedures Training Physical Safeguards Physical Access Controls Policy/Guidelines for Workstation Use Technical Services Access Control Authorization Control

16.0 - An Uncertain Balancing Act: State Pre-Emption

John S. Conniff

16.1 Introduction

The HIPAA Privacy Rule establishes a minimum set of requirements for the protection of individually identifiable health information. As a result, state laws are not pre-empted to the extent that they are stricter.

The following discussion reviews these areas of pre-emption and provides a framework for determining whether state or federal law will apply to a particular transaction.

16.2 State Privacy Laws

Hundreds of state laws govern or affect access to personal health information. These laws range from comprehensive to narrow and specific and often include state constitutional protection.[1]

Most states have laws covering medical records created and maintained by health care professionals. All states have laws governing use and disclosure of medical records in legal proceedings and in workers compensation claims.[2]

Most states have laws restricting access to health information that could lead to discrimination such as those regulating use and disclosure of HIV testing results. All states have laws that require the reporting of certain types of health information to public health officials and that limit government use and disclosure of this information. Some states have laws limiting insurer use and disclosure of health information.[3]

Some states allow minors to obtain certain types of health care without parental knowledge and therefore restrict disclosure of related health information. More recently, states have considered and adopted laws governing the use and disclosure of health information relating to genetic testing. These examples do not begin to exhaust the number and type of state laws governing health information.

The breadth of state law governing health information is complicated by the extreme variability in the level of privacy protection and by the lack of consistency among these laws within each state.

For example, while the Washington state medical records law requires authorization for release of medical records for insurance coverage,[4] no particular provision of the same law governs insurer procedures to protect privacy once the information is released.

In contrast, Washington restrictions on the release of information relating to sexually transmitted diseases specifically directs insurers to limit use and disclosure of information to those people involved in the evaluation and payment of a claim for benefits.[5]

16.3 Federal Pre-emption

16.3.1 Overview

Instead of pre-empting state laws and exercising exclusive jurisdiction, Congress established a federal "floor" below which no state could fall. Thus, the general standard for federal pre-emption applies and the federal law supersedes "contrary provision[s] of state law." [6] In adopting HIPAA, Congress expressly preserved more stringent state privacy laws while establishing standards for determining when federal privacy regulations would take precedence.

HIPAA establishes two standards for determining federal pre-emption of state law and two exceptions where state law takes precedence:

- Federal privacy regulations do not supersede *state laws determined by the Secretary of Health and Human Services (Secretary) to meet certain criteria* related to prevention of fraud and abuse, state health plan regulation, reporting on health care delivery, other public purposes, and regulation of controlled substances.[7]

- The regulations do not "supersede a contrary provision of State law, if the provision of *State law imposes requirements, standards, or implementation specifications that are more stringent* than the requirements, standards, or implementation specifications imposed under the [federal privacy regulations]."[8]

- HHS regulations do not limit *state public health laws* that require the reporting of disease or injury, child abuse, birth, or death, public health surveillance, or public health investigation or intervention.[9]

- Federal privacy regulations do not affect or pre-empt *state regulatory reporting laws* that require a "health plan to report, or to provide access to, information for management audits, financial audits, program monitoring and evaluation, facility licensure or certification, or individual licensure or certification."[10]

16.3.2 Privacy Rule Applicability

As with any legal determination, the first question to ask is whether the statute or regulation applies to the circumstances or whether there is a conflict at all. A state law may be pre-empted as to its application to one type of institution but this pre-emption will not prevent enforcement of the state law as to *other* types of institutions. Pre-emption does not "kill" a law; pre-emption substitutes the federal law for the state law under particular circumstances.

In many instances state laws will have broader application to a greater number of persons or circumstances addressing subjects not affected by the Privacy Rule.[11] Even where the state law is narrow, the Privacy Rule may not apply to the transaction, may not apply to the actor, or may be limited in scope.

Other sections of this book address particular requirements in greater detail; but these issues must be understood when analyzing pre-emption of state laws. Pre-emption involves a comparison of federal versus state requirements.

Three questions must be answered before determining the application of the federal versus state health information privacy law to a particular circumstance:

1. Does the state law apply to a "covered entity" as defined by the Privacy Rule?
2. Even if the state law applies to a covered entity, does the law apply to a function or activity governed by the federal regulation?
3. If the state law covers the entity and the activity, does the activity fall within one of the federal exceptions that preserve state laws?

The federal Privacy Rule applies only to health care providers, health plans, and health care clearinghouses who transmit health information electronically including providers on whose behalf someone has transmitted health information electronically (virtually all health providers).[12] Many types of insurance benefits are explicitly excluded under both HIPAA and by extension, the federal privacy regulation.[13]

For example, life insurers and workers compensation insurers are not covered by the federal regulation but will be covered to some extent under various state privacy laws. Thus, a state law governing privacy practices in the sale of life insurance is not pre-empted by the Privacy Rule.

Even if an "entity" is covered and must obtain consent or authorization for the use of protected health information, the function may be excluded. For example, an HMO is a covered entity but a disclosure of protected health information for a state workers compensation program is excluded from the regulations. No consent or authorization is necessary for disclosure and therefore, state law will exclusively govern the use and disclosure of health information for workers' compensation claims.[14]

Finally, even if an entity is covered or a function could be covered, the Privacy Rule creates explicit exceptions for certain state laws and activities. The two exceptions provided in HIPAA and carried over in the regulation govern state public health laws and state regulatory oversight of health plans.[15]

To provide guidance on these exceptions, HHS included specific exemptions from the consent and authorization provisions of the regulations.[16] A covered entity (e.g. a doctor or an HMO) may *disclose* protected health information (remember that the regulation make a distinction between "use" and "disclose" and must be followed accordingly) for at least five types of public health activities: disease and illness prevention and control, child abuse and neglect, limited Food & Drug Administration-related oversight functions, notification of individuals exposed to communicable disease, and limited workplace health and safety functions.[17]

A covered entity may also *disclose* protected health information to a "health oversight agency" for oversight activities including audits, investigations, and inspections relating to the health care system, government benefit programs.[18] These and other exemptions are discussed in other sections. They are discussed here as examples of laws that the Privacy Rule would classify as falling under either the public health or regulatory oversight exceptions.

16.3.3 Identifying the Conflict

Unless saved by an explicit exception noted above, the Privacy Rule pre-empts a state law if the state law is "contrary" to the regulation. As defined by the regulation, a state law is "contrary" when a covered entity "would find it impossible" to obey both state and federal laws or when the state law "stands as an obstacle" to the purpose of the federal privacy law.[19]

The definition incorporates the standard judicial test for determining when a state law conflicts with a federal law and is pre-empted.[20] Moreover, the definition of "state law" brings all types of state laws under the pre-emption provisions of the regulation.[21] Thus, state constitutional provisions, statutes, regulations, and common law as determined by state court decisions all face potential pre-emption under the regulation.

Despite this pre-emption of contrary state laws, the Secretary of HHS may make a determination that a state law is not pre-empted by the regulation if he finds that the state law meets certain conditions.

Keep in mind here the discussion only concerns "contrary state laws." If a covered entity can obey both the state and federal law and the federal purpose would not be thwarted, there is no pre-emption since the state law is not "contrary" to the regulation. Assuming that a state law is contrary to the regulations, the Secretary can yield to the state law upon a determination that the state law:

(1) Is necessary:
    (i) To prevent fraud and abuse related to the

provision of or payment for health care;
    (ii) To ensure appropriate State regulation of insurance and health plans to the extent expressly authorized by statute or regulation;
    (iii) For State reporting on health care delivery costs; or
    (iv) For purposes of serving a compelling need related to public health, safety, or welfare, and, if a standard, requirement, or implementation specification [of the privacy regulation] is at issue, if the Secretary determines that the intrusion into privacy is warranted when balanced against the need to be served; or
(2) Has as its principal purpose the regulation of the manufacture, registration, distribution, dispensing, or other control of any controlled substances [as defined under federal or state law].[22]

As noted above, other provisions of the Privacy Rule avoid conflict between federal and state law by providing various exceptions. For example, although a state may request an exception determination from HHS to ensure proper regulation of insurance § 164.512(d) of the regulation permits disclosure of protected health information for state regulatory oversight functions.

In short, an exception determination may not be required in all instances.

16.3.4 Requesting an Exception

Anyone can request that the Secretary make a determination.[23] If the request is made by a state, the request must come from the governor or his or her designee.[24] The request must be in writing, sent to an address published at a later date in the *Federal Register* and include the following information:

(1) State law to be saved;
(2) Particular federal standard for which an exception is requested;
(3) Provision of federal privacy rules that will not be implemented or the additional information the state will be able to collect with the exception;
(4) Effect of an exception on health plans and others;
(5) Reasons why the exception should be granted

including how it meets the conditions for exception laid out in the rule (see above);

(6) Other information the HHS requests.[25]

There is no timetable for HHS approval of a request for an exception.[26]

Until the Secretary makes a determination, the state law is pre-empted.[27]

When the exception is granted, the exception remains in effect until the federal or state law changes or the grounds upon which the exception was granted change.[28]

16.3.5 More Stringent State Privacy Laws

The Privacy Rule does not pre-empt tougher state privacy laws. A state law is saved from pre-emption if it "relates to the privacy of health information and is more stringent than a standard, requirement, or implementation specification" contained in the Privacy Rule.[29] A few observations are necessary before discussing these qualifications.

First, unlike the exception determinations, HHS will not and cannot make determinations as to whether a state law is or is not "more stringent." Although many commentators asked HHS to establish an advisory opinion process to determine whether state law was "more stringent," HHS noted that such an opinion would have little or no legal effect.[30]

If a covered entity chose to ignore a state privacy law and exclusively follow the federal regulation, only a state enforcement action against the entity and subsequent judicial decision would settle the matter of whether the state law was "more stringent" and therefore not pre-empted.

Only a competent legal review of state privacy laws by the entity can provide guidance. HHS has indicated that it will provide "technical assistance" to covered entities.[31]

Second, the Privacy Rule pre-empts on a provision-by-provision basis, not law-by-law.[32] In other words, if one provision of a state privacy law is pre-empted, another may not be.

For example, a state law may restrict disclosure in an instance permitted by federal law and may permit disclosure in an instance restricted by federal law. Only the more permissive state law would be pre-empted.

Parenthetically, states remain free to adopt new privacy laws or amend old ones to save them from pre-emption by making them "more stringent."

Nothing in HIPAA prevents future lawmaking by states; thus, covered entities must continue to pay attention to state laws governing health information privacy.[33]

Finally, to clarify the effect of pre-emption when federal and state laws conflict, when a state law avoids pre-emption by a conflicting federal law, the state law does not gain power beyond its original effect.

Many groups commenting on the proposed Privacy Rule were afraid that if a state privacy law took precedence over the federal Privacy Rule, the state law would extend to organizations previously exempt from state regulation.

This was particularly of concern for employers who worried that federal pre-emption of state laws regulating employer health plans would be diluted.[34] Because employer health plans are subject to the federal Privacy Rule and tougher state privacy laws take precedence over weaker federal provisions, perhaps employers would be required to follow the tougher state law. HHS expressed the opinion that neither HIPAA nor the federal Privacy Rule gave states new jurisdiction over employer health plans.[35]

A. "Relates to" Analysis: The first part of the test for determining whether a state law falls under the savings clause for tougher state laws is whether the law "relates to the privacy of health information." Under the federal Privacy Rule, a law "relates" if it "has the specific purpose of protecting the privacy of health information or affects the privacy of health information in a direct, clear, and substantial way."[36] HHS describes its intent in adopting this definition as restricting the type of state laws "that may potentially trump the federal standards to those that are clearly intended to establish state public policy and operate in the same areas as the federal standards."[37]

Thus, a state law need not be labeled a privacy law to survive pre-emption. For example, a state law that required reporting of health information and coincidentally restricted further disclosure would clearly and directly affect health information privacy even though the law's purpose was not to protect privacy.

B. "More Stringent" Analysis: At first glance, determining whether a state law survived pre-emption would seem an easy matter of asking whether the law was more restrictive of use and disclosure of information. However, "more stringent" is viewed from the consumer's perspective so that a state law that gave more access for individuals to view their own records is also "more stringent."

The federal Privacy Rule provides an extensive definition of what constitutes a "more stringent" state law. To survive pre-emption, the state privacy law must meet one or more criteria. Note in particular the last criterion that incorporates the general statutory standard:

(1) Restricts a use or disclosure that federal rules permit except for provisions that restrict required disclosure to HHS or individual access to her own information;

(2) Permits greater individual right to amend or access health information;

(3) Provides more information to individuals about health information use, disclosure, rights, or remedies;

(4) Imposes greater requirements for authorizations or consent to the release of health information including shorter durations for the validity of an authorization, impose greater restrictions, or reduce the ability of an entity to coerce an authorization;

(5) Requires higher record keeping standards that allow the individual to monitor disclosures; and

(6) Provides greater privacy protection for individuals.[38]

The definition includes a provision that explicitly preserves state laws that govern the rights of minors to obtain health care without parental knowledge:

"Nothing in this subchapter may be construed to pre-empt any State law to the extent that it authorizes or prohibits disclosure of protected health information about a minor to a parent, guardian, or person acting *in loco parentis* [as parent] of such minor."[39]

Thus, state laws governing these minor privacy rights take precedence over any provision of the Privacy Rule that either permits or restricts disclosure

in a manner that conflicts with these state laws.[40]

For example, under Washington statutes, a minor may consent to certain types of treatment for chemical dependency without parental consent.[41] No one may disclose protected health information to the parent without minor consent. The federal rule accommodates these state laws through explicit recognition of the ability of unemancipated minors to exercise rights under the federal rule to the extent that state law permits.[42, 43]

C. Pre-emption of State Penalties: The definition of pre-emption in the federal Privacy Rule makes no mention of state privacy law provisions that provide greater penalties than federal law. HIPAA imposes fines and imprisonment for violations of the privacy standards.[44]

A state law that provides different remedies for violations of a state privacy law does not conflict with the federal statute. The state remedy could be imposed on a violator without interference with any federal remedy. As noted earlier, state laws are considered provision by provision and thus, even if a substantive provision of state law were pre-empted as weaker (more permissive disclosure), the stronger penalty would not be pre-empted. HHS considered and removed a provision from the definition of "more stringent" that would have addressed penalties.[45] HHS went further to express its opinion that state laws that permit individuals to file suit to protect privacy rights "does not conflict with the HIPAA penalty provisions."[46]

16.4 Plan of Action

Without doubt, health plans, providers, and other organizations will face regulation of the use and disclosure of protected health information by both state and federal governments. Federal regulations will serve as a baseline with state laws filling the gaps or extending the federal standards. Persons and organizations should have already reviewed and complied with relevant state law.

The publicity surrounding the federal Privacy Rule has had the effect of alerting organizations to the need for state law compliance for the first time. Many organizations worried about the federal Privacy Rule already may be violating state laws now given the similarity between many state and federal requirements.

Review and compliance with state law will constitute an ongoing function for health care professionals, health plans, and others because states remain free to adopt or expand privacy laws.

Given the delayed effective date of the federal regulations, covered entities should start with a comprehensive review of state law and design a compliance strategy that satisfies state law then incorporate federal requirements.

The federal Privacy Rule tends more toward process than toward substance in states that have enacted privacy protections. Thus federal issues like employee training, privacy officials, form and content of authorizations, etc. will be unique while specific state prohibitions on certain disclosures, minor rights, and public reporting will not interfere with these federal process regulations.

When uncertainty exists as to whether and how to comply with conflicting federal and state standards, covered entities should pursue an HHS determination of pre-emption. However, HHS will not make the determination for issues relating to issues of the stringency of state privacy laws. In those instances, covered entities should pursue state legislative and regulatory clarification prior to federal effective dates.

When in doubt follow the state law and seek guidance from HHS, which has promised assistance and a cooperative approach to enforcement.[47]

16.5 Key Points

- Nothing in HIPAA prevents future lawmaking by states; thus, covered entities must continue to pay attention to state laws governing health information privacy.

- If health care providers and covered entities can obey both the state and federal law and the federal purpose would not be thwarted, there is no pre-emption since the state law is not "contrary" to the Privacy Rule.

- HIPAA does not pre-empt State penalties for noncompliance with health information protection requirements.

- Covered entities should start with a comprehensive review of state law and design a compliance strategy that satisfies those requirements then incorporate federal mandates.

Endnotes

[1] For example, Montana's constitution provides: "The right of individual privacy is essential to the well-being of a free society and shall not be infringed without the showing of a compelling state interest." Mont. Const. art. II § 10.

[2] Wisconsin's workers' compensation statute governing access to information is typical of state laws and provides at Wis. Stat. § 102.13(2)(a) (200): "An employee who reports an injury alleged to be work-related or files an application for hearing waives any physician-patient, psychologist-patient or chiropractor-patient privilege with respect to any condition or complaint reasonably related to the condition for which the employee claims compensation. Notwithstanding[…] any other law, any physician, chiropractor, psychologist, dentist, podiatrist, hospital or health care provider shall, within a reasonable time after written request by the employee, employer, worker's compensation insurer or department or its representative, *provide that person with any information or written material reasonably related to any injury for which the employee claims compensation.*" (emphasis added).

[3] Massachusetts has a comprehensive law governing insurer use and disclosure of information. *See* Mass. Gen. Laws Ann. ch. 175.

[4] Wash. Rev. Code § 70.02 (2001).

[5] Wash. Rev. Code § 70.24.105.

[6] Health Insurance Portability and Accountability Act of 1996, 42 U.S.C. § 1320d-7.

[7] *Id.* at 1320d-7(o)(2), which provides: "A provision or requirement under this part, or a standard or implementation specification adopted or established under sections 1172 through 1174, shall not supersede a contrary provision of State law, if the provision of State law—(A) is a provision the Secretary determines— (i) is necessary—(I) to prevent fraud and abuse; (II) to ensure appropriate State regulation of insurance and health plans; (III) for State reporting on health care delivery or costs; or (IV) for other purposes; or (ii) addresses controlled substances…"

[8] *Id.* at § 1320d-2.

[9] *Id.* at § 1320d-7 (b).

[10] *Id.* at § 1320d-7 (c).

[11] Where a state law governs a subject and there is no federal counterpart, HHS will not find pre-emption since there is no "contrary" state law. 65 Fed. Reg. at 82,581.

[12] "We [HHS] note that health care providers who do not submit HIPAA transactions in standard form become covered by this rule when other entities, such as a billing service or a hospital, transmit standard electronic transactions on their behalf." 65 Fed. Reg. at 82,477.

[13] The definition of "health plan" at 65 Fed. Reg. at 82,799 (to be codified at 45 C.F.R. pt. 160.103) excludes those insurance policies and plans that provide benefits excluded under 42 U.S.C. § 300gg-91(c)(1):

"(c) Excepted benefits: For purposes of this subchapter, the term 'excepted benefits' means benefits under one or more (or any combination thereof) of the following:

(1) Benefits not subject to requirements
   (A) Coverage only for accident, or disability income insurance, or any combination thereof.
   (B) Coverage issued as a supplement to liability insurance.
   (C) Liability insurance, including general liability insurance and automobile liability insurance.
   (D) Workers' compensation or similar insurance.
   (E) Automobile medical payment insurance.
   (F) Credit-only insurance.
   (G) Coverage for on-site medical clinics.
   (H) Other similar insurance coverage, specified in regulations, under which benefits for medical care are secondary or incidental to other insurance benefit."

[14] 65 Fed. Reg. at 82,818 (to be codified at 45 C.F.R. pt. 164.512(l)).

[15] 42 U.S.C. § 1320d-7 (b) and (c).

[16] *See* HHS comment at 65 Fed. Reg. at 82,588 (to be codified at 45 C.F.R. pt. 164.512 (b) and (d)).

[17] *See* HHS comment at 65 Fed. Reg. at page 82,668-70.

[18] 65 Fed. Reg. at 82,814 (to be codified at 45 C.F.R. pt. 164.512(d)).

[19] 65 Fed. Reg. at 82,800 (to be codified at 45 C.F.R. pt. 160.202.

[20] "We will find pre-emption where it is impossible for a private party to comply with both state and federal law [...] and where (under the circumstances of [a] particular case, [the challenged state law] stands as an obstacle to the accomplishment and execution of the full purposes and objectives of Congress) [...] What is a sufficient obstacle is a matter of judgment, to be informed by examining the federal statute as a whole and identifying its purpose and intended effects." *Crosby v. National Foreign Trade Council* (99-474) June 2000, 181 F.3d 38, affirmed. *See also Metropolitan Life Ins. Co. v. Massachusetts*, 471 U.S. 724 (1985).

[21] 65 Fed. Reg. at 82,801 (to be codified at 45 C.F.R. pt. 160.202).

[22] *id.* (to be codified at 45 C.F.R. pt. 160.203(a)).

[23] *id.* (to be codified at 45 C.F.R. pt. 160.204).

[24] *id.* (to be codified at 45 C.F.R. pt. 160.204(a)).

[25] *id.*

[26] Many commentators requested various time limits or suggested that silence from HHS meant the exception was automatically granted. While sympathetic to the need for speed, HHS noted that it had no idea how much time it would take to review exception requests because it had never done this sort of thing before and until it had some experience, HHS was making no promises. 65 Fed. Reg. at 82586.

[27] "...federal standards will pre-empt contrary state law and such pre-emption will not be removed unless and until the Secretary acts to grant an exception..." 65 Fed. Reg. at 82584.

[28] 65 Fed. Reg. at 82,801 (to be codified at 45 C.F.R. pt. 160.205).

[29] *id.* (to be codified at 45 C.F.R. pt. 160.203(b)).

[30] 65 Fed. Reg. at 82,580.

[31] "It is our intent to provide as much technical advice and assistance to the regulated community as we can with the resources available." 65 Fed. Reg. at 82,580.

[32] HHS acknowledged this fact in rejecting suggestions that if some parts of a state law were pre-empted all parts of the law should be pre-empted. Fed. Reg. at 82,582.

[33] "Nothing in the rules below prohibits or places any limits on states enacting stronger or more comprehensive privacy laws." 65 Fed. Reg. at 82,582.

[34] Employee Retirement Income Security Act (ERISA), 29 U.S.C. §§ 1001 *et seq.* (1985).

[35] 65 Fed. Reg. at 82,582.

[36] *id.* at 82,801 (to be codified at 45 C.F.R. pt. 160.202).

[37] *id.* at 82,583.

[38] id. at 82,800-01 (to be codified at 45 C.F.R. pt. 160.202).

[39] *id.*

[40] "Where states have considered the balance involved in protecting the confidentiality of minors' health information and have explicitly acted, for example, to authorize disclosure, defer the decision to disclose to the discretion of the health care provider, or prohibit disclosure of minors' protected health information to a parent, the rule defers to these decisions to the extent that they regulate such disclosures." 65 Fed. Reg. at 82,582.

[41] Wash. Rev. Code § 70.96A.095.

[42] 65 Fed. Reg. (to be codified at 45 C.F.R. pt. 164.502(g)(3)).

[43] As this book went to press, HHS Secretary Tommy Thompson issued a statement raising questions over whether HHS would maintain its stance in regard to the rights of minors.

[44] The HIPA statute provides: "(a) OFFENSE. A person who knowingly and in violation of this part [...] (1) uses or causes to be used a unique health identifier; (2) obtains individually identifiable health information relating to an individual; or (3) discloses individually identifiable health information to another person, shall be punished as provided in subsection (b).
(b) PENALTIES. A person described in subsection (a) shall (1) be fined not more than $50,000, imprisoned not more than 1 year, or both; (2) if the offense is committed under false pretenses, be fined not more than $100,000, imprisoned not more than 5 years, or both; and (3) if the offense is committed with intent to sell, transfer, or use individually identifiable health information for commercial advantage, personal gain, or malicious harm, be fined not more than $250,000, imprisoned not more than 10 years, or both." 42 U.S.C. §1320d–6.

[45] 65 Fed. Reg. at 82,582.

[46] *id.*

[47] id. at 82,801 (to be codified at 45 C.F.R. pt. 160.304).

Section 17.0 - HIPAA Lite: Gramm-Leach-Bliley

John Conniff

17.1 Federal Privacy Rule Relating to Financial Institutions

As health care prepares for the Privacy Rule, substantial attention is being paid to the privacy provisions of the Gramm-Leach-Bliley Act (GLB). Passed by Congress in 1999, GLB overhauled the regulation of banks and other financial institutions.[1]

The primary purpose of the law was to permit the creation of companies that combined banking, insurance and securities activities, including health insurers, who are covered by the HIPAA Privacy Rule as well. GLB repealed laws adopted in response to the financial depression of the 1930s that prohibited banks from engaging in the business of insurance.

Public concern over the sharing of information among these different types of companies led to a demand for privacy protection of sensitive financial information. These were protections included in Title V of GLB.

The financial privacy provisions govern all "financial institutions" which include insurance companies. Because GLB governs all insurance companies, an inherent conflict was created between regulations governing financial privacy and those adopted by the HHS governing health information privacy.[2] The health information privacy provisions only govern health insurance while the GLB covers all insurers.

17.2 Harmonizing HIPAA/GLB Enforcement

In proposing financial privacy regulations, the federal banking regulators noted that they would "consult with HHS to avoid the imposition of duplicative or inconsistent requirements."[3] The concern arose from the definition of financial information that included any information provided by a consumer to obtain an insurance product or service.[4]

The Federal Trade Commission noted that insurers would not be subject to dual federal regulation because each state had primary responsibility for adopting and enforcing GLB standards for insurers.[5]

Given the traditional state role of regulating insurance, this deference was part of the trade off in expanding bank powers to include insurance. While HHS will enforce its regulations against health insurers and sets a regulatory floor, GLB encourages states to take the lead and adopt financial privacy regulations for insurance.

GLB does not preempt stronger state privacy protections. The federal law preempts state law only to the extent that such law or regulation is inconsistent with the federal law. But a state financial privacy law stronger than GLB privacy provisions is not inconsistent and therefore not preempted.

However, unlike the HHS regulations, the Federal Trade Commission determines whether the state law provides greater protection while HHS does not make such determinations under health privacy standards. Although many commentators asked HHS to establish an advisory opinion process to determine whether state law was "more stringent," than health privacy provisions, HHS declared that such an opinion would have little or no legal effect since the federal statute authorized such findings only for other types of state laws.[6]

17.3 Assessing the Core Differences

Fundamentally, the greatest difference between GLB and the HHS regulations relate to their respective core requirements and philosophies.[7] GLB is essentially a notice statute requiring financial institutions (including insurers) to tell consumers (not businesses) about the institution's privacy policies.

GLB prevents only the sharing of financial information with nonaffiliates unless the disclosure is necessary to perform services and marketing for the financial institution. In short, GLB has few restrictions on the use of financial information. Consumers are permitted to "opt out" of (restrict) the institution's disclosure of information for a narrow range of marketing functions.

In contrast, the Privacy Rule begins with the premise that health insurers may not use or disclose information except as permitted under the regulation and as authorized by the individual. The regulations provide many exceptions for insurance functions; but the regulations establish a basic limit that prohibits the use and disclosure of information to the "minimum necessary to accomplish the intended purpose..."[8] In many respects, the Privacy Rule restricts use and disclosure of information to a far greater extent than the GLB regulations.

The complexity and cost of compliance with HHS regulations similarly differ from the GLB requirements. For example, HHS regulations require each health insurer account to consumers for disclosures of protected health information made over the prior six years except for disclosures relating to health care treatment, delivery, or health care operations.[9] Use of information for marketing purposes without explicit permission is strictly limited.[10]

Compared to the GLB standards, financial privacy is a simple "kiss and tell" rule while health information privacy is a "don't kiss and don't tell" policy. Add the typical layer of state health privacy laws and the differences between financial and health privacy become stark.

GLB specifically named the National Association of Insurance Commissioners (NAIC) as one of the organizations to be consulted for the development of regulations governing insurers.[11]

Consequently, the NAIC adopted a model GLB regulation urging its adoption by each of the state insurance regulatory agencies.[12] The NAIC model insurance regulation combines financial and health

information regulation patterned on the federal banking agencies' financial regulations.

Thus, life insurers (not covered by HHS regulations) must disclose privacy practices, provide opt out rights for financial, and obtain authorization for health information except for insurance functions. Insurers will be required to obtain authorizations for health information that will not be required of banks and securities firms under federal financial information privacy regulations.

As discussed in other sections, insurers must determine state standards and work to incorporate the federal requirements. Satisfying stricter state standards will satisfy federal standards including the financial standards.

Satisfying stricter federal health information standards will satisfy financial information standards. For example, the FTC noted in explaining its regulation that an insurer obtaining an authorization for use of health information satisfies the "opt out" requirement of the FTC regulation.[13]

17.4 Key Points

- The Gramm-Leach-Bliley Act covers all insurers, while the HIPAA Privacy Rule only covers health insurers.
- Compliance with the HIPAA Privacy Rule is likely to satisfy the requirements of the Gramm-Leach-Bliley Act for those organizations covered by both.
- Both HHS and financial regulators say they will harmonize enforcement to ensure that the two sets of regulations do not conflict.

Endnotes

[1] Pub. L. No. 106-102 113 Stat. (1999).

[2] *See* 65 Fed. Reg. at 82,483-84 for the relationship of HIPAA and the GLB. HHS notes: "GLB has caused concern and confusion among health plans that are subject to our privacy regulation."

[3] Privacy of Consumer Financial Information, 65 Fed. Reg. at 33,646, 33648 (May 24, 2000)(to be codified at 45 C.F.R. pt. 313).

[4] *id.* at 33,680 (to be codified at 16 C.F.R. pt. 313.3(o)). Federal regulators adopted essentially the same regulation for each of their respective jurisdictions. These rules are: Federal Trade Commission (FTC) 16 C.F.R. pt. 313; Office of Comptroller of Currency (OCC) 12 C.F.R. pt. 40;

Federal Reserve Board (FRB) 12 C.F.R. pt. 216; Federal
Deposit Insurance Corporation (FDIC) 12 C.F.R. pt. 332;
Office of Thrift Supervision (OTS) 12 C.F.R. pt. 573.

[5] *id.* at 33648.

[6] *id.* at 82,580. *See also* at 82,801(to be codified at 45
C.F.R. pt. 160.203(o)).

[7] *See* n. 4 above.

[8] 65 Fed. Reg. at 82,805-06 (to be codified at 45 C.F.R pt.
164.502 (a) and (b)).

[9] *id.* at 82,826 (to be codified at 45 C.F.R. pt. 164.528).

[10] *id.* at 82,819 (to be codiifed at 45 C.F.R. pt. 164.514(e)).

[11] Pub. L. No. 106-102, Tit. V, § 504 (a)(1).

[12] *See* NAIC Model Laws, Regulations, and Guidelines;,
Privacy of Consumer Financial and Health Information
Regulation, Vol. IV, no. 6724 (2000).

[13] 65 Fed. Reg. at 33648.

Part IV

Enforcement

Section 18.0 - Government Enforcement

Janet Newberg

18.1 Introduction

The Privacy Rule creates a new system for protecting individually identifiable health information. As a result, the federal government also assumed a new set of responsibilities for protecting this use of this information.

The scope and sheer size of the Privacy Rule have prompted the Department of Health and Human Services (HHS) to adjust the regulation as unintended consequences are discovered. HHS has already issued on round of clarifications, but health care providers and other covered entities can expect more guidances and advisories on how the federal government will enforce the regulatory requirements.

However, the Privacy Rule also creates a new set of crimes as well. Enforcement of law in this context will fall to the criminal justice system.

As complex and confusing as the rest of the Privacy Rule may appear, HHS is definitive in the way in which it intends to enforce the regulation. The department identified three ways in which the federal government intends to enforce the HIPAA Privacy Rule.

1. Violators will be subject to criminal investigation and prosecution;
2. HHS may impose civil monetary penalties on those who violate the privacy rule; and
3. HHS may take administrative action against covered entities to enforce the regulatory requirements.

The criminal and civil remedies were established in the HIPAA statute[1] itself and not by the regulation. Most of the administrative enforcement provisions are established in the regulation.

18.2 A New Crime - Wrongful Disclosure of Individually Identifiable Health Information

A. "Knowing" Violations: Congress in Section 262 of HIPAA created the crime of "Wrongful Disclosure of Individually Identifiable Health Information."[2] This provision makes it illegal for health care providers and other covered entities to knowingly obtain or disclose individually identifiable health information about an individual without the individual's consent or authorization. Conduct only falls within the parameters of this new offense if it is done "knowingly."[3] *Accidental or merely negligent conduct is not covered under this provision.*

Violation of this new crime will constitute either a federal misdemeanor or a federal felony depending on the state of mind of the individual committing the offense, or the purpose for which the offense was committed.

If a person knowingly obtains or discloses individually identifiable health information, that person will be subject to a fine of up to $50,000 and imprisonment for up to one year.[4]

According to definitions commonly used in federal litigation, a person acts "knowingly" by acting intentionally, or by acting in reckless disregard of or in deliberate ignorance of the truth.

Therefore, if a health care provider employee knows of the existence of the Privacy Rule, deliberately fails or refuses to become informed of the rule's provisions, and releases protected health information in violation of the Privacy Rule, that release could be viewed as a violation of this new criminal statute. Health care providers, plans, and clearinghouses should insure that they train all staff and employees on the new rules and put policies and procedures in place enforcing the rule's provisions.

B. False Pretences: If a person obtains or releases protected health information under false pretenses, the penalty increases to a fine of up to $100,000 and imprisonment of not more than five years.[5] A "false pretenses" offense could arise when, for example, an individual calls a local hospital seeking treatment information about his next-door-neighbor, and successfully obtains the information only by telling

C. Intent To Sell: Finally, if the offense is committed with the intent to sell, transfer, or use individually identifiable health information for commercial advantage, personal gain, or malicious harm, the perpetrator may be imprisoned for up to 10 years and fined not more than $250,000.[6] Hospitals that sell patient databases to health care products marketing firms could be liable under these "intent to sell, transfer or use" provisions.

The law refers to the perpetrator as a "person." However, federal criminal law makes it clear that a "person" can be an individual or a corporation. If a corporate entity is found guilty of committing this new offense, it will be subject to the sentencing provisions applicable to corporate entities set forth in the United States Sentencing Guidelines.

18.3 The Enforcers

A. Government Agencies: Special agents of HHS's Office of Inspector General (OIG) will probably bear the brunt of the responsibility for investigating criminal allegations of wrongful disclosure of protected health information. The only arm of the HHS that employs criminal special agents and is authorized to conduct investigations of crimes involving HHS programs is the OIG.

Therefore, although preliminary review of potential privacy rule violations may be conducted by the Office of Civil Rights (OCR), if and when the allegations rise to the level of a potential violation of this new crimi-

---

The U.S. Sentencing Commission and HIPAA

Although federal criminal statutes routinely establish the maximum penalties that can be imposed upon conviction (10 years in prison and a fine of $250,000 for example) only rarely do offenders receive the maximum penalties. Individuals found guilty of federal felonies and Class A misdemeanors receive sentences computed through application of the United States Sentencing Guidelines ("Guidelines").[1]

The Guidelines assign a sentencing range taking into account the severity of the offense (or offenses) of conviction, and the prior criminal history of the defendant. When Congress creates new federal crimes, the United States Sentencing Commission ("Commission") usually meets, considers the elements of the new crimes and what evil they were intended to address, and assigns an appropriate ranking of the offense's severity.

If the Commission does not rank a new offense, federal courts are instructed to find existing offenses with similar maximum penalties and use those severity levels to compute the offenders' sentences.

The Commission has not yet ranked the offense of Wrongful Disclosure of Individually Identifiable Health Information. The most serious violations of this new statute (those committed with intent to sell, transfer or use health information for commercial advantage, personal gain, or malicious harm) seem comparable to existing mail, wire, and health care fraud statutes.

If courts sentence these privacy offenders to sentences similar to those imposed on mail, wire, and health care fraud offenders, the sentences will increase with the amount of monetary gain to the offender.

- Janet Newberg

---

[1] Congress passed the Sentencing Reform Act of 1984, 18 U.S.C.A. §§ 3551 *et seq.* and 28 U.S.C.A. §§ 991-98, which, among other things, created the United States Sentencing Commission as an independent body in the Judicial Branch with power to promulgate binding sentencing guidelines establish a range of determinate sentences for all categories of federal offenses and defendants according to specific and detailed factors. *See generally* USSG, Ch. 1., Pt. A, 18 U.S.C.A.

An Immediate Impact: *U.S. v. Sutherland*

The Privacy Rule does not technically go into effect until April 2003, but that is not stopping courts from using it to make decisions now. Barely two weeks after HHS allowed the regulation to go into effect on April 14, a federal district court in Virginia used the regulation as the basis for requiring the federal government to give notice to patients whose records the federal prosecutors wanted to subpoena. The case involved a physician who was suspected of illegally dispensing controlled substances.

In *U.S. v. Sutherland*[1], the government sought hospital pharmacy records of some patients who had prescriptions issued by the physician filled at the facility. The hospital tried to quash the request based, in part, on confidentiality grounds.

While the HIPAA Privacy Rule did not bind the hospital, U.S. District Judge James P. Jones said he found the regulations "to be persuasive in that they demonstrate a strong federal policy of protection for patient medical records."[2]

Under the Privacy Rule, subpoenas not ordered by a court or administrative body require that the subjects of those subpoenas be given notice and an opportunity to object.[3]

As a result, he ordered the federal government to send written notices to the last known address of the affected patients to give them an opportunity to object to the request.

- Dennis Melamed

---

[1] *U.S. v. Sutherland*, 143 F. Supp. at 2d 609 (WD Va. 2001)

[2] *id.* 143 F. Supp. at 2d at 613.

[3] 65 Fed. Reg. at 82,814 (to be codified at 45 C.F.R. pt. 164.512 (e)(1)).

---

nal statute, it is likely that OCR will refer the matter to the OIG for investigation.

However, health care organizations also should expect other federal law enforcement agencies, including the Federal Bureau of Investigation (FBI), the Internal Revenue Service (IRS), and the U.S. Postal Inspection Service, to join in these investigations as well, particularly given the task force approach to federal law enforcement currently used in many of the federal districts around the country.

B. Federal Task Forces: Many federal prosecutors participate in "health care fraud task forces." Membership on these task forces generally consists of representatives from federal law enforcement agencies with some interest in prosecution of offenses related in some way to fraud in the health care delivery system.

The Minnesota Health Care Fraud Task Force, for example, has included a virtual alphabet soup of law enforcement members, including the HHS-OIG, FBI, U.S. Postal Inspection Service, the Department of Defense's Criminal Investigative Service, Drug En-

forcement Administration, Food and Drug Administration, IRS, state Medicaid Fraud Control Unit, and state Attorney General.

The FBI is almost always an active participant on such health care task forces around the country because of the Bureau's keen interest in investigating and prosecuting mail and wire fraud, money laundering, and related offenses. The IRS (tax fraud, money laundering) and U.S. Postal Inspection Service (mail fraud) frequently participate as well.

Providers, plans, and clearinghouses should expect that if the OIG commences an investigation into alleged criminal privacy violations, the district health care fraud task force is almost certain to determine if any other federal laws have been violated as well. Multiple alleged violations make a much more attractive package for a federal prosecutor and federal agents want their cases accepted for prosecution by their local federal prosecutors.

18.4 Civil Monetary Penalties

Congress authorized the HHS to impose "civil monetary penalties" on those who violate the Privacy Rule.[7] Generally, Section 1176 provides that HHS will impose on any person who violates a provision of the privacy rule a penalty of up to $100 for each violation.[8] This is capped at $25,000 per year per violation of an identical requirement or prohibition.[9]

Congress specifically directed, however, that HHS may not impose civil monetary penalties for an act that violates the new criminal wrongful disclosure statute.[10] This may be due to congressional concern over the possibility of "piling on" multiple penalties in multiple settings all based on the same underlying conduct. The U.S. government has been criticized by the federal courts in the past over the constitutional issues raised by prosecuting someone for a criminal offense and then imposing staggering civil penalties for the same offense.

In addition, the civil monetary penalties provision provides that HHS may not impose a civil fine if HHS believes that the person liable for the penalty did not know, and by exercising reasonable diligence would not have known, that someone violated the Privacy Rule.[11]

In essence, Congress explicitly refused to adopt a "strict liability" standard (where a person would be liable for even an accidental release of protected health information) and provided protection from liability for simply negligent releases. Therefore, if despite a health provider's best efforts to implement the necessary policies and procedures, train its employees, and conduct continuing monitoring, an employee still manages to release health care information in violation of the Privacy Rule, the provider itself will not be criminally or civilly liable for the release.

The imposition of fines is not automatic. Congress gave HHS some discretion by creating "reasonable cause" exemptions for all or part of a fine.[12] First, Congress authorized HHS to either not impose a fine at all, or to waive part of it, if HHS believes that the failure to comply was due to a reasonable cause and not willful neglect, and the covered entity corrected the failure to comply within 30 days.[13]

If, for example, a health care provider had policies in place providing for compliance and Privacy Rule training for all new employees within 24 hours of the date employment begins, but a new employee released protected health information after 21 hours of employment, HHS may find that the release was due to a reasonable cause, and not willful neglect, and may elect not to impose a fine.

Finally, the civil monetary provision allows HHS to waive part or all of a fine if the amount of the prospective penalty would be excessive relative to the compliance failure involved.[14]

Once again, the civil monetary penalty provision refers to violations by "persons." It is clear, however, that covered entities will be liable for civil penalties for the acts of their employees.

18.5 Administrative Actions

One provision of the Privacy Rule provides the general outline of HHS's administrative enforcement responsibilities.[15] HHS will provide much greater detail about its role in enforcing the Privacy Rule when it issues the final Enforcement Rule.

In the meantime, the compliance and enforcement section of the final Privacy Rule does outline some of these requirements. HHS describes how complaints must be filed with HHS, what HHS will do to investigate those complaints, what administrative responsibilities are borne by covered entities, and a suggestion that HHS may conduct "compliance reviews."

18.6 Complaints to the Secretary

The regulation provides that any person who believes that a covered entity has violated any requirement, standard, or implementation specification of the Privacy Rule may file a complaint with HHS.[16] The right to file is not limited to the individual whose health information was mishandled. HHS specifically extended the right to file to any person or entity, including competitors and whistleblowers.

All complaints must be filed in writing, either on paper or electronically.[17] The complaint must identify the entity that allegedly violated the Privacy Rule, and describe the acts or omissions believed to be in violation of the rule.[18] All complaints must be filed within 180 days of when the complainant knew or should have known that the act or omission complained of occurred, unless HHS decides to waive this time limit.[19]

HHS has the discretion to investigate complaints it receives, but it is not required to do so. If HHS decides to investigate, it may review the covered entity's pertinent policies, procedures and practices, and the circumstances regarding any alleged acts or omissions concerning compliance.[20]

If HHS investigates a complaint and finds that the covered entity failed to comply with the rule, HHS will inform both the covered entity and the complainant in writing of its findings. The Privacy Rule provides that HHS will, "attempt to resolve the matter by informal means whenever possible."[21]

Covered entities should adopt procedures for dealing with HHS privacy violation inquiries. In-house or outside counsel should be involved in developing these procedures, in order to ensure that all potentially serious allegations are routed to counsel as quickly as possible.

Until HHS through OCR or OIG develops a track record for handling allegations of Privacy Rule violation, counsel should be routinely involved in assessing and responding to HHS inquiries.

If HHS determines that the matter cannot be resolved by informal means, HHS will issue written findings documenting the noncompliance to the covered entity and the complainant.[22] *Covered entities should expect that the written findings also will be sent to those at HHS with responsibility for assessing civil monetary penalties and for conducting criminal investigations.* If the allegations involved were relatively serious, covered entities should expect litigation.

The Privacy Rule also provides that if, after investigation, HHS finds that no violation occurred, it will inform both the covered entity and the complainant of that finding in writing.[23]

Remember, though, that there is a difference between "not guilty" and "innocent." Just because the HHS made no finding that a violation occurred does not mean that the covered entity's privacy policies could not be improved. The entity's privacy officer should carefully review what possible deficiencies led to the allegations and institute necessary changes.

Investigations of non-criminal complaints of violation of the privacy rule will most likely be conducted by personnel within OCR. Although the rule does not specifically identify these options, HHS certainly reserves the right to seek civil monetary penalties upon finding a violation and to refer a complaint to the OIG for criminal investigation if such a referral is warranted.

Finally, the government remedies set forth in the HIPAA statute and the Privacy Rule are not the exclusive remedies available to address privacy violations. Expect Department of Justice attorneys to analyze, for example, whether violations of Privacy Rule provisions coupled with "claims" of some type submitted to the federal government might violate the federal False Claims Act.[24]

18.7 Compliance Reviews

The Privacy Rule's provisions on compliance and enforcement provide, in part, that, "The Secretary may conduct compliance reviews to determine whether covered entities are complying with the applicable requirements of [the Privacy Rule]."[25] HHS did not define the nature or extent of a compliance review, nor has it yet established the conditions under which it may choose to conduct these reviews.

The Privacy Rule governs all health care providers that conduct financial and administrative transactions electronically, all health plans, and all health care clearinghouses.

Many covered health care providers are also Medicaid or Medicare providers, and are more accustomed to the intense federal supervision and oversight associated with that status. However, many covered entities under the Privacy Rule may not historically have been subject to federal review of their business activities, and may find this regulatory intrusion confusing.

The Enforcement Rule is expected to contain much greater detail about exactly what a compliance review will be and how deeply HHS intends to probe into covered entities' day-to-day business operations in order to determine if they are complying with the Privacy Rule. In addition, HHS hinted that it may at a minimum piggyback on the efforts of various accrediting bodies, including Joint Commission on Accreditation of Healthcare Organizations, National Committee for Quality Assurance, and URAC, and utilize their survey work as part of these HHS compliance reviews.

18.8 Responsibilities of Covered Entities

HHS identified three administrative responsibilities of covered entities.[26] First, a covered entity must keep all records relating to its compliance with Privacy Rule requirements and must submit "compliance reports" in the time and manner to be specified by the Secretary.[27] At a minimum, covered entities should retain for six years patient consents, authorizations, Notices of Privacy Practices, privacy policies and procedures, disclosure logs, access requests, responses to access requests, and records of investigation relating to privacy issues.

Second, a covered entity must cooperate with HHS if the department undertakes an investigation or compliance review of the policies, procedures, or practices of the covered entity.[28]

Finally, a covered entity must give HHS access during "normal business hours" to its "facilities, books, records, accounts, and other sources of information, including protected health information, that are pertinent to ascertaining compliance with the [Privacy Rule]."[29]

If HHS believes that circumstances demand immediate action, such as when documents may be hidden or destroyed, the department has a right to access a covered entity's business records at any time and without notice.[30]

18.9 Key Points

- HIPAA creates a new crime: Wrongful Disclosure of Individually Identifiable Health Information.
- Accidental or merely negligent conduct in violating the Privacy Rule is generally not considered a federal criminal offense.
- Health care providers, plans, and clearing-houses should insure that they train all staff and employees on the new rules and put policies and procedures in place enforcing the rule's provisions to avoid the possibility of criminal prosecution.
- Hospitals that sell patient databases to health care products marketing firms could be liable

under the "intent to sell, transfer or use" provision of the Privacy Rule.

- Providers, plans, and clearinghouses should expect that if the HHS Office of Inspector General commences an investigation into alleged criminal privacy violations, federal health care fraud task forces will almost certainly look to see if any other federal laws have been violated as well.
- The civil monetary penalties provision under HIPAA provides that HHS may not impose a civil fine if HHS believes that the person liable for the penalty did not know, and by exercising reasonable diligence would not have known, that someone violated the Privacy Rule.
- The right to file a complaint with HHS is not limited to the individual whose health information was mishandled.
- If, after investigation, HHS finds that no violation occurred, it will inform both the covered entity and the complainant of that finding in writing.

Endnotes

[1] Health Insurance Portability and Accountability Act of 1996, 42 U.S.C. §§ 1320d-5 and 1320d-6.

[2] *id.* at § 1320d-6.

[3] *id.* at § 1320d-6(a).

[4] *id.* at § 1320d-6(b)(1).

[5] *id.* at § 1320d-6(b)(2).

[6] *id.* at § 1320d-6(b)(3).

[7] *id.* at § 1320d-5(a)(2).

[8] *id.* at § 1320d-5(a)(1).

[9] *id.*

[10] *id.* at § 1320d-5(b)(1).

[11] *id.* at § 1320d-5(b)(2).

[12] *id.* at § 1320d-5(b)(3).

[13] *id.* at § 1320d-5(b)(3)(A).

[14] *id.* at § 1320d-5(b)(4).

[15] 65 Fed. Reg. at 82,801-02(to be codified at 45 C.F.R. pts. 160.300-160.312).

[16] *id.* at 82,801-02 (to be codified at 45 C.F.R. pt. 160.306).

[17] *id.* at 82,801 (to be codified at 45 C.F.R. pt. 160.306(b)(1)).

[18] *id.* at 82,801 (to be codified at 45 C.F.R. pt. 160.306(b)(2)).

[19] *id.* at 82,801 (to be codified at 45 C.F.R. pt. 160.306(b)(3)).

[20] *id.* at 82,802 (to be codified at 45 C.F.R. pt. 160.306(c).

[21] *id.* at 82,802 (to be codified at 45 C.F.R. pt. 160.312(a)).

[22] *id.* at 82,802 (to be codified at 45 C.F.R. pt. 160.312(a)(2)).

[23] *id.* at 82,802 (to be codified at 45 C.F.R. pt. 160.312(b)).

[24] 31 U.S.C.A. §§ 3729-31 (2001).

[25] 65 Fed. Reg. at 82,802 (to be codified at 45 C.F.R. pt. 160.308).

[26] *id.* at 82,802 (to be codified at 45 C.F.R. pt. 160.310).

[27] *id.* at Reg. 82,802 (to be codified at 45 C.F.R. pt. 160.310(a)).

[28] *id.* at Reg. 82,802 (to be codified at 45 C.F.R. pt. 160.310(b)).

[29] *id.* at 82,802 (to be codified at 45 C.F.R. pt. 160.310(c)(1)).

[30] *id.*

Section 19.0 - Tort Liability and HIPAA

Theodore T. Martin

19.1 Introduction

Health care providers and other covered entities are concerned that the HIPAA Privacy Rule will increase their legal exposure. The criminal penalties discussed in the previous section outline specific penalties for failure to comply with the new regulation.

Wrongful use or disclosure of health care information in violation of the Privacy Rule, however, also can result in tort (civil) liability.[1]

Congress decided not to create a new private right of action allowing patients to sue over privacy breaches. Consequently, the Privacy Rule does not *directly* create new ways for patients to sue health care providers. This does not mean that providers cannot be sued in civil court for conduct that violates the regulation.

The Privacy Rule also does not preempt state law. Instead, as discussed in the Section 16.0 on preemption, it establishes a minimum set of privacy protection requirements or a "floor." States are free to impose stricter privacy regulations and free to permit plaintiffs to recover in tort for privacy violations. The existence of a new federal minimum set of standards also may make it easier for the plaintiff to prevail on the plaintiff's tort claim.

To understand this more clearly, a violation of the Privacy Rule can be compared to a driver who causes an expressway collision because he was driving over the speed limit. The speeding itself may not be subject to a lawsuit under state law, but the driver can still be held liable for negligence.

The absence of a traffic law granting a victim the right to file a lawsuit does not prevent the victim from going to court to seek damages on other grounds.

To carry this analogy further, the law designating the speed limit may make it easier for the innocent driver to win in court because the law established a standard of care, and the defendant simply cannot dispute the unreasonableness of his conduct.

Similarly, the same conduct that violates the Privacy Rule also may result in civil liability. The Privacy Rule establishes a minimum standard of conduct, a floor (but not a ceiling). Conduct that falls below that standard may be *per se* unreasonable.

19.2 The Likelihood of Tort Claims

Covered entities should not discount the likelihood that patients may sue them for conduct that falls short of the Privacy Rule. In fact, the U.S. government expects that the fear of lawsuits will help ensure patient privacy. The federal government's expectation was clearly expressed in 2000.

In response to the European Union's Directive on Data Privacy, the Commerce Department developed Safe Harbor principles. Companies that comply with these principles would be deemed to be compliance with EU requirements. In July 2000, the Department of Commerce explained that these principles should "be read against the US legal system and its well known features, such as class actions and contingency fees, which allow consumers even with novel claims relatively ready and inexpensive access to the courts and damages where justified."[2]

The Department of Commerce also commented, "Given the general applicability of tort law and the multiplicity of causes of action covering different aspects of privacy interest, monetary damages are likely to be available to those who suffer invasion of their privacy interest as a result of a failure to adhere to the safe harbor principles."

Prudence dictates that providers and other covered entities assume that the same features of our judicial system and the same legal principles that served to comfort the EU also will apply with equal force to conduct that violates the Privacy Rule.

19.3 The Nature of the Legal Threat: Key Theories of Tort Liability

At least five tort liability theories have evolved that directly relate to the HIPAA Privacy Rule and should be taken into account when planning your HIPAA compliance program.[3] These are:

1. Invasion of Privacy
   a. Unreasonable Intrusion
   b. Unreasonable Publicity
2. Breach of Confidence
3. Inducing Breach of Confidence
4. Negligence
5. Misrepresentation

The following sections provide a general overview of these theories to help health care organizations understand and successfully address these legal challenges.

19.3.1 Invasion of Privacy

Samuel D. Warren and Louis Brandeis in an article published in 1890 in the Harvard Law Review laid the foundation for the recognition of invasion of privacy as a tort. In their article, entitled "The Right to Privacy," Warren and Brandeis recognized the common law's ability to evolve in response to changing circumstances, "Political, social, and economic changes entail the recognition of new rights, and the common law, in its eternal youth, grows to meet the demands of society."[4] The law, they stated, already had developed to provide relief not only for batteries on persons and trespasses to property but also to intangible injuries to feelings and sensibilities.

Warren and Brandeis viewed with alarm recent inventions and new business methods that were leading to invasions of the sacred precincts of private life and feared that new mechanical devices "threatened to make good the prediction that 'what is whispered in the closet shall be proclaimed from the housetops.'" They argued in favor of explicit recognition of a right to privacy, a right to be let alone, noting that through invasion upon privacy, "modern enterprise and invention" had subjected individuals to "mental pain and distress, far greater than could be inflicted by mere bodily injury."

Since then, most states have recognized a number of separate types of claims for invasion of privacy. While each applies to some extent in the health care context, two types of invasion of privacy claims have the greatest applicability to situations involving the wrongful use or disclosure of health care information:

- Unreasonable intrusion upon one's seclusion
- Unreasonable publicity given to another's private life

The first claim generally refers to the unreasonable prying into another's private affairs; the second generally refers to unreasonable publicity given to another's private concerns.

A. Intrusions upon Seclusion: In most states, a patient or consumer can successfully sue a defendant that has intentionally intruded into his private affairs where the intrusion is highly offensive to a "reasonable" person. The invasion may involve a physical intrusion into an area where one reasonably expects privacy.

For example, a California appellate court in January 2001 upheld a jury's determination that the presence of a drug salesman during the breast examination of a partially disrobed cancer patient was a tortuous intrusion upon the patient's seclusion. The court stated, "A breast cancer patient who goes into an oncologist's office to be examined does not, nor should she, take a risk that what goes on in the examination room will be seen or heard by anyone other than medical personnel."[5]

In its decision, the court stressed that the patient alleged that she never consented to the presence of the male drug salesman during the examination and that neither the physician nor the salesman ever identified the salesman's occupation.

In most health care contexts, this kind of intrusion and the potential liabilities will be very rare.

However, health care providers would be wise to develop policies that clearly address the presence of medical product manufacturers and other third parties in health delivery settings.

It is important to note that courts have ruled that patients and consumers may successfully sue even in the absence of a physical intrusion where there has been some other form of investigation or examination of private concerns.

For example, a college was held liable for such an intrusion when it advised students that their blood was being tested for rubella when in fact the blood was positive for human immunodeficiency virus.[6] The court stated, "Although intrusion upon seclusion clearly encompasses an intrusion upon a physical space held in seclusion by a person, the element of seclusion also encompasses intrusions into a person's private concerns based upon a reasonable expectation of privacy in that area."

B. Unreasonable Publicity: The second type of invasion of privacy claim can arise when a health care provider or other covered entity releases information which is highly offensive to the public, and the matter is not of legitimate public interest.[7]

For a patient or consumer to have the basis to sue, the matter that is publicized must not be of a legitimate public interest. Generally, where a purely private aspect of a person's life is involved, the matter is not of legitimate public interest. This is often the case with medical treatment.

This invasion of privacy also requires that publicity must be about the private life of an individual. When strictly enforced, this can be a difficult element to establish.

Many courts have held that this "publicity" element requires that the matter must be communicated to the public at large or to so many people that the matter must be regarded as being substantially certain to become public knowledge.

For example, in a recent federal district court case in Minnesota, a woman sued her former employer claiming that her assistant manager had told co-workers that she had an abortion.[7] The court held that the woman had failed to meet this test because no reasonable person could infer from the allegations that the former employer had disclosed her abortion to a sufficiently large number of people that the public at large either knew or was substantially certain to

become aware of it.

However, some courts have relaxed the publicity requirement where a special relationship existed between the patient and the "public." For example, in an Illinois appellate court case a supervisor had disclosed information about an employee's mastectomy to fellow employees.[8] The Illinois court held that the public disclosure requirement was satisfied by proof that the woman had a special relationship with the "public," the co-workers.

A Colorado appellate court reached a similar result.[9] In the Colorado case, a law firm that employed the plaintiff disclosed to all its employees that the plaintiff had been exposed to the HIV virus even though the employees had no legitimate interest in this information.

The court held that the disclosure was actionable even though the information had not been disclosed to the public at large, noting that communication "to the general public has not been required by some courts because disclosure to those persons with whom the plaintiff has a special relationship may be just as devastating as disclosure to many."

19.3.2 Breach of Confidence

A patient who is injured by a covered entity's wrongful disclosure of identifiable health care information may have grounds to sue for breach of confidence. A majority of state courts that have addressed the issue have held that a patient can sue a physician for breach of confidence for an unauthorized, non-privileged disclosure to a third party of health care information that the physician learned within the physician-patient relationship.

Unlike invasion of privacy, breach of confidence does not require proof of either unreasonable intrusion upon one's seclusion or unreasonable publicity given to another's private life. A Washington case demonstrates that in some circumstances this difference can be crucial.[10] In that case, a patient, during her initial appointment with her physician, revealed information about her medical and personal history. She disclosed that she had previously been married to a physician and described her relationship with her ex-husband as extremely strained.

After meeting with the plaintiff, the physician contacted the woman's ex-husband and disclosed his patient's use of pain medicines. The ex-husband then used that information to support a motion to modify custody orders relating to the couple's two children. The physician had not intruded into the patient's personal affairs and there was no publicity, at least in the strict sense, of the patient's private life.

Nonetheless, the court held that for such a "palpable harm" there must be a legal remedy and held that the woman could proceed on a claim for breach of confidence.

A number of courts have held that physicians are not the only ones that can be held liable for breaches of confidence. The Ohio Supreme Court addressed whether a hospital could be sued for breach of confidence.[11] In that case the hospital had provided its law firm with patient registration forms containing medical information about its patients. The law firm reviewed these forms for the sole purpose of determining whether the patients were potential Social Security Income claimants.

The law firm then contacted patients and informed them how they could take legal action to obtain Social Security benefits. If the claim was covered, the hospital would receive payment for a claim that otherwise was not collectible.

Patients later sued claiming that the hospital had breached the patients' confidentiality. The Ohio court held that the hospital could be held liable for the unauthorized, non-privileged disclosure.

A Massachusetts court also recently held that a pharmacy could be sued for breach of confidence.[12] The prescription customers in that case alleged that CVS Pharmacy, Inc. had wrongfully disclosed information to third parties. The court admitted that it was not aware of any case which had held that pharmacists owe their customers a duty of confidentiality but concluded that in light of a state regulation requiring that pharmacists maintain patient confidentiality it was reasonable to infer that a person who provides private medical and prescription information to a pharmacist expects that the information will be maintained in confidence.

The Massachusetts court viewed the pharmacist-patient relationship as analogous to the physician -patient relationship and held that a breach of confidence by a pharmacist was actionable.

19.3.3 Inducing Breach of Confidence

Many state courts have recognized wrongfully inducing a breach of confidence as a separate claim. Patients may use this theory to pursue claims against business associates or other third parties that convince covered entities wrongfully to disclose protected health information.

In the Ohio hospital case discussed above, the Ohio Supreme Court not only held that the hospital *could* be held liable for the breach of confidence but also determined that law firm *could* be held liable for convincing the hospital to share the records, if the patients could establish that the law firm:

1. Knew or reasonably should have known of the existence of the patient-physician relationship;
2. Intended to induce the hospital to disclose information about the patient or should reasonably have anticipated that would induce the physician to disclose that information; and
3. Did not reasonably believe that the hospital could disclose the information without violating the duty of confidentiality.

The West Virginia Supreme Court adopted a similar standard in a case in which an employer had *ex parte* communications with the plaintiff's treating physician after the employee had filed a workers compensation claim.[13]

19.3.4 Negligence

Violation of the Privacy Rule also may give rise to a claim of negligence. In a negligence action, a plaintiff contends that the covered entity failed to exercise the skill that a reasonably prudent person would have exercised in a similar situation.

Traditionally, in order to prevail under a negligence theory, a plaintiff must establish four elements:

1. A legally recognized duty on the part of the defendant to the plaintiff to conform to a certain standard of conduct;
2. A breach of that duty;
3. A casual connection between that breach and resulting injuries, known as proximate cause; and
4. Actual loss or damage.

Those entrusted with health care information should recognize that some courts have granted recovery to patients and consumers injured as a result of a defendant's negligent health information practices.

For example in 2000, a California a plaintiff sued a pharmacy for damages resulting from the unauthorized disclosure of prescription drug information. In the midst of an acrimonious separation from her husband, the woman advised the pharmacy that she did not want her medical information disclosed to anyone, especially her husband.

The following day, the husband requested a medical expense report for the plaintiff purportedly for the purpose of preparing his tax returns. The pharmacy provided the husband with a printout listing all the prescription drugs ordered by the plaintiff from the pharmacy during the past year. The husband later contacted friends and family accusing the woman of being a drug abuser, filed court papers that alleged that the woman was a drug addict and a danger to their children, and attached the printout to a letter to the department of motor vehicles.

The jury returned a verdict in favor of the woman; and the court of appeals affirmed, noting that all of the woman's damages resulted from the pharmacy's original breach of its duty.

Patients may be able to use the Privacy Rule to establish the existence of a duty and the minimum standard of care where the Privacy Rule requires a covered entity to take certain steps to guard against wrongful use or disclosure of information.

For example, the Privacy Rule requires a covered entity to provide a certain level of initial and ongoing training of employees. A covered entity's failure to comply with this requirement may result in negligence *per se* where the patient can establish a causal relationship between the noncompliance and the patient's damages.

19.3.5 Misrepresentation

In most states, misrepresenting facts for the purpose of convincing another to act or to refrain from acting can lead to tort liability. A misrepresentation generally only is fraudulent if it is made with knowledge or the belief that it is false or, in some states, where the plaintiff makes the statement with reckless disregard

for its truth or falsity. Some states also permit recovery for negligent misrepresentation.

The Privacy Rule requires covered entities to provide individuals with notice of their information practices, and patients and consumers may pursue a misrepresentation claim where the covered entity uses or discloses the information in a manner inconsistent with the stated policy.

A recent Connecticut case outside the health care context provides additional cautionary guidance. In that case, the plaintiff contracted with an electricity company to buy service. After the plaintiff failed to make timely payments, the electricity company reported the lateness of the payments to credit agencies. The plaintiff later applied to a bank for a credit card, but the bank denied his application because of the reports of late payments. The plaintiff sued the electricity company under a variety of theories including misrepresentation. He claimed that the defendant had not informed him of its reporting practices at the time he opened his account. The court held that the plaintiff's allegations that the electricity company had failed to inform him of a material fact during the formation of their agreement sufficiently established a claim for negligent misrepresentation, noting that a claim for misrepresentation may be based on a defendant's failure to speak when he has a duty to do so.

In the health care context, the Privacy Rule may make it more difficult for covered entities to claim that they did not have a duty to disclose their information practices to individuals affected by those practices.

19.4 Damages

Patients and consumers who can establish wrongful use or disclosure of confidential information can recover compensatory damages for the injuries suffered. While traditionally many courts have imposed some limits on the recovery of damages for emotional distress, particularly where there is no physical injury, a number of courts have rejected such a rigid rule.

In addition, many courts have held in invasion of privacy and breach of confidence cases that patients and consumers can recover for emotional distress where they establish that they have actually suffered such injuries and where emotional distress normally would result from such conduct.

In a recent Virginia case the court permitted the recovery for damages for emotional distress in an action against a health care provider for the wrongful disclosure of medical records.[14] The court recognized that in many cases emotional distress damages are not recoverable where there is no accompanying physical harm.

The court, however, recognized that this rule should not apply where a health care provider has wrongfully disclosed medical records. The court wrote:

> Without question, a patient, whose intimate personal medical information is wrongfully disseminated to third parties, will experience some degree of humiliation, embarrassment, and hurt. Under these circumstances, we perceive no logical reason to refuse recovery of emotional distress damages[15]

In addition to compensatory damages, patients and consumers often claim punitive damages. Unlike compensatory damages, punitive damages are intended to punish the defendants.

Historically, the law limited punitive damages to intentional torts such as assault and battery and trespass. During the last 35 years, courts in a number of states have lowered the standard for recovery of punitive damages, and there has been a marked increase both in the number of punitive damage awards and the size of these awards.

19.5 New Threats and Societal Attitudes

Prudent risk management certainly requires an understanding of the elements of typical claims that may be brought for wrongful use or disclosure of health care information and the damages that may be recovered. But the dry recitation of legal principles is only a point of departure.

There also must be recognition of the fundamental changes that have occurred in the nature of health care and less tangible, but equally important, changes in public attitudes. Both individually and collectively these changes affect the magnitude of potential exposure.

Prompted both by technological innovation and government regulation, health care continues to

undergo a transition to digital information systems. These changes materially benefit not only health care organizations and society at large but also individual patients when they receive improved care and lead healthier lives. At the same time the transition to digital systems has given rise to new threats to the privacy of an individual's personal information. While the threat always has existed that someone would wrongfully use or disclose information to others, that risk was relatively localized. Those limits have disappeared. The collection of data in large electronic databases combined with the ability to transfer this data instantaneously around the world over public networks such as the Internet has increased exponentially both the number of people that can be damaged by a breach as well as the amount of damage per individual.

19.6 Managing the Risks of Tort Liability

Organizations can take a number of steps to reduce their tort liability exposure. Not surprisingly, these steps align closely with the multifaceted, organization-wide, protective measures mandated by the Privacy Rule, including restrictions on the use and disclosure of individually identifiable health information and the adoption of administrative, technical and physical safeguards.

Compliance with the Privacy Rule, however, only establishes minimum standards. For purposes of tort liability, the Privacy Rule establishes the floor, not the ceiling. Historically, in the aftermath of an injury, three questions are asked of organizations:

1. What did you know;
2. When did you know it; and
3. What did you do about it?

These questions do not follow with any precision or any rule of law. Nonetheless the answers are an important indication of a company's exposure to tort liability.

In light of the enormous publicity that has attended the issue of privacy and actual and proposed government regulations, it would be difficult for the health care industry not to acknowledge that they are aware of the sensitivity of health care information and the damages that can flow from a wrongful use or disclosure.

The Privacy Rule outlines at least the areas in which companies should continue to focus their attention with the recognition that all of these proactive measures, from the training of employees to the deployment of new technology enhanced solutions, involve not one time action but ongoing assessment and implementation.

19.7 Key Points

- Although HIPAA does not give patients and consumers a new right to sue for violations, it does establish a minimum standard of conduct, and violation of that standard may result in tort liability.
- At least five tort liability theories have evolved that directly relate to the HIPAA Privacy Rule and should be taken into account when planning HIPAA compliance programs. These are:
  1. Invasion of privacy (which can be broken down into unreasonable intrusion and unreasonable publicity),
  2. Breach of confidence,
  3. Inducing breach of confidence,
  4. Negligence, and
  5. Misrepresentation.
- In most health care contexts, unreasonable physical intrusion upon seclusion will be rare. Health care providers, however, should develop policies that clearly address the presence of medical product manufacturers and other third parties in health delivery settings.
- Some courts have held that even in the absence of physical intrusion, an unreasonable intrusion into a person's private concerns can give rise to tort liability.
- Unreasonable publicity can result when a health care provider or other covered entity releases information to the public, which is highly offensive, and the matter is not of legitimate public interest.[17]
- An unauthorized, non-privileged disclosure to a third party of health care information that the physician learned within the physician-patient relationship may be a tortuous breach of confidence.
- Business associates or other third parties that convince covered entities wrongfully to disclose protected health information may be liable for inducing a breach of confidence.

- A covered entity's failure to comply with the Privacy Rule requirement may result in negligence *per se* where person injured can establish a causal relationship between the noncompliance and damages.
- To avoid a misrepresentation claim, health care providers and other covered entities should make sure that they strictly comply with their published policies concerning their information practices.
- Organizations can take a number of steps to reduce their tort liability exposure. These steps, which involve ongoing assessment and implementation, align closely with the multifaceted, organization-wide, protective measures mandated by the Privacy Rule

Endnotes

[1] A tort is "Damage, injury, or a wrongful act done willfully, negligently, or in circumstances involving strict liability, but not involving breach of contract, for which a civil suit can be brought." *The American Heritage Dictionary of The English Language.* (2000) at1823.

[2] EU, US Seal Deal on Data Privacy, *Health Info. Privacy Alert,* July 2000, at 4.

[3] While this list does not describe the universe of legal vulnerabilities, these are the most common claims.

[4] Louis D. Brandeis and Samuel D. Warren, The Right to Privacy, 4 *Harv. L. Rev.* 193 (1890).

[5] *Sanchez-Scott v. Alza Pharmaceutical,* 86 Cal App. 4th 365, 103 Cal Rptr. 2d 410, 418 (2001).

[6] *Doe v. High-Tech Institute, Inc.,* 972 P.2d 1060 (Colo. App. 1998).

[7] *C.L.D. v. Wall-Mart Stores, Inc.,* 79 F. Supp. 2d 1080 (D. Minn. 1999).

[8] *Miller v. Motorola, Inc.,* 202 Ill. App. 3d 976, 560 N.E. 2d 900 (1990).

[9] *Borquez v. Ozer,* 923 P.2d 166 (Colo. Ct. App. 1995).

[10] *Berger v. Sonneland,* 101 Wn. App. 141, 2000 WL 75844 (Wash. App. Div. 3 June 13, 2000).

[11] *Biddle v. Warren General Hosp.,* 86 Ohio St. 3d 395, 715 N.E.2d 518 (1999).

[12] *Weld v. CVS Pharmacy, Inc.,* 1999 Mass. Super. LEXIS 261 (June 1, 1999).

[13] *Morris v. Consolidation Coal Co.,* 191 W. Va. 426, 446 S.E.2d 648 (1994).

[14] *Fairfax Hosp. v. Curtis,* 254 Va. 437, 492 S.E. 2d 642 (1997).

[15] 254 Va. at 446, 492 S.E. 2d at 647.

Part V

Appendices

Appendix A

Text of the
Federal Privacy Rule

**Thursday,
December 28, 2000**

Part II

Department of Health and Human Services

Office of the Secretary

45 CFR Parts 160 and 164
Standards for Privacy of Individually Identifiable Health Information; Final Rule

all state privacy laws. As explained in this section, the regulation would only preempt state laws where there is a direct conflict between state laws and the regulation, and where the regulation provides more stringent privacy protection than state law. We discussed this issue during our consultation with state representatives, who generally accepted our approach to the preemption issue. During the consultation, we requested further information from the states about whether they currently have laws requiring that providers have a "duty to warn" family members or third parties about a patient's condition other than in emergency circumstances. Since the consultation, we have not received additional comments or questions from the states.

X. Executive Order 13086; Consultation and Coordination With Indian Tribal Governments

In drafting the proposed rule, the Department consulted with representatives of the National Congress of American Indians and the National Indian Health Board, as well as with a representative of the self-governance Tribes. During the consultation, we discussed issues regarding the application of Title II of HIPAA to the Tribes, and potential variations based on the relationship of each Tribe with the IHS for the purpose of providing health services. Participants raised questions about the status of Tribal laws regarding the privacy of health information.

List of Subjects

45 CFR Part 160

Electronic transactions, Employer benefit plan, Health, Health care, Health facilities, Health insurance, Health records, Medicaid, Medical research, Medicare, Privacy, Reporting and record keeping requirements.

45 CFR Part 164

Electronic transactions, Employer benefit plan, Health, Health care, Health facilities, Health insurance, Health records, Medicaid, Medical research, Medicare, Privacy, Reporting and record keeping requirements.

Note: to reader: This final rule is one of several proposed and final rules that are being published to implement the Administrative Simplification provisions of the Health Insurance Portability and Accountability Act of 1996. 45 CFR subchapter C consisting of Parts 160 and 162 was added at 65 FR 50365, Aug. 17, 2000. Part 160 consists of general provisions, Part 162 consists of the various administrative simplification regulations relating to

transactions and identifiers, and new Part 164 consists of the regulations implementing the security and privacy requirements of the legislation.

Dated: December 19, 2000.

Donna Shalala,

Secretary,

For the reasons set forth in the preamble, 45 CFR Subtitle A, Subchapter C, is amended as follows:

1. Part 160 is revised to read as follows:

PART 160—GENERAL ADMINISTRATIVE REQUIREMENTS

Subpart A—General Provisions

160.101 Statutory basis and purpose.
160.102 Applicability.
160.103 Definitions.
160.104 Modifications.

Subpart B—Preemption of State Law

160.201 Applicability.
160.202 Definitions.
160.203 General rule and exceptions.
160.204 Process for requesting exception determinations.
160.205 Duration of effectiveness of exception determinations.

Subpart C—Compliance and Enforcement

160.300 Applicability.
160.302 Definitions.
160.304 Principles for achieving compliance.
160.306 Complaints to the Secretary.
160.308 Compliance reviews.
160.310 Responsibilities of covered entities.
160.312 Secretarial action regarding complaints and compliance reviews.

Authority: Sec. 1171 through 1179 of the Social Security Act, (42 U.S.C. 1320d–1329d–8) as added by sec. 262 of Pub. L. 104–191, 110 Stat. 2021–2031 and sec. 264 of Pub. L. 104–191 (42 U.S.C. 1320d–2(note)).

Subpart A—General Provisions

§ 160.101 Statutory basis and purpose.

The requirements of this subchapter implement sections 1171 through 1179 of the Social Security Act (the Act), as added by section 262 of Public Law 104–191, and section 264 of Public Law 104–191.

§ 160.102 Applicability.

(a) Except as otherwise provided, the standards, requirements, and implementation specifications adopted under this subchapter apply to the following entities:

(1) A health plan.

(2) A health care clearinghouse.

(3) A health care provider who transmits any health information in electronic form in connection with a transaction covered by this subchapter.

(b) To the extent required under section 201(a)(5) of the Health Insurance

Portability Act of 1996, (Pub. L. 104–191), nothing in this subchapter shall be construed to diminish the authority of any Inspector General, including such authority as provided in the Inspector General Act of 1978, as amended (5 U.S.C. App.).

§ 160.103 Definitions.

Except as otherwise provided, the following definitions apply to this subchapter:

Act means the Social Security Act.

ANSI stands for the American National Standards Institute.

Business associate: (1) Except as provided in paragraph (2) of this definition, *business associate* means, with respect to a covered entity, a person who:

(i) On behalf of such covered entity or of an organized health care arrangement (as defined in § 164.501 of this subchapter) in which the covered entity participates, but other than in the capacity of a member of the workforce of such covered entity or arrangement, performs, or assists in the performance of:

(A) A function or activity involving the use or disclosure of individually identifiable health information, including claims processing or administration, data analysis, processing or administration, utilization review, quality assurance, billing, benefit management, practice management, and repricing; or

(B) Any other function or activity regulated by this subchapter; or

(ii) Provides, other than in the capacity of a member of the workforce of such covered entity, legal, actuarial, accounting, consulting, data aggregation (as defined in § 164.501 of this subchapter), management, administrative, accreditation, or financial services to or for such covered entity, or to or for an organized health care arrangement in which the covered entity participates, where the provision of the service involves the disclosure of individually identifiable health information from such covered entity or arrangement, or from another business associate of such covered entity or arrangement, to the person.

(2) A covered entity participating in an organized health care arrangement that performs a function or activity as described by paragraph (1)(i) of this definition for or on behalf of such organized health care arrangement, or that provides a service as described in paragraph (1)(ii) of this definition to or for such organized health care arrangement, does not, simply through the performance of such function or activity or the provision of such service,

become a business associate of other covered entities participating in such organized health care arrangement.

(3) A covered entity may be a business associate of another covered entity.

Compliance date means the date by which a covered entity must comply with a standard, implementation specification, requirement, or modification adopted under this subchapter.

Covered entity means:

(1) A health plan.

(2) A health care clearinghouse.

(3) A health care provider who transmits any health information in electronic form in connection with a transaction covered by this subchapter.

Group health plan (also see definition of *health plan* in this section) means an employee welfare benefit plan (as defined in section 3(1) of the Employee Retirement Income and Security Act of 1974 (ERISA), 29 U.S.C. 1002(1)), including insured and self-insured plans, to the extent that the plan provides medical care (as defined in section 2791(a)(2) of the Public Health Service Act (PHS Act), 42 U.S.C. 300gg–91(a)(2)), including items and services paid for as medical care, to employees or their dependents directly or through insurance, reimbursement, or otherwise, that:

(1) Has 50 or more participants (as defined in section 3(7) of ERISA, 29 U.S.C. 1002(7)); or

(2) Is administered by an entity other than the employer that established and maintains the plan.

HCFA stands for Health Care Financing Administration within the Department of Health and Human Services.

HHS stands for the Department of Health and Human Services.

Health care means care, services, or supplies related to the health of an individual. *Health care* includes, but is not limited to, the following:

(1) Preventive, diagnostic, therapeutic, rehabilitative, maintenance, or palliative care, and counseling, service, assessment, or procedure with respect to the physical or mental condition, or functional status, of an individual or that affects the structure or function of the body; and

(2) Sale or dispensing of a drug, device, equipment, or other item in accordance with a prescription.

Health care clearinghouse means a public or private entity, including a billing service, repricing company, community health management information system or community health information system, and "value-added" networks and switches, that does either of the following functions:

(1) Processes or facilitates the processing of health information received from another entity in a nonstandard format or containing nonstandard data content into standard data elements or a standard transaction.

(2) Receives a standard transaction from another entity and processes or facilitates the processing of health information into nonstandard format or nonstandard data content for the receiving entity.

Health care provider means a provider of services (as defined in section 1861(u) of the Act, 42 U.S.C. 1395x(u)), a provider of medical or health services (as defined in section 1861(s) of the Act, 42 U.S.C. 1395x(s)), and any other person or organization who furnishes, bills, or is paid for health care in the normal course of business.

Health information means any information, whether oral or recorded in any form or medium, that:

(1) Is created or received by a health care provider, health plan, public health authority, employer, life insurer, school or university, or health care clearinghouse; and

(2) Relates to the past, present, or future physical or mental health or condition of an individual; the provision of health care to an individual; or the past, present, or future payment for the provision of health care to an individual.

Health insurance issuer (as defined in section 2791(b)(2) of the PHS Act, 42 U.S.C. 300gg–91(b)(2) and used in the definition of *health plan* in this section) means an insurance company, insurance service, or insurance organization (including an HMO) that is licensed to engage in the business of insurance in a State and is subject to State law that regulates insurance. Such term does not include a group health plan.

Health maintenance organization (HMO) (as defined in section 2791(b)(3) of the PHS Act, 42 U.S.C. 300gg–91(b)(3) and used in the definition of *health plan* in this section) means a federally qualified HMO, an organization recognized as an HMO under State law, or a similar organization regulated for solvency under State law in the same manner and to the same extent as such an HMO.

Health plan means an individual or group plan that provides, or pays the cost of, medical care (as defined in section 2791(a)(2) of the PHS Act, 42 U.S.C. 300gg–91(a)(2)).

(1) *Health plan* includes the following, singly or in combination:

(i) A group health plan, as defined in this section.

(ii) A health insurance issuer, as defined in this section.

(iii) An HMO, as defined in this section.

(iv) Part A or Part B of the Medicare program under title XVIII of the Act.

(v) The Medicaid program under title XIX of the Act, 42 U.S.C. 1396, *et seq.*

(vi) An issuer of a Medicare supplemental policy (as defined in section 1882(g)(1) of the Act, 42 U.S.C. 1395ss(g)(1)).

(vii) An issuer of a long-term care policy, excluding a nursing home fixed-indemnity policy.

(viii) An employee welfare benefit plan or any other arrangement that is established or maintained for the purpose of offering or providing health benefits to the employees of two or more employers.

(ix) The health care program for active military personnel under title 10 of the United States Code.

(x) The veterans health care program under 38 U.S.C. chapter 17.

(xi) The Civilian Health and Medical Program of the Uniformed Services (CHAMPUS) (as defined in 10 U.S.C. 1072(4)).

(xii) The Indian Health Service program under the Indian Health Care Improvement Act, 25 U.S.C. 1601, *et seq.*

(xiii) The Federal Employees Health Benefits Program under 5 U.S.C. 8902, *et seq.*

(xiv) An approved State child health plan under title XXI of the Act, providing benefits for child health assistance that meet the requirements of section 2103 of the Act, 42 U.S.C. 1397, *et seq.*

(xv) The Medicare+Choice program under Part C of title XVIII of the Act, 42 U.S.C. 1395w–21 through 1395w–28.

(xvi) A high risk pool that is a mechanism established under State law to provide health insurance coverage or comparable coverage to eligible individuals.

(xvii) Any other individual or group plan, or combination of individual or group plans, that provides or pays for the cost of medical care (as defined in section 2791(a)(2) of the PHS Act, 42 U.S.C. 300gg–91(a)(2)).

(2) *Health plan* excludes:

(i) Any policy, plan, or program to the extent that it provides, or pays for the cost of, excepted benefits that are listed in section 2791(c)(1) of the PHS Act, 42 U.S.C. 300gg–91(c)(1); and

(ii) A government-funded program (other than one listed in paragraph (1)(i)–(xvi) of this definition):

(A) Whose principal purpose is other than providing, or paying the cost of, health care; or

(B) Whose principal activity is:

(1) The direct provision of health care to persons; or

(2) The making of grants to fund the direct provision of health care to persons.

Implementation specification means specific requirements or instructions for implementing a standard.

Modify or *modification* refers to a change adopted by the Secretary, through regulation, to a standard or an implementation specification.

Secretary means the Secretary of Health and Human Services or any other officer or employee of HHS to whom the authority involved has been delegated.

Small health plan means a health plan with annual receipts of $5 million or less.

Standard means a rule, condition, or requirement:

(1) Describing the following information for products, systems, services or practices:

(i) Classification of components.

(ii) Specification of materials, performance, or operations; or

(iii) Delineation of procedures; or

(2) With respect to the privacy of individually identifiable health information.

Standard setting organization (SSO) means an organization accredited by the American National Standards Institute that develops and maintains standards for information transactions or data elements, or any other standard that is necessary for, or will facilitate the implementation of, this part.

State refers to one of the following:

(1) For a health plan established or regulated by Federal law, State has the meaning set forth in the applicable section of the United States Code for such health plan.

(2) For all other purposes, *State* means any of the several States, the District of Columbia, the Commonwealth of Puerto Rico, the Virgin Islands, and Guam.

Trading partner agreement means an agreement related to the exchange of information in electronic transactions, whether the agreement is distinct or part of a larger agreement, between each party to the agreement. (For example, a trading partner agreement may specify, among other things, the duties and responsibilities of each party in conducting a standard transaction.)

Transaction means the transmission of information between two parties to carry out financial or administrative activities related to health care. It includes the following types of information transmissions:

(1) Health care claims or equivalent encounter information.

(2) Health care payment and remittance advice.

(3) Coordination of benefits.

(4) Health care claim status.

(5) Enrollment and disenrollment in a health plan.

(6) Eligibility for a health plan.

(7) Health plan premium payments.

(8) Referral certification and authorization.

(9) First report of injury.

(10) Health claims attachments.

(11) Other transactions that the Secretary may prescribe by regulation.

Workforce means employees, volunteers, trainees, and other persons whose conduct, in the performance of work for a covered entity, is under the direct control of such entity, whether or not they are paid by the covered entity.

§ 160.104 Modifications.

(a) Except as provided in paragraph (b) of this section, the Secretary may adopt a modification to a standard or implementation specification adopted under this subchapter no more frequently than once every 12 months.

(b) The Secretary may adopt a modification at any time during the first year after the standard or implementation specification is initially adopted, if the Secretary determines that the modification is necessary to permit compliance with the standard or implementation specification.

(c) The Secretary will establish the compliance date for any standard or implementation specification modified under this section.

(1) The compliance date for a modification is no earlier than 180 days after the effective date of the final rule in which the Secretary adopts the modification.

(2) The Secretary may consider the extent of the modification and the time needed to comply with the modification in determining the compliance date for the modification.

(3) The Secretary may extend the compliance date for small health plans, as the Secretary determines is appropriate.

Subpart B—Preemption of State Law

§ 160.201 Applicability.

The provisions of this subpart implement section 1178 of the Act, as added by section 262 of Public Law 104–191.

§ 160.202 Definitions.

For purposes of this subpart, the following terms have the following meanings:

Contrary, when used to compare a provision of State law to a standard, requirement, or implementation specification adopted under this subchapter, means:

(1) A covered entity would find it impossible to comply with both the State and federal requirements; or

(2) The provision of State law stands as an obstacle to the accomplishment and execution of the full purposes and objectives of part C of title XI of the Act or section 264 of Pub. L. 104–191, as applicable.

More stringent means, in the context of a comparison of a provision of State law and a standard, requirement, or implementation specification adopted under subpart E of part 164 of this subchapter, a State law that meets one or more of the following criteria:

(1) With respect to a use or disclosure, the law prohibits or restricts a use or disclosure in circumstances under which such use or disclosure otherwise would be permitted under this subchapter, except if the disclosure is:

(i) Required by the Secretary in connection with determining whether a covered entity is in compliance with this subchapter; or

(ii) To the individual who is the subject of the individually identifiable health information.

(2) With respect to the rights of an individual who is the subject of the individually identifiable health information of access to or amendment of individually identifiable health information, permits greater rights of access or amendment, as applicable; provided that, nothing in this subchapter may be construed to preempt any State law to the extent that it authorizes or prohibits disclosure of protected health information about a minor to a parent, guardian, or person acting *in loco parentis* of such minor.

(3) With respect to information to be provided to an individual who is the subject of the individually identifiable health information about a use, a disclosure, rights, and remedies, provides the greater amount of information.

(4) With respect to the form or substance of an authorization or consent for use or disclosure of individually identifiable health information, provides requirements that narrow the scope or duration, increase the privacy protections afforded (such as by expanding the criteria for), or reduce the coercive effect of the circumstances surrounding the authorization or consent, as applicable.

(5) With respect to recordkeeping or requirements relating to accounting of disclosures, provides for the retention or reporting of more detailed information or for a longer duration.

145

(6) With respect to any other matter, provides greater privacy protection for the individual who is the subject of the individually identifiable health information.

Relates to the privacy of individually identifiable health information means, with respect to a State law, that the State law has the specific purpose of protecting the privacy of health information or affects the privacy of health information in a direct, clear, and substantial way.

State law means a constitution, statute, regulation, rule, common law, or other State action having the force and effect of law.

§ 160.203 General rule and exceptions.

A standard, requirement, or implementation specification adopted under this subchapter that is contrary to a provision of State law preempts the provision of State law. This general rule applies, except if one or more of the following conditions is met:

(a) A determination is made by the Secretary under § 160.204 that the provision of State law:

(1) Is necessary:

(i) To prevent fraud and abuse related to the provision of or payment for health care;

(ii) To ensure appropriate State regulation of insurance and health plans to the extent expressly authorized by statute or regulation;

(iii) For State reporting on health care delivery or costs; or

(iv) For purposes of serving a compelling need related to public health, safety, or welfare, and, if a standard, requirement, or implementation specification under part 164 of this subchapter is at issue, if the Secretary determines that the intrusion into privacy is warranted when balanced against the need to be served; or

(2) Has as its principal purpose the regulation of the manufacture, registration, distribution, dispensing, or other control of any controlled substances (as defined in 21 U.S.C. 802), or that is deemed a controlled substance by State law.

(b) The provision of State law relates to the privacy of health information and is more stringent than a standard, requirement, or implementation specification adopted under subpart E of part 164 of this subchapter.

(c) The provision of State law, including State procedures established under such law, as applicable, provides for the reporting of disease or injury, child abuse, birth, or death, or for the conduct of public health surveillance, investigation, or intervention.

(d) The provision of State law requires a health plan to report, or to provide access to, information for the purpose of management audits, financial audits, program monitoring and evaluation, or the licensure or certification of facilities or individuals.

§ 160.204 Process for requesting exception determinations.

(a) A request to except a provision of State law from preemption under § 160.203(a) may be submitted to the Secretary. A request by a State must be submitted through its chief elected official, or his or her designee. The request must be in writing and include the following information:

(1) The State law for which the exception is requested;

(2) The particular standard, requirement, or implementation specification for which the exception is requested;

(3) The part of the standard or other provision that will not be implemented based on the exception or the additional data to be collected based on the exception, as appropriate;

(4) How health care providers, health plans, and other entities would be affected by the exception;

(5) The reasons why the State law should not be preempted by the federal standard, requirement, or implementation specification, including how the State law meets one or more of the criteria at § 160.203(a); and

(6) Any other information the Secretary may request in order to make the determination.

(b) Requests for exception under this section must be submitted to the Secretary at an address that will be published in the **Federal Register**. Until the Secretary's determination is made, the standard, requirement, or implementation specification under this subchapter remains in effect.

(c) The Secretary's determination under this section will be made on the basis of the extent to which the information provided and other factors demonstrate that one or more of the criteria at § 160.203(a) has been met.

§ 160.205 Duration of effectiveness of exception determinations.

An exception granted under this subpart remains in effect until:

(a) Either the State law or the federal standard, requirement, or implementation specification that provided the basis for the exception is materially changed such that the ground for the exception no longer exists; or

(b) The Secretary revokes the exception, based on a determination that the ground supporting the need for the exception no longer exists.

Subpart C—Compliance and Enforcement

§ 160.300 Applicability.

This subpart applies to actions by the Secretary, covered entities, and others with respect to ascertaining the compliance by covered entities with and the enforcement of the applicable requirements of this part 160 and the applicable standards, requirements, and implementation specifications of subpart E of part 164 of this subchapter.

§ 160.302 Definitions.

As used in this subpart, terms defined in § 164.501 of this subchapter have the same meanings given to them in that section.

§ 160.304 Principles for achieving compliance.

(a) *Cooperation.* The Secretary will, to the extent practicable, seek the cooperation of covered entities in obtaining compliance with the applicable requirements of this part 160 and the applicable standards, requirements, and implementation specifications of subpart E of part 164 of this subchapter.

(b) *Assistance.* The Secretary may provide technical assistance to covered entities to help them comply voluntarily with the applicable requirements of this part 160 or the applicable standards, requirements, and implementation specifications of subpart E of part 164 of this subchapter.

§ 160.306 Complaints to the Secretary.

(a) *Right to file a complaint.* A person who believes a covered entity is not complying with the applicable requirements of this part 160 or the applicable standards, requirements, and implementation specifications of subpart E of part 164 of this subchapter may file a complaint with the Secretary.

(b) *Requirements for filing complaints.* Complaints under this section must meet the following requirements:

(1) A complaint must be filed in writing, either on paper or electronically.

(2) A complaint must name the entity that is the subject of the complaint and describe the acts or omissions believed to be in violation of the applicable requirements of this part 160 or the applicable standards, requirements, and implementation specifications of subpart E of part 164 of this subchapter.

(3) A complaint must be filed within 180 days of when the complainant knew or should have known that the act or omission complained of occurred, unless this time limit is waived by the Secretary for good cause shown.

(4) The Secretary may prescribe additional procedures for the filing of complaints, as well as the place and manner of filing, by notice in the **Federal Register**.

(c) *Investigation.* The Secretary may investigate complaints filed under this section. Such investigation may include a review of the pertinent policies, procedures, or practices of the covered entity and of the circumstances regarding any alleged acts or omissions concerning compliance.

§ 160.308 Compliance reviews.

The Secretary may conduct compliance reviews to determine whether covered entities are complying with the applicable requirements of this part 160 and the applicable standards, requirements, and implementation specifications of subpart E of part 164 of this subchapter.

§ 160.310 Responsibilities of covered entities.

(a) *Provide records and compliance reports.* A covered entity must keep such records and submit such compliance reports, in such time and manner and containing such information, as the Secretary may determine to be necessary to enable the Secretary to ascertain whether the covered entity has complied or is complying with the applicable requirements of this part 160 and applicable standards, requirements, and implementation specifications of subpart E of part 164 of this subchapter.

(b) *Cooperate with complaint investigations and compliance reviews.* A covered entity must cooperate with the Secretary, if the Secretary undertakes an investigation or compliance review of the policies, procedures, or practices of a covered entity to determine whether it is complying with the applicable requirements of this part 160 and the standards, requirements, and implementation specifications of subpart E of part 164 of this subchapter.

(c) *Permit access to information.* (1) A covered entity must permit access by the Secretary during normal business hours to its facilities, books, records, accounts, and other sources of information, including protected health information, that are pertinent to ascertaining compliance with the applicable requirements of this part 160 and the applicable standards, requirements, and implementation specifications of subpart E of part 164 of this subchapter. If the Secretary determines that exigent circumstances exist, such as when documents may be hidden or destroyed, a covered entity

must permit access by the Secretary at any time and without notice.

(2) If any information required of a covered entity under this section is in the exclusive possession of any other agency, institution, or person and the other agency, institution, or person fails or refuses to furnish the information, the covered entity must so certify and set forth what efforts it has made to obtain the information.

(3) Protected health information obtained by the Secretary in connection with an investigation or compliance review under this subpart will not be disclosed by the Secretary, except if necessary for ascertaining or enforcing compliance with the applicable requirements of this part 160 and the applicable standards, requirements, and implementation specifications of subpart E of part 164 of this subchapter, or if otherwise required by law.

§ 160.312 Secretarial action regarding complaints and compliance reviews.

(a) *Resolution where noncompliance is indicated.* (1) If an investigation pursuant to § 160.306 or a compliance review pursuant to § 160.308 indicates a failure to comply, the Secretary will so inform the covered entity and, if the matter arose from a complaint, the complainant, in writing and attempt to resolve the matter by informal means whenever possible.

(2) If the Secretary finds the covered entity is not in compliance and determines that the matter cannot be resolved by informal means, the Secretary may issue to the covered entity and, if the matter arose from a complaint, to the complainant written findings documenting the non-compliance.

(b) *Resolution when no violation is found.* If, after an investigation or compliance review, the Secretary determines that further action is not warranted, the Secretary will so inform the covered entity and, if the matter arose from a complaint, the complainant in writing.

2. A new Part 164 is added to read as follows:

PART 164—SECURITY AND PRIVACY

Subpart A—General Provisions
Sec.

Authority: 42 U.S.C. 1320d–2 and 1320d–4, sec. 264 of Pub. L. 104–191, 110 Stat. 2033–2034 (42 U.S.C. 1320(d–2(note)).

Subpart A—General Provisions

§ 164.102 Statutory basis.

The provisions of this part are adopted pursuant to the Secretary's authority to prescribe standards, requirements, and implementation standards under part C of title XI of the Act and section 264 of Public Law 104–191.

§ 164.104 Applicability.

Except as otherwise provided, the provisions of this part apply to covered entities: health plans, health care clearinghouses, and health care providers who transmit health information in electronic form in connection with any transaction referred to in section 1173(a)(1) of the Act.

§ 164.106 Relationship to other parts.

In complying with the requirements of this part, covered entities are required to comply with the applicable provisions of parts 160 and 162 of this subchapter.

Subpart B–D—[Reserved]

Subpart E—Privacy of Individually Identifiable Health Information

§ 164.500 Applicability.

(a) Except as otherwise provided herein, the standards, requirements, and

147

implementation specifications of this subpart apply to covered entities with respect to protected health information.

(b) Health care clearinghouses must comply with the standards, requirements, and implementation specifications as follows:

(1) When a health care clearinghouse creates or receives protected health information as a business associate of another covered entity, the clearinghouse must comply with:

(i) Section 164.500 relating to applicability;

(ii) Section 164.501 relating to definitions;

(iii) Section 164.502 relating to uses and disclosures of protected health information, except that a clearinghouse is prohibited from using or disclosing protected health information other than as permitted in the business associate contract under which it created or received the protected health information;

(iv) Section 164.504 relating to the organizational requirements for covered entities, including the designation of health care components of a covered entity;

(v) Section 164.512 relating to uses and disclosures for which consent, individual authorization or an opportunity to agree or object is not required, except that a clearinghouse is prohibited from using or disclosing protected health information other than as permitted in the business associate contract under which it created or received the protected health information;

(vi) Section 164.532 relating to transition requirements; and

(vii) Section 164.534 relating to compliance dates for initial implementation of the privacy standards.

(2) When a health care clearinghouse creates or receives protected health information other than as a business associate of a covered entity, the clearinghouse must comply with all of the standards, requirements, and implementation specifications of this subpart.

(c) The standards, requirements, and implementation specifications of this subpart do not apply to the Department of Defense or to any other federal agency, or non-governmental organization acting on its behalf, when providing health care to overseas foreign national beneficiaries.

§ 164.501 Definitions.

As used in this subpart, the following terms have the following meanings:

Correctional institution means any penal or correctional facility, jail, reformatory, detention center, work farm, halfway house, or residential community program center operated by, or under contract to, the United States, a State, a territory, a political subdivision of a State or territory, or an Indian tribe, for the confinement or rehabilitation of persons charged with or convicted of a criminal offense or other persons held in lawful custody. *Other persons* held in lawful custody includes juvenile offenders adjudicated delinquent, aliens detained awaiting deportation, persons committed to mental institutions through the criminal justice system, witnesses, or others awaiting charges or trial.

Covered functions means those functions of a covered entity the performance of which makes the entity a health plan, health care provider, or health care clearinghouse.

Data aggregation means, with respect to protected health information created or received by a business associate in its capacity as the business associate of a covered entity, the combining of such protected health information by the business associate with the protected health information received by the business associate in its capacity as a business associate of another covered entity, to permit data analyses that relate to the health care operations of the respective covered entities.

Designated record set means:

(1) A group of records maintained by or for a covered entity that is:

(i) The medical records and billing records about individuals maintained by or for a covered health care provider;

(ii) The enrollment, payment, claims adjudication, and case or medical management record systems maintained by or for a health plan; or

(iii) Used, in whole or in part, by or for the covered entity to make decisions about individuals.

(2) For purposes of this paragraph, the term record means any item, collection, or grouping of information that includes protected health information and is maintained, collected, used, or disseminated by or for a covered entity.

Direct treatment relationship means a treatment relationship between an individual and a health care provider that is not an indirect treatment relationship.

Disclosure means the release, transfer, provision of access to, or divulging in any other manner of information outside the entity holding the information.

Health care operations means any of the following activities of the covered entity to the extent that the activities are related to covered functions, and any of the following activities of an organized health care arrangement in which the covered entity participates:

(1) Conducting quality assessment and improvement activities, including outcomes evaluation and development of clinical guidelines, provided that the obtaining of generalizable knowledge is not the primary purpose of any studies resulting from such activities; population-based activities relating to improving health or reducing health care costs, protocol development, case management and care coordination, contacting of health care providers and patients with information about treatment alternatives; and related functions that do not include treatment;

(2) Reviewing the competence or qualifications of health care professionals, evaluating practitioner and provider performance, health plan performance, conducting training programs in which students, trainees, or practitioners in areas of health care learn under supervision to practice or improve their skills as health care providers, training of non-health care professionals, accreditation, certification, licensing, or credentialing activities;

(3) Underwriting, premium rating, and other activities relating to the creation, renewal or replacement of a contract of health insurance or health benefits, and ceding, securing, or placing a contract for reinsurance of risk relating to claims for health care (including stop-loss insurance and excess of loss insurance), provided that the requirements of § 164.514(g) are met, if applicable;

(4) Conducting or arranging for medical review, legal services, and auditing functions, including fraud and abuse detection and compliance programs;

(5) Business planning and development, such as conducting cost-management and planning-related analyses related to managing and operating the entity, including formulary development and administration, development or improvement of methods of payment or coverage policies; and

(6) Business management and general administrative activities of the entity, including, but not limited to:

(i) Management activities relating to implementation of and compliance with the requirements of this subchapter;

(ii) Customer service, including the provision of data analyses for policy holders, plan sponsors, or other customers, provided that protected health information is not disclosed to such policy holder, plan sponsor, or customer.

(iii) Resolution of internal grievances;

(iv) Due diligence in connection with the sale or transfer of assets to a potential successor in interest, if the potential successor in interest is a covered entity or, following completion of the sale or transfer, will become a covered entity; and

(v) Consistent with the applicable requirements of § 164.514, creating de-identified health information, fundraising for the benefit of the covered entity, and marketing for which an individual authorization is not required as described in § 164.514(e)(2).

Health oversight agency means an agency or authority of the United States, a State, a territory, a political subdivision of a State or territory, or an Indian tribe, or a person or entity acting under a grant of authority from or contract with such public agency, including the employees or agents of such public agency or its contractors or persons or entities to whom it has granted authority, that is authorized by law to oversee the health care system (whether public or private) or government programs in which health information is necessary to determine eligibility or compliance, or to enforce civil rights laws for which health information is relevant.

Indirect treatment relationship means a relationship between an individual and a health care provider in which:

(1) The health care provider delivers health care to the individual based on the orders of another health care provider; and

(2) The health care provider typically provides services or products, or reports the diagnosis or results associated with the health care, directly to another health care provider, who provides the services or products or reports to the individual.

Individual means the person who is the subject of protected health information.

Individually identifiable health information is information that is a subset of health information, including demographic information collected from an individual, and:

(1) Is created or received by a health care provider, health plan, employer, or health care clearinghouse; and

(2) Relates to the past, present, or future physical or mental health or condition of an individual; the provision of health care to an individual; or the past, present, or future payment for the provision of health care to an individual; and

(i) That identifies the individual; or

(ii) With respect to which there is a reasonable basis to believe the information can be used to identify the individual.

Inmate means a person incarcerated in or otherwise confined to a correctional institution.

Law enforcement official means an officer or employee of any agency or authority of the United States, a State, a territory, a political subdivision of a State or territory, or an Indian tribe, who is empowered by law to:

(1) Investigate or conduct an official inquiry into a potential violation of law; or

(2) Prosecute or otherwise conduct a criminal, civil, or administrative proceeding arising from an alleged violation of law.

Marketing means to make a communication about a product or service a purpose of which is to encourage recipients of the communication to purchase or use the product or service.

(1) *Marketing* does not include communications that meet the requirements of paragraph (2) of this definition and that are made by a covered entity:

(i) For the purpose of describing the entities participating in a health care provider network or health plan network, or for the purpose of describing if and the extent to which a product or service (or payment for such product or service) is provided by a covered entity or included in a plan of benefits; or

(ii) That are tailored to the circumstances of a particular individual and the communications are:

(A) Made by a health care provider to an individual as part of the treatment of the individual, and for the purpose of furthering the treatment of that individual; or

(B) Made by a health care provider or health plan to an individual in the course of managing the treatment of that individual, or for the purpose of directing or recommending to that individual alternative treatments, therapies, health care providers, or settings of care.

(2) A communication described in paragraph (1) of this definition is not included in marketing if:

(i) The communication is made orally; or

(ii) The communication is in writing and the covered entity does not receive direct or indirect remuneration from a third party for making the communication.

Organized health care arrangement means:

(1) A clinically integrated care setting in which individuals typically receive health care from more than one health care provider;

(2) An organized system of health care in which more than one covered entity participates, and in which the participating covered entities:

(i) Hold themselves out to the public as participating in a joint arrangement; and

(ii) Participate in joint activities that include at least one of the following:

(A) Utilization review, in which health care decisions by participating covered entities are reviewed by other participating covered entities or by a third party on their behalf;

(B) Quality assessment and improvement activities, in which treatment provided by participating covered entities is assessed by other participating covered entities or by a third party on their behalf; or

(C) Payment activities, if the financial risk for delivering health care is shared, in part or in whole, by participating covered entities through the joint arrangement and if protected health information created or received by a covered entity is reviewed by other participating covered entities or by a third party on their behalf for the purpose of administering the sharing of financial risk.

(3) A group health plan and a health insurance issuer or HMO with respect to such group health plan, but only with respect to protected health information created or received by such health insurance issuer or HMO that relates to individuals who are or who have been participants or beneficiaries in such group health plan;

(4) A group health plan and one or more other group health plans each of which are maintained by the same plan sponsor; or

(5) The group health plans described in paragraph (4) of this definition and health insurance issuers or HMOs with respect to such group health plans, but only with respect to protected health information created or received by such health insurance issuers or HMOs that relates to individuals who are or have been participants or beneficiaries in any of such group health plans.

Payment means:

(1) The activities undertaken by:

(i) A health plan to obtain premiums or to determine or fulfill its responsibility for coverage and provision of benefits under the health plan; or

(ii) A covered health care provider or health plan to obtain or provide reimbursement for the provision of health care; and

(2) The activities in paragraph (1) of this definition relate to the individual to whom health care is provided and include, but are not limited to:

149

(i) Determinations of eligibility or coverage (including coordination of benefits or the determination of cost sharing amounts), and adjudication or subrogation of health benefit claims;

(ii) Risk adjusting amounts due based on enrollee health status and demographic characteristics;

(iii) Billing, claims management, collection activities, obtaining payment under a contract for reinsurance (including stop-loss insurance and excess of loss insurance), and related health care data processing;

(iv) Review of health care services with respect to medical necessity, coverage under a health plan, appropriateness of care, or justification of charges;

(v) Utilization review activities, including precertification and preauthorization of services, concurrent and retrospective review of services; and

(vi) Disclosure to consumer reporting agencies of any of the following protected health information relating to collection of premiums or reimbursement:

(A) Name and address;

(B) Date of birth;

(C) Social security number;

(D) Payment history;

(E) Account number; and

(F) Name and address of the health care provider and/or health plan.

Plan sponsor is defined as defined at section 3(16)(B) of ERISA, 29 U.S.C. 1002(16)(B).

Protected health information means individually identifiable health information:

(1) Except as provided in paragraph (2) of this definition, that is:

(i) Transmitted by electronic media;

(ii) Maintained in any medium described in the definition of *electronic media* at § 162.103 of this subchapter; or

(iii) Transmitted or maintained in any other form or medium.

(2) *Protected health information* excludes individually identifiable health information in:

(i) Education records covered by the Family Educational Right and Privacy Act, as amended, 20 U.S.C. 1232g; and

(ii) Records described at 20 U.S.C. 1232g(a)(4)(B)(iv).

Psychotherapy notes means notes recorded (in any medium) by a health care provider who is a mental health professional documenting or analyzing the contents of conversation during a private counseling session or a group, joint, or family counseling session and that are separated from the rest of the individual's medical record.

Psychotherapy notes excludes medication prescription and monitoring, counseling session start and stop times, the modalities and frequencies of treatment furnished, results of clinical tests, and any summary of the following items: Diagnosis, functional status, the treatment plan, symptoms, prognosis, and progress to date.

Public health authority means an agency or authority of the United States, a State, a territory, a political subdivision of a State or territory, or an Indian tribe, or a person or entity acting under a grant of authority from or contract with such public agency, including the employees or agents of such public agency or its contractors or persons or entities to whom it has granted authority, that is responsible for public health matters as part of its official mandate.

Required by law means a mandate contained in law that compels a covered entity to make a use or disclosure of protected health information and that is enforceable in a court of law. *Required by law* includes, but is not limited to, court orders and court-ordered warrants; subpoenas or summons issued by a court, grand jury, a governmental or tribal inspector general, or an administrative body authorized to require the production of information; a civil or an authorized investigative demand; Medicare conditions of participation with respect to health care providers participating in the program; and statutes or regulations that require the production of information, including statutes or regulations that require such information if payment is sought under a government program providing public benefits.

Research means a systematic investigation, including research development, testing, and evaluation, designed to develop or contribute to generalizable knowledge.

Treatment means the provision, coordination, or management of health care and related services by one or more health care providers, including the coordination or management of health care by a health care provider with a third party; consultation between health care providers relating to a patient; or the referral of a patient for health care from one health care provider to another.

Use means, with respect to individually identifiable health information, the sharing, employment, application, utilization, examination, or analysis of such information within an entity that maintains such information.

§ 164.502 Uses and disclosures of protected health information: general rules.

(a) *Standard.* A covered entity may not use or disclose protected health information, except as permitted or required by this subpart or by subpart C of part 160 of this subchapter.

(1) *Permitted uses and disclosures.* A covered entity is permitted to use or disclose protected health information as follows:

(i) To the individual;

(ii) Pursuant to and in compliance with a consent that complies with § 164.506, to carry out treatment, payment, or health care operations;

(iii) Without consent, if consent is not required under § 164.506(a) and has not been sought under § 164.506(a)(4), to carry out treatment, payment, or health care operations, except with respect to psychotherapy notes;

(iv) Pursuant to and in compliance with a valid authorization under § 164.508;

(v) Pursuant to an agreement under, or as otherwise permitted by, § 164.510; and

(vi) As permitted by and in compliance with this section, § 164.512, or § 164.514(e), (f), and (g).

(2) *Required disclosures.* A covered entity is required to disclose protected health information:

(i) To an individual, when requested under, and required by § 164.524 or § 164.528; and

(ii) When required by the Secretary under subpart C of part 160 of this subchapter to investigate or determine the covered entity's compliance with this subpart.

(b) *Standard: Minimum necessary.* (1) *Minimum necessary applies.* When using or disclosing protected health information or when requesting protected health information from another covered entity, a covered entity must make reasonable efforts to limit protected health information to the minimum necessary to accomplish the intended purpose of the use, disclosure, or request.

(2) *Minimum necessary does not apply.* This requirement does not apply to:

(i) Disclosures to or requests by a health care provider for treatment;

(ii) Uses or disclosures made to the individual, as permitted under paragraph (a)(1)(i) of this section, as required by paragraph (a)(2)(i) of this section, or pursuant to an authorization under § 164.508, except for authorizations requested by the covered entity under § 164.508(d), (e), or (f);

(iii) Disclosures made to the Secretary in accordance with subpart C of part 160 of this subchapter;

(iv) Uses or disclosures that are required by law, as described by § 164.512(a); and

(v) Uses or disclosures that are required for compliance with applicable requirements of this subchapter.

(c) *Standard: Uses and disclosures of protected health information subject to an agreed upon restriction.* A covered entity that has agreed to a restriction pursuant to § 164.522(a)(1) may not use or disclose the protected health information covered by the restriction in violation of such restriction, except as otherwise provided in § 164.522(a).

(d) *Standard: Uses and disclosures of de-identified protected health information.*

(1) *Uses and disclosures to create de-identified information.* A covered entity may use protected health information to create information that is not individually identifiable health information or disclose protected health information only to a business associate for such purpose, whether or not the de-identified information is to be used by the covered entity.

(2) *Uses and disclosures of de-identified information.* Health information that meets the standard and implementation specifications for de-identification under § 164.514(a) and (b) is considered not to be individually identifiable health information, *i.e.*, de-identified. The requirements of this subpart do not apply to information that has been de-identified in accordance with the applicable requirements of § 164.514, provided that:

(i) Disclosure of a code or other means of record identification designed to enable coded or otherwise de-identified information to be re-identified constitutes disclosure of protected health information; and

(ii) If de-identified information is re-identified, a covered entity may use or disclose such re-identified information only as permitted or required by this subpart.

(e)(1) *Standard: Disclosures to business associates.* (i) A covered entity may disclose protected health information to a business associate and may allow a business associate to create or receive protected health information on its behalf, if the covered entity obtains satisfactory assurance that the business associate will appropriately safeguard the information.

(ii) This standard does not apply:

(A) With respect to disclosures by a covered entity to a health care provider concerning the treatment of the individual;

(B) With respect to disclosures by a group health plan or a health insurance issuer or HMO with respect to a group

health plan to the plan sponsor, to the extent that the requirements of § 164.504(f) apply and are met; or

(C) With respect to uses or disclosures by a health plan that is a government program providing public benefits, if eligibility for, or enrollment in, the health plan is determined by an agency other than the agency administering the health plan, or if the protected health information used to determine enrollment or eligibility in the health plan is collected by an agency other than the agency administering the health plan, and such activity is authorized by law, with respect to the collection and sharing of individually identifiable health information for the performance of such functions by the health plan and the agency other than the agency administering the health plan.

(iii) A covered entity that violates the satisfactory assurances it provided as a business associate of another covered entity will be in noncompliance with the standards, implementation specifications, and requirements of this paragraph and § 164.504(e).

(2) *Implementation specification: documentation.* A covered entity must document the satisfactory assurances required by paragraph (e)(1) of this section through a written contract or other written agreement or arrangement with the business associate that meets the applicable requirements of § 164.504(e).

(f) *Standard: Deceased individuals.* A covered entity must comply with the requirements of this subpart with respect to the protected health information of a deceased individual.

(g)(1) *Standard: Personal representatives.* As specified in this paragraph, a covered entity must, except as provided in paragraphs (g)(3) and (g)(5) of this section, treat a personal representative as the individual for purposes of this subchapter.

(2) *Implementation specification: adults and emancipated minors.* If under applicable law a person has authority to act on behalf of an individual who is an adult or an emancipated minor in making decisions related to health care, a covered entity must treat such person as a personal representative under this subchapter, with respect to protected health information relevant to such personal representation.

(3) *Implementation specification: unemancipated minors.* If under applicable law a parent, guardian, or other person acting *in loco parentis* has authority to act on behalf of an individual who is an unemancipated minor in making decisions related to

health care, a covered entity must treat such person as a personal representative under this subchapter, with respect to protected health information relevant to such personal representation, except that such person may not be a personal representative of an unemancipated minor, and the minor has the authority to act as an individual, with respect to protected health information pertaining to a health care service, if:

(i) The minor consents to such health care service; no other consent to such health care service is required by law, regardless of whether the consent of another person has also been obtained; and the minor has not requested that such person be treated as the personal representative;

(ii) The minor may lawfully obtain such health care service without the consent of a parent, guardian, or other person acting *in loco parentis*, and the minor, a court, or another person authorized by law consents to such health care service; or

(iii) A parent, guardian, or other person acting *in loco parentis* assents to an agreement of confidentiality between a covered health care provider and the minor with respect to such health care service.

(4) *Implementation specification: Deceased individuals.* If under applicable law an executor, administrator, or other person has authority to act on behalf of a deceased individual or of the individual's estate, a covered entity must treat such person as a personal representative under this subchapter, with respect to protected health information relevant to such personal representation.

(5) *Implementation specification: Abuse, neglect, endangerment situations.* Notwithstanding a State law or any requirement of this paragraph to the contrary, a covered entity may elect not to treat a person as the personal representative of an individual if:

(i) The covered entity has a reasonable belief that:

(A) The individual has been or may be subjected to domestic violence, abuse, or neglect by such person; or

(B) Treating such person as the personal representative could endanger the individual; and

(ii) The covered entity, in the exercise of professional judgment, decides that it is not in the best interest of the individual to treat the person as the individual's personal representative.

(h) *Standard: Confidential communications.* A covered health care provider or health plan must comply with the applicable requirements of § 164.522(b) in communicating protected health information.

151

(i) *Standard: Uses and disclosures consistent with notice.* A covered entity that is required by § 164.520 to have a notice may not use or disclose protected health information in a manner inconsistent with such notice. A covered entity that is required by § 164.520(b)(1)(iii) to include a specific statement in its notice if it intends to engage in an activity listed in § 164.520(b)(1)(iii)(A)–(C), may not use or disclose protected health information for such activities, unless the required statement is included in the notice.

(j) *Standard: Disclosures by whistleblowers and workforce member crime victims.*

(1) *Disclosures by whistleblowers.* A covered entity is not considered to have violated the requirements of this subpart if a member of its workforce or a business associate discloses protected health information, provided that:

(i) The workforce member or business associate believes in good faith that the covered entity has engaged in conduct that is unlawful or otherwise violates professional or clinical standards, or that the care, services, or conditions provided by the covered entity potentially endangers one or more patients, workers, or the public; and

(ii) The disclosure is to:

(A) A health oversight agency or public health authority authorized by law to investigate or otherwise oversee the relevant conduct or conditions of the covered entity or to an appropriate health care accreditation organization for the purpose of reporting the allegation of failure to meet professional standards or misconduct by the covered entity; or

(B) An attorney retained by or on behalf of the workforce member or business associate for the purpose of determining the legal options of the workforce member or business associate with regard to the conduct described in paragraph (j)(1)(i) of this section.

(2) *Disclosures by workforce members who are victims of a crime.* A covered entity is not considered to have violated the requirements of this subpart if a member of its workforce who is the victim of a criminal act discloses protected health information to a law enforcement official, provided that:

(i) The protected health information disclosed is about the suspected perpetrator of the criminal act; and

(ii) The protected health information disclosed is limited to the information listed in § 164.512(f)(2)(i).

§ 164.504 Uses and disclosures: Organizational requirements.

(a) *Definitions.* As used in this section:

Common control exists if an entity has the power, directly or indirectly, significantly to influence or direct the actions or policies of another entity.

Common ownership exists if an entity or entities possess an ownership or equity interest of 5 percent or more in another entity.

Health care component has the following meaning:

(1) Components of a covered entity that perform covered functions are part of the health care component.

(2) Another component of the covered entity is part of the entity's health care component to the extent that:

(i) It performs, with respect to a component that performs covered functions, activities that would make such other component a business associate of the component that performs covered functions if the two components were separate legal entities; and

(ii) The activities involve the use or disclosure of protected health information that such other component creates or receives from or on behalf of the component that performs covered functions.

Hybrid entity means a single legal entity that is a covered entity and whose covered functions are not its primary functions.

Plan administration functions means administration functions performed by the plan sponsor of a group health plan on behalf of the group health plan and excludes functions performed by the plan sponsor in connection with any other benefit or benefit plan of the plan sponsor.

Summary health information means information, that may be individually identifiable health information, and:

(1) That summarizes the claims history, claims expenses, or type of claims experienced by individuals for whom a plan sponsor has provided health benefits under a group health plan; and

(2) From which the information described at § 164.514(b)(2)(i) has been deleted, except that the geographic information described in § 164.514(b)(2)(i)(B) need only be aggregated to the level of a five digit zip code.

(b) *Standard: Health care component.* If a covered entity is a hybrid entity, the requirements of this subpart, other than the requirements of this section, apply only to the health care component(s) of the entity, as specified in this section.

(c)(1) *Implementation specification: Application of other provisions.* In applying a provision of this subpart, other than this section, to a hybrid entity:

(i) A reference in such provision to a "covered entity" refers to a health care component of the covered entity;

(ii) A reference in such provision to a "health plan," "covered health care provider," or "health care clearinghouse" refers to a health care component of the covered entity if such health care component performs the functions of a health plan, covered health care provider, or health care clearinghouse, as applicable; and

(iii) A reference in such provision to "protected health information" refers to protected health information that is created or received by or on behalf of the health care component of the covered entity.

(2) *Implementation specifications: Safeguard requirements.* The covered entity that is a hybrid entity must ensure that a health care component of the entity complies with the applicable requirements of this subpart. In particular, and without limiting this requirement, such covered entity must ensure that:

(i) Its health care component does not disclose protected health information to another component of the covered entity in circumstances in which this subpart would prohibit such disclosure if the health care component and the other component were separate and distinct legal entities;

(ii) A component that is described by paragraph (2)(i) of the definition of *health care component* in this section does not use or disclose protected health information that is within paragraph (2)(ii) of such definition for purposes of its activities other than those described by paragraph (2)(i) of such definition in a way prohibited by this subpart; and

(iii) If a person performs duties for both the health care component in the capacity of a member of the workforce of such component and for another component of the entity in the same capacity with respect to that component, such workforce member must not use or disclose protected health information created or received in the course of or incident to the member's work for the health care component in a way prohibited by this subpart.

(3) *Implementation specifications: Responsibilities of the covered entity.* A covered entity that is a hybrid entity has the following responsibilities:

(i) For purposes of subpart C of part 160 of this subchapter, pertaining to compliance and enforcement, the covered entity has the responsibility to comply with this subpart.

(ii) The covered entity has the responsibility for complying with

§ 164.530(i), pertaining to the implementation of policies and procedures to ensure compliance with this subpart, including the safeguard requirements in paragraph (c)(2) of this section.

(iii) The covered entity is responsible for designating the components that are part of one or more health care components of the covered entity and documenting the designation as required by § 164.530(j).

(d)(1) *Standard: Affiliated covered entities.* Legally separate covered entities that are affiliated may designate themselves as a single covered entity for purposes of this subpart.

(2) *Implementation specifications: Requirements for designation of an affiliated covered entity.* (i) Legally separate covered entities may designate themselves (including any health care component of such covered entity) as a single affiliated covered entity, for purposes of this subpart, if all of the covered entities designated are under common ownership or control.

(ii) The designation of an affiliated covered entity must be documented and the documentation maintained as required by § 164.530(j).

(3) *Implementation specifications: Safeguard requirements.* An affiliated covered entity must ensure that:

(i) The affiliated covered entity's use and disclosure of protected health information comply with the applicable requirements of this subpart; and

(ii) If the affiliated covered entity combines the functions of a health plan, health care provider, or health care clearinghouse, the affiliated covered entity complies with paragraph (g) of this section.

(e)(1) *Standard: Business associate contracts.* (i) The contract or other arrangement between the covered entity and the business associate required by § 164.502(e)(2) must meet the requirements of paragraph (e)(2) or (e)(3) of this section, as applicable.

(ii) A covered entity is not in compliance with the standards in § 164.502(e) and paragraph (e) of this section, if the covered entity knew of a pattern of activity or practice of the business associate that constituted a material breach or violation of the business associate's obligation under the contract or other arrangement, unless the covered entity took reasonable steps to cure the breach or end the violation, as applicable, and, if such steps were unsuccessful:

(A) Terminated the contract or arrangement, if feasible; or

(B) If termination is not feasible, reported the problem to the Secretary.

(2) *Implementation specifications: Business associate contracts.* A contract between the covered entity and a business associate must:

(i) Establish the permitted and required uses and disclosures of such information by the business associate. The contract may not authorize the business associate to use or further disclose the information in a manner that would violate the requirements of this subpart, if done by the covered entity, except that:

(A) The contract may permit the business associate to use and disclose protected health information for the proper management and administration of the business associate, as provided in paragraph (e)(4) of this section; and

(B) The contract may permit the business associate to provide data aggregation services relating to the health care operations of the covered entity.

(ii) Provide that the business associate will:

(A) Not use or further disclose the information other than as permitted or required by the contract or as required by law;

(B) Use appropriate safeguards to prevent use or disclosure of the information other than as provided for by its contract;

(C) Report to the covered entity any use or disclosure of the information not provided for by its contract of which it becomes aware;

(D) Ensure that any agents, including a subcontractor, to whom it provides protected health information received from, or created or received by the business associate on behalf of, the covered entity agrees to the same restrictions and conditions that apply to the business associate with respect to such information;

(E) Make available protected health information in accordance with § 164.524;

(F) Make available protected health information for amendment and incorporate any amendments to protected health information in accordance with § 164.526;

(G) Make available the information required to provide an accounting of disclosures in accordance with § 164.528;

(H) Make its internal practices, books, and records relating to the use and disclosure of protected health information received from, or created or received by the business associate on behalf of, the covered entity available to the Secretary for purposes of determining the covered entity's compliance with this subpart; and

(I) At termination of the contract, if feasible, return or destroy all protected health information received from, or created or received by the business associate on behalf of, the covered entity that the business associate still maintains in any form and retain no copies of such information or, if such return or destruction is not feasible, extend the protections of the contract to the information and limit further uses and disclosures to those purposes that make the return or destruction of the information infeasible.

(iii) Authorize termination of the contract by the covered entity, if the covered entity determines that the business associate has violated a material term of the contract.

(3) *Implementation specifications: Other arrangements.* (i) If a covered entity and its business associate are both governmental entities:

(A) The covered entity may comply with paragraph (e) of this section by entering into a memorandum of understanding with the business associate that contains terms that accomplish the objectives of paragraph (e)(2) of this section.

(B) The covered entity may comply with paragraph (e) of this section, if other law (including regulations adopted by the covered entity or its business associate) contains requirements applicable to the business associate that accomplish the objectives of paragraph (e)(2) of this section.

(ii) If a business associate is required by law to perform a function or activity on behalf of a covered entity or to provide a service described in the definition of *business associate* in § 160.103 of this subchapter to a covered entity, such covered entity may disclose protected health information to the business associate to the extent necessary to comply with the legal mandate without meeting the requirements of this paragraph (e), provided that the covered entity attempts in good faith to obtain satisfactory assurances as required by paragraph (e)(3)(i) of this section, and, if such attempt fails, documents the attempt and the reasons that such assurances cannot be obtained.

(iii) The covered entity may omit from its other arrangements the termination authorization required by paragraph (e)(2)(iii) of this section, if such authorization is inconsistent with the statutory obligations of the covered entity or its business associate.

(4) *Implementation specifications: Other requirements for contracts and other arrangements.* (i) The contract or other arrangement between the covered entity and the business associate may

153

permit the business associate to use the information received by the business associate in its capacity as a business associate to the covered entity, if necessary:

(A) For the proper management and administration of the business associate; or

(B) To carry out the legal responsibilities of the business associate.

(ii) The contract or other arrangement between the covered entity and the business associate may permit the business associate to disclose the information received by the business associate in its capacity as a business associate for the purposes described in paragraph (e)(4)(i) of this section, if:

(A) The disclosure is required by law; or

(B)(1) The business associate obtains reasonable assurances from the person to whom the information is disclosed that it will be held confidentially and used or further disclosed only as required by law or for the purpose for which it was disclosed to the person; and

(2) The person notifies the business associate of any instances of which it is aware in which the confidentiality of the information has been breached.

(f)(1) *Standard: Requirements for group health plans.* (i) Except as provided under paragraph (f)(1)(ii) of this section or as otherwise authorized under § 164.508, a group health plan, in order to disclose protected health information to the plan sponsor or to provide for or permit the disclosure of protected health information to the plan sponsor by a health insurance issuer or HMO with respect to the group health plan, must ensure that the plan documents restrict uses and discloses of such information by the plan sponsor consistent with the requirements of this subpart.

(ii) The group health plan, or a health insurance issuer or HMO with respect to the group health plan, may disclose summary health information to the plan sponsor, if the plan sponsor requests the summary health information for the purpose of :

(A) Obtaining premium bids from health plans for providing health insurance coverage under the group health plan; or

(B) Modifying, amending, or terminating the group health plan.

(2) *Implementation specifications: Requirements for plan documents.* The plan documents of the group health plan must be amended to incorporate provisions to:

(i) Establish the permitted and required uses and disclosures of such information by the plan sponsor, provided that such permitted and required uses and disclosures may not be inconsistent with this subpart.

(ii) Provide that the group health plan will disclose protected health information to the plan sponsor only upon receipt of a certification by the plan sponsor that the plan documents have been amended to incorporate the following provisions and that the plan sponsor agrees to:

(A) Not use or further disclose the information other than as permitted or required by the plan documents or as required by law;

(B) Ensure that any agents, including a subcontractor, to whom it provides protected health information received from the group health plan agree to the same restrictions and conditions that apply to the plan sponsor with respect to such information;

(C) Not use or disclose the information for employment-related actions and decisions or in connection with any other benefit or employee benefit plan of the plan sponsor;

(D) Report to the group health plan any use or disclosure of the information that is inconsistent with the uses or disclosures provided for of which it becomes aware;

(E) Make available protected health information in accordance with § 164.524;

(F) Make available protected health information for amendment and incorporate any amendments to protected health information in accordance with § 164.526;

(G) Make available the information required to provide an accounting of disclosures in accordance with § 164.528;

(H) Make its internal practices, books, and records relating to the use and disclosure of protected health information received from the group health plan available to the Secretary for purposes of determining compliance by the group health plan with this subpart;

(I) If feasible, return or destroy all protected health information received from the group health plan that the sponsor still maintains in any form and retain no copies of such information when no longer needed for the purpose for which disclosure was made, except that, if such return or destruction is not feasible, limit further uses and disclosures to those purposes that make the return or destruction of the information infeasible; and

(J) Ensure that the adequate separation required in paragraph (f)(2)(iii) of this section is established.

(iii) Provide for adequate separation between the group health plan and the plan sponsor. The plan documents must:

(A) Describe those employees or classes of employees or other persons under the control of the plan sponsor to be given access to the protected health information to be disclosed, provided that any employee or person who receives protected health information relating to payment under, health care operations of, or other matters pertaining to the group health plan in the ordinary course of business must be included in such description;

(B) Restrict the access to and use by such employees and other persons described in paragraph (f)(2)(iii)(A) of this section to the plan administration functions that the plan sponsor performs for the group health plan; and

(C) Provide an effective mechanism for resolving any issues of noncompliance by persons described in paragraph (f)(2)(iii)(A) of this section with the plan document provisions required by this paragraph.

(3) *Implementation specifications: Uses and disclosures.* A group health plan may:

(i) Disclose protected health information to a plan sponsor to carry out plan administration functions that the plan sponsor performs only consistent with the provisions of paragraph (f)(2) of this section;

(ii) Not permit a health insurance issuer or HMO with respect to the group health plan to disclose protected health information to the plan sponsor except as permitted by this paragraph;

(iii) Not disclose and may not permit a health insurance issuer or HMO to disclose protected health information to a plan sponsor as otherwise permitted by this paragraph unless a statement required by § 164.520(b)(1)(iii)(C) is included in the appropriate notice; and

(iv) Not disclose protected health information to the plan sponsor for the purpose of employment-related actions or decisions or in connection with any other benefit or employee benefit plan of the plan sponsor.

(g) *Standard: Requirements for a covered entity with multiple covered functions.*

(1) A covered entity that performs multiple covered functions that would make the entity any combination of a health plan, a covered health care provider, and a health care clearinghouse, must comply with the standards, requirements, and implementation specifications of this subpart, as applicable to the health plan, health care provider, or health care clearinghouse covered functions performed.

(2) A covered entity that performs multiple covered functions may use or disclose the protected health information of individuals who receive the covered entity's health plan or health care provider services, but not both, only for purposes related to the appropriate function being performed.

§ 164.506 Consent for uses or disclosures to carry out treatment, payment, or health care operations.

(a) *Standard: Consent requirement.* (1) Except as provided in paragraph (a)(2) or (a)(3) of this section, a covered health care provider must obtain the individual's consent, in accordance with this section, prior to using or disclosing protected health information to carry out treatment, payment, or health care operations.

(2) A covered health care provider may, without consent, use or disclose protected health information to carry out treatment, payment, or health care operations, if:

(i) The covered health care provider has an indirect treatment relationship with the individual; or

(ii) The covered health care provider created or received the protected health information in the course of providing health care to an individual who is an inmate.

(3)(i) A covered health care provider may, without prior consent, use or disclose protected health information created or received under paragraph (a)(3)(i)(A)–(C) of this section to carry out treatment, payment, or health care operations:

(A) In emergency treatment situations, if the covered health care provider attempts to obtain such consent as soon as reasonably practicable after the delivery of such treatment;

(B) If the covered health care provider is required by law to treat the individual, and the covered health care provider attempts to obtain such consent but is unable to obtain such consent; or

(C) If a covered health care provider attempts to obtain such consent from the individual but is unable to obtain such consent due to substantial barriers to communicating with the individual, and the covered health care provider determines, in the exercise of professional judgment, that the individual's consent to receive treatment is clearly inferred from the circumstances.

(ii) A covered health care provider that fails to obtain such consent in accordance with paragraph (a)(3)(i) of this section must document its attempt to obtain consent and the reason why consent was not obtained.

(4) If a covered entity is not required to obtain consent by paragraph (a)(1) of this section, it may obtain an individual's consent for the covered entity's own use or disclosure of protected health information to carry out treatment, payment, or health care operations, provided that such consent meets the requirements of this section.

(5) Except as provided in paragraph (f)(1) of this section, a consent obtained by a covered entity under this section is not effective to permit another covered entity to use or disclose protected health information.

(b) *Implementation specifications: General requirements.* (1) A covered health care provider may condition treatment on the provision by the individual of a consent under this section.

(2) A health plan may condition enrollment in the health plan on the provision by the individual of a consent under this section sought in conjunction with such enrollment.

(3) A consent under this section may not be combined in a single document with the notice required by § 164.520.

(4)(i) A consent for use or disclosure may be combined with other types of written legal permission from the individual (*e.g.,* an informed consent for treatment or a consent to assignment of benefits), if the consent under this section:

(A) Is visually and organizationally separate from such other written legal permission; and

(B) Is separately signed by the individual and dated.

(ii) A consent for use or disclosure may be combined with a research authorization under § 164.508(f).

(5) An individual may revoke a consent under this section at any time, except to the extent that the covered entity has taken action in reliance thereon. Such revocation must be in writing.

(6) A covered entity must document and retain any signed consent under this section as required by § 164.530(j).

(c) *Implementation specifications: Content requirements.* A consent under this section must be in plain language and:

(1) Inform the individual that protected health information may be used and disclosed to carry out treatment, payment, or health care operations;

(2) Refer the individual to the notice required by § 164.520 for a more complete description of such uses and disclosures and state that the individual has the right to review the notice prior to signing the consent;

(3) If the covered entity has reserved the right to change its privacy practices that are described in the notice in accordance with § 164.520(b)(1)(v)(C), state that the terms of its notice may change and describe how the individual may obtain a revised notice;

(4) State that:

(i) The individual has the right to request that the covered entity restrict how protected health information is used or disclosed to carry out treatment, payment, or health care operations;

(ii) The covered entity is not required to agree to requested restrictions; and

(iii) If the covered entity agrees to a requested restriction, the restriction is binding on the covered entity;

(5) State that the individual has the right to revoke the consent in writing, except to the extent that the covered entity has taken action in reliance thereon; and

(6) Be signed by the individual and dated.

(d) *Implementation specifications: Defective consents.* There is no consent under this section, if the document submitted has any of the following defects:

(1) The consent lacks an element required by paragraph (c) of this section, as applicable; or

(2) The consent has been revoked in accordance with paragraph (b)(5) of this section.

(e) *Standard: Resolving conflicting consents and authorizations.* (1) If a covered entity has obtained a consent under this section and receives any other authorization or written legal permission from the individual for a disclosure of protected health information to carry out treatment, payment, or health care operations, the covered entity may disclose such protected health information only in accordance with the more restrictive consent, authorization, or other written legal permission from the individual.

(2) A covered entity may attempt to resolve a conflict between a consent and an authorization or other written legal permission from the individual described in paragraph (e)(1) of this section by:

(i) Obtaining a new consent from the individual under this section for the disclosure to carry out treatment, payment, or health care operations; or

(ii) Communicating orally or in writing with the individual in order to determine the individual's preference in resolving the conflict. The covered entity must document the individual's preference and may only disclose protected health information in accordance with the individual's preference.

(f)(1) *Standard: Joint consents.* Covered entities that participate in an organized health care arrangement and that have a joint notice under § 164.520(d) may comply with this section by a joint consent.

(2) *Implementation specifications: Requirements for joint consents.* (i) A joint consent must:

(A) Include the name or other specific identification of the covered entities, or classes of covered entities, to which the joint consent applies; and

(B) Meet the requirements of this section, except that the statements required by this section may be altered to reflect the fact that the consent covers more than one covered entity.

(ii) If an individual revokes a joint consent, the covered entity that receives the revocation must inform the other entities covered by the joint consent of the revocation as soon as practicable.

§ 164.508 Uses and disclosures for which an authorization is required.

(a) *Standard: Authorizations for uses and disclosures.* (1) *Authorization required: General rule.* Except as otherwise permitted or required by this subchapter, a covered entity may not use or disclose protected health information without an authorization. that is valid under this section. When a covered entity obtains or receives a valid authorization for its use or disclosure of protected health information, such use or disclosure must be consistent with such authorization.

(2) *Authorization required: psychotherapy notes.* Notwithstanding any other provision of this subpart, other than transition provisions provided for in § 164.532, a covered entity must obtain an authorization for any use or disclosure of psychotherapy notes, except:

(i) To carry out the following treatment, payment, or health care operations, consistent with consent requirements in § 164.506:

(A) Use by originator of the psychotherapy notes for treatment;

(B) Use or disclosure by the covered entity in training programs in which students, trainees, or practitioners in mental health learn under supervision to practice or improve their skills in group, joint, family, or individual counseling; or

(C) Use or disclosure by the covered entity to defend a legal action or other proceeding brought by the individual; and

(ii) A use or disclosure that is required by § 164.502(a)(2)(ii) or permitted by § 164.512(a); § 164.512(d) with respect to the oversight of the originator of the psychotherapy notes; § 164.512(g)(1); or § 164.512(j)(1)(i).

(b) *Implementation specifications: General requirements.*—(1) *Valid authorizations.*

(i) A valid authorization is a document that contains the elements listed in paragraph (c) and, as applicable, paragraph (d), (e), or (f) of this section.

(ii) A valid authorization may contain elements or information in addition to the elements required by this section, provided that such additional elements or information are not be inconsistent with the elements required by this section.

(2) *Defective authorizations.* An authorization is not valid, if the document submitted has any of the following defects:

(i) The expiration date has passed or the expiration event is known by the covered entity to have occurred;

(ii) The authorization has not been filled out completely, with respect to an element described by paragraph (c), (d), (e), or (f) of this section, if applicable;

(iii) The authorization is known by the covered entity to have been revoked;

(iv) The authorization lacks an element required by paragraph (c), (d), (e), or (f) of this section, if applicable;

(v) The authorization violates paragraph (b)(3) of this section, if applicable;

(vi) Any material information in the authorization is known by the covered entity to be false.

(3) *Compound authorizations.* An authorization for use or disclosure of protected health information may not be combined with any other document to create a compound authorization, except as follows:

(i) An authorization for the use or disclosure of protected health information created for research that includes treatment of the individual may be combined as permitted by § 164.506(b)(4)(ii) or paragraph (f) of this section;

(ii) An authorization for a use or disclosure of psychotherapy notes may only be combined with another authorization for a use or disclosure of psychotherapy notes;

(iii) An authorization under this section, other than an authorization for a use or disclosure of psychotherapy notes may be combined with any other such authorization under this section, except when a covered entity has conditioned the provision of treatment, payment, enrollment in the health plan, or eligibility for benefits under paragraph (b)(4) of this section on the provision of one of the authorizations.

(4) *Prohibition on conditioning of authorizations.* A covered entity may not condition the provision to an individual of treatment, payment, enrollment in the health plan, or eligibility for benefits on the provision of an authorization, except:

(i) A covered health care provider may condition the provision of research-related treatment on provision of an authorization under paragraph (f) of this section;

(ii) A health plan may condition enrollment in the health plan or eligibility for benefits on provision of an authorization requested by the health plan prior to an individual's enrollment in the health plan, if:

(A) The authorization sought is for the health plan's eligibility or enrollment determinations relating to the individual or for its underwriting or risk rating determinations; and

(B) The authorization is not for a use or disclosure of psychotherapy notes under paragraph (a)(2) of this section;

(iii) A health plan may condition payment of a claim for specified benefits on provision of an authorization under paragraph (e) of this section, if:

(A) The disclosure is necessary to determine payment of such claim; and

(B) The authorization is not for a use or disclosure of psychotherapy notes under paragraph (a)(2) of this section; and

(iv) A covered entity may condition the provision of health care that is solely for the purpose of creating protected health information for disclosure to a third party on provision of an authorization for the disclosure of the protected health information to such third party.

(5) *Revocation of authorizations.* An individual may revoke an authorization provided under this section at any time, provided that the revocation is in writing, except to the extent that:

(i) The covered entity has taken action in reliance thereon; or

(ii) If the authorization was obtained as a condition of obtaining insurance coverage, other law provides the insurer with the right to contest a claim under the policy.

(6) *Documentation.* A covered entity must document and retain any signed authorization under this section as required by § 164.530(j).

(c) *Implementation specifications: Core elements and requirements.* (1) *Core elements.* A valid authorization under this section must contain at least the following elements:

(i) A description of the information to be used or disclosed that identifies the information in a specific and meaningful fashion;

(ii) The name or other specific identification of the person(s), or class of persons, authorized to make the requested use or disclosure;

(iii) The name or other specific identification of the person(s), or class of persons, to whom the covered entity may make the requested use or disclosure;

(iv) An expiration date or an expiration event that relates to the individual or the purpose of the use or disclosure;

(v) A statement of the individual's right to revoke the authorization in writing and the exceptions to the right to revoke, together with a description of how the individual may revoke the authorization;

(vi) A statement that information used or disclosed pursuant to the authorization may be subject to redisclosure by the recipient and no longer be protected by this rule;

(vii) Signature of the individual and date; and

(viii) If the authorization is signed by a personal representative of the individual, a description of such representative's authority to act for the individual.

(2) *Plain language requirement.* The authorization must be written in plain language.

(d) *Implementation specifications: Authorizations requested by a covered entity for its own uses and disclosures.* If an authorization is requested by a covered entity for its own use or disclosure of protected health information that it maintains, the covered entity must comply with the following requirements.

(1) *Required elements.* The authorization for the uses or disclosures described in this paragraph must, in addition to meeting the requirements of paragraph (c) of this section, contain the following elements:

(i) For any authorization to which the prohibition on conditioning in paragraph (b)(4) of this section applies, a statement that the covered entity will not condition treatment, payment, enrollment in the health plan, or eligibility for benefits on the individual's providing authorization for the requested use or disclosure;

(ii) A description of each purpose of the requested use or disclosure;

(iii) A statement that the individual may:

(A) Inspect or copy the protected health information to be used or disclosed as provided in § 164.524; and

(B) Refuse to sign the authorization; and

(iv) If use or disclosure of the requested information will result in

direct or indirect remuneration to the covered entity from a third party, a statement that such remuneration will result.

(2) *Copy to the individual.* A covered entity must provide the individual with a copy of the signed authorization.

(e) *Implementation specifications: Authorizations requested by a covered entity for disclosures by others.* If an authorization is requested by a covered entity for another covered entity to disclose protected health information to the covered entity requesting the authorization to carry out treatment, payment, or health care operations, the covered entity requesting the authorization must comply with the following requirements.

(1) *Required elements.* The authorization for the disclosures described in this paragraph must, in addition to meeting the requirements of paragraph (c) of this section, contain the following elements:

(i) A description of each purpose of the requested disclosure;

(ii) Except for an authorization on which payment may be conditioned under paragraph (b)(4)(iii) of this section, a statement that the covered entity will not condition treatment, payment, enrollment in the health plan, or eligibility for benefits on the individual's providing authorization for the requested use or disclosure; and

(iii) A statement that the individual may refuse to sign the authorization.

(2) *Copy to the individual.* A covered entity must provide the individual with a copy of the signed authorization.

(f) *Implementation specifications: Authorizations for uses and disclosures of protected health information created for research that includes treatment of the individual.*

(1) *Required elements.* Except as otherwise permitted by § 164.512(i), a covered entity that creates protected health information for the purpose, in whole or in part, of research that includes treatment of individuals must obtain an authorization for the use or disclosure of such information. Such authorization must:

(i) For uses and disclosures not otherwise permitted or required under this subpart, meet the requirements of paragraphs (c) and (d) of this section; and

(ii) Contain:

(A) A description of the extent to which such protected health information will be used or disclosed to carry out treatment, payment, or health care operations;

(B) A description of any protected health information that will not be used or disclosed for purposes permitted in

accordance with §§ 164.510 and 164.512, provided that the covered entity may not include a limitation affecting its right to make a use or disclosure that is required by law or permitted by § 164.512(j)(1)(i); and

(C) If the covered entity has obtained or intends to obtain the individual's consent under § 164.506, or has provided or intends to provide the individual with a notice under § 164.520, the authorization must refer to that consent or notice, as applicable, and state that the statements made pursuant to this section are binding.

(2) *Optional procedure.* An authorization under this paragraph may be in the same document as:

(i) A consent to participate in the research;

(ii) A consent to use or disclose protected health information to carry out treatment, payment, or health care operations under § 164.506; or

(iii) A notice of privacy practices under § 164.520.

§ 164.510 Uses and disclosures requiring an opportunity for the individual to agree or to object.

A covered entity may use or disclose protected health information without the written consent or authorization of the individual as described by §§ 164.506 and 164.508, respectively, provided that the individual is informed in advance of the use or disclosure and has the opportunity to agree to or prohibit or restrict the disclosure in accordance with the applicable requirements of this section. The covered entity may orally inform the individual of and obtain the individual's oral agreement or objection to a use or disclosure permitted by this section.

(a) *Standard: use and disclosure for facility directories.* (1) *Permitted uses and disclosure.* Except when an objection is expressed in accordance with paragraphs (a)(2) or (3) of this section, a covered health care provider may:

(i) Use the following protected health information to maintain a directory of individuals in its facility:

(A) The individual's name;

(B) The individual's location in the covered health care provider's facility;

(C) The individual's condition described in general terms that does not communicate specific medical information about the individual; and

(D) The individual's religious affiliation; and

(ii) Disclose for directory purposes such information:

(A) To members of the clergy; or

(B) Except for religious affiliation, to other persons who ask for the individual by name.

(2) *Opportunity to object.* A covered health care provider must inform an individual of the protected health information that it may include in a directory and the persons to whom it may disclose such information (including disclosures to clergy of information regarding religious affiliation) and provide the individual with the opportunity to restrict or prohibit some or all of the uses or disclosures permitted by paragraph (a)(1) of this section.

(3) *Emergency circumstances.* (i) If the opportunity to object to uses or disclosures required by paragraph (a)(2) of this section cannot practicably be provided because of the individual's incapacity or an emergency treatment circumstance, a covered health care provider may use or disclose some or all of the protected health information permitted by paragraph (a)(1) of this section for the facility's directory, if such disclosure is:

(A) Consistent with a prior expressed preference of the individual, if any, that is known to the covered health care provider; and

(B) In the individual's best interest as determined by the covered health care provider, in the exercise of professional judgment.

(ii) The covered health care provider must inform the individual and provide an opportunity to object to uses or disclosures for directory purposes as required by paragraph (a)(2) of this section when it becomes practicable to do so.

(b) *Standard: uses and disclosures for involvement in the individual's care and notification purposes.* (1) *Permitted uses and disclosures.* (i) A covered entity may, in accordance with paragraphs (b)(2) or (3) of this section, disclose to a family member, other relative, or a close personal friend of the individual, or any other person identified by the individual, the protected health information directly relevant to such person's involvement with the individual's care or payment related to the individual's health care.

(ii) A covered entity may use or disclose protected health information to notify, or assist in the notification of (including identifying or locating), a family member, a personal representative of the individual, or another person responsible for the care of the individual of the individual's location, general condition, or death. Any such use or disclosure of protected health information for such notification purposes must be in accordance with

paragraphs (b)(2), (3), or (4) of this section, as applicable.

(2) *Uses and disclosures with the individual present.* If the individual is present for, or otherwise available prior to, a use or disclosure permitted by paragraph (b)(1) of this section and has the capacity to make health care decisions, the covered entity may use or disclose the protected health information if it:

(i) Obtains the individual's agreement;

(ii) Provides the individual with the opportunity to object to the disclosure, and the individual does not express an objection; or

(iii) Reasonably infers from the circumstances, based the exercise of professional judgment, that the individual does not object to the disclosure.

(3) *Limited uses and disclosures when the individual is not present.* If the individual is not present for, or the opportunity to agree or object to the use or disclosure cannot practicably be provided because of the individual's incapacity or an emergency circumstance, the covered entity may, in the exercise of professional judgment, determine whether the disclosure is in the best interests of the individual and, if so, disclose only the protected health information that is directly relevant to the person's involvement with the individual's health care. A covered entity may use professional judgment and its experience with common practice to make reasonable inferences of the individual's best interest in allowing a person to act on behalf of the individual to pick up filled prescriptions, medical supplies, X-rays, or other similar forms of protected health information.

(4) *Use and disclosures for disaster relief purposes.* A covered entity may use or disclose protected health information to a public or private entity authorized by law or by its charter to assist in disaster relief efforts, for the purpose of coordinating with such entities the uses or disclosures permitted by paragraph (b)(1)(ii) of this section. The requirements in paragraphs (b)(2) and (3) of this section apply to such uses and disclosure to the extent that the covered entity, in the exercise of professional judgment, determines that the requirements do not interfere with the ability to respond to the emergency circumstances.

§ 164.512   Uses and disclosures for which consent, an authorization, or opportunity to agree or object is not required.

A covered entity may use or disclose protected health information without the written consent or authorization of

the individual as described in §§ 164.506 and 164.508, respectively, or the opportunity for the individual to agree or object as described in § 164.510, in the situations covered by this section, subject to the applicable requirements of this section. When the covered entity is required by this section to inform the individual of, or when the individual may agree to, a use or disclosure permitted by this section, the covered entity's information and the individual's agreement may be given orally.

(a) *Standard: Uses and disclosures required by law.* (1) A covered entity may use or disclose protected health information to the extent that such use or disclosure is required by law and the use or disclosure complies with and is limited to the relevant requirements of such law.

(2) A covered entity must meet the requirements described in paragraph (c), (e), or (f) of this section for uses or disclosures required by law.

(b) *Standard: uses and disclosures for public health activities.* (1) *Permitted disclosures.* A covered entity may disclose protected health information for the public health activities and purposes described in this paragraph to:

(i) A public health authority that is authorized by law to collect or receive such information for the purpose of preventing or controlling disease, injury, or disability, including, but not limited to, the reporting of disease, injury, vital events such as birth or death, and the conduct of public health surveillance, public health investigations, and public health interventions; or, at the direction of a public health authority, to an official of a foreign government agency that is acting in collaboration with a public health authority;

(ii) A public health authority or other appropriate government authority authorized by law to receive reports of child abuse or neglect;

(iii) A person subject to the jurisdiction of the Food and Drug Administration:

(A) To report adverse events (or similar reports with respect to food or dietary supplements), product defects or problems (including problems with the use or labeling of a product), or biological product deviations if the disclosure is made to the person required or directed to report such information to the Food and Drug Administration;

(B) To track products if the disclosure is made to a person required or directed by the Food and Drug Administration to track the product;

(C) To enable product recalls, repairs, or replacement (including locating and notifying individuals who have received products of product recalls, withdrawals, or other problems); or

(D) To conduct post marketing surveillance to comply with requirements or at the direction of the Food and Drug Administration;

(iv) A person who may have been exposed to a communicable disease or may otherwise be at risk of contracting or spreading a disease or condition, if the covered entity or public health authority is authorized by law to notify such person as necessary in the conduct of a public health intervention or investigation; or

(v) An employer, about an individual who is a member of the workforce of the employer, if:

(A) The covered entity is a covered health care provider who is a member of the workforce of such employer or who provides a health care to the individual at the request of the employer:

(1) To conduct an evaluation relating to medical surveillance of the workplace; or

(2) To evaluate whether the individual has a work-related illness or injury;

(B) The protected health information that is disclosed consists of findings concerning a work-related illness or injury or a workplace-related medical surveillance;

(C) The employer needs such findings in order to comply with its obligations, under 29 CFR parts 1904 through 1928, 30 CFR parts 50 through 90, or under state law having a similar purpose, to record such illness or injury or to carry out responsibilities for workplace medical surveillance;

(D) The covered health care provider provides written notice to the individual that protected health information relating to the medical surveillance of the workplace and work-related illnesses and injuries is disclosed to the employer:

(1) By giving a copy of the notice to the individual at the time the health care is provided; or

(2) If the health care is provided on the work site of the employer, by posting the notice in a prominent place at the location where the health care is provided.

(2) *Permitted uses.* If the covered entity also is a public health authority, the covered entity is permitted to use protected health information in all cases in which it is permitted to disclose such information for public health activities under paragraph (b)(1) of this section.

(c) *Standard: Disclosures about victims of abuse, neglect or domestic violence.* (1) *Permitted disclosures.*

Except for reports of child abuse or neglect permitted by paragraph (b)(1)(ii) of this section, a covered entity may disclose protected health information about an individual whom the covered entity reasonably believes to be a victim of abuse, neglect, or domestic violence to a government authority, including a social service or protective services agency, authorized by law to receive reports of such abuse, neglect, or domestic violence:

(i) To the extent the disclosure is required by law and the disclosure complies with and is limited to the relevant requirements of such law;

(ii) If the individual agrees to the disclosure; or

(iii) To the extent the disclosure is expressly authorized by statute or regulation and:

(A) The covered entity, in the exercise of professional judgment, believes the disclosure is necessary to prevent serious harm to the individual or other potential victims; or

(B) If the individual is unable to agree because of incapacity, a law enforcement or other public official authorized to receive the report represents that the protected health information for which disclosure is sought is not intended to be used against the individual and that an immediate enforcement activity that depends upon the disclosure would be materially and adversely affected by waiting until the individual is able to agree to the disclosure.

(2) *Informing the individual.* A covered entity that makes a disclosure permitted by paragraph (c)(1) of this section must promptly inform the individual that such a report has been or will be made, except if:

(i) The covered entity, in the exercise of professional judgment, believes informing the individual would place the individual at risk of serious harm; or

(ii) The covered entity would be informing a personal representative, and the covered entity reasonably believes the personal representative is responsible for the abuse, neglect, or other injury, and that informing such person would not be in the best interests of the individual as determined by the covered entity, in the exercise of professional judgment.

(d) *Standard: Uses and disclosures for health oversight activities.* (1) *Permitted disclosures.* A covered entity may disclose protected health information to a health oversight agency for oversight activities authorized by law, including audits; civil, administrative, or criminal investigations; inspections; licensure or disciplinary actions; civil, administrative, or criminal proceedings

or actions; or other activities necessary for appropriate oversight of:

(i) The health care system;

(ii) Government benefit programs for which health information is relevant to beneficiary eligibility;

(iii) Entities subject to government regulatory programs for which health information is necessary for determining compliance with program standards; or

(iv) Entities subject to civil rights laws for which health information is necessary for determining compliance.

(2) *Exception to health oversight activities.* For the purpose of the disclosures permitted by paragraph (d)(1) of this section, a health oversight activity does not include an investigation or other activity in which the individual is the subject of the investigation or activity and such investigation or other activity does not arise out of and is not directly related to:

(i) The receipt of health care;

(ii) A claim for public benefits related to health; or

(iii) Qualification for, or receipt of, public benefits or services when a patient's health is integral to the claim for public benefits or services.

(3) *Joint activities or investigations.* Nothwithstanding paragraph (d)(2) of this section, if a health oversight activity or investigation is conducted in conjunction with an oversight activity or investigation relating to a claim for public benefits not related to health, the joint activity or investigation is considered a health oversight activity for purposes of paragraph (d) of this section.

(4) *Permitted uses.* If a covered entity also is a health oversight agency, the covered entity may use protected health information for health oversight activities as permitted by paragraph (d) of this section.

(e) *Standard: Disclosures for judicial and administrative proceedings.*

(1) *Permitted disclosures.* A covered entity may disclose protected health information in the course of any judicial or administrative proceeding:

(i) In response to an order of a court or administrative tribunal, provided that the covered entity discloses only the protected health information expressly authorized by such order; or

(ii) In response to a subpoena, discovery request, or other lawful process, that is not accompanied by an order of a court or administrative tribunal, if:

(A) The covered entity receives satisfactory assurance, as described in paragraph (e)(1)(iii) of this section, from the party seeking the information that reasonable efforts have been made by

159

such party to ensure that the individual who is the subject of the protected health information that has been requested has been given notice of the request; or

(B) The covered entity receives satisfactory assurance, as described in paragraph (e)(1)(iv) of this section, from the party seeking the information that reasonable efforts have been made by such party to secure a qualified protective order that meets the requirements of paragraph (e)(1)(v) of this section.

(iii) For the purposes of paragraph (e)(1)(ii)(A) of this section, a covered entity receives satisfactory assurances from a party seeking protecting health information if the covered entity receives from such party a written statement and accompanying documentation demonstrating that:

(A) The party requesting such information has made a good faith attempt to provide written notice to the individual (or, if the individual's location is unknown, to mail a notice to the individual's last known address);

(B) The notice included sufficient information about the litigation or proceeding in which the protected health information is requested to permit the individual to raise an objection to the court or administrative tribunal; and

(C) The time for the individual to raise objections to the court or administrative tribunal has elapsed, and:

(1) No objections were filed; or

(2) All objections filed by the individual have been resolved by the court or the administrative tribunal and the disclosures being sought are consistent with such resolution.

(iv) For the purposes of paragraph (e)(1)(ii)(B) of this section, a covered entity receives satisfactory assurances from a party seeking protected health information, if the covered entity receives from such party a written statement and accompanying documentation demonstrating that:

(A) The parties to the dispute giving rise to the request for information have agreed to a qualified protective order and have presented it to the court or administrative tribunal with jurisdiction over the dispute; or

(B) The party seeking the protected health information has requested a qualified protective order from such court or administrative tribunal.

(v) For purposes of paragraph (e)(1) of this section, a qualified protective order means, with respect to protected health information requested under paragraph (e)(1)(ii) of this section, an order of a court or of an administrative tribunal or

a stipulation by the parties to the litigation or administrative proceeding that:

(A) Prohibits the parties from using or disclosing the protected health information for any purpose other than the litigation or proceeding for which such information was requested; and

(B) Requires the return to the covered entity or destruction of the protected health information (including all copies made) at the end of the litigation or proceeding.

(vi) Nothwithstanding paragraph (e)(1)(ii) of this section, a covered entity may disclose protected health information in response to lawful process described in paragraph (e)(1)(ii) of this section without receiving satisfactory assurance under paragraph (e)(1)(ii)(A) or (B) of this section, if the covered entity makes reasonable efforts to provide notice to the individual sufficient to meet the requirements of paragraph (e)(1)(iii) of this section or to seek a qualified protective order sufficient to meet the requirements of paragraph (e)(1)(iv) of this section.

(2) *Other uses and disclosures under this section.* The provisions of this paragraph do not supersede other provisions of this section that otherwise permit or restrict uses or disclosures of protected health information.

(f) *Standard: Disclosures for law enforcement purposes.* A covered entity may disclose protected health information for a law enforcement purpose to a law enforcement official if the conditions in paragraphs (f)(1) through (f)(6) of this section are met, as applicable.

(1) *Permitted disclosures: Pursuant to process and as otherwise required by law.* A covered entity may disclose protected health information:

(i) As required by law including laws that require the reporting of certain types of wounds or other physical injuries, except for laws subject to paragraph (b)(1)(ii) or (c)(1)(i) of this section; or

(ii) In compliance with and as limited by the relevant requirements of:

(A) A court order or court-ordered warrant, or a subpoena or summons issued by a judicial officer;

(B) A grand jury subpoena; or

(C) An administrative request, including an administrative subpoena or summons, a civil or an authorized investigative demand, or similar process authorized under law, provided that:

(1) The information sought is relevant and material to a legitimate law enforcement inquiry;

(2) The request is specific and limited in scope to the extent reasonably

practicable in light of the purpose for which the information is sought; and

(3) De-identified information could not reasonably be used.

(2) *Permitted disclosures: Limited information for identification and location purposes.* Except for disclosures required by law as permitted by paragraph (f)(1) of this section, a covered entity may disclose protected health information in response to a law enforcement official's request for such information for the purpose of identifying or locating a suspect, fugitive, material witness, or missing person, provided that:

(i) The covered entity may disclose only the following information:

(A) Name and address;

(B) Date and place of birth;

(C) Social security number;

(D) ABO blood type and rh factor;

(E) Type of injury;

(F) Date and time of treatment;

(G) Date and time of death, if applicable; and

(H) A description of distinguishing physical characteristics, including height, weight, gender, race, hair and eye color, presence or absence of facial hair (beard or moustache), scars, and tattoos.

(ii) Except as permitted by paragraph (f)(2)(i) of this section, the covered entity may not disclose for the purposes of identification or location under paragraph (f)(2) of this section any protected health information related to the individual's DNA or DNA analysis, dental records, or typing, samples or analysis of body fluids or tissue.

(3) *Permitted disclosure: Victims of a crime.* Except for disclosures required by law as permitted by paragraph (f)(1) of this section, a covered entity may disclose protected health information in response to a law enforcement official's request for such information about an individual who is or is suspected to be a victim of a crime, other than disclosures that are subject to paragraph (b) or (c) of this section, if:

(ii) The individual agrees to the disclosure; or

(iii) The covered entity is unable to obtain the individual's agreement because of incapacity or other emergency circumstance, provided that:

(A) The law enforcement official represents that such information is needed to determine whether a violation of law by a person other than the victim has occurred, and such information is not intended to be used against the victim;

(B) The law enforcement official represents that immediate law enforcement activity that depends upon the disclosure would be materially and adversely affected by waiting until the individual is able to agree to the disclosure; and

(C) The disclosure is in the best interests of the individual as determined by the covered entity, in the exercise of professional judgment.

(4) *Permitted disclosure: Decedents.* A covered entity may disclose protected health information about an individual who has died to a law enforcement official for the purpose of alerting law enforcement of the death of the individual if the covered entity has a suspicion that such death may have resulted from criminal conduct.

(5) *Permitted disclosure: Crime on premises.* A covered entity may disclose to a law enforcement official protected health information that the covered entity believes in good faith constitutes evidence of criminal conduct that occurred on the premises of the covered entity.

(6) *Permitted disclosure: Reporting crime in emergencies.* (i) A covered health care provider providing emergency health care in response to a medical emergency, other than such emergency on the premises of the covered health care provider, may disclose protected health information to a law enforcement official if such disclosure appears necessary to alert law enforcement to:

(A) The commission and nature of a crime;

(B) The location of such crime or of the victim(s) of such crime; and

(C) The identity, description, and location of the perpetrator of such crime.

(ii) If a covered health care provider believes that the medical emergency described in paragraph (f)(6)(i) of this section is the result of abuse, neglect, or domestic violence of the individual in need of emergency health care, paragraph (f)(6)(i) of this section does not apply and any disclosure to a law enforcement official for law enforcement purposes is subject to paragraph (c) of this section.

(g) *Standard: Uses and disclosures about decedents.* (1) *Coroners and medical examiners.* A covered entity may disclose protected health information to a coroner or medical examiner for the purpose of identifying a deceased person, determining a cause of death, or other duties as authorized by law. A covered entity that also performs the duties of a coroner or medical examiner may use protected health information for the purposes described in this paragraph.

(2) *Funeral directors.* A covered entity may disclose protected health information to funeral directors,

consistent with applicable law, as necessary to carry out their duties with respect to the decedent. If necessary for funeral directors carry out their duties, the covered entity may disclose the protected health information prior to, and in reasonable anticipation of, the individual's death.

(h) *Standard: Uses and disclosures for cadaveric organ, eye or tissue donation purposes.* A covered entity may use or disclose protected health information to organ procurement organizations or other entities engaged in the procurement, banking, or transplantation of cadaveric organs, eyes, or tissue for the purpose of facilitating organ, eye or tissue donation and transplantation.

(i) *Standard: Uses and disclosures for research purposes.* (1) *Permitted uses and disclosures.* A covered entity may use or disclose protected health information for research, regardless of the source of funding of the research, provided that:

(i) *Board approval of a waiver of authorization.* The covered entity obtains documentation that an alteration to or waiver, in whole or in part, of the individual authorization required by § 164.508 for use or disclosure of protected health information has been approved by either:

(A) An Institutional Review Board (IRB), established in accordance with 7 CFR lc.107, 10 CFR 745.107, 14 CFR 1230.107, 15 CFR 27.107, 16 CFR 1028.107, 21 CFR 56.107, 22 CFR 225.107, 24 CFR 60.107, 28 CFR 46.107, 32 CFR 219.107, 34 CFR 97.107, 38 CFR 16.107, 40 CFR 26.107, 45 CFR 46.107, 45 CFR 690.107, or 49 CFR 11.107; or

(B) A privacy board that:

(*1*) Has members with varying backgrounds and appropriate professional competency as necessary to review the effect of the research protocol on the individual's privacy rights and related interests;

(*2*) Includes at least one member who is not affiliated with the covered entity, not affiliated with any entity conducting or sponsoring the research, and not related to any person who is affiliated with any of such entities; and

(*3*) Does not have any member participating in a review of any project in which the member has a conflict of interest.

(ii) *Reviews preparatory to research.* The covered entity obtains from the researcher representations that:

(A) Use or disclosure is sought solely to review protected health information as necessary to prepare a research protocol or for similar purposes preparatory to research;

(B) No protected health information is to be removed from the covered entity by the researcher in the course of the review; and

(C) The protected health information for which use or access is sought is necessary for the research purposes.

(iii) *Research on decedent's information.* The covered entity obtains from the researcher:

(A) Representation that the use or disclosure is sought is solely for research on the protected health information of decedents;

(B) Documentation, at the request of the covered entity, of the death of such individuals; and

(C) Representation that the protected health information for which use or disclosure is sought is necessary for the research purposes.

(2) *Documentation of waiver approval.* For a use or disclosure to be permitted based on documentation of approval of an alteration or waiver, under paragraph (i)(1)(i) of this section, the documentation must include all of the following:

(i) *Identification and date of action.* A statement identifying the IRB or privacy board and the date on which the alteration or waiver of authorization was approved;

(ii) *Waiver criteria.* A statement that the IRB or privacy board has determined that the alteration or waiver, in whole or in part, of authorization satisfies the following criteria:

(A) The use or disclosure of protected health information involves no more than minimal risk to the individuals;

(B) The alteration or waiver will not adversely affect the privacy rights and the welfare of the individuals;

(C) The research could not practicably be conducted without the alteration or waiver;

(D) The research could not practicably be conducted without access to and use of the protected health information;

(E) The privacy risks to individuals whose protected health information is to be used or disclosed are reasonable in relation to the anticipated benefits if any to the individuals, and the importance of the knowledge that may reasonably be expected to result from the research;

(F) There is an adequate plan to protect the identifiers from improper use and disclosure;

(G) There is an adequate plan to destroy the identifiers at the earliest opportunity consistent with conduct of the research, unless there is a health or research justification for retaining the identifiers, or such retention is otherwise required by law; and

(H) There are adequate written assurances that the protected health information will not be reused or disclosed to any other person or entity, except as required by law, for authorized oversight of the research project, or for other research for which the use or disclosure of protected health information would be permitted by this subpart.

(iii) *Protected health information needed.* A brief description of the protected health information for which use or access has been determined to be necessary by the IRB or privacy board has determined, pursuant to paragraph (i)(2)(ii)(D) of this section;

(iv) *Review and approval procedures.* A statement that the alteration or waiver of authorization has been reviewed and approved under either normal or expedited review procedures, as follows:

(A) An IRB must follow the requirements of the Common Rule, including the normal review procedures (7 CFR 1c.108(b), 10 CFR 745.108(b), 14 CFR 1230.108(b), 15 CFR 27.108(b), 16 CFR 1028.108(b), 21 CFR 56.108(b), 22 CFR 225.108(b), 24 CFR 60.108(b), 28 CFR 46.108(b), 32 CFR 219.108(b), 34 CFR 97.108(b), 38 CFR 16.108(b), 40 CFR 26.108(b), 45 CFR 46.108(b), 45 CFR 690.108(b), or 49 CFR 11.108(b)) or the expedited review procedures (7 CFR 1c.110, 10 CFR 745.110, 14 CFR 1230.110, 15 CFR 27.110, 16 CFR 1028.110, 21 CFR 56.110, 22 CFR 225.110, 24 CFR 60.110, 28 CFR 46.110, 32 CFR 219.110, 34 CFR 97.110, 38 CFR 16.110, 40 CFR 26.110, 45 CFR 46.110, 45 CFR 690.110, or 49 CFR 11.110);

(B) A privacy board must review the proposed research at convened meetings at which a majority of the privacy board members are present, including at least one member who satisfies the criterion stated in paragraph (i)(1)(i)(B)(2) of this section, and the alteration or waiver of authorization must be approved by the majority of the privacy board members present at the meeting, unless the privacy board elects to use an expedited review procedure in accordance with paragraph (i)(2)(iv)(C) of this section;

(C) A privacy board may use an expedited review procedure if the research involves no more than minimal risk to the privacy of the individuals who are the subject of the protected health information for which use or disclosure is being sought. If the privacy board elects to use an expedited review procedure, the review and approval of the alteration or waiver of authorization may be carried out by the chair of the privacy board, or by one or more members of the privacy board as designated by the chair; and

(v) *Required signature.* The documentation of the alteration or waiver of authorization must be signed by the chair or other member, as designated by the chair, of the IRB or the privacy board, as applicable.

(j) *Standard: Uses and disclosures to avert a serious threat to health or safety.* (1) *Permitted disclosures.* A covered entity may, consistent with applicable law and standards of ethical conduct, use or disclose protected health information, if the covered entity, in good faith, believes the use or disclosure:

(i)(A) Is necessary to prevent or lessen a serious and imminent threat to the health or safety of a person or the public; and

(B) Is to a person or persons reasonably able to prevent or lessen the threat, including the target of the threat; or

(ii) Is necessary for law enforcement authorities to identify or apprehend an individual:

(A) Because of a statement by an individual admitting participation in a violent crime that the covered entity reasonably believes may have caused serious physical harm to the victim; or

(B) Where it appears from all the circumstances that the individual has escaped from a correctional institution or from lawful custody, as those terms are defined in § 164.501.

(2) *Use or disclosure not permitted.* A use or disclosure pursuant to paragraph (j)(1)(ii)(A) of this section may not be made if the information described in paragraph (j)(1)(ii)(A) of this section is learned by the covered entity:

(i) In the course of treatment to affect the propensity to commit the criminal conduct that is the basis for the disclosure under paragraph (j)(1)(ii)(A) of this section, or counseling or therapy; or

(ii) Through a request by the individual to initiate or to be referred for the treatment, counseling, or therapy described in paragraph (j)(2)(i) of this section.

(3) *Limit on information that may be disclosed.* A disclosure made pursuant to paragraph (j)(1)(ii)(A) of this section shall contain only the statement described in paragraph (j)(1)(ii)(A) of this section and the protected health information described in paragraph (f)(2)(i) of this section.

(4) *Presumption of good faith belief.* A covered entity that uses or discloses protected health information pursuant to paragraph (j)(1) of this section is presumed to have acted in good faith with regard to a belief described in paragraph (j)(1)(i) or (ii) of this section, if the belief is based upon the covered entity's actual knowledge or in reliance on a credible representation by a person with apparent knowledge or authority.

(k) *Standard: Uses and disclosures for specialized government functions.* (1) *Military and veterans activities.* (i) *Armed Forces personnel.* A covered entity may use and disclose the protected health information of individuals who are Armed Forces personnel for activities deemed necessary by appropriate military command authorities to assure the proper execution of the military mission, if the appropriate military authority has published by notice in the **Federal Register** the following information:

(A) Appropriate military command authorities; and

(B) The purposes for which the protected health information may be used or disclosed.

(ii) *Separation or discharge from military service.* A covered entity that is a component of the Departments of Defense or Transportation may disclose to the Department of Veterans Affairs (DVA) the protected health information of an individual who is a member of the Armed Forces upon the separation or discharge of the individual from military service for the purpose of a determination by DVA of the individual's eligibility for or entitlement to benefits under laws administered by the Secretary of Veterans Affairs.

(iii) *Veterans.* A covered entity that is a component of the Department of Veterans Affairs may use and disclose protected health information to components of the Department that determine eligibility for or entitlement to, or that provide, benefits under the laws administered by the Secretary of Veterans Affairs.

(iv) *Foreign military personnel.* A covered entity may use and disclose the protected health information of individuals who are foreign military personnel to their appropriate foreign military authority for the same purposes for which uses and disclosures are permitted for Armed Forces personnel under the notice published in the **Federal Register** pursuant to paragraph (k)(1)(i) of this section.

(2) *National security and intelligence activities.* A covered entity may disclose protected health information to authorized federal officials for the conduct of lawful intelligence, counter-intelligence, and other national security activities authorized by the National Security Act (50 U.S.C. 401, *et seq.*) and implementing authority (*e.g.,* Executive Order 12333).

(3) *Protective services for the President and others.* A covered entity may disclose protected health

information to authorized federal officials for the provision of protective services to the President or other persons authorized by 18 U.S.C. 3056, or to foreign heads of state or other persons authorized by 22 U.S.C. 2709(a)(3), or to for the conduct of investigations authorized by 18 U.S.C. 871 and 879.

(4) *Medical suitability determinations.* A covered entity that is a component of the Department of State may use protected health information to make medical suitability determinations and may disclose whether or not the individual was determined to be medically suitable to the officials in the Department of State who need access to such information for the following purposes:

(i) For the purpose of a required security clearance conducted pursuant to Executive Orders 10450 and 12698;

(ii) As necessary to determine worldwide availability or availability for mandatory service abroad under sections 101(a)(4) and 504 of the Foreign Service Act; or

(iii) For a family to accompany a Foreign Service member abroad, consistent with section 101(b)(5) and 904 of the Foreign Service Act.

(5) *Correctional institutions and other law enforcement custodial situations.* (i) *Permitted disclosures.* A covered entity may disclose to a correctional institution or a law enforcement official having lawful custody of an inmate or other individual protected health information about such inmate or individual, if the correctional institution or such law enforcement official represents that such protected health information is necessary for:

(A) The provision of health care to such individuals;

(B) The health and safety of such individual or other inmates;

(C) The health and safety of the officers or employees of or others at the correctional institution;

(D) The health and safety of such individuals and officers or other persons responsible for the transporting of inmates or their transfer from one institution, facility, or setting to another;

(E) Law enforcement on the premises of the correctional institution; and

(F) The administration and maintenance of the safety, security, and good order of the correctional institution.

(ii) *Permitted uses.* A covered entity that is a correctional institution may use protected health information of individuals who are inmates for any purpose for which such protected health information may be disclosed.

(iii) *No application after release.* For the purposes of this provision, an individual is no longer an inmate when released on parole, probation, supervised release, or otherwise is no longer in lawful custody.

(6) *Covered entities that are government programs providing public benefits.* (i) A health plan that is a government program providing public benefits may disclose protected health information relating to eligibility for or enrollment in the health plan to another agency administering a government program providing public benefits if the sharing of eligibility or enrollment information among such government agencies or the maintenance of such information in a single or combined data system accessible to all such government agencies is required or expressly authorized by statute or regulation.

(ii) A covered entity that is a government agency administering a government program providing public benefits may disclose protected health information relating to the program to another covered entity that is a government agency administering a government program providing public benefits if the programs serve the same or similar populations and the disclosure of protected health information is necessary to coordinate the covered functions of such programs or to improve administration and management relating to the covered functions of such programs.

(l) *Standard: Disclosures for workers' compensation.* A covered entity may disclose protected health information as authorized by and to the extent necessary to comply with laws relating to workers' compensation or other similar programs, established by law, that provide benefits for work-related injuries or illness without regard to fault.

§ 164.514 Other requirements relating to uses and disclosures of protected health information.

(a) *Standard: de-identification of protected health information.* Health information that does not identify an individual and with respect to which there is no reasonable basis to believe that the information can be used to identify an individual is not individually identifiable health information.

(b) *Implementation specifications: requirements for de-identification of protected health information.* A covered entity may determine that health information is not individually identifiable health information only if:

(1) A person with appropriate knowledge of and experience with generally accepted statistical and scientific principles and methods for rendering information not individually identifiable:

(i) Applying such principles and methods, determines that the risk is very small that the information could be used, alone or in combination with other reasonably available information, by an anticipated recipient to identify an individual who is a subject of the information; and

(ii) Documents the methods and results of the analysis that justify such determination; or

(2)(i) The following identifiers of the individual or of relatives, employers, or household members of the individual, are removed:

(A) Names;

(B) All geographic subdivisions smaller than a State, including street address, city, county, precinct, zip code, and their equivalent geocodes, except for the initial three digits of a zip code if, according to the current publicly available data from the Bureau of the Census:

(*1*) The geographic unit formed by combining all zip codes with the same three initial digits contains more than 20,000 people; and

(*2*) The initial three digits of a zip code for all such geographic units containing 20,000 or fewer people is changed to 000.

(C) All elements of dates (except year) for dates directly related to an individual, including birth date, admission date, discharge date, date of death; and all ages over 89 and all elements of dates (including year) indicative of such age, except that such ages and elements may be aggregated into a single category of age 90 or older;

(D) Telephone numbers;

(E) Fax numbers;

(F) Electronic mail addresses;

(G) Social security numbers;

(H) Medical record numbers;

(I) Health plan beneficiary numbers;

(J) Account numbers;

(K) Certificate/license numbers;

(L) Vehicle identifiers and serial numbers, including license plate numbers;

(M) Device identifiers and serial numbers;

(N) Web Universal Resource Locators (URLs);

(O) Internet Protocol (IP) address numbers;

(P) Biometric identifiers, including finger and voice prints;

(Q) Full face photographic images and any comparable images; and

(R) Any other unique identifying number, characteristic, or code; and

163

(ii) The covered entity does not have actual knowledge that the information could be used alone or in combination with other information to identify an individual who is a subject of the information.

(c) *Implementation specifications: re-identification.* A covered entity may assign a code or other means of record identification to allow information de-identified under this section to be re-identified by the covered entity, provided that:

(1) *Derivation.* The code or other means of record identification is not derived from or related to information about the individual and is not otherwise capable of being translated so as to identify the individual; and

(2) *Security.* The covered entity does not use or disclose the code or other means of record identification for any other purpose, and does not disclose the mechanism for re-identification.

(d)(1) *Standard: minimum necessary requirements.* A covered entity must reasonably ensure that the standards, requirements, and implementation specifications of § 164.502(b) and this section relating to a request for or the use and disclosure of the minimum necessary protected health information are met.

(2) *Implementation specifications: minimum necessary uses of protected health information.* (i) A covered entity must identify:

(A) Those persons or classes of persons, as appropriate, in its workforce who need access to protected health information to carry out their duties; and

(B) For each such person or class of persons, the category or categories of protected health information to which access is needed and any conditions appropriate to such access.

(ii) A covered entity must make reasonable efforts to limit the access of such persons or classes identified in paragraph (d)(2)(i)(A) of this section to protected health information consistent with paragraph (d)(2)(i)(B) of this section.

(3) *Implementation specification: Minimum necessary disclosures of protected health information.* (i) For any type of disclosure that it makes on a routine and recurring basis, a covered entity must implement policies and procedures (which may be standard protocols) that limit the protected health information disclosed to the amount reasonably necessary to achieve the purpose of the disclosure.

(ii) For all other disclosures, a covered entity must:

(A) Develop criteria designed to limit the protected health information

disclosed to the information reasonably necessary to accomplish the purpose for which disclosure is sought; and

(B) Review requests for disclosure on an individual basis in accordance with such criteria.

(iii) A covered entity may rely, if such reliance is reasonable under the circumstances, on a requested disclosure as the minimum necessary for the stated purpose when:

(A) Making disclosures to public officials that are permitted under § 164.512, if the public official represents that the information requested is the minimum necessary for the stated purpose(s);

(B) The information is requested by another covered entity;

(C) The information is requested by a professional who is a member of its workforce or is a business associate of the covered entity for the purpose of providing professional services to the covered entity, if the professional represents that the information requested is the minimum necessary for the stated purpose(s); or

(D) Documentation or representations that comply with the applicable requirements of § 164.512(i) have been provided by a person requesting the information for research purposes.

(4) *Implementation specifications: Minimum necessary requests for protected health information.* (i) A covered entity must limit any request for protected health information to that which is reasonably necessary to accomplish the purpose for which the request is made, when requesting such information from other covered entities.

(ii) For a request that is made on a routine and recurring basis, a covered entity must implement policies and procedures (which may be standard protocols) that limit the protected health information requested to the amount reasonably necessary to accomplish the purpose for which the request is made.

(iii) For all other requests, a covered entity must review the request on an individual basis to determine that the protected health information sought is limited to the information reasonably necessary to accomplish the purpose for which the request is made.

(5) *Implementation specification: Other content requirement.* For all uses, disclosures, or requests to which the requirements in paragraph (d) of this section apply, a covered entity may not use, disclose or request an entire medical record, except when the entire medical record is specifically justified as the amount that is reasonably necessary to accomplish the purpose of the use, disclosure, or request.

(e)(1) *Standard: Uses and disclosures of protected health information for marketing.* A covered entity may not use or disclose protected health information for marketing without an authorization that meets the applicable requirements of § 164.508, except as provided for by paragraph (e)(2) of this section.

(2) *Implementation specifications: Requirements relating to marketing.* (i) A covered entity is not required to obtain an authorization under § 164.508 when it uses or discloses protected health information to make a marketing communication to an individual that:

(A) Occurs in a face-to-face encounter with the individual;

(B) Concerns products or services of nominal value; or

(C) Concerns the health-related products and services of the covered entity or of a third party and the communication meets the applicable conditions in paragraph (e)(3) of this section.

(ii) A covered entity may disclose protected health information for purposes of such communications only to a business associate that assists the covered entity with such communications.

(3) *Implementation specifications: Requirements for certain marketing communications.* For a marketing communication to qualify under paragraph (e)(2)(i) of this section, the following conditions must be met:

(i) The communication must:

(A) Identify the covered entity as the party making the communication;

(B) If the covered entity has received or will receive direct or indirect remuneration for making the communication, prominently state that fact; and

(C) Except when the communication is contained in a newsletter or similar type of general communication device that the covered entity distributes to a broad cross-section of patients, enrollees, or other broad groups of individuals, contain instructions describing how the individual may opt out of receiving future such communications.

(ii) If the covered entity uses or discloses protected health information to target the communication to individuals based on their health status or condition:

(A) The covered entity must make a determination prior to making the communication that the product or service being marketed may be beneficial to the health of the type or class of individual targeted; and

(B) The communication must explain why the individual has been targeted and how the product or service relates to the health of the individual.

(iii) The covered entity must make reasonable efforts to ensure that individuals who decide to opt out of receiving future marketing communications, under paragraph (e)(3)(i)(C) of this section, are not sent such communications.

(f)(1) *Standard: Uses and disclosures for fundraising.* A covered entity may use, or disclose to a business associate or to an institutionally related foundation, the following protected health information for the purpose of raising funds for its own benefit, without an authorization meeting the requirements of § 164.508:

(i) Demographic information relating to an individual; and

(ii) Dates of health care provided to an individual.

(2) *Implementation specifications: Fundraising requirements.* (i) The covered entity may not use or disclose protected health information for fundraising purposes as otherwise permitted by paragraph (f)(1) of this section unless a statement required by § 164.520(b)(1)(iii)(B) is included in the covered entity's notice;

(ii) The covered entity must include in any fundraising materials it sends to an individual under this paragraph a description of how the individual may opt out of receiving any further fundraising communications.

(iii) The covered entity must make reasonable efforts to ensure that individuals who decide to opt out of receiving future fundraising communications are not sent such communications.

(g) *Standard: Uses and disclosures for underwriting and related purposes.* If a health plan receives protected heath information for the purpose of underwriting, premium rating, or other activities relating to the creation, renewal, or replacement of a contract of health insurance or health benefits, and if such health insurance or health benefits are not placed with the health plan, such health plan may not use or disclose such protected health information for any other purpose, except as may be required by law.

(h)(1) *Standard: Verification requirements.* Prior to any disclosure permitted by this subpart, a covered entity must:

(i) Except with respect to disclosures under § 164.510, verify the identity of a person requesting protected health information and the authority of any such person to have access to protected health information under this subpart, if the identity or any such authority of

such person is not known to the covered entity; and

(ii) Obtain any documentation, statements, or representations, whether oral or written, from the person requesting the protected health information when such documentation, statement, or representation is a condition of the disclosure under this subpart.

(2) *Implementation specifications: Verification.* (i) *Conditions on disclosures.* If a disclosure is conditioned by this subpart on particular documentation, statements, or representations from the person requesting the protected health information, a covered entity may rely, if such reliance is reasonable under the circumstances, on documentation, statements, or representations that, on their face, meet the applicable requirements.

(A) The conditions in § 164.512(f)(1)(ii)(C) may be satisfied by the administrative subpoena or similar process or by a separate written statement that, on its face, demonstrates that the applicable requirements have been met.

(B) The documentation required by § 164.512(i)(2) may be satisfied by one or more written statements, provided that each is appropriately dated and signed in accordance with § 164.512(i)(2)(i) and (v).

(ii) *Identity of public officials.* A covered entity may rely, if such reliance is reasonable under the circumstances, on any of the following to verify identity when the disclosure of protected health information is to a public official or a person acting on behalf of the public official:

(A) If the request is made in person, presentation of an agency identification badge, other official credentials, or other proof of government status;

(B) If the request is in writing, the request is on the appropriate government letterhead; or

(C) If the disclosure is to a person acting on behalf of a public official, a written statement on appropriate government letterhead that the person is acting under the government's authority or other evidence or documentation of agency, such as a contract for services, memorandum of understanding, or purchase order, that establishes that the person is acting on behalf of the public official.

(iii) *Authority of public officials.* A covered entity may rely, if such reliance is reasonable under the circumstances, on any of the following to verify authority when the disclosure of protected health information is to a

public official or a person acting on behalf of the public official:

(A) A written statement of the legal authority under which the information is requested, or, if a written statement would be impracticable, an oral statement of such legal authority;

(B) If a request is made pursuant to legal process, warrant, subpoena, order, or other legal process issued by a grand jury or a judicial or administrative tribunal is presumed to constitute legal authority.

(iv) *Exercise of professional judgment.* The verification requirements of this paragraph are met if the covered entity relies on the exercise of professional judgment in making a use or disclosure in accordance with § 164.510 or acts on a good faith belief in making a disclosure in accordance with § 164.512(j).

§ 164.520 Notice of privacy practices for protected health information.

(a) *Standard: notice of privacy practices.* (1) *Right to notice.* Except as provided by paragraph (a)(2) or (3) of this section, an individual has a right to adequate notice of the uses and disclosures of protected health information that may be made by the covered entity, and of the individual's rights and the covered entity's legal duties with respect to protected health information.

(2) *Exception for group health plans.* (i) An individual enrolled in a group health plan has a right to notice:

(A) From the group health plan, if, and to the extent that, such an individual does not receive health benefits under the group health plan through an insurance contract with a health insurance issuer or HMO; or

(B) From the health insurance issuer or HMO with respect to the group health plan through which such individuals receive their health benefits under the group health plan.

(ii) A group health plan that provides health benefits solely through an insurance contract with a health insurance issuer or HMO, and that creates or receives protected health information in addition to summary health information as defined in § 164.504(a) or information on whether the individual is participating in the group health plan, or is enrolled in or has disenrolled from a health insurance issuer or HMO offered by the plan, must:

(A) Maintain a notice under this section; and

(B) Provide such notice upon request to any person. The provisions of paragraph (c)(1) of this section do not apply to such group health plan.

165

(iii) A group health plan that provides health benefits solely through an insurance contract with a health insurance issuer or HMO, and does not create or receive protected health information other than summary health information as defined in § 164.504(a) or information on whether an individual is participating in the group health plan, or is enrolled in or has disenrolled from a health insurance issuer or HMO offered by the plan, is not required to maintain or provide a notice under this section.

(3) *Exception for inmates.* An inmate does not have a right to notice under this section, and the requirements of this section do not apply to a correctional institution that is a covered entity.

(b) *Implementation specifications: content of notice.*

(1) *Required elements.* The covered entity must provide a notice that is written in plain language and that contains the elements required by this paragraph.

(i) *Header.* The notice must contain the following statement as a header or otherwise prominently displayed: "THIS NOTICE DESCRIBES HOW MEDICAL INFORMATION ABOUT YOU MAY BE USED AND DISCLOSED AND HOW YOU CAN GET ACCESS TO THIS INFORMATION. PLEASE REVIEW IT CAREFULLY."

(ii) *Uses and disclosures.* The notice must contain:

(A) A description, including at least one example, of the types of uses and disclosures that the covered entity is permitted by this subpart to make for each of the following purposes: treatment, payment, and health care operations.

(B) A description of each of the other purposes for which the covered entity is permitted or required by this subpart to use or disclose protected health information without the individual's written consent or authorization.

(C) If a use or disclosure for any purpose described in paragraphs (b)(1)(ii)(A) or (B) of this section is prohibited or materially limited by other applicable law, the description of such use or disclosure must reflect the more stringent law as defined in § 160.202 of this subchapter.

(D) For each purpose described in paragraph (b)(1)(ii)(A) or (B) of this section, the description must include sufficient detail to place the individual on notice of the uses and disclosures that are permitted or required by this subpart and other applicable law.

(E) A statement that other uses and disclosures will be made only with the individual's written authorization and

that the individual may revoke such authorization as provided by § 164.508(b)(5).

(iii) *Separate statements for certain uses or disclosures.* If the covered entity intends to engage in any of the following activities, the description required by paragraph (b)(1)(ii)(A) of this section must include a separate statement, as applicable, that:

(A) The covered entity may contact the individual to provide appointment reminders or information about treatment alternatives or other health-related benefits and services that may be of interest to the individual;

(B) The covered entity may contact the individual to raise funds for the covered entity; or

(C) A group health plan, or a health insurance issuer or HMO with respect to a group health plan, may disclose protected health information to the sponsor of the plan.

(iv) *Individual rights.* The notice must contain a statement of the individual's rights with respect to protected health information and a brief description of how the individual may exercise these rights, as follows:

(A) The right to request restrictions on certain uses and disclosures of protected health information as provided by § 164.522(a), including a statement that the covered entity is not required to agree to a requested restriction;

(B) The right to receive confidential communications of protected health information as provided by § 164.522(b), as applicable;

(C) The right to inspect and copy protected health information as provided by § 164.524;

(D) The right to amend protected health information as provided by § 164.526;

(E) The right to receive an accounting of disclosures of protected health information as provided by § 164.528; and

(F) The right of an individual, including an individual who has agreed to receive the notice electronically in accordance with paragraph (c)(3) of this section, to obtain a paper copy of the notice from the covered entity upon request.

(v) *Covered entity's duties.* The notice must contain:

(A) A statement that the covered entity is required by law to maintain the privacy of protected health information and to provide individuals with notice of its legal duties and privacy practices with respect to protected health information;

(B) A statement that the covered entity is required to abide by the terms of the notice currently in effect; and

(C) For the covered entity to apply a change in a privacy practice that is described in the notice to protected health information that the covered entity created or received prior to issuing a revised notice, in accordance with § 164.530(i)(2)(ii), a statement that it reserves the right to change the terms of its notice and to make the new notice provisions effective for all protected health information that it maintains. The statement must also describe how it will provide individuals with a revised notice.

(vi) *Complaints.* The notice must contain a statement that individuals may complain to the covered entity and to the Secretary if they believe their privacy rights have been violated, a brief description of how the individual may file a complaint with the covered entity, and a statement that the individual will not be retaliated against for filing a complaint.

(vii) *Contact.* The notice must contain the name, or title, and telephone number of a person or office to contact for further information as required by § 164.530(a)(1)(ii).

(viii) *Effective date.* The notice must contain the date on which the notice is first in effect, which may not be earlier than the date on which the notice is printed or otherwise published.

(2) *Optional elements.* (i) In addition to the information required by paragraph (b)(1) of this section, if a covered entity elects to limit the uses or disclosures that it is permitted to make under this subpart, the covered entity may describe its more limited uses or disclosures in its notice, provided that the covered entity may not include in its notice a limitation affecting its right to make a use or disclosure that is required by law or permitted by § 164.512(j)(1)(i).

(ii) For the covered entity to apply a change in its more limited uses and disclosures to protected health information created or received prior to issuing a revised notice, in accordance with § 164.530(i)(2)(ii), the notice must include the statements required by paragraph (b)(1)(v)(C) of this section.

(3) *Revisions to the notice.* The covered entity must promptly revise and distribute its notice whenever there is a material change to the uses or disclosures, the individual's rights, the covered entity's legal duties, or other privacy practices stated in the notice. Except when required by law, a material change to any term of the notice may not be implemented prior to the effective date of the notice in which such material change is reflected.

(c) *Implementation specifications: Provision of notice.* A covered entity must make the notice required by this section available on request to any person and to individuals as specified in paragraphs (c)(1) through (c)(4) of this section, as applicable.

(1) *Specific requirements for health plans.* (i) A health plan must provide notice:

(A) No later than the compliance date for the health plan, to individuals then covered by the plan;

(B) Thereafter, at the time of enrollment, to individuals who are new enrollees; and

(C) Within 60 days of a material revision to the notice, to individuals then covered by the plan.

(ii) No less frequently than once every three years, the health plan must notify individuals then covered by the plan of the availability of the notice and how to obtain the notice.

(iii) The health plan satisfies the requirements of paragraph (c)(1) of this section if notice is provided to the named insured of a policy under which coverage is provided to the named insured and one or more dependents.

(iv) If a health plan has more than one notice, it satisfies the requirements of paragraph (c)(1) of this section by providing the notice that is relevant to the individual or other person requesting the notice.

(2) *Specific requirements for certain covered health care providers.* A covered health care provider that has a direct treatment relationship with an individual must:

(i) Provide the notice no later than the date of the first service delivery, including service delivered electronically, to such individual after the compliance date for the covered health care provider;

(ii) If the covered health care provider maintains a physical service delivery site:

(A) Have the notice available at the service delivery site for individuals to request to take with them; and

(B) Post the notice in a clear and prominent location where it is reasonable to expect individuals seeking service from the covered health care provider to be able to read the notice; and

(iii) Whenever the notice is revised, make the notice available upon request on or after the effective date of the revision and promptly comply with the requirements of paragraph (c)(2)(ii) of this section, if applicable.

(3) *Specific requirements for electronic notice.* (i) A covered entity that maintains a web site that provides information about the covered entity's customer services or benefits must prominently post its notice on the web site and make the notice available electronically through the web site.

(ii) A covered entity may provide the notice required by this section to an individual by e-mail, if the individual agrees to electronic notice and such agreement has not been withdrawn. If the covered entity knows that the e-mail transmission has failed, a paper copy of the notice must be provided to the individual. Provision of electronic notice by the covered entity will satisfy the provision requirements of paragraph (c) of this section when timely made in accordance with paragraph (c)(1) or (2) of this section.

(iii) For purposes of paragraph (c)(2)(i) of this section, if the first service delivery to an individual is delivered electronically, the covered health care provider must provide electronic notice automatically and contemporaneously in response to the individual's first request for service.

(iv) The individual who is the recipient of electronic notice retains the right to obtain a paper copy of the notice from a covered entity upon request.

(d) *Implementation specifications: Joint notice by separate covered entities.* Covered entities that participate in organized health care arrangements may comply with this section by a joint notice, provided that:

(1) The covered entities participating in the organized health care arrangement agree to abide by the terms of the notice with respect to protected health information created or received by the covered entity as part of its participation in the organized health care arrangement;

(2) The joint notice meets the implementation specifications in paragraph (b) of this section, except that the statements required by this section may be altered to reflect the fact that the notice covers more than one covered entity; and

(i) Describes with reasonable specificity the covered entities, or class of entities, to which the joint notice applies;

(ii) Describes with reasonable specificity the service delivery sites, or classes of service delivery sites, to which the joint notice applies; and

(iii) If applicable, states that the covered entities participating in the organized health care arrangement will share protected health information with each other, as necessary to carry out treatment, payment, or health care operations relating to the organized health care arrangement.

(3) The covered entities included in the joint notice must provide the notice to individuals in accordance with the applicable implementation specifications of paragraph (c) of this section. Provision of the joint notice to an individual by any one of the covered entities included in the joint notice will satisfy the provision requirement of paragraph (c) of this section with respect to all others covered by the joint notice.

(e) *Implementation specifications: Documentation.* A covered entity must document compliance with the notice requirements by retaining copies of the notices issued by the covered entity as required by § 164.530(j).

§ 164.522 Rights to request privacy protection for protected health information.

(a)(1) *Standard: Right of an individual to request restriction of uses and disclosures.* (i) A covered entity must permit an individual to request that the covered entity restrict:

(A) Uses or disclosures of protected health information about the individual to carry out treatment, payment, or health care operations; and

(B) Disclosures permitted under § 164.510(b).

(ii) A covered entity is not required to agree to a restriction.

(iii) A covered entity that agrees to a restriction under paragraph (a)(1)(i) of this section may not use or disclose protected health information in violation of such restriction, except that, if the individual who requested the restriction is in need of emergency treatment and the restricted protected health information is needed to provide the emergency treatment, the covered entity may use the restricted protected health information, or may disclose such information to a health care provider, to provide such treatment to the individual.

(iv) If restricted protected health information is disclosed to a health care provider for emergency treatment under paragraph (a)(1)(iii) of this section, the covered entity must request that such health care provider not further use or disclose the information.

(v) A restriction agreed to by a covered entity under paragraph (a) of this section, is not effective under this subpart to prevent uses or disclosures permitted or required under §§ 164.502(a)(2)(i), 164.510(a) or 164.512.

(2) *Implementation specifications: Terminating a restriction.* A covered entity may terminate its agreement to a restriction, if :

(i) The individual agrees to or requests the termination in writing;

(ii) The individual orally agrees to the termination and the oral agreement is documented; or

(iii) The covered entity informs the individual that it is terminating its agreement to a restriction, except that such termination is only effective with respect to protected health information created or received after it has so informed the individual.

(3) *Implementation specification: Documentation.* A covered entity that agrees to a restriction must document the restriction in accordance with § 164.530(j).

(b)(1) *Standard: Confidential communications requirements.* (i) A covered health care provider must permit individuals to request and must accommodate reasonable requests by individuals to receive communications of protected health information from the covered health care provider by alternative means or at alternative locations.

(ii) A health plan must permit individuals to request and must accommodate reasonable requests by individuals to receive communications of protected health information from the health plan by alternative means or at alternative locations, if the individual clearly states that the disclosure of all or part of that information could endanger the individual.

(2) *Implementation specifications: Conditions on providing confidential communications.*

(i) A covered entity may require the individual to make a request for a confidential communication described in paragraph (b)(1) of this section in writing.

(ii) A covered entity may condition the provision of a reasonable accommodation on:

(A) When appropriate, information as to how payment, if any, will be handled; and

(B) Specification of an alternative address or other method of contact.

(iii) A covered health care provider may not require an explanation from the individual as to the basis for the request as a condition of providing communications on a confidential basis.

(iv) A health plan may require that a request contain a statement that disclosure of all or part of the information to which the request pertains could endanger the individual.

§ 164.524 Access of individuals to protected health information.

(a) *Standard: Access to protected health information.* (1) *Right of access.* Except as otherwise provided in paragraph (a)(2) or (a)(3) of this section, an individual has a right of access to inspect and obtain a copy of protected health information about the individual in a designated record set, for as long as the protected health information is

maintained in the designated record set, except for:

(i) Psychotherapy notes;

(ii) Information compiled in reasonable anticipation of, or for use in, a civil, criminal, or administrative action or proceeding; and

(iii) Protected health information maintained by a covered entity that is:

(A) Subject to the Clinical Laboratory Improvements Amendments of 1988, 42 U.S.C. 263a, to the extent the provision of access to the individual would be prohibited by law; or

(B) Exempt from the Clinical Laboratory Improvements Amendments of 1988, pursuant to 42 CFR 493.3(a)(2).

(2) *Unreviewable grounds for denial.* A covered entity may deny an individual access without providing the individual an opportunity for review, in the following circumstances.

(i) The protected health information is excepted from the right of access by paragraph (a)(1) of this section.

(ii) A covered entity that is a correctional institution or a covered health care provider acting under the direction of the correctional institution may deny, in whole or in part, an inmate's request to obtain a copy of protected health information, if obtaining such copy would jeopardize the health, safety, security, custody, or rehabilitation of the individual or of other inmates, or the safety of any officer, employee, or other person at the correctional institution or responsible for the transporting of the inmate.

(iii) An individual's access to protected health information created or obtained by a covered health care provider in the course of research that includes treatment may be temporarily suspended for as long as the research is in progress, provided that the individual has agreed to the denial of access when consenting to participate in the research that includes treatment, and the covered health care provider has informed the individual that the right of access will be reinstated upon completion of the research.

(iv) An individual's access to protected health information that is contained in records that are subject to the Privacy Act, 5 U.S.C. 552a, may be denied, if the denial of access under the Privacy Act would meet the requirements of that law.

(v) An individual's access may be denied if the protected health information was obtained from someone other than a health care provider under a promise of confidentiality and the access requested would be reasonably likely to reveal the source of the information.

(3) *Reviewable grounds for denial.* A covered entity may deny an individual access, provided that the individual is given a right to have such denials reviewed, as required by paragraph (a)(4) of this section, in the following circumstances:

(i) A licensed health care professional has determined, in the exercise of professional judgment, that the access requested is reasonably likely to endanger the life or physical safety of the individual or another person;

(ii) The protected health information makes reference to another person (unless such other person is a health care provider) and a licensed health care professional has determined, in the exercise of professional judgment, that the access requested is reasonably likely to cause substantial harm to such other person; or

(iii) The request for access is made by the individual's personal representative and a licensed health care professional has determined, in the exercise of professional judgment, that the provision of access to such personal representative is reasonably likely to cause substantial harm to the individual or another person.

(4) *Review of a denial of access.* If access is denied on a ground permitted under paragraph (a)(3) of this section, the individual has the right to have the denial reviewed by a licensed health care professional who is designated by the covered entity to act as a reviewing official and who did not participate in the original decision to deny. The covered entity must provide or deny access in accordance with the determination of the reviewing official under paragraph (d)(4) of this section.

(b) *Implementation specifications: requests for access and timely action.* (1) *Individual's request for access.* The covered entity must permit an individual to request access to inspect or to obtain a copy of the protected health information about the individual that is maintained in a designated record set. The covered entity may require individuals to make requests for access in writing, provided that it informs individuals of such a requirement.

(2) *Timely action by the covered entity.* (i) Except as provided in paragraph (b)(2)(ii) of this section, the covered entity must act on a request for access no later than 30 days after receipt of the request as follows.

(A) If the covered entity grants the request, in whole or in part, it must inform the individual of the acceptance of the request and provide the access requested, in accordance with paragraph (c) of this section.

(B) If the covered entity denies the request, in whole or in part, it must provide the individual with a written denial, in accordance with paragraph (d) of this section.

(ii) If the request for access is for protected health information that is not maintained or accessible to the covered entity on-site, the covered entity must take an action required by paragraph (b)(2)(i) of this section by no later than 60 days from the receipt of such a request.

(iii) If the covered entity is unable to take an action required by paragraph (b)(2)(i)(A) or (B) of this section within the time required by paragraph (b)(2)(i) or (ii) of this section, as applicable, the covered entity may extend the time for such actions by no more than 30 days, provided that:

(A) The covered entity, within the time limit set by paragraph (b)(2)(i) or (ii) of this section, as applicable, provides the individual with a written statement of the reasons for the delay and the date by which the covered entity will complete its action on the request; and

(B) The covered entity may have only one such extension of time for action on a request for access.

(c) *Implementation specifications:* *Provision of access.* If the covered entity provides an individual with access, in whole or in part, to protected health information, the covered entity must comply with the following requirements.

(1) *Providing the access requested.* The covered entity must provide the access requested by individuals, including inspection or obtaining a copy, or both, of the protected health information about them in designated record sets. If the same protected health information that is the subject of a request for access is maintained in more than one designated record set or at more than one location, the covered entity need only produce the protected health information once in response to a request for access.

(2) *Form of access requested.* (i) The covered entity must provide the individual with access to the protected health information in the form or format requested by the individual, if it is readily producible in such form or format; or, if not, in a readable hard copy form or such other form or format as agreed to by the covered entity and the individual.

(ii) The covered entity may provide the individual with a summary of the protected health information requested, in lieu of providing access to the protected health information or may provide an explanation of the protected

health information to which access has been provided, if:

(A) The individual agrees in advance to such a summary or explanation; and

(B) The individual agrees in advance to the fees imposed, if any, by the covered entity for such summary or explanation.

(3) *Time and manner of access.* The covered entity must provide the access as requested by the individual in a timely manner as required by paragraph (b)(2) of this section, including arranging with the individual for a convenient time and place to inspect or obtain a copy of the protected health information, or mailing the copy of the protected health information at the individual's request. The covered entity may discuss the scope, format, and other aspects of the request for access with the individual as necessary to facilitate the timely provision of access.

(4) *Fees.* If the individual requests a copy of the protected health information or agrees to a summary or explanation of such information, the covered entity may impose a reasonable, cost-based fee, provided that the fee includes only the cost of:

(i) Copying, including the cost of supplies for and labor of copying, the protected health information requested by the individual;

(ii) Postage, when the individual has requested the copy, or the summary or explanation, be mailed; and

(iii) Preparing an explanation or summary of the protected health information, if agreed to by the individual as required by paragraph (c)(2)(ii) of this section.

(d) *Implementation specifications:* *Denial of access.* If the covered entity denies access, in whole or in part, to protected health information, the covered entity must comply with the following requirements.

(1) *Making other information accessible.* The covered entity must, to the extent possible, give the individual access to any other protected health information requested, after excluding the protected health information as to which the covered entity has a ground to deny access.

(2) *Denial.* The covered entity must provide a timely, written denial to the individual, in accordance with paragraph (b)(2) of this section. The denial must be in plain language and contain:

(i) The basis for the denial;

(ii) If applicable, a statement of the individual's review rights under paragraph (a)(4) of this section, including a description of how the individual may exercise such review rights; and

(iii) A description of how the individual may complain to the covered entity pursuant to the complaint procedures in § 164.530(d) or to the Secretary pursuant to the procedures in § 160.306. The description must include the name, or title, and telephone number of the contact person or office designated in § 164.530(a)(1)(ii).

(3) *Other responsibility.* If the covered entity does not maintain the protected health information that is the subject of the individual's request for access, and the covered entity knows where the requested information is maintained, the covered entity must inform the individual where to direct the request for access.

(4) Review of denial requested. If the individual has requested a review of a denial under paragraph (a)(4) of this section, the covered entity must designate a licensed health care professional, who was not directly involved in the denial to review the decision to deny access. The covered entity must promptly refer a request for review to such designated reviewing official. The designated reviewing official must determine, within a reasonable period of time, whether or not to deny the access requested based on the standards in paragraph (a)(3) of this section. The covered entity must promptly provide written notice to the individual of the determination of the designated reviewing official and take other action as required by this section to carry out the designated reviewing official's determination.

(e) *Implementation specification:* *Documentation.* A covered entity must document the following and retain the documentation as required by § 164.530(j):

(1) The designated record sets that are subject to access by individuals; and

(2) The titles of the persons or offices responsible for receiving and processing requests for access by individuals.

§ 164.526   Amendment of protected health information.

(a) *Standard: Right to amend.* (1) *Right to amend.* An individual has the right to have a covered entity amend protected health information or a record about the individual in a designated record set for as long as the protected health information is maintained in the designated record set.

(2) *Denial of amendment.* A covered entity may deny an individual's request for amendment, if it determines that the protected health information or record that is the subject of the request:

(i) Was not created by the covered entity, unless the individual provides a reasonable basis to believe that the

169

originator of protected health information is no longer available to act on the requested amendment;

(ii) Is not part of the designated record set;

(iii) Would not be available for inspection under § 164.524; or

(iv) Is accurate and complete.

(b) *Implementation specifications: requests for amendment and timely action.* (1) *Individual's request for amendment.* The covered entity must permit an individual to request that the covered entity amend the protected health information maintained in the designated record set. The covered entity may require individuals to make requests for amendment in writing and to provide a reason to support a requested amendment, provided that it informs individuals in advance of such requirements.

(2) *Timely action by the covered entity.* (i) The covered entity must act on the individual's request for an amendment no later than 60 days after receipt of such a request, as follows.

(A) If the covered entity grants the requested amendment, in whole or in part, it must take the actions required by paragraphs (c)(1) and (2) of this section.

(B) If the covered entity denies the requested amendment, in whole or in part, it must provide the individual with a written denial, in accordance with paragraph (d)(1) of this section.

(ii) If the covered entity is unable to act on the amendment within the time required by paragraph (b)(2)(i) of this section, the covered entity may extend the time for such action by no more than 30 days, provided that:

(A) The covered entity, within the time limit set by paragraph (b)(2)(i) of this section, provides the individual with a written statement of the reasons for the delay and the date by which the covered entity will complete its action on the request; and

(B) The covered entity may have only one such extension of time for action on a request for an amendment.

(c) *Implementation specifications: Accepting the amendment.* If the covered entity accepts the requested amendment, in whole or in part, the covered entity must comply with the following requirements.

(1) *Making the amendment.* The covered entity must make the appropriate amendment to the protected health information or record that is the subject of the request for amendment by, at a minimum, identifying the records in the designated record set that are affected by the amendment and appending or otherwise providing a link to the location of the amendment.

(2) *Informing the individual.* In accordance with paragraph (b) of this section, the covered entity must timely inform the individual that the amendment is accepted and obtain the individual's identification of and agreement to have the covered entity notify the relevant persons with which the amendment needs to be shared in accordance with paragraph (c)(3) of this section.

(3) *Informing others.* The covered entity must make reasonable efforts to inform and provide the amendment within a reasonable time to:

(i) Persons identified by the individual as having received protected health information about the individual and needing the amendment; and

(ii) Persons, including business associates, that the covered entity knows have the protected health information that is the subject of the amendment and that may have relied, or could foreseeably rely, on such information to the detriment of the individual.

(d) *Implementation specifications: Denying the amendment.* If the covered entity denies the requested amendment, in whole or in part, the covered entity must comply with the following requirements.

(1) *Denial.* The covered entity must provide the individual with a timely, written denial, in accordance with paragraph (b)(2) of this section. The denial must use plain language and contain:

(i) The basis for the denial, in accordance with paragraph (a)(2) of this section;

(ii) The individual's right to submit a written statement disagreeing with the denial and how the individual may file such a statement;

(iii) A statement that, if the individual does not submit a statement of disagreement, the individual may request that the covered entity provide the individual's request for amendment and the denial with any future disclosures of the protected health information that is the subject of the amendment; and

(iv) A description of how the individual may complain to the covered entity pursuant to the complaint procedures established in § 164.530(d) or to the Secretary pursuant to the procedures established in § 160.306. The description must include the name, or title, and telephone number of the contact person or office designated in § 164.530(a)(1)(ii).

(2) *Statement of disagreement.* The covered entity must permit the individual to submit to the covered entity a written statement disagreeing with the denial of all or part of a requested amendment and the basis of such disagreement. The covered entity may reasonably limit the length of a statement of disagreement.

(3) *Rebuttal statement.* The covered entity may prepare a written rebuttal to the individual's statement of disagreement. Whenever such a rebuttal is prepared, the covered entity must provide a copy to the individual who submitted the statement of disagreement.

(4) *Recordkeeping.* The covered entity must, as appropriate, identify the record or protected health information in the designated record set that is the subject of the disputed amendment and append or otherwise link the individual's request for an amendment, the covered entity's denial of the request, the individual's statement of disagreement, if any, and the covered entity's rebuttal, if any, to the designated record set.

(5) *Future disclosures.* (i) If a statement of disagreement has been submitted by the individual, the covered entity must include the material appended in accordance with paragraph (d)(4) of this section, or, at the election of the covered entity, an accurate summary of any such information, with any subsequent disclosure of the protected health information to which the disagreement relates.

(ii) If the individual has not submitted a written statement of disagreement, the covered entity must include the individual's request for amendment and its denial, or an accurate summary of such information, with any subsequent disclosure of the protected health information only if the individual has requested such action in accordance with paragraph (d)(1)(iii) of this section.

(iii) When a subsequent disclosure described in paragraph (d)(5)(i) or (ii) of this section is made using a standard transaction under part 162 of this subchapter that does not permit the additional material to be included with the disclosure, the covered entity may separately transmit the material required by paragraph (d)(5)(i) or (ii) of this section, as applicable, to the recipient of the standard transaction.

(e) *Implementation specification: Actions on notices of amendment.* A covered entity that is informed by another covered entity of an amendment to an individual's protected health information, in accordance with paragraph (c)(3) of this section, must amend the protected health information in designated record sets as provided by paragraph (c)(1) of this section.

(f) *Implementation specification: Documentation.* A covered entity must document the titles of the persons or offices responsible for receiving and processing requests for amendments by individuals and retain the documentation as required by § 164.530(j).

§ 164.528 Accounting of disclosures of protected health information.

(a) *Standard: Right to an accounting of disclosures of protected health information.* (1) An individual has a right to receive an accounting of disclosures of protected health information made by a covered entity in the six years prior to the date on which the accounting is requested, except for disclosures:

(i) To carry out treatment, payment and health care operations as provided in § 164.502;

(ii) To individuals of protected health information about them as provided in § 164.502;

(iii) For the facility's directory or to persons involved in the individual's care or other notification purposes as provided in § 164.510;

(iv) For national security or intelligence purposes as provided in § 164.512(k)(2);

(v) To correctional institutions or law enforcement officials as provided in § 164.512(k)(5); or

(vi) That occurred prior to the compliance date for the covered entity.

(2)(i) The covered entity must temporarily suspend an individual's right to receive an accounting of disclosures to a health oversight agency or law enforcement official, as provided in § 164.512(d) or (f), respectively, for the time specified by such agency or official, if such agency or official provides the covered entity with a written statement that such an accounting to the individual would be reasonably likely to impede the agency's activities and specifying the time for which such a suspension is required.

(ii) If the agency or official statement in paragraph (a)(2)(i) of this section is made orally, the covered entity must:

(A) Document the statement, including the identity of the agency or official making the statement;

(B) Temporarily suspend the individual's right to an accounting of disclosures subject to the statement; and

(C) Limit the temporary suspension to no longer than 30 days from the date of the oral statement, unless a written statement pursuant to paragraph (a)(2)(i) of this section is submitted during that time.

(3) An individual may request an accounting of disclosures for a period of time less than six years from the date of the request.

(b) *Implementation specifications: Content of the accounting.* The covered entity must provide the individual with a written accounting that meets the following requirements.

(1) Except as otherwise provided by paragraph (a) of this section, the accounting must include disclosures of protected health information that occurred during the six years (or such shorter time period at the request of the individual as provided in paragraph (a)(3) of this section) prior to the date of the request for an accounting, including disclosures to or by business associates of the covered entity.

(2) The accounting must include for each disclosure:

(i) The date of the disclosure;

(ii) The name of the entity or person who received the protected health information and, if known, the address of such entity or person;

(iii) A brief description of the protected health information disclosed; and

(iv) A brief statement of the purpose of the disclosure that reasonably informs the individual of the basis for the disclosure; or, in lieu of such statement:

(A) A copy of the individual's written authorization pursuant to § 164.508; or

(B) A copy of a written request for a disclosure under §§ 164.502(a)(2)(ii) or 164.512, if any.

(3) If, during the period covered by the accounting, the covered entity has made multiple disclosures of protected health information to the same person or entity for a single purpose under §§ 164.502(a)(2)(ii) or 164.512, or pursuant to a single authorization under § 164.508, the accounting may, with respect to such multiple disclosures, provide:

(i) The information required by paragraph (b)(2) of this section for the first disclosure during the accounting period;

(ii) The frequency, periodicity, or number of the disclosures made during the accounting period; and

(iii) The date of the last such disclosure during the accounting period.

(c) *Implementation specifications: Provision of the accounting.* (1) The covered entity must act on the individual's request for an accounting, no later than 60 days after receipt of such a request, as follows.

(i) The covered entity must provide the individual with the accounting requested; or

(ii) If the covered entity is unable to provide the accounting within the time required by paragraph (c)(1) of this section, the covered entity may extend the time to provide the accounting by no more than 30 days, provided that:

(A) The covered entity, within the time limit set by paragraph (c)(1) of this section, provides the individual with a written statement of the reasons for the delay and the date by which the covered entity will provide the accounting; and

(B) The covered entity may have only one such extension of time for action on a request for an accounting.

(2) The covered entity must provide the first accounting to an individual in any 12 month period without charge. The covered entity may impose a reasonable, cost-based fee for each subsequent request for an accounting by the same individual within the 12 month period, provided that the covered entity informs the individual in advance of the fee and provides the individual with an opportunity to withdraw or modify the request for a subsequent accounting in order to avoid or reduce the fee.

(d) *Implementation specification: Documentation.* A covered entity must document the following and retain the documentation as required by § 164.530(j):

(1) The information required to be included in an accounting under paragraph (b) of this section for disclosures of protected health information that are subject to an accounting under paragraph (a) of this section;

(2) The written accounting that is provided to the individual under this section; and

(3) The titles of the persons or offices responsible for receiving and processing requests for an accounting by individuals.

§ 164.530 Administrative requirements.

(a)(1) *Standard: Personnel designations.* (i) A covered entity must designate a privacy official who is responsible for the development and implementation of the policies and procedures of the entity.

(ii) A covered entity must designate a contact person or office who is responsible for receiving complaints under this section and who is able to provide further information about matters covered by the notice required by § 164.520.

(2) *Implementation specification: Personnel designations.* A covered entity must document the personnel designations in paragraph (a)(1) of this section as required by paragraph (j) of this section.

(b)(1) Standard: Training. A covered entity must train all members of its workforce on the policies and procedures with respect to protected health information required by this subpart, as necessary and appropriate for the members of the workforce to carry out their function within the covered entity.

(2) *Implementation specifications: Training.* (i) A covered entity must provide training that meets the requirements of paragraph (b)(1) of this section, as follows:

(A) To each member of the covered entity's workforce by no later than the compliance date for the covered entity;

(B) Thereafter, to each new member of the workforce within a reasonable period of time after the person joins the covered entity's workforce; and

(C) To each member of the covered entity's workforce whose functions are affected by a material change in the policies or procedures required by this subpart, within a reasonable period of time after the material change becomes effective in accordance with paragraph (i) of this section.

(ii) A covered entity must document that the training as described in paragraph (b)(2)(i) of this section has been provided, as required by paragraph (j) of this section.

(c)(1) *Standard: Safeguards.* A covered entity must have in place appropriate administrative, technical, and physical safeguards to protect the privacy of protected health information.

(2) *Implementation specification: Safeguards.* A covered entity must reasonably safeguard protected health information from any intentional or unintentional use or disclosure that is in violation of the standards, implementation specifications or other requirements of this subpart.

(d)(1) *Standard: Complaints to the covered entity.* A covered entity must provide a process for individuals to make complaints concerning the covered entity's policies and procedures required by this subpart or its compliance with such policies and procedures or the requirements of this subpart.

(2) *Implementation specification: Documentation of complaints.* As required by paragraph (j) of this section, a covered entity must document all complaints received, and their disposition, if any.

(e)(1) *Standard: Sanctions.* A covered entity must have and apply appropriate sanctions against members of its workforce who fail to comply with the privacy policies and procedures of the covered entity or the requirements of this subpart. This standard does not apply to a member of the covered entity's workforce with respect to actions that are covered by and that meet the conditions of § 164.502(j) or paragraph (g)(2) of this section.

(2) *Implementation specification: Documentation.* As required by

paragraph (j) of this section, a covered entity must document the sanctions that are applied, if any.

(f) *Standard: Mitigation.* A covered entity must mitigate, to the extent practicable, any harmful effect that is known to the covered entity of a use or disclosure of protected health information in violation of its policies and procedures or the requirements of this subpart by the covered entity or its business associate.

(g) *Standard: Refraining from intimidating or retaliatory acts.* A covered entity may not intimidate, threaten, coerce, discriminate against, or take other retaliatory action against:

(1) *Individuals.* Any individual for the exercise by the individual of any right under, or for participation by the individual in any process established by this subpart, including the filing of a complaint under this section;

(2) *Individuals and others.* Any individual or other person for:

(i) Filing of a complaint with the Secretary under subpart C of part 160 of this subchapter;

(ii) Testifying, assisting, or participating in an investigation, compliance review, proceeding, or hearing under Part C of Title XI; or

(iii) Opposing any act or practice made unlawful by this subpart, provided the individual or person has a good faith belief that the practice opposed is unlawful, and the manner of the opposition is reasonable and does not involve a disclosure of protected health information in violation of this subpart.

(h) *Standard: Waiver of rights.* A covered entity may not require individuals to waive their rights under § 160.306 of this subchapter or this subpart as a condition of the provision of treatment, payment, enrollment in a health plan, or eligibility for benefits.

(i)(1) *Standard: Policies and procedures.* A covered entity must implement policies and procedures with respect to protected health information that are designed to comply with the standards, implementation specifications, or other requirements of this subpart. The policies and procedures must be reasonably designed, taking into account the size of and the type of activities that relate to protected health information undertaken by the covered entity, to ensure such compliance. This standard is not to be construed to permit or excuse an action that violates any other standard, implementation specification, or other requirement of this subpart.

(2) *Standard: Changes to policies or procedures.* (i) A covered entity must change its policies and procedures as

necessary and appropriate to comply with changes in the law, including the standards, requirements, and implementation specifications of this subpart;

(ii) When a covered entity changes a privacy practice that is stated in the notice described in § 164.520, and makes corresponding changes to its policies and procedures, it may make the changes effective for protected health information that it created or received prior to the effective date of the notice revision, if the covered entity has, in accordance with § 164.520(b)(1)(v)(C), included in the notice a statement reserving its right to make such a change in its privacy practices; or

(iii) A covered entity may make any other changes to policies and procedures at any time, provided that the changes are documented and implemented in accordance with paragraph (i)(5) of this section.

(3) *Implementation specification: Changes in law.* Whenever there is a change in law that necessitates a change to the covered entity's policies or procedures, the covered entity must promptly document and implement the revised policy or procedure. If the change in law materially affects the content of the notice required by § 164.520, the covered entity must promptly make the appropriate revisions to the notice in accordance with § 164.520(b)(3). Nothing in this paragraph may be used by a covered entity to excuse a failure to comply with the law.

(4) *Implementation specifications: Changes to privacy practices stated in the notice.* (i) To implement a change as provided by paragraph (i)(2)(ii) of this section, a covered entity must:

(A) Ensure that the policy or procedure, as revised to reflect a change in the covered entity's privacy practice as stated in its notice, complies with the standards, requirements, and implementation specifications of this subpart;

(B) Document the policy or procedure, as revised, as required by paragraph (j) of this section; and

(C) Revise the notice as required by § 164.520(b)(3) to state the changed practice and make the revised notice available as required by § 164.520(c). The covered entity may not implement a change to a policy or procedure prior to the effective date of the revised notice.

(ii) If a covered entity has not reserved its right under § 164.520(b)(1)(v)(C) to change a privacy practice that is stated in the notice, the covered entity is bound by the privacy practices as stated in the notice with respect to protected health information created or received while such notice is in effect. A covered entity may change a privacy practice that is stated in the notice, and the related policies and procedures, without having reserved the right to do so, provided that:

(A) Such change meets the implementation the requirements in paragraphs (i)(4)(i)(A)–(C) of this section; and

(B) Such change is effective only with respect to protected health information created or received after the effective date of the notice.

(5) *Implementation specification: Changes to other policies or procedures.* A covered entity may change, at any time, a policy or procedure that does not materially affect the content of the notice required by § 164.520, provided that:

(i) The policy or procedure, as revised, complies with the standards, requirements, and implementation specifications of this subpart; and

(ii) Prior to the effective date of the change, the policy or procedure, as revised, is documented as required by paragraph (j) of this section.

(j)(1) *Standard: Documentation.* A covered entity must:

(i) Maintain the policies and procedures provided for in paragraph (i) of this section in written or electronic form;

(ii) If a communication is required by this subpart to be in writing, maintain such writing, or an electronic copy, as documentation; and

(iii) If an action, activity, or designation is required by this subpart to be documented, maintain a written or electronic record of such action, activity, or designation.

(2) *Implementation specification: Retention period.* A covered entity must retain the documentation required by paragraph (j)(1) of this section for six years from the date of its creation or the date when it last was in effect, whichever is later.

(k) *Standard: Group health plans.* (1) A group health plan is not subject to the standards or implementation specifications in paragraphs (a) through (f) and (i) of this section, to the extent that:

(i) The group health plan provides health benefits solely through an insurance contract with a health insurance issuer or an HMO; and

(ii) The group health plan does not create or receive protected health information, except for:

(A) Summary health information as defined in § 164.504(a); or

(B) Information on whether the individual is participating in the group health plan, or is enrolled in or has disenrolled from a health insurance issuer or HMO offered by the plan.

(2) A group health plan described in paragraph (k)(1) of this section is subject to the standard and implementation specification in paragraph (j) of this section only with respect to plan documents amended in accordance with § 164.504(f).

§ 164.532 Transition provisions.

(a) *Standard: Effect of prior consents and authorizations.* Notwithstanding other sections of this subpart, a covered entity may continue to use or disclose protected health information pursuant to a consent, authorization, or other express legal permission obtained from an individual permitting the use or disclosure of protected health information that does not comply with §§ 164.506 or 164.508 of this subpart consistent with paragraph (b) of this section.

(b) *Implementation specification: Requirements for retaining effectiveness of prior consents and authorizations.* Notwithstanding other sections of this subpart, the following provisions apply to use or disclosure by a covered entity of protected health information pursuant to a consent, authorization, or other express legal permission obtained from an individual permitting the use or disclosure of protected health information, if the consent, authorization, or other express legal permission was obtained from an individual before the applicable compliance date of this subpart and does not comply with §§ 164.506 or 164.508 of this subpart.

(1) If the consent, authorization, or other express legal permission obtained from an individual permits a use or disclosure for purposes of carrying out treatment, payment, or health care operations, the covered entity may, with respect to protected health information that it created or received before the applicable compliance date of this subpart and to which the consent, authorization, or other express legal permission obtained from an individual applies, use or disclose such information for purposes of carrying out treatment, payment, or health care operations, provided that:

(i) The covered entity does not make any use or disclosure that is expressly excluded from the a consent, authorization, or other express legal permission obtained from an individual; and

(ii) The covered entity complies with all limitations placed by the consent,

authorization, or other express legal permission obtained from an individual.

(2) If the consent, authorization, or other express legal permission obtained from an individual specifically permits a use or disclosure for a purpose other than to carry out treatment, payment, or health care operations, the covered entity may, with respect to protected health information that it created or received before the applicable compliance date of this subpart and to which the consent, authorization, or other express legal permission obtained from an individual applies, make such use or disclosure, provided that:

(i) The covered entity does not make any use or disclosure that is expressly excluded from the consent, authorization, or other express legal permission obtained from an individual; and

(ii) The covered entity complies with all limitations placed by the consent, authorization, or other express legal permission obtained from an individual.

(3) In the case of a consent, authorization, or other express legal permission obtained from an individual that identifies a specific research project that includes treatment of individuals:

(i) If the consent, authorization, or other express legal permission obtained from an individual specifically permits a use or disclosure for purposes of the project, the covered entity may, with respect to protected health information that it created or received either before or after the applicable compliance date of this subpart and to which the consent or authorization applies, make such use or disclosure for purposes of that project, provided that the covered entity complies with all limitations placed by the consent, authorization, or other express legal permission obtained from an individual.

(ii) If the consent, authorization, or other express legal permission obtained from an individual is a general consent to participate in the project, and a covered entity is conducting or participating in the research, such covered entity may, with respect to protected health information that it created or received as part of the project before or after the applicable compliance date of this subpart, make a use or disclosure for purposes of that project, provided that the covered entity complies with all limitations placed by the consent, authorization, or other express legal permission obtained from an individual.

(4) If, after the applicable compliance date of this subpart, a covered entity agrees to a restriction requested by an individual under § 164.522(a), a subsequent use or disclosure of

protected health information that is subject to the restriction based on a consent, authorization, or other express legal permission obtained from an individual as given effect by paragraph (b) of this section, must comply with such restriction.

§ 164.534   Compliance dates for initial implementation of the privacy standards.

(a) *Health care providers.* A covered health care provider must comply with the applicable requirements of this subpart no later than February 26, 2003.

(b) *Health plans.* A health plan must comply with the applicable requirements of this subpart no later than the following date, as applicable:

(1) *Health plans other than small health plans*—February 26, 2003.

(2) *Small health plans*—February 26, 2004.

(c) *Health care clearinghouses.* A health care clearinghouse must comply with the applicable requirements of this subpart no later than February 26, 2003.

[FR Doc. 00–32678 Filed 12–20–00; 11:21 am]

BILLING CODE 4150–04–P

Appendix B

HHS Clarification of the Federal Privacy Rule

HHS Clarification of the Federal Privacy Rule

[45 CFR Parts 160 and 164]

General Overview

The following is an overview that provides answers to general questions regarding the regulation entitled, Standards for Privacy of Individually Identifiable Health Information (the Privacy Rule), promulgated by the Department of Health and Human Services (HHS), and process for modifications to that rule. Detailed guidance on specific requirements in the regulation is presented in subsequent sections, each of which addresses a different standard. The Privacy Rule provides the first comprehensive federal protection for the privacy of health information. All segments of the health care industry have expressed their support for the objective of enhanced patient privacy in the health care system. At the same time, HHS and most parties agree that privacy protections must not interfere with a patient's access to or the quality of health care delivery.

The guidance provided in this section and those that follow is meant to communicate as clearly as possible the privacy policies contained in the rule. Each section has a short summary of a particular standard in the Privacy Rule, followed by "Frequently Asked Questions" about that provision. In some cases, the guidance identifies areas of the Privacy Rule where a modification or change to the rule is necessary. These areas are summarized below in response to the question "What changes might you make to the final rule?" and discussed in more detail in the subsequent sections of this guidance. We emphasize that this guidance document is only the first of several technical assistance materials that we will issue to provide clarification and help covered entities implement the rule. We anticipate that there will be many questions that will arise on an ongoing basis which we will need to answer in future guidance. In addition, the Department will issue proposed modifications as necessary in one or more rulemakings to ensure that patients' privacy

needs are appropriately met. The Department plans to work expeditiously to address these additional questions and propose modifications as necessary.

Frequently Asked Questions

Q: What does this regulation do?

A: The Privacy Rule became effective on April 14, 2001. Most health plans and health care providers that are covered by the new rule must comply with the new requirements by April 2003.

The Privacy Rule for the first time creates national standards to protect individuals' medical records and other personal health information.

- It gives patients more control over their health information.
- It sets boundaries on the use and release of health records.
- It establishes appropriate safeguards that health care providers and others must achieve to protect the privacy of health information.
- It holds violators accountable, with civil and criminal penalties that can be imposed if they violate patients' privacy rights.
- And it strikes a balance when public responsibility requires disclosure of some forms of data - for example, to protect public health.

For patients - it means being able to make informed choices when seeking care and reimbursement for care based on how personal health information may be used.

- It enables patients to find out how their information may be used and what disclosures of their information have been made.

- It generally limits release of information to the minimum reasonably needed for the purpose of the disclosure.
- It gives patients the right to examine and obtain a copy of their own health records and request corrections.

Q: Why is this regulation needed?

A: In enacting the Health Insurance Portability and Accountability Act of 1996 (HIPAA), Congress mandated the establishment of standards for the privacy of individually identifiable health information.

When it comes to personal information that moves across hospitals, doctors' offices, insurers or third party payers, and state lines, our country has relied on a patchwork of federal and state laws. Under the current patchwork of laws, personal health information can be distributed - without either notice or consent - for reasons that have nothing to do with a patient's medical treatment or health care reimbursement. Patient information held by a health plan may be passed on to a lender who may then deny the patient's application for a home mortgage or a credit card - or to an employer who may use it in personnel decisions. The Privacy Rule establishes a federal floor of safeguards to protect the confidentiality of medical information. State laws which provide stronger privacy protections will continue to apply over and above the new federal privacy standards.

Health care providers have a strong tradition of safeguarding private health information. But in today's world, the old system of paper records in locked filing cabinets is not enough. With information broadly held and transmitted electronically, the rule provides clear standards for all parties regarding protection of personal health information.

Q: What does this regulation require the average provider or health plan to do?

A: For the average health care provider or health plan, the Privacy Rule requires activities, such as:

- Providing information to patients about their privacy rights and how their information can be used.
- Adopting clear privacy procedures for its practice, hospital, or plan.
- Training employees so that they understand the privacy procedures.

- Designating an individual to be responsible for seeing that the privacy procedures are adopted and followed.
- Securing patient records containing individually identifiable health information so that they are not readily available to those who do not need them.

Responsible health care providers and businesses already take many of the kinds of steps required by the rule to protect patients' privacy. Covered entities of all types and sizes are required to comply with the final Privacy Rule. To ease the burden of complying with the new requirements, the Privacy Rule gives needed flexibility for providers and plans to create their own privacy procedures, tailored to fit their size and needs. The scalability of the rules provides a more efficient and appropriate means of safeguarding protected health information than would any single standard. For example,

- The privacy official at a small physician practice may be the office manager, who will have other non-privacy related duties; the privacy official at a large health plan may be a full-time position, and may have the regular support and advice of a privacy staff or board.
- The training requirement may be satisfied by a small physician practice's providing each new member of the workforce with a copy of its privacy policies and documenting that new members have reviewed the policies; whereas a large health plan may provide training through live instruction, video presentations, or interactive software programs.
- The policies and procedures of small providers may be more limited under the rule than those of a large hospital or health plan, based on the volume of health information maintained and the number of interactions with those within and outside of the health care system.

Q. Who must comply with these new privacy standards?

A: As required by Congress in HIPAA, the Privacy Rule covers health plans, health care clearinghouses, and those health care providers who conduct certain financial and administrative transactions electronically. These electronic transactions are those for which standards are required to be adopted by the Secretary under HIPAA, such as electronic billing and fund transfers. These entities (collectively called "covered entities") are bound by the new privacy standards even if they contract with others (called "business associates") to perform some of their essential functions. The law does not give HHS the authority to regulate other types of private businesses or public agencies through this regulation. For example, HHS does not have the authority to regulate employers, life insurance companies, or public agencies that deliver social security or welfare benefits. The "Business associate" section of this guidance provides a more detailed discussion of the covered entities' responsibilities when they engage others to perform essential functions or services for them.

Q: When will covered entities have to meet these standards?

A: As Congress required in HIPAA, most covered entities have two full years from the date that the regulation took effect - or, until April 14, 2003 - to come into compliance with these standards. Under the law, small health plans will have three full years - or, until April 14, 2004 - to come into compliance.

The HHS Office for Civil Rights (OCR) will provide assistance to help covered entities prepare to comply with the rule. OCR maintains a Web site with information on the new regulation, including guidance for industry, such as these frequently asked questions, at http://www.hhs.gov/ocr/hipaa/.

Q: Do you expect to make any changes to this rule before the compliance date?

A: We can and will issue proposed modifications to correct any unintended negative effects of the Privacy Rule on health care quality or on access to such care.

In February 2001, Secretary Thompson requested public comments on the final rule to help HHS assess the rule's real-world impact in health care delivery. During the 30-day comment period, we received more than 11,000 letters or comments - including some petitions with thousands of names. These comments are helping to guide the Department's efforts to clarify areas of the rule to eliminate uncertainties and to help covered entities begin their implementation efforts.

Q: What changes might you make in the final rule?

A: We continue to review the input received during the recent public comment period to determine what changes are appropriate to ensure that the rule protects patient privacy as intended without harming consumers' access to care or the quality of that care.

Examples of standards in the Privacy Rule for which we will propose changes are:

- Phoned-in Prescriptions - A change will permit pharmacists to fill prescriptions phoned in by a patient's doctor before obtaining the patient's written consent (see the "Consent" section of this guidance for more discussion).
- Referral Appointments - A change will permit direct treatment providers receiving a first time patient referral to schedule appointments, surgery, or other procedures before obtaining the patient's signed consent (see the "Consent" section of this guidance for more discussion).
- Allowable Communications - A change will increase the confidence of covered entities that they are free to engage in whatever communications are required for quick, effective, high quality health care, including routine oral communications with family members, treatment discussions with staff involved
- in coordination of patient care, and using patient names to locate them in waiting areas (see the "Oral Communications" section of this guidance for more discussion).
- Minimum Necessary Scope - A change will increase covered entities' confidence that certain common practices, such as use of sign-up sheets and X-ray lightboards, and maintenance of patient medical charts at bedside, are not prohibited under the rule (see the "Minimum Necessary" section of this guidance for more discussion).

In addition, HHS may reevaluate the Privacy Rule to ensure that parents have appropriate access to information about the health and well-being of their children. This issue is discussed further in the "Parents and Minors" section of this guidance.

Other changes to the Privacy Rule also may be considered as appropriate.

Q: How will you make any changes?

A: Any changes to the final rule must be made in accordance with the Administrative Procedures Act (APA). HHS intends to comply with the APA by publishing its rule changes in the Federal Register through a Notice of Proposed Rulemaking and will invite comment from the public. After reviewing and addressing those comments, HHS will issue a final rule to implement appropriate modifications.

Congress specifically authorized HHS to make appropriate modifications in the first year after the final rule took effect in order to ensure the rule could be properly implemented in the real world. We are working as quickly as we can to identify where modifications are needed and what corrections need to be made so as to give covered entities as much time as possible to implement the rule.

Covered entities can and should begin the process of implementing the privacy standards in order to meet their compliance dates.

Consent [45 CFR § 164.506]

Background

The Privacy Rule establishes a federal requirement that most doctors, hospitals, or other health care providers obtain a patient's written consent before using or disclosing the patient's personal health information to carry out treatment, payment, or health care operations (TPO). Today, many health care providers, for professional or ethical reasons, routinely obtain a patient's consent for disclosure of information to insurance companies or for other purposes. The Privacy Rule builds on these practices by establishing a uniform standard for certain health care providers to obtain their patients' consent for uses and disclosures of health information about the patient to carry out TPO.

General Provisions

- Patient consent is required before a covered health care provider that has a direct treatment relationship with the patient may use or disclose protected health information (PHI) for purposes of TPO. Exceptions to this standard are shown in the next bullet.
- Uses and disclosures for TPO may be permitted without prior consent in an emergency,

when a provider is required by law to treat the individual, or when there are substantial communication barriers.
- Health care providers that have indirect treatment relationships with patients (such as laboratories that only interact with physicians and not patients), health plans, and health care clearinghouses may use and disclose PHI for purposes of TPO without obtaining a patient's consent. The rule permits such entities to obtain consent, if they choose.
- If a patient refuses to consent to the use or disclosure of their PHI to carry out TPO, the health care provider may refuse to treat the patient.
- A patient's written consent need only be obtained by a provider one time.
- The consent document may be brief and may be written in general terms. It must be written in plain language, inform the individual that information may be used and disclosed for TPO, state the patient's rights to review the provider's privacy notice, to request restrictions and to revoke consent, and be dated and signed by the individual (or his or her representative).

Individual Rights

- An individual may revoke consent in writing, except to the extent that the covered entity has taken action in reliance on the consent.
- An individual may request restrictions on uses or disclosures of health information for TPO. The covered entity need not agree to the restriction requested, but is bound by any restriction to which it agrees.
- An individual must be given a notice of the covered entity's privacy practices and may review that notice prior to signing a consent.

Administrative Issues

- A covered entity must retain the signed consent for 6 years from the date it was last in effect. The Privacy Rule does not dictate the form in which these consents are to be retained by the covered entity.
- Certain integrated covered entities may obtain one joint consent for multiple entities.
- If a covered entity obtains consent and also

receives an authorization to disclose PHI for TPO, the covered entity may disclose information only in accordance with the more restrictive document, unless the covered entity resolves the conflict with the individual.

- Transition provisions allow providers to rely on consents received prior to April 14, 2003 (the compliance date of the Privacy Rule for most covered entities), for uses and disclosures of health information obtained prior to that date.

Frequently Asked Questions

Q. Are health plans or clearinghouses required to obtain an individual's consent to use or disclose PHI to carry out TPO?

A: No. Health plans and clearinghouses may use and disclose PHI for these purposes without obtaining consent. These entities are permitted to obtain consent. If they choose to seek individual consent for these uses and disclosures, the consent must meet the standards, requirements, and implementation specifications for consents set forth under the rule.

Q: Can a pharmacist use PHI to fill a prescription that was telephoned in by a patient's physician if the patient is a new patient to the pharmacy and has not yet provided written consent to the pharmacy?

A: The Privacy Rule, as written, does not permit this activity without prior patient consent. It poses a problem for first-time users of a particular pharmacy or pharmacy chain. The Department of Health and Human Services did not intend the rule to interfere with a pharmacist's normal activities in this way.

The Secretary is aware of this problem, and will propose modifications to fix it to ensure ready patient access to high quality health care.

Q: Can direct treatment providers, such as a specialist or hospital, to whom a patient is referred for the first time, use PHI to set up appointments or schedule surgery or other procedures before obtaining the patient's written consent?

A: As in the pharmacist example above, the Privacy Rule, as written, does not permit uses of PHI prior to obtaining the patient's written consent for TPO. This unintended problem potentially exists in any circumstance when a patient's first contact with a direct

treatment provider is not in person. As noted above, the Secretary is aware of this problem and will propose modifications to fix it.

Q: Will the consent requirement restrict the ability of providers to consult with other providers about a patient's condition?

A: No. A provider with a direct treatment relationship with a patient would have to have initially obtained consent to use that patient's health information for treatment purposes. Consulting with another health care provider about the patient's case falls within the definition of "treatment" and, therefore, is permissible. If the provider being consulted does not otherwise have a direct treatment relationship with the patient, that provider does not need to obtain the patient's consent to engage in the consultation.

Q: Does a pharmacist have to obtain a consent under the Privacy Rule in order to provide advice about over-the-counter medicines to customers?

A: No. A pharmacist may provide advice about over-the-counter medicines without obtaining the customers' prior consent, provided that the pharmacist does not create or keep a record of any PHI. In this case, the only interaction or disclosure of information is a conversation between the pharmacist and the customer. The pharmacist may disclose PHI about the customer to the customer without obtaining his or her consent (§ 164.502(a)(1)(i)), but may not otherwise use or disclose that information.

Q: Can a patient have a friend or family member pick up a prescription for her?

A: Yes. A pharmacist may use professional judgment and experience with common practice to make reasonable inferences of the patient's best interest in allowing a person, other than the patient, to pick up a prescription (see § 164.510(b)). For example, the fact that a relative or friend arrives at a pharmacy and asks to pick up a specific prescription for an individual effectively verifies that he or she is involved in the individual's care, and the rule allows the pharmacist to give the filled prescription to the relative or friend. The individual does not need to provide the pharmacist with the names of such persons in advance.

Q: The rule provides an exception to the prior consent requirement for "emergency treatment situations." How will a provider know when the situation is an "emergency treatment situation" and, therefore, is exempt from the Privacy Rule's prior consent requirement?

A: Health care providers must exercise their professional judgment to determine whether obtaining a consent would interfere with the timely delivery of necessary health care. If, based on professional judgment, a provider reasonably believes at the time the patient presents for treatment that a delay involved in obtaining the patient's consent to use or disclose information would compromise the patient's care, the provider may use or disclose PHI that was obtained during the emergency treatment, without prior consent, to carry out TPO. The provider must attempt to obtain consent as soon as reasonably practicable after the provision of treatment. If the provider is able to obtain the patient's consent to use or disclose information before providing care, without compromising the patient's care, we require the provider to do so.

Q: Does the exception to the consent requirement regarding substantial barriers to communication with the individual affect requirements under Title VI of the Civil Rights Act of 1964 or the Americans with Disabilities Act?

A: No. The provision of the Privacy Rule regarding substantial barriers to communication does not affect covered entities' obligations under Title VI or the Americans with Disabilities Act. Entities that are covered by these statutes must continue to meet the requirements of the statutes. The Privacy Rule works in conjunction with these laws to remove impediments to access to necessary health care for all individuals.

Q: What is the difference between "consent" and "authorization" under the Privacy Rule?

A: A consent is a general document that gives health care providers, which have a direct treatment relationship with a patient, permission to use and disclose all PHI for TPO. It gives permission only to that provider, not to any other person. Health care providers may condition the provision of treatment on the individual providing this consent. One consent may cover all uses and disclosures for TPO by that provider, indefinitely. A consent need not specify the particular information to be used or disclosed, nor the recipients of disclosed information. Only doctors or

other health care providers with a direct treatment relationship with a patient are required to obtain consent. Generally, a "direct treatment provider" is one that treats a patient directly, rather than based on the orders of another provider, and/or provides health care services or test results directly to patients. Other health care providers, health plans, and health care clearinghouses may use or disclose information for TPO without consent, or may choose to obtain a consent.

An authorization is a more customized document that gives covered entities permission to use specified PHI for specified purposes, which are generally other than TPO, or to disclose PHI to a third party specified by the individual.

Covered entities may not condition treatment or coverage on the individual providing an authorization. An authorization is more detailed and specific than a consent. It covers only the uses and disclosures and only the PHI stipulated in the authorization; it has an expiration date; and, in some cases, it also states the purpose for which the information may be used or disclosed.

An authorization is required for use and disclosure of PHI not otherwise allowed by the rule. In general, this means an authorization is required for purposes that are not part of TPO and not described in § 164.510 (uses and disclosures that require an opportunity for the individual to agree or to object) or § 164.512 (uses and disclosures for which consent, authorization, or an opportunity to agree or to object is not required). Situations in which an authorization is required for TPO purposes are identified and discussed in the next question.

All covered entities, not just direct treatment providers, must obtain an authorization to use or disclose PHI for these purposes. For example, a covered entity would need an authorization from individuals to sell a patient mailing list, to disclose information to an employer for employment decisions, or to disclose information for eligibility for life insurance. A covered entity will never need to obtain both an individual's consent and authorization for a single use or disclosure. However, a provider may have to obtain consent and authorization from the same patient for different uses or disclosures. For example, an obstetrician may, under the consent obtained from the patient, send an appointment reminder to the patient, but would need authorization from the patient to send her name and address to a company marketing a diaper service.

Q: Would a covered entity ever need an authorization rather than a consent for uses or disclosures of PHI for TPO?

A: Yes. The Privacy Rule requires providers to obtain authorization and not consent to use or disclose PHI maintained in psychotherapy notes for treatment by persons other than the originator of the notes, for payment, or for health care operations purposes, except as specified in the Privacy Rule (§ 164.508(a)(2)). In addition, because the consent is only for a use or disclosure of PHI for the TPO purposes of the covered entity obtaining the consent, an authorization is also required if the disclosure is for the TPO purposes of an entity other than the provider who obtained the consent. For example, a health plan seeking payment for a particular service from a second health plan, such as in coordination of benefits or secondary payer situations, may need PHI from a physician who rendered the health care services. In this case, the provider typically has been paid, and the transaction is between the plans. Since the provider's disclosure is for the TPO purposes of the plan, it would not be covered by the provider's consent. Rather, an authorization, and not a consent, would be the proper document for the plan to use when requesting such a disclosure.

Q: Will health care providers be required to determine whether another covered entity has a more restrictive consent form before disclosing information to that entity for TPO purposes?

A: No. Generally, a consent permits only the covered entity that obtains the consent to use or disclose PHI for its own TPO purposes. Under the Privacy Rule, one covered entity is not bound by a consent or any restrictions on that consent agreed to by another covered entity, with one exception. A covered entity would be bound by the consent of another covered entity if the entities use a "joint consent," as permitted by the Privacy Rule (§ 164.506(f)).

In addition, it is possible for several entities to choose to be treated as a single covered entity under the rule, as "affiliated entities." Because affiliated entities are considered to be one covered entity under the rule, there would be only one consent and each entity would be bound by that consent (§ 164.504(d)).

Q: What is the interaction between "consent" and "notice"?

A: The consent and the notice of privacy practices are two distinct documents. A consent document is brief (may be less than one page). It must refer to the notice and must inform the individual that he has the opportunity to review the notice prior to signing the consent. The Privacy Rule does not require that the individual read the notice or that the covered entity explain each item in the notice before the individual provides consent. We expect that some patients will simply sign the consent while others will read the notice carefully and discuss some of the practices with the covered entity.

Q: May consent for use or disclosure of PHI be provided electronically?

A: Yes. The covered entity may choose to obtain and store consents in paper or electronic form, provided that the consent meets all of the requirements under the Privacy Rule, including that it be signed by the individual. Paper is not required.

Q: Must a covered entity verify a signature on a consent form if the individual is not present when he signs it?

A: No.

Q: May consent be obtained by a health care provider only one time if there is a single connected course of treatment involving multiple visits?

A: Yes. A health care provider needs to obtain consent from a patient for use or disclosure of PHI only one time. This is true regardless of whether there is a connected course of treatment or treatment for unrelated conditions. A provider will need to obtain a new consent from a patient only if the patient has revoked the consent between treatments.

Q: If an individual consents to the use or disclosure of PHI for TPO purposes, obtains a health care service, and then revokes consent before the provider bills for such service, is the provider precluded from billing for such service?

A: No. A health care provider that provides a health care service to an individual after obtaining consent from the individual, may bill for such service even if the individual immediately revokes consent after the service has been provided. The Privacy Rule requires that an individual be permitted to revoke consent, but provides that the revocation is not effective to the extent that the health care provider has acted in reliance on the consent. Where the provider has obtained a consent and provided a health care service pursuant to that consent with the expectation that he or she could bill for the service, the health care provider has acted in reliance on the consent. The revocation would not interfere with the billing or reimbursement for that care.

Q: If covered providers that are affiliated or part of an organized health care arrangement are located in different states with different laws regarding uses and disclosures of health information (e.g., a chain of pharmacies), do they need to obtain a consent in each state that the patient obtains treatment?

A: No. The consent is general and only needs to be obtained by a covered entity (or by affiliated entities or entities that are part of an organized health care arrangement) one time. The Privacy Rule does not require that the consent include any details about state law, and therefore, does not require different consent forms in each state. State law may impose additional requirements for consent forms on covered entities.

Q: Must a revocation of a consent be in writing?

A: Yes.

Q: The Privacy Rule permits a covered entity to continue to use or disclose health information which it has on the compliance date pursuant to express legal permission obtained from an individual prior to the compliance date. Is a form, signed by a patient prior to the compliance date of the rule, that permits a provider to use or disclose information for the limited purpose of payment sufficient to meet these transition provision requirements?

A: Yes. A provider that obtains permission from a patient prior to the compliance date to use or disclose information for payment purposes may use the PHI about that patient collected pursuant to that permission for purposes of TPO. Under the transition provisions, if prior to the compliance date, a provider

obtained a consent for the use or disclosure of health information for any one of the TPO purposes, the provider may use the health information collected pursuant to that consent for all three purposes after the compliance date (§ 164.532(b)).

Thus, a provider that obtained consent for use or disclosure for billing purposes would be able to draw on the data obtained prior to the compliance date and covered by the consent form for all TPO activities to the extent not expressly excluded by the terms of the consent.

Q: Are health plans and health care clearinghouses required by the Privacy Rule to have some form of express legal permission to use and disclose health information obtained prior to the compliance date for TPO purposes?

A: No. Health plans and health care clearinghouses are not required to have express legal permission from individuals to use or disclose health information obtained prior to the compliance date for their own TPO purposes.

Minimum Necessary
[45 CFR §§ 164.502(b), 164.514(d)]

General Requirement

The Privacy Rule generally requires covered entities to take reasonable steps to limit the use or disclosure of, and requests for protected health information (PHI) to the minimum necessary to accomplish the intended purpose. The minimum necessary provisions do not apply to the following:

- Disclosures to or requests by a health care provider for treatment purposes.
- Disclosures to the individual who is the subject of the information.
- Uses or disclosures made pursuant to an authorization requested by the individual.
- Uses or disclosures required for compliance with the standardized Health Insurance Portability and Accountability Act (HIPAA) transactions.
- Disclosures to the Department of Health and Human Services (HHS) when disclosure of information is required under the rule for enforcement purposes.
- Uses or disclosures that are required by other law.

The implementation specifications for this provision require a covered entity to develop and implement policies and procedures appropriate for its own organization, reflecting the entity's business practices and workforce. We understand this guidance will not answer all questions pertaining to the minimum necessary standard, especially as applied to specific industry practices. As more questions arise with regard to application of the minimum necessary standard to particular circumstances, we will provide more detailed guidance and clarification on this issue.

Uses and Disclosures of and Requests for PHI

For uses of PHI, the policies and procedures must identify the persons or classes of persons within the covered entity who need access to the information to carry out their job duties, the categories or types of PHI needed, and conditions appropriate to such access. For example, hospitals may implement policies that permit doctors, nurses, or others involved in treatment to have access to the entire medical record, as needed. Case-by-case review of each use is not required. Where the entire medical record is necessary, the covered entity's policies and procedures must state so explicitly and include a justification.

For routine or recurring requests and disclosures, the policies and procedures may be standard protocols and must limit PHI disclosed or requested to that which is the minimum necessary for that particular type of disclosure or request. Individual review of each disclosure or request is not required.

For non-routine disclosures, covered entities must develop reasonable criteria for determining, and limiting disclosure to, only the minimum amount of PHI necessary to accomplish the purpose of a non-routine disclosure. Non-routine disclosures must be reviewed on an individual basis in accordance with these criteria. When making non-routine requests for PHI, the covered entity must review each request so as to ask for only that information reasonably necessary for the purpose of the request.

Reasonable Reliance

In certain circumstances, the Privacy Rule permits a covered entity to rely on the judgment of the party requesting the disclosure as to the minimum amount of information that is needed. Such reliance must be reasonable under the particular circumstances of the request. This reliance is permitted when the request is made by:

- A public official or agency for a disclosure permitted under § 164.512 of the rule.
- Another covered entity.
- A professional who is a workforce member or business associate of the covered entity holding the information.
- A researcher with appropriate documentation from an Institutional Review Board (IRB) or Privacy Board.

The rule does not require such reliance, however, and the covered entity always retains discretion to make its own minimum necessary determination for disclosures to which the standard applies.

Treatment Settings

We understand that medical information must be conveyed freely and quickly in treatment settings, and thus understand the heightened concern that covered entities have about how the minimum necessary standard applies in such settings.

Therefore, we are taking the following steps to clarify the application of the minimum necessary standard in treatment settings. First, we clarify some of the issues here, including the application of minimum necessary to specific practices, so that covered entities may begin implementation of the Privacy Rule. Second, we will propose corresponding changes to the regulation text, to increase the confidence of covered entities that they are free to engage in whatever communications are required for quick, effective, high quality health care. We understand that issues of this importance need to be addressed directly and clearly to eliminate any ambiguities.

Frequently Asked Questions

Q: How are covered entities expected to determine what is the minimum necessary information that can be used, disclosed, or requested for a particular purpose?

A: The Privacy Rule requires a covered entity to make reasonable efforts to limit use, disclosure of, and requests for PHI to the minimum necessary to accomplish the intended purpose. To allow covered entities the flexibility to address their unique circumstances, the rule requires covered entities to make their own assessment of what PHI is reasonably necessary for a particular purpose, given the characteristics of their business and workforce, and to implement policies and procedures accordingly. This is not a strict standard and covered entities need not limit information uses or disclosures to those that are absolutely needed to serve the purpose. Rather, this is a reasonableness standard that calls for an approach consistent with the best practices and guidelines already used by many providers today to limit the unnecessary sharing of medical information.

The minimum necessary standard is intended to make covered entities evaluate their practices and enhance protections as needed to prevent unnecessary or inappropriate access to PHI. It is intended to reflect and be consistent with, not override, professional judgment and standards. Therefore, we expect that covered entities will utilize the input of prudent professionals involved in health care activities when developing policies and procedures that appropriately will limit access to personal health information without sacrificing the quality of health care.

Q: Won't the minimum necessary restrictions impede the delivery of quality health care by preventing or hindering necessary exchanges of patient medical information among health care providers involved in treatment?

A: No. Disclosures for treatment purposes (including requests for disclosures) between health care providers are explicitly exempted from the minimum necessary requirements.

The Privacy Rule provides the covered entity with substantial discretion as to how to implement the minimum necessary standard, and appropriately and reasonably limit access to the use of identifiable health information within the covered entity. The rule recognizes that the covered entity is in the best position to know and determine who in its workforce needs access to personal health information to perform their jobs. Therefore, the covered entity can develop role-based access policies that allow its health care providers and other employees, as appropriate, access to patient information, including entire medical records, for treatment purposes.

Q: Do the minimum necessary requirements prohibit medical residents, medical students, nursing students, and other medical trainees from accessing patients' medical information in the course of their training?

A: No. The definition of "health care operations" in the rule provides for "conducting training programs in which students, trainees, or practitioners in areas of health care learn under supervision to practice or improve their skills as health care providers." Covered entities can shape their policies and procedures for minimum necessary uses and disclosures to permit medical trainees access to patients' medical information, including entire medical records.

Q: Must minimum necessary be applied to disclosures to third parties that are authorized by an individual?

A: No, unless the authorization was requested by a covered entity for its own purposes. The Privacy Rule exempts from the minimum necessary requirements most uses or disclosures that are authorized by an individual. This includes authorizations covered entities may receive directly from third parties, such as life, disability, or casualty insurers pursuant to the patient's application for or claim under an insurance policy. For example, if a covered health care provider receives an individual's authorization to disclose medical information to a life insurer for underwriting purposes, the provider is permitted to disclose the information requested on the authorization without making any minimum necessary determination. The authorization must meet the requirements of § 164.508.

However, minimum necessary does apply to authorizations requested by the covered entity for its own purposes (see § 164.508(d), (e), and (f)).

Q: Are providers required to make a minimum necessary determination to disclose to federal or state agencies, such as the Social Security Administration (SSA) or its affiliated state agencies, for individuals' applications for federal or state benefits?

A: No. These disclosures must be authorized by an individual and, therefore, are exempt from the minimum necessary requirements. Further, use of the provider's own authorization form is not required. Providers can accept an agency's authorization form as long as it meets the requirements of § 164.508 of the rule. For example, disclosures to SSA (or its affiliated state agencies) for purposes of determining eligibility for disability benefits are currently made subject to an individual's completed SSA authorization form. After the compliance date, the current process may continue subject only to modest changes in the SSA authoriza-

tion form to conform to the requirements in §
164.508.

Q: Doesn't the minimum necessary standard conflict with the Transactions standards? Does minimum necessary apply to the standard transactions?

A: No, because the Privacy Rule exempts from the minimum necessary standard any uses or disclosures that are required for compliance with the applicable requirements of the subchapter. This includes all data elements that are required or situationally required in the standard transactions. However, in many cases, covered entities have significant discretion as to the information included in these transactions. This standard does apply to those optional data elements.

Q: Does the rule strictly prohibit use, disclosure, or requests of an entire medical record? Does the rule prevent use, disclosure, or requests of entire medical records without case-by-case justification?

A: No. The Privacy Rule does not prohibit use, disclosure, or requests of an entire medical record. A covered entity may use, disclose, or request an entire medical record, without a case-by-case justification, if the covered entity has documented in its policies and procedures that the entire medical record is the amount reasonably necessary for certain identified purposes. For uses, the policies and procedures would identify those persons or classes of person in the workforce that need to see the entire medical record and the conditions, if any, that are appropriate for such access. Policies and procedures for routine disclosures and requests and the criteria used for non-routine disclosures would identify the circumstances under which disclosing or requesting the entire medical record is reasonably necessary for particular purposes. In making non-routine requests, the covered entity may also establish and utilize criteria to assist in determining when to request the entire medical record.

The Privacy Rule does not require that a justification be provided with respect to each distinct medical record.

Finally, no justification is needed in those instances where the minimum necessary standard does not apply, such as disclosures to or requests by a health care provider for treatment or disclosures to the individual.

Q: In limiting access, are covered entities required to completely restructure existing workflow systems, including redesigns of office space and upgrades of computer systems, in order to comply with the minimum necessary requirements?

A: No. The basic standard for minimum necessary uses requires that covered entities make reasonable efforts to limit access to PHI to those in the workforce that need access based on their roles in the covered entity.

The Department generally does not consider facility redesigns as necessary to meet the reasonableness standard for minimum necessary uses. However, covered entities may need to make certain adjustments to their facilities to minimize access, such as isolating and locking file cabinets or records rooms, or providing additional security, such as passwords, on computers maintaining personal information.

Covered entities should also take into account their ability to configure their record systems to allow access to only certain fields, and the practicality of organizing systems to allow this capacity. For example, it may not be reasonable for a small, solo practitioner who has largely a paper-based records system to limit access of employees with certain functions to only limited fields in a patient record, while other employees have access to the complete record.

Alternatively, a hospital with an electronic patient record system may reasonably implement such controls, and therefore, may choose to limit access in this manner to comply with the rule.

Q: Do the minimum necessary requirements prohibit covered entities from maintaining patient medical charts at bedside, require that covered entities shred empty prescription vials, or require that X-ray light boards be isolated?

A: No. The minimum necessary standards do not require that covered entities take any of these specific measures. Covered entities must, in accordance with other provisions of the Privacy Rule, take reasonable precautions to prevent inadvertent or unnecessary disclosures. For example, while the Privacy Rule does not require that X-ray boards be totally isolated from all other functions, it does require covered entities to take reasonable precautions to protect X-rays from being accessible to the public. We understand that these and similar matters are of special concern to many covered entities, and we will propose modifications to the rule to increase covered entities' confidence that these practices are not prohibited.

Q: Will doctors' and physicians' offices be allowed to continue using sign-in sheets in waiting rooms?

A: We did not intend to prohibit the use of sign-in sheets, but understand that the Privacy Rule is ambiguous about this common practice. We, therefore, intend to propose modifications to the rule to clarify that this and similar practices are permissible.

Q: What happens when a covered entity believes that a request is seeking more than the minimum necessary PHI?

A: In such a situation, the Privacy Rule requires a covered entity to limit the disclosure to the minimum necessary as determined by the disclosing entity.

Where the rule permits covered entities to rely on the judgment of the person requesting the information, and if such reliance is reasonable despite the covered entity's concerns, the covered entity may make the disclosure as requested.

Nothing in the Privacy Rule prevents a covered entity from discussing its concerns with the person making the request, and negotiating an information exchange that meets the needs of both parties. Such discussions occur today and may continue after the compliance date of the Privacy Rule.

Oral Communications
[45 CFR §§ 160.103, 164.501]

Background

The Privacy Rule applies to individually identifiable health information in all forms, electronic, written, oral, and any other. Coverage of oral (spoken) information ensures that information retains protections when discussed or read aloud from a computer screen or a written document. If oral communications were not covered, any health information could be disclosed to any person, so long as the disclosure was spoken. Providers and health plans understand the sensitivity of oral information. For example, many hospitals already have confidentiality policies and concrete procedures for addressing privacy, such as posting signs in elevators that remind employees to protect patient confidentiality.

We also understand that oral communications must occur freely and quickly in treatment settings, and thus understand the heightened concern that covered entities have about how the rule applies. Therefore, we are taking a two-step approach to clarifying the regulation with respect to these communications.

First, we provide some clarification of these issues here, so that covered entities may begin implementing the rule by the compliance date. Second, we will propose appropriate changes to the regulation text to clarify the regulatory basis for the policies discussed below in order to minimize confusion and to increase the confidence of covered entities that they are free to engage in communications as required for quick, effective, and high quality health care.

We understand that issues of this importance need to be addressed directly and clearly in the Privacy Rule and that any ambiguities need to be eliminated.

General Requirements

- Covered entities must reasonably safeguard protected health information (PHI) including oral information - from any intentional or unintentional use or disclosure that is in violation of the rule (see § 164.530(c)(2)). They must have in place appropriate administrative, technical, and physical safeguards to protect the privacy of PHI. "Reasonably safeguard" means that covered entities must make reasonable efforts to prevent uses and disclosures not permitted by the rule. However, we do not expect reasonable safeguards to guarantee the privacy of PHI from any and all potential risks. In determining whether a covered entity has provided reasonable safeguards, the Department will take into account all the circumstances, including the potential effects on patient care and the financial and administrative burden of any safeguards.

- Covered entities must have policies and procedures that reasonably limit access to and use of PHI to the minimum necessary given the job responsibilities of the workforce and the nature of their business (see §§ 164.502(b), 164.514(d)). The minimum necessary standard does not apply to disclosures, including oral disclosures, among providers for treatment purposes. For a more complete discussion of the minimum necessary requirements, see the fact sheet and frequently asked questions titled "Minimum Necessary."

- Many health care providers already make it a practice to ensure reasonable safeguards for oral information - for instance, by speaking quietly when discussing a patient's condition with family members in a waiting room or other public area, and by avoiding using patients' names in public hallways and elevators. Protection of patient confidentiality is an important practice for many health care and health information management professionals; covered entities can build upon those codes of conduct to develop the reasonable safeguards required by the Privacy Rule.

Frequently Asked Questions

Q: If health care providers engage in confidential conversations with other providers or with patients, have they violated the rule if there is a possibility that they could be overheard?

A: The Privacy Rule is not intended to prohibit providers from talking to each other and to their patients. Provisions of this rule requiring covered entities to implement reasonable safeguards that reflect their particular circumstances and exempting treatment disclosures from certain requirements are intended to ensure that providers' primary consideration is the appropriate treatment of their patients. We also understand that overheard communications are unavoidable. For example, in a busy emergency room, it may be necessary for providers to speak loudly in order to ensure appropriate treatment. The Privacy Rule is not intended to prevent this appropriate behavior. We would consider the following practices to be permissible, if reasonable precautions are taken to minimize the chance of inadvertent disclosures to others who may be nearby (such as using lowered voices, talking apart):

- Health care staff may orally coordinate services at hospital nursing stations.
- Nurses or other health care professionals may discuss a patient's condition over the phone with the patient, a provider, or a family member.
- A health care professional may discuss lab test results with a patient or other provider in a joint treatment area.
- Health care professionals may discuss a patient's condition during training rounds in an academic or training institution.

We will propose regulatory language to reinforce and clarify that these and similar oral communications (such as calling out patient names in a waiting room) are permissible.

Q: Does the Privacy Rule require hospitals and doctors' offices to be retrofitted, to provide private rooms, and soundproof walls to avoid any possibility that a conversation is overheard?

A: No, the Privacy Rule does not require these types of structural changes be made to facilities. Covered entities must have in place appropriate administrative, technical, and physical safeguards to protect the privacy of PHI. "Reasonable safeguards" mean that covered entities must make reasonable efforts to prevent uses and disclosures not permitted by the rule. The Department does not consider facility restructuring to be a requirement under this standard. In determining what is reasonable, the Department will take into account the concerns of covered entities regarding potential effects on patient care and financial burden.

For example, the Privacy Rule does not require the following types of structural or systems changes:

- Private rooms.
- Soundproofing of rooms.
- Encryption of wireless or other emergency medical radio communications which can be intercepted by scanners.
- Encryption of telephone systems.

Covered entities must provide reasonable safeguards to avoid prohibited disclosures. The rule does not require that all risk be eliminated to satisfy this standard. Covered entities must review their own practices and determine what steps are reasonable to safeguard their patient information.

Examples of the types of adjustments or modifications to facilities or systems that may constitute reasonable safeguards are:

- Pharmacies could ask waiting customers to stand a few feet back from a counter used for patient counseling.
- Providers could add curtains or screens to areas where oral communications often occur between doctors and patients or among professionals treating the patient.
- In an area where multiple patient-staff communications routinely occur, use of cubicles, dividers, shields, or similar barriers may constitute a reasonable safeguard. For example, a large clinic intake area may reasonably use cubicles or shield-type dividers, rather than separate rooms.

In assessing what is "reasonable," covered entities may consider the viewpoint of prudent professionals.

Q: Do covered entities need to provide patients access to oral information?

A: No. The Privacy Rule requires covered entities to provide individuals with access to PHI about themselves that is contained in their "designated record sets." The term "record" in the term "designated record set" does not include oral information; rather, it connotes information that has been recorded in some manner.

The rule does not require covered entities to tape or digitally record oral communications, nor retain digitally or tape recorded information after transcription. But if such records are maintained and used to make decisions about the individual, they may meet the definition of "designated record set." For example, a health plan is not required to provide a member access to tapes of a telephone "advice line" interaction if the tape is only maintained for customer service review and not to make decisions about the member.

Q: Do covered entities have to document all oral communications?

A: No. The Privacy Rule does not require covered entities to document any information, including oral information, that is used or disclosed for treatment, payment or health care operations (TPO).

The rule includes, however, documentation requirements for some information disclosures for other purposes. For example, some disclosures must be documented in order to meet the standard for providing a disclosure history to an individual upon request.

Where a documentation requirement exists in the rule, it applies to all relevant communications, whether in oral or some other form.

For example, if a covered physician discloses information about a case of tuberculosis to a public health authority as permitted by the rule in § 164.512, then he or she must maintain a record of that disclosure regardless of whether the disclosure was made orally by phone or in writing.

Q: Did the Department change its position from the proposed rule by covering oral communications in the final Privacy Rule?

A: No. The proposed rule would have covered information in any form or medium, as long as it had at some point been maintained or transmitted electronically. Once information had been electronic, it would have continued to be covered as long as it was held by a covered entity, whether in electronic, written, or oral form.

The final Privacy Rule eliminates this nexus to electronic information. All individually identifiable health information of the covered entity is covered by the rule.

Business Associates
[45 CFR §§ 160.103, 164.502(e), 164.514(e)]

Background

By law, the Privacy Rule applies only to health plans, health care clearinghouses, and certain health care providers. In today's health care system, however, most health care providers and health plans do not carry out all of their health care activities and functions by themselves; they require assistance from a variety of contractors and other businesses. In allowing providers and plans to give protected health information (PHI) to these "business associates," the Privacy Rule conditions such disclosures on the provider or plan obtaining, typically by contract, satisfactory assurances that the business associate will use the information only for the purposes for which they were engaged by the covered entity, will safeguard the information from misuse, and will help the covered entity comply with the covered entity's duties to provide individuals with access to health information about them and a history of certain disclosures (e.g., if the business associate maintains the only copy of information, it must promise to cooperate with the covered entity to provide individuals access to information upon request). PHI may be disclosed to a business associate only to help the providers and plans carry out their health care functions - not for independent use by the business associate.

What is a "business associate"

- A business associate is a person or entity who provides certain functions, activities, or services for or to a covered entity, involving the use and/or disclosure of PHI.
- A business associate is not a member of the health care provider, health plan, or other covered entity's workforce.
- A health care provider, health plan, or other covered entity can also be a business associate to another covered entity.
- The rule includes exceptions. The business associate requirements do not apply to covered entities who disclose PHI to providers for treatment purposes - for example, information exchanges between a hospital and physicians with admitting privileges at the hospital.

Frequently Asked Questions

Q: Has the Secretary exceeded the statutory authority by requiring "satisfactory assurances" for disclosures to business associates?

A: No. The Health Insurance Portability and Accountability Act of 1996 (HIPAA) gives the Secretary authority to directly regulate health care providers, health plans, and health care clearinghouses. It also grants the Department explicit authority to regulate the uses and disclosures of PHI maintained and transmitted by covered entities. Therefore, we do have the authority to condition the disclosure of PHI by a covered entity to a business associate on the covered entity's having a contract with that business associate.

Q: Has the Secretary exceeded the HIPAA statutory authority by requiring "business associates" to comply with the Privacy Rule, even if that requirement is through a contract?

A: The Privacy Rule does not "pass through" its requirements to business associates or otherwise cause business associates to comply with the terms of the rule. The assurances that covered entities must obtain prior to disclosing PHI to business associates create a set of contractual obligations far narrower than the provisions of the rule, to protect information generally and help the covered entity comply with its obligations under the rule.

For example, covered entities do not need to ask their business associates to agree to appoint a privacy officer, or develop policies and procedures for use and disclosure of PHI.

Q: Is it reasonable for covered entities to be held liable for the privacy violations of business associates?

A: A health care provider, health plan, or other covered entity is not liable for privacy violations of a business associate. Covered entities are not required to actively monitor or oversee the means by which the business associate carries out safeguards or the extent to which the business associate abides by the requirements of the contract.

Moreover, a business associate's violation of the terms of the contract does not, in and of itself, constitute a violation of the rule by the covered entity. The contract must obligate the business associate to advise the covered entity when violations have occurred.

If the covered entity becomes aware of a pattern or practice of the business associate that constitutes a material breach or violation of the business associate's obligations under its contract, the covered entity must take "reasonable steps" to cure the breach or to end the violation. Reasonable steps will vary with the circumstances and nature of the business relationship.

If such steps are not successful, the covered entity must terminate the contract if feasible. The rule also provides for circumstances in which termination is not feasible, for example, where there are no other viable business alternatives for the covered entity. In such circumstances where termination is not feasible, the covered entity must report the problem to the Department.Only if the covered entity fails to take the kinds of steps described above would it be considered to be out of compliance with the requirements of the rule.

Parents and Minors
[45 CFR § 164.502(g)]

General Requirements

The Privacy Rule provides individuals with certain rights with respect to their personal health information, including the right to obtain access to and to request amendment of health information about themselves. These rights rest with that individual, or with the "personal representative" of that individual. In general, a person's right to control protected health information (PHI) is based on that person's right (under state or other applicable law, e.g., tribal or military law) to control the health care itself.

Because a parent usually has authority to make health care decisions about his or her minor child, a parent is generally a "personal representative" of his or her minor child under the Privacy Rule and has the right to obtain access to health information about his or her minor child. This would also be true in the case of a guardian or other person acting in loco parentis of a minor.

There are exceptions in which a parent might not be the "personal representative" with respect to certain health information about a minor child. In the following situations, the Privacy Rule defers to determinations under other law that the parent does not control the minor's health care decisions and, thus, does not control the PHI related to that care.

- When state or other law does not require consent of a parent or other person before a minor can obtain a particular health care service, and the minor consents to the health care service, the parent is not the minor's personal representative under the Privacy Rule. For example, when a state law provides an adolescent the right to consent to mental health treatment without the consent of his or her parent, and the adolescent obtains such treatment without the consent of the parent, the parent is not the personal representative under the Privacy Rule for that treatment. The minor may choose to involve a parent in these health care decisions without giving up his or her right to control the related health information. Of course, the minor may always have the parent continue to be his or her personal

representative even in these situations.
- When a court determines or other law authorizes someone other than the parent to make treatment decisions for a minor, the parent is not the personal representative of the minor for the relevant services. For example, courts may grant authority to make health care decisions for the minor to an adult other than the parent, to the minor, or the court may make the decision(s) itself. In order to not undermine these court decisions, the parent is not the personal representative under the Privacy Rule in these circumstances.

In the following situations, the Privacy Rule reflects current professional practice in determining that the parent is not the minor's personal representative with respect to the relevant PHI:

- When a parent agrees to a confidential relationship between the minor and the physician, the parent does not have access to the health information related to that conversation or relationship. For example, if a physician asks the parent of a 16-year old if the physician can talk with the child confidentially about a medical condition and the parent agrees, the parent would not control the PHI that was discussed during that confidential conference.
- When a physician (or other covered entity) reasonably believes in his or her professional judgment that the child has been or may be subjected to abuse or neglect, or that treating the parent as the child's personal representative could endanger the child, the physician may choose not to treat the parent as the personal representative of the child.

Relation to State Law

In addition to the provisions (described above) tying the right to control information to the right to control treatment, the Privacy Rule also states that it does not preempt state laws that specifically address disclosure of health information about a minor to a parent (§ 160.202). This is true whether the state law authorizes or prohibits such disclosure. Thus, if a physician believes that disclosure of information about a minor would endanger that minor, but a state law requires disclosure to a parent, the physician may comply with the state law without violating the Privacy Rule. Similarly, a provider may comply with a state law that requires disclosure to a parent and would not have to accommodate a request for confidential communications that would be contrary to state law.

Frequently Asked Questions

Q: Does the Privacy Rule allow parents the right to see their children's medical records?

A: The Privacy Rule generally allows parents, as their minor children's personal representatives, to have access to information about the health and well-being of their children when state or other underlying law allows parents to make treatment decisions for the child. There are two exceptions: (1) when the parent agrees that the minor and the health care provider may have a confidential relationship, the provider is allowed to withhold information from the parent to the extent of that agreement; and (2) when the provider reasonably believes in his or her professional judgment that the child has been or may be subjected to abuse or neglect, or that treating the parent as the child's personal representative could endanger the child, the provider is permitted not to treat the parent as the child's personal representative with respect to health information.

Secretary Thompson has stated that he is reassessing these provisions of the regulation.

Q: Does the Privacy Rule provide rights for children to be treated without parental consent?

A: No. The Privacy Rule does not address consent to treatment, nor does it preempt or change state or other laws that address consent to treatment. The Rule addresses access to health information, not the underlying treatment.

Q: If a child receives emergency medical care without a parent's consent, can the parent get all information about the child's treatment and condition?

A: Generally, yes. Even though the parent did not provide consent to the treatment in this situation, under the Privacy Rule, the parent would still be the child's personal representative. This would not be so only when the minor provided consent (and no other consent is required) or the treating physician suspects abuse or neglect or reasonably believes that releasing the information to the parent will endanger the child.

Health-Related Communications and Marketing
[45 CFR §§ 164.501, 164.514(e)]

General Requirements

The Privacy Rule addresses the use and disclosure of protected health information (PHI) for marketing purposes in the following ways:

- Defines what is "marketing" under the rule; Removes from that definition certain treatment or health care operations activities;
- Set limits on the kind of marketing that can be done as a health care operation; and
- Requires individual authorization for all other uses or disclosures of PHI for marketing purposes.

What is Marketing

The Privacy Rule defines "marketing" as "a communication about a product or service a purpose of which is to encourage recipients of the communication to purchase or use the product or service." To make this definition easier for covered entities to understand and comply with, we specified what "marketing" is not, as well as generally defined what it is. As questions arise about what activities are "marketing" under the Privacy Rule, we will provide additional clarification regarding such activities.

Communications that are Not Marketing

The Privacy Rule carves out activities that are not considered marketing under this definition. In recommending treatments or describing available services, health care providers and health plans are advising us to purchase goods and services. To prevent any interference with essential treatment or similar health-related communications with a patient, the rule identifies the following activities as not subject to the marketing provision, even if the activity otherwise meets the definition of marketing. (Written communications for which the covered entity is compensated by a third party are not carved out of the marketing definition.) Thus, a covered entity is not "marketing" when it:

- Describes the participating providers or plans in a network. For example, a health plan is not marketing when it tells its enrollees about which doctors and hospitals are preferred providers, which are included in its network, or which providers offer a particular service. Similarly, a health insurer notifying enrollees of a new pharmacy that has begun to accept its drug coverage is not engaging in marketing.

- Describes the services offered by a provider or the benefits covered by a health plan. For example, informing a plan enrollee about drug formulary coverage is not marketing.

Furthermore, it is not marketing for a covered entity to use an individual's PHI to tailor a health-related communication to that individual, when the communication is:

- Part of a provider's treatment of the patient and for the purpose of furthering that treatment. For example, recommendations of specific brand-name or over-the-counter pharmaceuticals or referrals of patients to other providers are not marketing.
- Made in the course of managing the individual's treatment or recommending alternative treatment. For example, reminder notices for appointments, annual exams, or prescription refills are not marketing. Similarly, informing an individual who is a smoker about an effective smoking-cessation program is not marketing, even if that program is offered by someone other than the provider or plan making the recommendation.

Limitations on Marketing Communications

If a communication is marketing, a covered entity may use or disclose PHI to create or make the communication, pursuant to any applicable consent obtained under § 164.506, only in the following circumstances:

- It is a face-to-face communication with the individual. For example, sample products may be provided to a patient during an office visit.
- It involves products or services of nominal value. For example, a provider can distribute pens, toothbrushes, or key chains with the name of the covered entity or a health care product manufacturer on it.
- It concerns the health-related products and services of the covered entity or a third party, and only if the communication:

 - Identifies the covered entity that is making the communication. Thus, consumers will know the source of these marketing calls or materials.- States that the covered entity is being compensated for making the communication, when that is so.
 - Tells individuals how to opt out of further marketing communications, with some exceptions as provided in the rule. The covered entity must make reasonable efforts to honor requests to opt-out.
 - Explains why individuals with specific conditions or characteristics (e.g., diabetics, smokers) have been targeted, if that is so, and how the product or service relates to the health of the individual. The covered entity must also have made a determination that the product or service may be of benefit to individuals with that condition or characteristic.

For all other communications that are "marketing" under the Privacy Rule, the covered entity must obtain the individual's authorization to use or disclose PHI to create or make the marketing communication.

Business Associates

Disclosure of PHI for marketing purposes is limited to disclosure to business associates that undertake marketing activities on behalf of the covered entity. No other disclosure for marketing is permitted. Covered entities may not give away or sell lists of patients or enrollees without obtaining authorization from each person on the list. As with any disclosure to a business associate, the covered entity must obtain the business associate's agreement to use the PHI only for the covered entity's marketing activities. A covered entity may not give PHI to a business associate for the business associate's own purposes.

Frequently Asked Questions

Q: Does this rule expand the ability of providers, plans, marketers and others to use my PHI to market goods and services to me? Does the Privacy Rule make it easier for health care businesses to engage in door-to-door sales and marketing efforts?

A: No. The provisions described above impose limits on the use or disclosure of PHI for marketing that do not exist in most states today. For example, the rule requires patients' authorization for the following types of uses or disclosures of PHI for marketing:

- Selling PHI to third parties for their use and re-use. Under the rule, a hospital or other provider may not sell names of pregnant women to baby formula manufacturers or magazines.
- Disclosing PHI to outsiders for the outsiders' independent marketing use. Under the rule, doctors may not provide patient lists to pharmaceutical companies for those companies' drug promotions.

These activities can occur today with no authorization from the individual. In addition, for the marketing activities that are allowed by the rule without authorization from the individual, the Privacy Rule requires covered entities to offer individuals the ability to opt-out of further marketing communications.

Similarly, under the business associate provisions of the rule, a covered entity may not give PHI to a telemarketer, door-to-door salesperson, or other marketer it has hired unless that marketer has agreed by contract to use the information only for marketing on behalf of the covered entity. Today, there may be no restrictions on how marketers re-use information they obtain from health plans and providers.

Q: Can telemarketers gain access to PHI and call individuals to sell goods and services?

A: Under the rule, unless the covered entity obtains the individual's authorization, it may only give health information to a telemarketer that it has hired to undertake marketing on its behalf. The telemarketer must be a business associate under the rule, which means that it must agree by contract to use the information only for marketing on behalf of the covered entity, and not to market its own goods or services (or those of another third party). The caller must identify the covered entity that is sponsoring the marketing call. The caller must provide individuals the opportunity to opt-out of further marketing.

Q: When is an authorization required from the patient before a provider or health plan engages in marketing to that individual?

A: An authorization for use or disclosure of PHI for marketing is always required, unless one of the following three exceptions apply:

- The marketing occurs during an in-person meeting with the patient (e.g., during a medical appointment).
- The marketing concerns products or services of nominal value.
- The covered entity is marketing health-related products and services (of either the covered entity or a third party), the marketing identifies the covered entity that is responsible for the marketing, and the individual is offered an opportunity to opt-out of further marketing. In addition, the marketing must tell people if they have been targeted based on their health status, and must also tell people when the covered entity is compensated (directly or indirectly) for making the communication.

Q: How can I distinguish between activities for treatment, payment or health care operations (TPO) versus marketing activities?

A: There is no need for covered entities to make this distinction. In recommending treatments, providers and health plans advise us to purchase good and services. The overlap between "treatment," "health care operations," and "marketing" is unavoidable. Instead of creating artificial distinctions, the rule imposes requirements that do not require such distinctions. Specifically:

- If the activity is included in the rule's definition of "marketing," the rule's provisions restricting the use or disclosure of PHI for marketing purposes will apply, whether or not that communication also meets the rule's definition of "treatment," "payment," or "health care operations." For these communications, the individual's authorization is required before a covered entity may use or disclose PHI for marketing unless one of the exceptions to the authorization requirement (described above) applies.
- The rule exempts certain activities from the definition of "marketing." If an activity falls into one of the definition's exemptions, the marketing rules do not apply. In these cases, covered entities may engage in the activity

without first obtaining an authorization if the activity meets the definition of "treatment," "payment," or "health care operations." These exemptions are described above, in the section titled "Communications That Are Not Marketing," and are designed to ensure that nothing in this rule interferes with treatment activities.

Q: Do disease management, health promotion, preventive care, and wellness programs fall under the definition of "marketing"?

A: Whether these kinds of activities fall under the rule's definition of "marketing" depends on the specifics of how the activity is conducted. The activities currently undertaken under these rubrics are diverse. Covered entities must examine the particular activities they undertake, and compare these to the activities that are exempt from the definition of "marketing."

Q: Can contractors (business associates) use PHI to market to individuals for their own business purposes?

A: The Privacy Rule prohibits health plans and covered health care providers from giving PHI to third parties for the third party's own business purposes, absent authorization from the individuals. Under the statute, this regulation cannot govern contractors directly.

Research
[45 CFR §§ 164.501, 164.508(f), 164.512(i)]

Background

The Privacy Rule establishes the conditions under which protected health information (PHI) may be used or disclosed by covered entities for research purposes. A covered entity may always use or disclose for research purposes health information which has been de-identified (in accordance with §§ 164.502(d), 164.514(a)-(c) of the rule) without regard to the provisions below.

The Privacy Rule also defines the means by which individuals/human research subjects are informed of how medical information about themselves will be used or disclosed and their rights with regard to gaining access to information about themselves, when such information is held by covered entities. Where

research is concerned, the Privacy Rule protects the privacy of individually identifiable health information, while at the same time, ensuring that researchers continue to have access to medical information necessary to conduct vital research.

Currently, most research involving human subjects operates under the Common Rule (codified for the Department of Health and Human Services (HHS) at Title 45 Code of Federal Regulations Part 46) and/or the Food and Drug Administration's (FDA) human subjects protection regulations, which have some provisions that are similar to, but more stringent than and separate from, the Privacy Rule's provisions for research.

Using and Disclosing PHI for Research

In the course of conducting research, researchers may create, use, and/or disclose individually identifiable health information. Under the Privacy Rule, covered entities are permitted to use and disclose PHI for research with individual authorization, or without individual authorization under limited circumstances set forth in the Privacy Rule.

Research Use/Disclosure without Authorization:

To use or disclose PHI without authorization by the research participant, a covered entity must obtain one of the following:

- Documentation that an alteration or waiver of research participants' authorization for use/disclosure of information about them for research purposes has been approved by an Institutional Review Board (IRB) or a Privacy Board. This provision of the Privacy Rule might be used, for example, to conduct records research, when researchers are unable to use de-identified information and it is not practicable to obtain research participants' authorization.

Or

- Representations from the researcher, either in writing or orally, that the use or disclosure of the PHI is solely to prepare a research protocol or for similar purposes preparatory to research, that the researcher will not remove any PHI from the covered entity, and representation that PHI for which access is sought is necessary for the research purpose. This provision might be used, for example, to design a research study or to assess the feasibility of conducting a study.

Or

- Representations from the researcher, either in writing or orally, that the use or disclosure being sought is solely for research on the PHI of decedents, that the PHI being sought is necessary for the research, and, at the request of the covered entity, documentation of the death of the individuals about whom information is being sought.

A covered entity may use or disclose PHI for research purposes pursuant to a waiver of authorization by an IRB or Privacy Board provided it has obtained documentation of all of the following:

- A statement that the alteration or waiver of authorization was approved by an IRB or Privacy Board that was composed as stipulated by the Privacy Rule;
- A statement identifying the IRB or Privacy Board and the date on which the alteration or waiver of authorization was approved;
- A statement that the IRB or Privacy Board has determined that the alteration or waiver of authorization, in whole or in part, satisfies the following eight criteria:

  - The use or disclosure of PHI involves no more than minimal risk to the individuals;
  - The alteration or waiver will not adversely affect the privacy rights and the welfare of the individuals;
  - The research could not practicably be conducted without the alteration or waiver;
  - The research could not practicably be conducted without access to and use of the PHI;
  - The privacy risks to individuals whose PHI is to be used or disclosed are reasonable in relation to the anticipated benefits, if any, to the individuals, and the importance of the knowledge that may reasonably be expected to result from the research;

  - here is an adequate plan to protect the identifiers from improper use and disclosure;
  - There is an adequate plan to destroy the identifiers at the earliest opportunity consistent with conduct of the research, unless there is a health or research justification for retaining the identifiers or such retention is otherwise required by law; and
  - There are adequate written assurances that the PHI will not be reused or disclosed to any other person or entity, except as required by law, for authorized oversight of the research project, or for other research for which the use or disclosure of PHI would be permitted by this subpart.

- A brief description of the PHI for which use or access has been determined to be necessary by the IRB or Privacy Board;
- A statement that the alteration or waiver of authorization has been reviewed and approved under either normal or expedited review procedures as stipulated by the Privacy Rule; and
- The signature of the chair or other member, as designated by the chair, of the IRB or the Privacy Board, as applicable.

Research Use/Disclosure with Individual Authorization:

The Privacy Rule also permits covered entities to use and disclose PHI for research purposes when a research participant authorizes the use or disclosure of information about him or herself. Today, for example, a research participant's authorization will typically be sought for most clinical trials and some records research. In this case, documentation of IRB or Privacy Board approval of a waiver of authorization is not required for the use or disclosure of PHI.

To use or disclose PHI created from a research study that includes treatment (e.g., a clinical trial), additional research-specific elements must be included in the authorization form required under § 164.508, which describe how PHI created for the research study will be used or disclosed. For example, if the covered entity/researcher intends to seek reimbursement from the research subject's health plan for the routine costs of care associated with the protocol, the authorization must describe types of information that will be provided to the health plan. This authorization may be combined with the traditional informed consent document used in research.

The Privacy Rule permits, but does not require, the disclosure of PHI for specified public policy purposes in § 164.512. With few exceptions, the covered entity/ researcher may choose to limit its right to disclose information created for a research study that includes treatment to purposes narrower than those permitted by the rule, in accordance with his or her own professional standards.

Frequently Asked Questions

Q: Will the rule hinder medical research by making doctors and others less willing and/or able to share information about individual patients?

A: We do not believe that the Privacy Rule will hinder medical research. Indeed, patients and health plan members should be more willing to participate in research when they know their information is protected. For example, in genetic studies at the National Institutes of Health (NIH), nearly 32 percent of eligible people offered a test for breast cancer risk decline to take it. The overwhelming majority of those who refuse cite concerns about health insurance discrimination and loss of privacy as the reason. The Privacy Rule both permits important research and, at the same time, encourages patients to participate in research by providing much needed assurances about the privacy of their health information.

The Privacy Rule will require some covered health care providers and health plans to change their current practices related to documenting research uses and disclosures. It is possible that some covered health care providers and health plans may conclude that the rule's requirements for research uses and disclosures are too burdensome and will choose to limit researchers' access to PHI. We believe few providers will take this route, however, because the Common Rule includes similar, and more stringent requirements, that have not impaired the willingness of researchers to undertake federally-funded research. For example, unlike the Privacy Rule, the Common Rule requires IRB review for all research proposals under its purview, even if informed consent is to be sought.

The Privacy Rule requires documentation of IRB or Privacy Board approval only if patient authorization for the use or disclosure of PHI for research purposes is to be altered or waived.

Q: Are some of the criteria so subjective that inconsistent determinations may be made by IRBs and Privacy Boards reviewing similar or identical research projects?

A: Under the Privacy Rule, IRBs and Privacy Boards need to use their judgment as to whether the waiver criteria have been satisfied. Several of the waiver criteria are closely modeled on the Common Rule's criteria for the waiver of informed consent and for the approval of a research study. Thus, it is anticipated that IRBs already have experience in making the necessarily subjective assessments of risks and benefits. While IRBs or Privacy Boards may reach different determinations, the assessment of the waiver criteria through this deliberative process is a crucial element in the current system of safeguarding research participants' privacy. The entire system of local IRBs is, in fact, predicated on a deliberative process that permits local IRB autonomy. The Privacy Rule builds upon this principle; it does not change it.

In addition, for multi-site research that requires PHI from two or more covered entities, the Privacy Rule permits covered entities to accept documentation of IRB or Privacy Board approval from a single IRB or Privacy Board.

Q: Does the Privacy Rule prohibit researchers from conditioning participation in a clinical trial on an authorization to use/disclose existing PHI?

A: No. The Privacy Rule does not address conditions for enrollment in a research study. Therefore, the Privacy Rule in no way prohibits researchers from conditioning enrollment in a research study on the execution of an authorization for the use of pre-existing health information.

Q: Does the Privacy Rule permit the creation of a database for research purposes through an IRB or Privacy Board waiver of individual authorization?

A: Yes. A covered entity may use or disclose PHI without individuals' authorizations for the creation of a research database, provided the covered entity obtains documentation that an IRB or Privacy Board has determined that the specified waiver criteria were satisfied. PHI maintained in such a research database could be used or disclosed for future research studies as permitted by the Privacy Rule - that is, for future studies in which individual authorization has been obtained or where the rule would permit research without an authorization, such as pursuant to an IRB or Privacy Board waiver.

Q: Will IRBs be able to handle the additional responsibilities imposed by the Privacy Rule?

A: Recognizing that some institutions may not have IRBs, or that some IRBs may not have the expertise needed to review research that requires consideration of risks to privacy, the Privacy Rule permits the covered entity to accept documentation of waiver of authorization from an alternative body called a Privacy Board-which could have fewer members, and members with different expertise than IRBs.

In addition, for research that is determined to be of no more than minimal risk, IRBs and Privacy Boards could use an expedited review process, which permits covered entities to accept documentation when only one or more members of the IRB or Privacy Board have conducted the review.

Q: By establishing new waiver criteria and authorization requirements, hasn't the Privacy Rule, in effect, modified the Common Rule?

A: No. Where both the Privacy Rule and the Common Rule apply, both regulations must be followed. The Privacy Rule regulates only the content and conditions of the documentation that covered entities must obtain before using or disclosing PHI for research purposes.

Q: Is documentation of IRB and Privacy Board approval required before a covered entity would be permitted to disclose PHI for research purposes without an individual's authorization?

A: No. The Privacy Rule requires documentation of waiver approval by either an IRB or a Privacy Board, not both.

Q: Does a covered entity need to create an IRB or Privacy Board before using or disclosing PHI for research?

A: No. The IRB or Privacy Board could be created by the covered entity or the recipient researcher, or it could be an independent board.

Q: What does the Privacy Rule say about a research participant's right of access to research records or results?

A: With few exceptions, the Privacy Rule gives patients the right to inspect and obtain a copy of health information about themselves that is maintained in a "designated record set." A designated record set is basically a group of records which a covered entity uses to make decisions about individuals, and includes a health care provider's medical records and billing records, and a health plan's enrollment, payment, claims adjudication, and case or medical management record systems. Research records or results maintained in a designated record set are accessible to research participants unless one of the Privacy Rule's permitted exceptions applies.

One of the permitted exceptions applies to PHI created or obtained by a covered health care provider/researcher for a clinical trial. The Privacy Rule permits the individual's access rights in these cases to be suspended while the clinical trial is in progress, provided the research participant agreed to this denial of access when consenting to participate in the clinical trial. In addition, the health care provider/researcher must inform the research participant that the right to access PHI will be reinstated at the conclusion of the clinical trial.

Q: Are the Privacy Rule's requirements regarding patient access in harmony with the Clinical Laboratory Improvements Amendments of 1988 (CLIA)?

A: Yes. The Privacy Rule does not require clinical laboratories that are also covered health care providers to provide an individual access to information if CLIA prohibits them from doing so. CLIA permits clinical laboratories to provide clinical laboratory test records and reports only to "authorized persons," as defined primarily by state law. The individual who is the subject of the information is not always included as an authorized person. Therefore, the Privacy Rule includes an exception to individuals' general right to access PHI about themselves if providing an individual such access would be in conflict with CLIA.

In addition, for certain research laboratories that are exempt from the CLIA regulations, the Privacy Rule does not require such research laboratories if they are also a covered health care provider to provide individuals with access to PHI because doing so may result in the research laboratory losing its CLIA exemption.

Q: Do the Privacy Rule's requirements for authorization and the Common Rule's requirements for informed consent differ?

A: Yes. Under the Privacy Rule, a patient's authorization will be used for the use and disclosure of PHI for research purposes. In contrast, an individual's informed consent as required by the Common Rule and FDA's human subjects regulations is a consent to participate in the research study as a whole, not simply a consent for the research use or disclosure of PHI. For this reason, there are important differences between the Privacy Rule's requirements for individual authorization, and the Common Rule's and FDA's requirements for informed consent. Where the Privacy Rule, the Common Rule, and/or FDA's human subjects regulations are applicable, each of the applicable regulations will need to be followed.

Restrictions on Government Access to Health Information
[45 CFR §§ 160.300; 164.512(b); 164.512(f)]

Background

Under the Privacy Rule, government-operated health plans and health care providers must meet substantially the same requirements as private ones for protecting the privacy of individual identifiable health information. For instance, government-run health plans, such as Medicare and Medicaid, must take virtually the same steps to protect the claims and health information that they receive from beneficiaries as private insurance plans or health maintenance organizations (HMO). In addition, all federal agencies must also meet the requirements of the Privacy Act of 1974, which restricts what information about individual citizens - including any personal health information - can be shared with other agencies and with the public.

The only new authority for government involves enforcement of the Privacy Rule itself. In order to ensure covered entities protect patients' privacy as required, the rule provides that health plans, hospitals, and other covered entities cooperate with the Department's efforts to investigate complaints or otherwise ensure compliance. The Department of Health and Human Services (HHS) Office for Civil Rights (OCR) is responsible for enforcing the privacy protections and access rights for consumers under this rule.

Frequently Asked Questions

Q: Does the rule require my doctor to send my medical records to the government?

A: No. The rule does not require a physician or any other covered entity to send medical information to the government for a government data base or similar operation. This rule does not require or allow any new government access to medical information, with one exception: the rule does give OCR the authority to investigate complaints and to otherwise ensure that covered entities comply with the rule.

OCR has been assigned the responsibility of enforcing the Privacy Rule. As is typical in many enforcement settings, OCR may need to look at how a covered entity handled medical records and other personal health information. The Privacy Rule limits disclosure to OCR to information that is "pertinent to ascertaining compliance." OCR will maintain stringent controls to safeguard any individually identifiable health information that it receives. If covered entities could avoid or ignore enforcement requests, consumers would not have a way to ensure an independent review of their concerns about privacy violations under the rule.

Q: Why would a Privacy Rule require covered entities to turn over anybody's personal health information as part of a government enforcement process?

A: An important ingredient in ensuring compliance with the Privacy Rule is the Department's responsibility to investigate complaints that the rule has been violated and to follow up on other information regarding noncompliance. At times, this responsibility entails seeing personal health information, such as when an individual indicates to the Department that they believe a covered entity has not properly handled their medical records.

What information would be needed depends on the circumstances and the alleged violations. The Privacy Rule limits OCR's access to information that is "pertinent to ascertaining compliance." In some cases, no personal health information would be needed. For instance, OCR may need to review only a business contract to determine whether a health plan included appropriate language to protect privacy when it hired an outside company to help process claims.

Examples of investigations that may require OCR to have access to protected health information (PHI) include:

- Allegations that a covered entity refused to note a request for correction in   a patient's medical record, or did not provide complete access to a patient's   medical records to that patient.
- Allegations that a covered entity used health information for marketing purposes without first obtaining the individuals' authorization when required by the rule. OCR may need to review information in the marketing department that contains personal health information, to determine whether a violation has occurred.

Q: Will this rule make it easier for police and law enforcement agencies to get my medical information?

A: No. The rule does not expand current law enforcement access to individually identifiable health information. In fact, it limits access to a greater degree than currently exists. Today, law enforcement officers obtain health information for many purposes, sometimes without a warrant or other prior process. The rule establishes new procedures and safeguards to restrict the circumstances under which a covered entity may give such information to law enforcement officers.

For example, the rule limits the type of information that covered entities may disclose to law enforcement, absent a warrant or other prior process, when law enforcement is seeking to identify or locate a suspect. It specifically prohibits disclosure of DNA information for this purpose, absent some other legal requirements such as a warrant. Similarly, under most circumstances, the Privacy Rule requires covered entities to obtain permission from persons who have been the victim of domestic violence or abuse before disclosing information about them to law enforcement. In most states, such permission is not required today.

Where state law imposes additional restrictions on disclosure of health information to law enforcement,

those state laws continue to apply. This rule sets a national floor of legal protections; it is not a set of "best practices."

Even in those circumstances when disclosure to law enforcement is permitted by the rule, the Privacy Rule does not require covered entities to disclose any information. Some other federal or state law may require a disclosure, and the Privacy Rule does not interfere with the operation of these other laws. However, unless the disclosure is required by some other law, covered entities should use their professional judgment to decide whether to disclose information, reflecting their own policies and ethical principles. In other words, doctors, hospitals, and health plans could continue to follow their own policies to protect privacy in such instances.

Q: Must a health care provider or other covered entity obtain permission from a patient prior to notifying public health authorities of the occurrence of a reportable disease?

A: No. All states have laws that require providers to report cases of specific diseases to public health officials. The Privacy Rule allows disclosures that are required by law. Furthermore, disclosures to public health authorities that are authorized by law to collect or receive information for public health purposes are also permissible under the Privacy Rule. In order to do their job of protecting the health of the public, it is frequently necessary for public health officials to obtain information about the persons affected by a disease.

In some cases they may need to contact those affected in order to determine the cause of the disease to allow for actions to prevent further illness. The Privacy Rule continues to allow for the existing practice of sharing PHI with public health authorities that are authorized by law to collect or receive such information to aid them in their mission of protecting the health of the public. Examples of such activities include those directed at the reporting of disease or injury, reporting deaths and births, investigating the occurrence and cause of injury and disease, and monitoring adverse outcomes related to food, drugs, biological products, and dietary supplements.

Q: How does the rule affect my rights under the federal Privacy Act?

A: The Privacy Act of 1974 protects personal information about individuals held by the federal government. Covered entities that are federal agencies or federal contractors that maintain records that are covered by the Privacy Act not only must obey the Privacy Rule's requirements but also must comply with the Privacy Act.

Payment [45 CFR 164.501]

General Requirements

As provided for by the Privacy Rule, a covered entity may use and disclose protected health information (PHI) for payment purposes. "Payment" is a defined term that encompasses the various activities of health care providers to obtain payment or be reimbursed for their services and for a health plan to obtain premiums, to fulfill their coverage responsibilities and provide benefits under the plan, and to obtain or provide reimbursement for the provision of health care.

In addition to the general definition, the Privacy Rule provides examples of common payment activities which include, but are not limited to:

- Determining eligibility or coverage under a plan and adjudicating claims; Risk adjustments;
- Billing and collection activities;
- Reviewing health care services for medical necessity, coverage, justification of charges, and the like;
- Utilization review activities; and
- Disclosures to consumer reporting agencies (limited to specified identifying information about the individual, his or her payment history, and identifying information about the covered entity).

Frequently Asked Questions

Q: Does the rule prevent reporting to consumer credit reporting agencies or otherwise create any conflict with the Fair Credit Reporting Act (FCRA)?

A: No. The Privacy Rule's definition of "payment" includes disclosures to consumer reporting agencies. These disclosures, however, are limited to the following PHI about the individual: name and address; date of birth; social security number; payment history; account number. In addition, disclosure of the name and address of the health care provider or health plan making the report is allowed. The covered entity may perform this payment activity directly or may carry out this function through a third party, such as a collection agency, under a business associate arrangement.

We are not aware of any conflict in the consumer credit reporting disclosures permitted by the Privacy Rule and FCRA. The Privacy Rule permits uses and disclosures by the covered entity or its business associate as may be required by FCRA or other law. Therefore, we do not believe there would be a conflict between the Privacy Rule and legal duties imposed on data furnishers by FCRA.

Q: Does the Privacy Rule prevent health plans and providers from using debt collection agencies? Does the rule conflict with the Fair Debt Collection Practices Act?

A: The Privacy Rule permits covered entities to continue to use the services of debt collection agencies. Debt collection is recognized as a payment activity within the "payment" definition. Through a business associate arrangement, the covered entity may engage a debt collection agency to perform this function on its behalf. Disclosures to collection agencies under a business associate agreement are governed by other provisions of the rule, including consent (where consent is required) and the minimum necessary requirements.

We are not aware of any conflict between the Privacy Rule and the Fair Debt Collection Practices Act. Where a use or disclosure of PHI is necessary for the covered entity to fulfill a legal duty, the Privacy Rule would permit such use or disclosure as required by law.

Q: Are location information services of collection agencies, which are required under the Fair Debt Collection Practices Act, permitted under the Privacy Rule?

A: "Payment" is broadly defined as activities by health plans or health care providers to obtain premiums or obtain or provide reimbursements for the provision of health care. The activities specified are by way of example and are not intended to be an exclusive listing. Billing, claims management, collection activities and related data processing are expressly included in the definition of "payment." Obtaining information about the location of the individual is a routine activity to facilitate the collection of amounts owed and the management of accounts receivable, and, therefore, would constitute a payment activity. The covered entity and its business associate would also have to comply with any limitations placed on location information services by the Fair Debt Collection Practices Act.

Appendix C

Model
Business Associate Contract

This model business associate contract has been prepared by Alex Brittin of the Brittin Law Group, P.L.L.C.
This does not constitute nor substitute the need for legal advice. For further information about HIPAA see:

http://privacysecuritynetwork.com/healthcare

PrivacySecurityNetwork's Model Business Associate Contract

MODEL BUSINESS ASSOCIATE CONTRACT

THIS CONTRACT is entered into on this _____ day of _____, 2001, between Provider/ Plan/Clearinghouse ("COVERED ENTITIY") and Vendor/Person(s) ("BUSINESS ASSOCIATE").

WITNESSETH:

WHEREAS, COVERED ENTITY will make available and/or transfer to BUSINESS ASSOCIATE certain Information, in conjunction with goods or services that are being provided by BUSINESS ASSOCIATE to COVERED ENTITY, that is confidential and must be afforded special treatment and protection.

WHEREAS, BUSINESS ASSOCIATE will have access to and/or receive from COVERED ENTITY certain Information that can be used or disclosed only in accordance with this Contract and the HHS Privacy Regulations.

NOW, THEREFORE, COVERED ENTITY and BUSINESS ASSOCIATE agree as follows:

1   **Definitions.** The following terms shall have the meaning ascribed to them in this Section. Other capitalized terms shall have the meaning ascribed to them in the context in which they first appear.

2   **Contract** shall refer to this document.

3   **BUSINESS ASSOCIATE** shall mean [name of organization receiving the Information]

4   **COVERED ENTITY** shall mean [name of organization providing/making available the Information]

5   **HHS Privacy Regulations** shall mean the Code of Federal Regulations ("C.F.R.") at Title 45, Sections 160 and 164.

6   **Individual** shall mean the person who is the subject of the Information, and has the same meaning as the term "individual" is defined by 45 C.F.R. 164.501.

7   **Information** shall mean any "health information" provided and/or made available by COVERED ENTITY to BUSINESS ASSOCIATE, and has the same meaning as the term "health information"

is defined by 45 C.F.R. 160.103.

8   **Parties** shall mean BUSINESS ASSOCIATE and COVERED ENTITY.

9   **Secretary** shall mean the Secretary of the Department of Health and Human Services ("HHS") and any other officer or employee of HHS to whom the authority involved has been delegated.

10 **Term.** The term of this Contract shall be from _____ (the "Effective Date") until [date/either party submits written notice to the other of its intent to terminate this Contract/upon termination of the underlying agreement/when all of the Information provided by COVERED ENTITY to BUSINESS ASSOCIATE is destroyed or returned to COVERED ENTITY pursuant to Clause 6.9].

11 **Limits On Use And Disclosure Established By Terms Of Contract.** BUSINESS ASSOCIATE hereby agrees that it shall be prohibited from using or disclosing the Information provided or made available by COVERED ENTITIY for any purpose other than as expressly permitted or required by this Contract. (ref. 45 C.F.R. 164.504(e)(2)(i).)

12 **Stated Purposes For Which BUSINESS ASSOCIATE May Use Or Disclose Information.** The Parties hereby agree that BUSINESS ASSOCIATE shall be permitted to use and/or disclose Information provided or made available from COVERED ENTITY for the following stated purposes:

> [Include a general statement describing the stated purposes that BUSINESS ASSOCIATE may use or disclose the Information. These uses and disclosures must be within the scope of the BUSINESS ASSOCIATE's representation of the COVERED ENTITY.]

(ref. 45 C.F.R. 164.504(e)(2)(i); 65 Fed. Reg. 82505.)

13 **Additional Purposes For Which BUSINESS ASSOCIATE May Use Or Disclose Information.** In addition to the Stated Purposes for which BUSINESS ASSOCIATE may use or disclose Information described in clause 4, BUSINESS ASSOCIATE may use or disclose Information provided or made available from COVERED ENTITY for the following additional purpose(s):

14 **Use of Information For Management, Administration and Legal Responsibilities.** BUSINESS ASSOCIATE is permitted to use Information if necessary for the proper management and administration of BUSINESS ASSOCIATE or to carry out legal responsibilities of BUSINESS ASSOCIATE. (ref. 45 C.F.R. 164.504(e)(4)(i)(A-B)).

15 **Disclosure of Information For Management, Administration and Legal Responsibilities.** BUSINESS ASSICIATE is permitted to disclose Information received from COVERED ENTITY for the proper management and administration of BUSINESS ASSOCIATE or to carry out legal responsibilities of BUSINESS ASSOCIATE, provided:

16 The disclosure is required by law; or

17 The BUSINESS ASSOCIATE obtains reasonable assurances from the person to whom the information is disclosed that it will be held confidentially and used or further disclosed only as required by law or for the purposes for which it was disclosed to the person, the person will use appropriate safeguards to prevent use or disclosure of the information, and the person immediately notifies the BUSINESS ASSOCIATE of any instance of which it is aware in which the confidentiality of the information has been breached. (ref. 45 C.F.R. 164.504(e)(4)(ii).

18 **Data Aggregation Services.** BUSINESS ASSOCIATE is also permitted to use or disclose Information to provide data aggregation services, as that term is defined by 45 C.F.R. 164.501, relating to the health care operations of COVERED ENTITY. **(Optional)**(ref. 45 C.F.R. 164.504(e)(2)(i)(B).

19 BUSINESS ASSOCIATE OBLIGATIONS:

20 **Limits On Use And Further Disclosure Established By Contract And Law.** BUSINESS ASSOCIATE hereby agrees that the Information provided or made available by COVERED ENTITY shall not be further used or disclosed other than as permitted or required by the Contract or as required by law. (ref. 45 C.F.R. 164.504(e)(2)(ii)(A))

21 **Appropriate Safeguards.** BUSINESS ASSOCIATE will establish and maintain appropriate safeguards to prevent any use or disclosure of the Information, other than as provided for by this Contract. (ref. 164.504(e)(2)(ii)(B))

22 **Reports Of Improper Use Or Disclosure.** BUSINESS ASSOCIATE hereby agrees that it shall report to COVERED ENTITY [within a reasonable period of time after discovery/within two (2) days of discovery] of any use or disclosure of Information not provided for or allowed by this Contract. (ref. 45 C.F.R. 164.504(e)(2)(ii)(C))

23 **Subcontractors And Agents.** BUSINESS ASSOCIATE hereby agrees that anytime Information is provided or made available to any subcontractors or agents, BUSINESS ASSOCIATE must enter into a subcontract with the subcontractor or agent that contains the same terms, conditions and restrictions on the use and disclosure of Information as contained in this Contract. (ref. 45 C.F.R. 164.504(e)(2)(ii)(D))

24 **Right of Access to Information.** BUSINESS ASSOCIATE hereby agrees to make available and provide a right of access to Information by an Individual. This right of access shall conform with and meet all of the requirements of 45 C.F.R. 164.524, including substitution of the words "Covered Entity" with BUSINESS ASSOCIATE where appropriate. (ref. 45 C.F.R. 164.504(e)(2)(ii)(E))

25 **Amendment and Incorporation of Amendments.** BUSINESS ASSOCIATE agrees to make Information available for amendment and to incorporate any amendments to Information in accordance with 45 C.F.R. 164.526, including substitution of the words "Covered Entity" with BUSINESS ASSOCIATE where appropriate. (ref. 164.504(e)(2)(ii)(F))

26 **Provide Accounting.** BUSINESS ASSOCIATE agrees to make Information available as required to provide an accounting of disclosures in accordance with 45 C.F.R. 164.528, including substitution of the words "Covered Entity" with BUSINESS ASSOCIATE where appropriate. (ref. 45 C.F.R. 164.504(e)(2)(ii)(G))

27 **Access to Books and Records.** BUSINESS ASSOCIATE hereby agrees to make its internal practices, books, and records relating to the use or disclosure of Information received from, or created or received by BUSINESS ASSOCIATE on behalf of the COVERED ENTITY, available to the Secretary or the Secretary's designee for purposes of determining compliance with the HHS Privacy Regulations. (ref. 45 C.F.R. 164.504(e)(2)(ii)(H))

28 **Return or Destruction of Information.** At termination of this Contract, BUSINESS ASSOCIATE hereby agrees to return or destroy all Information received from, or created or received by BUSINESS ASSOCIATE on behalf of COVERED ENTITY. BUSINESS ASSOCIATE agrees not to retain any copies of the Information after termination of this Contract. If return or destruction of the Information is not feasible, BUSINESS ASSOCIATE agrees to extend the protections of this Contract for as long as necessary to protect the Information and to limit any further use or disclosure. If BUSINESS ASSOCIATE elects to destroy the Information, it shall certify to COVERED

ENTITY that the Information has been destroyed. (ref. 45 C.F.R. 164.504(e)(2)(ii)(I))

29 **Mitigation Procedures.** BUSINESS ASSOCIATE agrees to have procedures in place for mitigating, to the maximum extent practicable, any deleterious effect from the use or disclosure of Information in a manner contrary to this Contract or the HHS Privacy Regulations. (ref. 45 C.F.R. 164.530(f))

30 **Sanction Procedures.** BUSINESS ASSOCIATE agrees and understands that it must develop and implement a system of sanctions for any employee, subcontractor or agent who violates this Agreement or the HHS Privacy Regulations. (**optional,** *see* 45 C.F.R. 164.530(e)(1))

31 **Property Rights.** The Information shall be and remain the property of COVERED ENTITY. BUSINESS ASSOCIATE agrees that it acquires no title or rights to the Information, including any de-identified information, as a result of this Contract. (**optional**)

32 **Termination of Contract.** BUSINESS ASSOCIATE agrees that COVERED ENTITY has the right to immediately terminate this Contract and seek relief under the Disputes Article if COVERED ENTITY determines that BUSINESS ASSOCIATE has violated a material term of this Contract. (ref. 45 C.F.R. 164.506(e)(2)(iii).

33 **Grounds For Breach.** Any non-compliance by BUSINESS ASSOCIATE with this Contract or the HHS Privacy Regulations will automatically be considered to be a Grounds For Breach, if BUSINESS ASSOCIATE knew or reasonably should have known of such non-compliance and failed to immediately take reasonable steps to cure the non-compliance. (**optional**).

34 **Choice of Law.** The law of the State of _____ shall govern this Contract. (**optional**)

35 **Disputes.** Any controversy or claim arising out of or relating to the Contract will be finally settled by compulsory arbitration in accordance with the Commercial Arbitration Rules of the American Arbitration Association ("AAA"), except for injunctive relief as described below in article [or in court of competent jurisdiction]. (**optional**)

36 **Injunctive Relief.** Notwithstanding any rights or remedies provided for in this Contract, COVERED ENTITY retains all rights to seek injunctive relief to prevent or stop the unauthorized use or disclosure of Information by BUSINESS ASSOCIATE or any agent, contractor or third party that received Information from BUSINESS ASSOCIATE. (**optional**)

37 **Miscellaneous:**

38 **Binding Nature and Assignment.** This Contract shall be binding on the Parties hereto and their successors and assigns, but neither Party may assign this Agreement without the prior written consent of the other, which consent shall not be unreasonably withheld. (**optional**)

39 **Notices.** Whenever under this Contract one party is required to give notice to the other, such notice shall be deemed given if mailed by First Class United States mail, postage prepaid, and addressed as follows: (**optional**)

COVERED ENTITY:

[Name/Address]

BUSINESS ASSOCIATE

[Name/Address]

Either Party may at any time change its address for notification purposes by mailing a notice stating the change and setting forth the new address.

40 **Good Faith.** The Parties agree to exercise good faith in the performance of this Contract. **(optional)**

41 **Article Headings.** The article headings used are for reference and convenience only, and shall not enter into the interpretation of this Contract. **(optional)**

42 **Force Majeure.** BUSINESS ASSOCIATE shall be excused from performance under this Contract for any period BUSINESS ASSOCIATE is prevented from performing any services pursuant hereto, in whole or in part, as a result of an Act of God, war, civil disturbance, court order, labor dispute or other cause beyond its reasonable control, and such nonperformance shall not be grounds for termination. **(optional)**

43 **Attorney's fees.** Except as otherwise specified in this Contract, if any legal action or other proceeding is brought for the enforcement of this Contract, or because of an alleged dispute, breach, default, misrepresentation, or injunctive action, in connection with any of the provisions of this Contract, each party shall bear their own legal expenses and the other cost incurred in that action or proceeding. **(optional)**

44 **Entire Agreement.** This Contract consists of this document, and constitutes the entire agreement between the Parties. There are no understandings or agreements relating to this Agreement which are not fully expressed in this Contract and no change, waiver or discharge of obligations arising under this Contract shall be valid unless in writing and executed by the Party against whom such change, waiver or discharge is sought to be enforced. **(optional)**

45 **Limitation of Liability (optional)**

46 **Insurance (optional)**

47 **Indemnification (optional)**

48 **Payment (optional)**

49 **New Statutory and Legislative Requirements (optional)**

   IN WITNESS WHEREOF, BUSINESS ASSOCIATE and COVERED ENTITY have caused this Contract to be signed and delivered by their duly authorized representatives, as of the date set forth above.

BUSINESS ASSOCIATE   COVERED ENTITY
By:_____   By:_____
Print Name:_____   Print Name:_____
Title:_____   Title:_____

Appendix D

Model Request for Proposal to Conduct HIPAA Assessment

This model Request for Proposal has been prepared by Alex Brittin of the Brittin Law Group, P.L.L.C.
This does not constitute nor substitute the need for legal advice. For further information about HIPAA see:

http://privacysecuritynetwork.com/healthcare

PrivacySecurityNetwork's Model Request for Proposal to Conduct HIPAA Assessment

Table of Contents

Request for Proposal

1 Request for Proposal Specifications

1.1.1 Purpose

The purpose of this RFP is to engage an organization that will provide [YOUR COMPANY] with an assessment of the impact of the Health Insurance Portability and Accountability Act ("HIPAA") (Public Law 104-191) to [YOUR COMPANY]. The assessment should look at the business, technical and physical aspects of [YOUR COMPANY]. The goal is to have a cost-effective strategy, and develop a detailed work plan to meet the HIPAA requirements within the required timeframes.

1.1.2 Key Dates

Week 0	Request for Information sent to potential Vendors
Week 3	Deadline for Questions from Vendors
Week 4	Responses to Vendor questions
Week 5	Deadline for Vendor proposals
Week 6	Notify short list of Vendors for final presentation
Week 7-Week 9	Presentations
Week 10	Final selection of Vendors

1.1.3 Qs & As

Any questions or requests for clarification in connection with this Request for Proposal should be directed to:

[YOUR COMPANY'S CONTACT PERSON]

Questions should be received by the question deadline date. Answers to certain Vendor inquiries may be distributed by e-mail to all Vendors if they clarify [YOUR COMPANY's] requirements.

1.1.4 Copies of Proposal

Submit three copies of the proposal to the following address no later than the deadline date.

[YOUR COMPANY'S ADDRESS]

1.1.5 Negotiation of Contract

A contract will be executed between the parties upon the terms and conditions stated in this RFP and as such other terms and conditions as required or necessary by [YOUR COMPANY].

2 Request for Proposal Information

2.1 Statement of Need

[YOUR COMPANY'S] need to create a detailed strategy and set of work plans to implement the necessary changes to meet the HIPAA regulations within the specified time frames. [YOUR COMPANY] needs to:

- To be in compliance with the regulations
- To meet accreditation requirements, e.g., the American Health Care Accreditation Commission/URAC or the Joint Commission of Accreditation of Hospitals (JCAHO)
- To remain a competitive healthcare organization

2.2 Objectives and Goals of Assessment

[YOUR COMPANY] wants to partner with a Vendor experienced with the HIPAA regulations, security issues, e-business, healthcare operations and information technology. The Vendor must be able to assist [YOUR COMPANY] in identifying what needs to be done to become HIPAA compliant. The Vendor must assist [YOUR COMPANY] in developing a cost-effective strategy to become HIPAA compliant and in developing the roadmap (detailed work plans and a budget) to get [YOUR COMPANY] HIPAA compliant within the required timeframes established by HHS.

To accomplish the goals and objectives applicable, the Vendor will need to bring the following expertise to the
engagement:

- A methodology and tool set used to complete HIPAA assessments at other healthcare organizations
- A detailed understanding of the HIPAA regulations
- Legal expertise in interpreting HIPAA regulations
- Understanding applicable State Laws
- Healthcare knowledge and experience, including

  - awareness of trends related to HIPAA in health care organizations ("HCO") across the country
  - a familiarity with and understanding of security and confidentiality issues
  - knowledge and understanding of the flow of patient information within a HCO and with business partners.
  - knowledge and understanding of the relationships between various business partners, e.g., medical centers, physicians, clearinghouses and payers.
  - knowledge of the information technology trends within healthcare

- Expertise in e-business
- Expertise in physical and administrative security policies and procedures, such as those used in the military or banking industry that need to be adopted by HCOs
- Project Management Experience
- Expertise in information technology in the areas of:

  - data security
  - technical security mechanisms
  - healthcare applications

In an effort to reduce costs, [YOUR COMPANY] wishes to partner with a Vendor that is willing to share tools and methodologies and allow [YOUR COMPANY] to work with and receive training and guidance from the Vendor.

2.3 Vendor Responsibilities

The HIPAA regulations are not final and may not be final for several months. [YOUR COMPANY] wants to complete the assessment process and begin implementation when it makes sense. The Vendor must work with [YOUR COMPANY] to complete all of the tasks listed in the Scope of Work section to meet the schedule for implementation of the HIPAA regulations.

The Vendor must provide tools and methodologies that train and guide [YOUR COMPANY's] project team members to participate in the assessment process and to reduce the cost of this effort.

The Vendor must identify interpretations of the HIPAA standards to [YOUR COMPANY] and allow [YOUR COMPANY] to agree with the interpretation or ask the Vendor to use a different interpretation of the standard. [YOUR COMPANY] wants to avoid Vendor recommendations that are based on the Vendor's interpretation of a standard that may be different from [YOUR COMPANY's] interpretation of the same standard.

2.3.1 Scope of Work

2.3.1.1 HIPAA Education and Training

2.3.1.1.1 Education for Managers and Staff Involved in Assessment

Provide HIPAA education and training for managers and staff across the organization that will be involved in the HIPAA assessment and planning process. One objective of the training should be to give the managers and staff a detailed understanding of the HIPAA regulation so that when they participate in the assessment process they are better able to contribute, knowing what requirements the organization has to meet and why. [YOUR COMPANY] will provide managers with an overview of HIPAA awareness training in advance.

2.3.1.1.2 Education for HIPAA Core Team

Provide in depth HIPAA education and training for the core HIPAA project team. Another objective of the training is to give the team a detailed understanding of the HIPAA regulation so they have the background needed to supervise and do the work required on the project.

2.3.1.2 Baseline Privacy and Security Assessment

Assist [YOUR COMPANY'S] team in identifying and documenting the potential security and privacy threats and risks in [YOUR COMPANY'S] current technology infrastructure and business operations practices. Survey [YOUR COMPANY'S] current technology infrastructure, security and privacy policies and practices, and identify gaps in relationship to the HIPAA Security, electronic signature and privacy standards. List the current vulnerabilities and areas of exposure in the technology infrastructure and business operational practices. Assess the potential risks and consequences of the identified gaps.

Recommend technologies and Vendors that are needed to close the gaps and reduce the risks. Identify practices, policies and procedures that need to be developed to close the gaps and reduce risks.

2.3.1.3 E-Business Assessment and Strategic Approach for HIPAA

[YOUR COMPANY] is in the process of formalizing e-business opportunities and e-business strategies. The Vendor must provide general recommendations and observations that [YOUR COMPANY] may consider when developing an e-business strategy and identify key issues and considerations for [YOUR COMPANY] as it moves forward in the area of e-business.

2.3.1.4 Development of a Strategic Approach for HIPAA

Assist [YOUR COMPANY'S] team in developing alternative strategies for implementing solutions (technical and administrative) for HIPAA compliance based on the outcomes of the baseline security and privacy assessment. The strategies should also include ideas on implementation approaches and solutions for other HIPAA regulations, including:

- Standards for Electronic Transaction and Code Sets
- National Identifiers

Identify solution alternatives, address key issues and identify trends in health care organizations across the country. Develop a high-level implementation plan identifying the duration of the HIPAA program, overall budget and resource requirements.

2.3.1.5 Development of Detailed Implementation Plans and Budget

Assist [YOUR COMPANY'S] team in developing detailed project plans that will need to be implemented to accomplish the overall HIPAA strategy. The detailed plans should include detailed budget and staffing requirements.

2.3.2 Deliverables

1. Training presentation and handouts for the management and staff training classes.
2. Training presentation and handouts for the HIPAA project team training classes.
3. Tools and methodologies for [YOUR COMPANY'S] staff to use with guidance from the Vendor in accomplishing parts of the assessment.
4. Diagram and document the flow of patient information for [YOUR COMPANY].
5. Diagram and document the electronic data interchanges [YOUR COMPANY] has with business partners.
6. Document the relationships with trading partners.
7. Document the gaps, vulnerabilities, and risks discovered during the baseline assessment in technology and application infrastructures and in operational practices.
8. HIPAA strategy documents identifying recommended alternatives and solutions.
9. E-business assessment and strategy document.
10. High-level HIPAA project work plan, budget and staffing plan based on the selected strategy.
11. Detailed work plans, budget and staffing plan for the selected strategy for the HIPAA Program. The detailed work plans are for each subproject within the HIPAA program. The collection of detailed plans will serve as the road map for [YOUR COMPANY] to implement items required to be compliant with HIPAA regulations, in the required time frames.

2.4 [YOUR COMPANY'S] Environment

2.4.1 Overview of [YOUR COMPANY]

[Generally describe YOUR COMPANY]

Here are some statistics on [YOUR COMPANY]:

Number of Employees
Gross Revenue
Number of Locations
Numer of Affiliated Physicians
Number of Hospital Admissions
Number of Outpatient Visits
Number of ER Visits

2.4.2 Overview of Current Technical Environment

The data communication network is [describe].
The network is [describe].

The internet capabilities are [describe].
Legacy systems are [describe].

Graphically describe [YOUR COMPANY'S] system.

2.4.3 Overview of Current Applications Environment

[YOUR COMPANY] uses the [describe] information system.
The Clinical information system is [describe].
Electronic billing system is [describe] and it goes to a clearinghouse through [describe] application.
The clearinghouse formats the transactions [describe].
[YOUR COMPANY] uses [describe] software.
[YOUR COMPANY] does/does not have in-house developed applications
[YOUR COMPANY] uses the Internet for [describe purposes].
[YOUR COMPANY] does not have an electronic medical record system or an enterprise wide master person index.

3 Response Guidelines

3.1 Response Guidelines

3.1.1 Preparation Costs Borne By Vendor

Neither [YOUR COMPANY], nor its representatives, nor employees shall be liable for the costs incurred by a Vendor in preparing or submitting a response to this solicitation.

3.1.2 Rights of Non-Response

[YOUR COMPANY] reserves the right to not take action on any Vendor's proposal.

3.2 Contents of the Response

3.2.1 Section I – Introduction

The introduction should include:

- The Title Page identifying your organization's name and address, name of the contact person, telephone and fax numbers, e-mail address, and proposal date.
- Table of contents including a clear identification of the material by section and page number

3.2.2 Section II — Vendor Qualifications

3.2.2.1 Qualifications and Experience of the Company

Demonstrate [YOUR COMPANY'S] experience and qualifications in the following areas. It is preferred that [YOUR COMPANY] have experience in completing HIPAA assessments. Include the following information:

- A detailed understanding of the HIPAA regulations and contacts in Washington D.C. to organizations involved in shaping the legislation
- Legal expertise in interpreting HIPAA regulations
- Healthcare knowledge and experience, including

  - awareness of trends related to HIPAA in HCOs across the country
  - familiarity with and understanding of security and confidentiality issues from the perspective of a HCO

- knowledge and understanding of the flow of patient information within a HCO and with Business partners.
- knowledge and understanding of the relationships between various business partners, e.g., medical centers, physicians, clearinghouses and payers.
- knowledge of the information technology trends within healthcare

- Expertise in physical security and in administrative security policies and procedures, such as those used in the military or banking industry which need to be adopted by HCOs
- Expertise in information technology in the areas of:
  - data security
  - technical security mechanisms
  - healthcare applications

3.2.2.2 Management Capability

Demonstrate [YOUR COMPANY'S] management qualifications and capabilities to staff and supervise the engagement. Describe the management approach that will be used to ensure successful completion of the effort required by the Scope of Work. Describe your process for monitoring and controlling both progress and financial resources.

[YOUR COMPANY] requests that the Vendor provide resumes of the engagement manager and personnel who will be assigned to this engagement. No substitutions should be made without the prior consent of [YOUR COMPANY].

3.2.2.3 References

Provide a list of up to three references for which similar engagements have been completed. The list should provide the name, title, telephone number and address of an appropriate person to be contacted.

3.2.2.4 Subcontractors

The response may include the use of subcontractors, headed by the primary Vendor who will be responsible for the entire engagement and guarantee performance of all subcontractors. In such a case, the response should include all information on subcontractors, including management, experience, references and expertise. Prior to the initiation of the project, any subcontractor/partner must be approved by [YOUR COMPANY].

3.2.3 Section III – Understanding of Requirements, Scope of Work & Deliverables

This section should include your understanding of the work to be performed and the results to be achieved. Discuss the detailed approach that will be used to ensure successful completion of the effort required by the scope of work. Itemize and describe the work to be done and the deliverables to be produced. Discuss the methods and tools that will be used to accomplish the work.

3.2.4 Section IV – Provide Work Plan and Schedule

Provide a work plan and schedule for completing the Scope of Work & Deliverables. Discuss the approach that will be used to ensure successful completion of the work required by the scope of work.

Define the requirement for resources from [YOUR COMPANY] to work on the assessment process. What type of resource (skills needed) will be needed from [YOUR COMPANY] and for what amount of time and what duration. [YOUR COMPANY] would like to use its resources to do the assessment where possible to keep costs down.

3.2.5 Section V – Proposed Costs

The proposal should clearly identify all related costs including travel and other reimbursable expense. Provide a detailed cost breakdown by type of resource indicating the rate per hour and estimated hours for the engagement. Prices should include all costs to be charged to the engagement. Costs should be itemized for each of the following five scope of work items. The following chart provides an example of how the figures should be broken out for two of the Work items. The Scope of Work items are:

Items listed in the scope of work:

1. HIPAA Education & Training
2. Baseline Privacy & Security Assessment
3. E-Business Assessment & Strategic Approach for HIPAA
4. Development of a Strategic Approach
5. Development of Detailed Implementation Plans
6. Others you may have added

Scope of Work Items	Description of Costs	Rate Per Hour	Total Hours	Total Dollars
2. Baseline Privacy & Security Assessment				
	Resources			
	Senior Manager			
	Project Manager			
	Technical Analyst			
	Travel & Expense (Explain)			
	Other Billable Expenses (Describe)			
Total for Item 2				
5. Development of Detailed Implementation Plans				
	Resources			
	Resource 1			
	Resource 2			
	Travel & Expenses (Explain)			
	Other Expenses (Explain)			
Total for Item 5				
TOTAL FOR ALL ITEMS				

4   Evaluation of Proposal

Proposals will be evaluated in the following categories with a possible 100 points in the rating score.

1.   Qualification & Experience of the Company (20)

Demonstration of:

- A methodology and tool set successfully used to complete HIPAA assessments at other HCOs
- A detailed understanding of the HIPAA regulations
- Legal expertise in interpreting HIPAA regulations
- Familiarity with State Laws
- Healthcare knowledge and experience, including

  - awareness of trends related to HIPAA in HCO across the country
  - familiarity with and understand security and confidentiality issues
  - knowledge and understanding of the flow of patient information within a HCO and with Business partners such as physicians and payers.
  - knowledge and understanding of the relationships between various business partners, e.g., medical centers, physicians, clearinghouses and payers.
  - knowledge of information technology trends within healthcare

- Expertise in e-business
- Expertise in physical security and in administrative security policies and procedures, such as those used in the military or banking industry which need to be adopted by HCOs
- Project Management Experience
- Expertise in information technology in the areas of:

  - data security
  - technical security mechanisms
  - healthcare applications

1.   Management Capabilities (20)

Demonstration of:

- Management qualifications and capabilities to staff and supervise the engagement
- A management approach that will ensure successful completion of the work required by the scope of work
- A process for monitoring and controlling both progress and financial resources
- Qualified engagement managers and personnel being assigned to the engagement

1.   References (10)

Demonstration of:

- Satisfied customers at other sites for which similar engagements have been completed

1.   Understanding Requirements, Scope of Work and Deliverables (20)

Demonstration of:

- An understanding of the work to be performed and the results to be achieved.
- An understanding of the deliverables to be produced
- Availability of methods and tools that will be used to accomplish the work

- Sample deliverables from other engagements

1. Work Plan and Schedule (10)

   Demonstration of:

   - Tasks and time frames detailing the approach that will be used to ensure successful completion of the work required by the scope of work.
   - Resource requirements of [YOUR COMPANY'S] Staff defined

1. Proposed Costs (20)

   Demonstration of:

   - A clear and cost-effective budget for accomplishing the scope of work
   - Costs itemized for each item listed under the scope of work

5   Appendix: [YOUR COMPANY's] Organization Chart

Application	Vendor	Operating System	Department

6   Appendix: [YOUR COMPANY'S] Core Application Inventory and Schematic

7   Appendix: [YOUR COMPANY'S] Current Privacy and Security Policies

List your company's current privacy and security policies

		Existing Policies

Appendix E

Internet Resources

Internet Resources

Government

HHS Website on Administrative Simplification
http://aspe.hhs.gov/admnsimp/

HHS Office for Civil Rights
www.hhs.gov/ocr/hipaa.html

National Committee on Vital and Health Statistics
http://ncvhs.hhs.gov/

Associations

American Health Information Management Association
www.ahima.org/hot.topics/hipaa.html#pb

American Hospital Association
www.aha.org/hipaa/

Association for Electronic Health Care Transactions
www.afehct.org/

URAC/American Accreditation Healthcare Commission
www.urac.org

WEDI's Strategic National Implementation Process (SNIP) Implementation of HIPAA Standards
http://snip.wedi.org/

Public Interest Groups

Center for Democracy and Technology
www.cdt.org/privacy/medical/

Electronic Privacy Information Center
www.epic.org/privacy/medical/

Health Privacy Project, Institute for Health Care Research and Policy, Georgetown University
www.healthprivacy.org/

Other

PrivacySecurityNetwork.com
www.privacysecuritynetwork.com

HIPAAdvisory.com
http://hipaadvisory.com/live/

AHIMA Sample (Chief) Privacy Officer Job Description
http://www.ahima.org/infocenter/models/PrivacyOfficer2001.htm

HEALTH INFORMATION PRIVACY
ALERT

THE NEWSLETTER OF CHOICE FOR EARLY HIPAA ADOPTERS

DISCOVER:

- New strategies for coordinating your health data protection efforts;
- Where privacy issues affect compliance with the HIPAA data security requirements;
- How to balance your HIPAA duties with other corporate and regulatory responsibilities;
- Where HHS is focusing its HIPAA enforcement resources;
- How to easily access the key documents you need for HIPAA compliance and planning;
- When and why you need business associate agreements;
- Effective strategies for coping with patient access to records;
- How to protect yourself from the new legal liabilities created by HIPAA;

and much, much more.

Call (202) 296-3069 or Fax This Order Form to (202) 466-8032

Name: _____

Title: _____

Company: _____

Address 1: _____

Address 2: _____

City: _____

State: _____

Zip Code: _____

Email: _____

Signature _____

Tel. #: _____

Fax #: _____

Charge It To My

☐ Amex ☐ MasterCard ☐ Visa

Card # _____

Signature _____

Exp. Date_____

☐ Bill Me

QTY	DESCRIPTION	AMOUNT
1	Annual Subscription (12 issues) to Health Information Privacy Alert	$516.00
	Special Professional Discount for HIPAA Privacy Book Purchasers	**- $50.00**
	Subscribe Today!	
	TOTAL DUE WHEN ORDERED	$466.00